THE BEST OF
FAVORITE
BRAND NAME
RECIPES

COLLECTOR'S EDITION
VOLUME ONE

Publications International, Ltd.

Nutritional Analysis: Nutritional information is given for some of the recipes in this publication. Each analysis is based on the food items in the ingredient list, except ingredients labeled as "optional" or "for garnish." When more than one ingredient choice is listed, the first ingredient is used for analysis. If a range for the amount of an ingredient is given, the nutritional analysis is based on the lowest amount. Foods offered as "serve with" suggestions are not included in the analysis unless otherwise stated.

Microwave Cooking: Microwave ovens vary in wattage. The microwave cooking times given in this publication are approximate. Use the cooking times as guidelines and check for doneness before adding more time. Consult manufacturer's instructions for suitable microwave-safe cooking dishes.

THE BEST OF
FAVORITE
BRAND NAME
RECIPES

→ INTRODUCTION ←

The hardest part of producing a "best of the best" cookbook is narrowing down which recipes to include. We couldn't possibly choose all the outstanding recipes we've published throughout the year. What we've selected is an extraordinary array of more than 200 recipes from the most trusted and admired brand name food companies, such as Hershey, Kraft, Contadina, Quaker Oats, Sargento, StarKist, Nestlé and so many more. *The Best of Favorite Brand Name Recipes* is also brimming with more than 75 gorgeous full-color photographs that will inspire you to start cooking—and eating! We've included helpful hints in every chapter so you can make the most of your time in the kitchen. Each year's edition will serve as a reminder of favorite dishes and food trends for that year. As you purchase new volumes, you'll begin to collect recipes and memories to last a lifetime.

The recipes are organized by season so you can find exactly the right recipe for any day of the year. As you page through the book, you'll see many fabulous holiday menu suggestions to help plan those special occasions, such as Christmas, Valentine's Day, Mother's Day and Thanksgiving. We've also included fun ideas for graduation and Halloween parties, plus picnic suggestions.

Within each chapter, recipes are divided into Starters, Entrées & Sides and Desserts for easier reference. We've specially marked low-fat recipes with green boxes so you can spot them right away. They all have less than 15 grams of fat per serving. Blue boxes indicate recipes that can be completed in 30 minutes or less—great for the end of a particularly busy day! Whether you're searching for summertime salads or complete winter meals, you'll be able to find everything quickly with our easy reference system.

When you think of wintertime, you think first of the hectic holiday season and second of the quiet times that follow the holidays. The recipes we've included will carry you through both phases of the season. The volume contains a large selection of festive holiday recipes to meet all your entertaining needs. There are plenty of delectable holiday baking ideas, including White Chocolate Bavarian Christmas Tree, Chocolate-Dipped Almond Horns, Eggnog Cheesecake and Candy Cane & Wreath Ornaments. You can make a family brunch truly special by serving the Cherry, Almond & Chocolate Breakfast Wreath. If you'd like to host an elegant New Year's Eve dinner for friends, start the celebration with a beautiful Roasted Pepper and Avocado Salad. As the cold snowy nights of February approach, a comforting supper always helps to chase away the chill. Spicy Kielbasa & Chicken Gumbo or satisfying Macaroni and Cheese Dijon will surely warm you right up. And, for those famous New Year's resolutions, Chicken Enchiladas or Beef 'n' Broccoli will satisfy your diet needs and your need for appealing entrées.

Once spring flowers start blooming, you'll want to take advantage of fresh fruits and vegetables and serve lighter meals. The spring chapter is overflowing with imaginative salads, such as Seafood Louis, California Apricot Fruit Salad, Curried Tuna Salad and Thai Beef Salad.

If you have a pasta craving, try the delicious Penne Primavera with Sundried Tomato Sauce or the fast and tasty Linguine with Asparagus and Asiago. For a quick bite, there are lots of savory sandwiches and tempting pizzas, including Mediterranean Pita Pizzas, Provençal Chicken Sandwiches and Vegetarian Burgers. Tired of serving the same old holiday menus? Take a look at our innovative ideas for Easter, Mother's Day and Memorial Day.

In summer, what's more tantalizing than the aroma of outdoor cooking? We've included plenty of barbecue and outdoor grilling recipes to help you enjoy the season. Invite some friends to drop by and share Country Glazed Ribs, Grilled Rosemary Chicken, Savory Grilled Potatoes in Foil or America's Favorite Cheddar Beef Burgers. In the heat of summer, there's nothing more refreshing than cold summer

soups, such as Cool Italian Tomato Soup and Gazpacho. What goes better with soup than salad? Try Albacore and White Bean Salad with Orange Dressing, Garden Party Pasta Salad or a hearty Kielbasa Tomato Salad. We haven't neglected dessert either! Complete your meal with Creamy Cappuccino Frozen Dessert, Fabulous Fondue or Wisconsin Ricotta Tart with Kiwi and Raspberry Sauce.

Autumn means going back indoors, back to school and back to those fast-paced fall days. When time is short, try one of our quick meal recipes such as Mexican Beef Stir-Fry, Chicken with Walnuts or Szechuan Vegetable Lo Mein. We've also included a selection of warm and satisfying fare such as California Turkey Chili, Meat and Potato Stir-Fry and Cheese and Bean Quesadillas. No autumn recipe collection would be complete without special Thanksgiving recipes. Along with traditional Roast Turkey with Fresh Herb Stuffing, there are new baking ideas, such as Pumpkin Pecan Pie, Pumpkin Harvest Bread and Golden Apple Buttermilk Bread.

No matter what the temperature is outside or how many people drop by to share a meal, you'll always be prepared with the right recipe. Look through the photos, daydream about your favorite time of year and head to the kitchen for a year's worth of unbeatable brand name recipes.

Winter

"Winter is the time for comfort,
for good food and warmth, for
the touch of a friendly hand and
for a talk beside the fire: it is the
time for home."

Edith Stiwell

Party Cheese Wreath (page 13)

→ STARTERS ←

Zesty Zucchini Chick-Pea Salad

  3 medium zucchini
½ teaspoon salt
  5 tablespoons white vinegar
  1 clove garlic, minced
¼ teaspoon dried thyme leaves
½ cup olive oil
  1 cup canned chick-peas, drained
½ cup sliced pitted black olives
  3 green onions, minced
  1 canned chipotle chili pepper in adobo sauce,
     drained, seeded and minced
  1 ripe avocado
⅓ cup crumbled feta *or* 3 tablespoons grated
     Romano cheese
     Boston lettuce leaves
     Sliced tomatoes and cilantro sprigs, for garnish

Cut zucchini lengthwise into halves; cut halves crosswise into ¼-inch-thick slices. Place slices in medium bowl; sprinkle with salt. Toss to mix. Spread zucchini on several layers of paper towels. Let stand at room temperature 30 minutes to drain.

Combine vinegar, garlic and thyme in large bowl. Gradually add oil in thin, steady stream, whisking continuously until dressing is thoroughly blended.

Pat zucchini dry; add to dressing. Add chick-peas, olives and onions; toss lightly to coat. Cover; refrigerate at least 30 minutes or up to 4 hours, stirring occasionally.

Add chili pepper to salad just before serving. Stir gently to mix. Peel, pit and cut avocado into ½-inch cubes. Add avocado and cheese; toss lightly to mix.

Serve salad in lettuce-lined bowl or plate. Garnish, if desired. *Makes 4 to 6 servings*

Singapore Spicy Noodles

1¼ cups water
  2 tablespoons ketchup
2½ teaspoons packed brown sugar
1½ teaspoons chopped cilantro
  1 teaspoon cornstarch
¾ teaspoon LAWRY'S® Seasoned Salt
¾ teaspoon LAWRY'S® Garlic Powder with Parsley
¼ teaspoon crushed red pepper
2½ tablespoons chunky peanut butter
  8 ounces linguine, cooked, drained and kept
     warm
  1 cup shredded red cabbage
¼ cup sliced green onions with tops

In medium saucepan, combine water, ketchup, sugar, cilantro, cornstarch, Seasoned Salt, Garlic Powder with Parsley and red pepper. Bring to a boil over medium-high heat. Reduce heat to low; simmer, uncovered, 5 minutes. Cool 10 minutes; blend in peanut butter. Add to linguine with cabbage and onions; toss lightly.
Makes 4 servings

Presentation: *Garnish with green onion curls. Serve with a marinated cucumber salad.*

Hint: *For a heartier entrée, add shredded cooked chicken or pork.*

Singapore Spicy Noodles

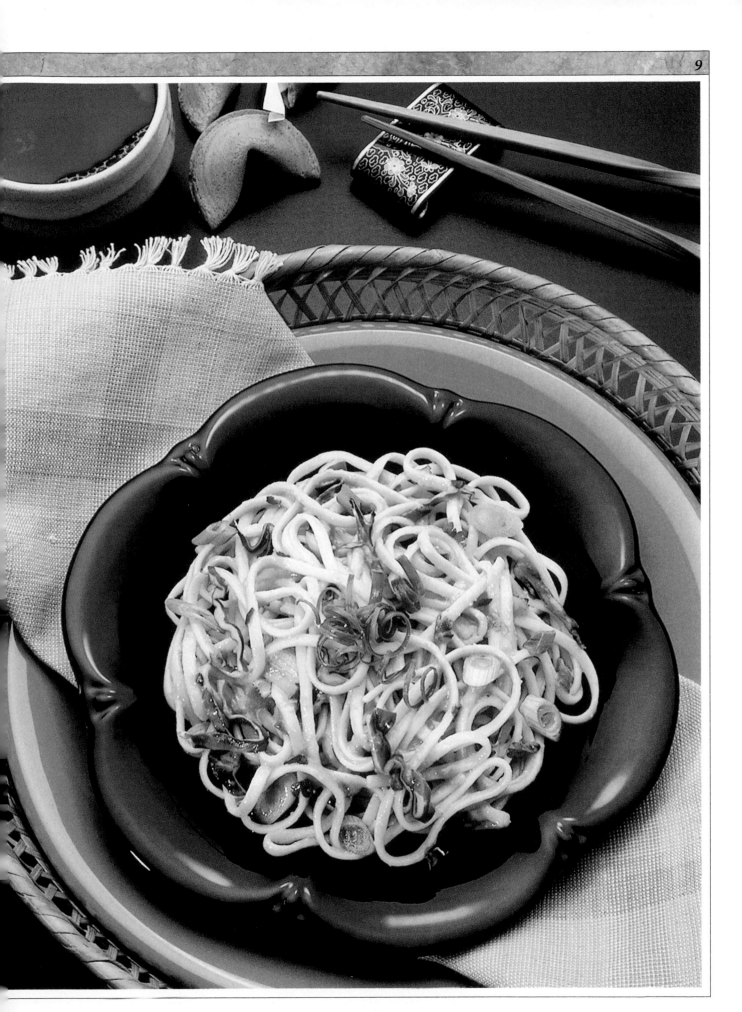

Orange-Berry Salad

½ cup prepared HIDDEN VALLEY RANCH®
    Original Ranch® salad dressing
2 tablespoons orange juice
1 teaspoon grated orange peel
½ cup heavy cream, whipped
1 can (11 ounces) mandarin orange segments
2 packages (3 ounces each) strawberry- or
    raspberry-flavored gelatin
1 can (16 ounces) whole-berry cranberry sauce
½ cup walnut pieces
    Mint sprigs
    Whole fresh strawberries and raspberries

In large bowl, whisk together salad dressing, orange juice and peel. Fold in whipped cream; cover and refrigerate. Drain oranges, reserving juice. Add water to juice to measure 3 cups; pour into large saucepan and bring to a boil. Stir in gelatin until dissolved. Cover and refrigerate until partially set. Fold orange segments, cranberry sauce and walnuts into gelatin. Pour into lightly oiled 6-cup ring mold. Cover and refrigerate until firm; unmold. Garnish with mint, fresh strawberries and raspberries. Serve with chilled dressing.   *Makes 8 servings*

⁙ COOK'S TIP ⁙

Grating and shredding cheeses are often confused. Only hard cheeses, like Parmesan and Romano, are grated. Semisoft and semifirm cheeses, like Cheddar, Swiss and mozzarella are shredded. Blue, feta and goat cheeses are crumbled.

Barley Mounds in Avocado Pears

2¼ cups water, divided
½ cup medium pearled barley
1 package (8 to 10 ounces) frozen mixed
    vegetables
2 tablespoons margarine
1 clove garlic, minced
2 tablespoons flour
¼ teaspoon salt
¼ teaspoon dry mustard
¼ teaspoon black pepper
½ cup milk
½ cup sliced fresh mushrooms
¾ cup (3 ounces) shredded Gruyère cheese,
    divided
2 tablespoons chopped fresh parsley
3 avocado pears, Winter Nellis pears or other firm
    green winter pears

1. In medium saucepan, bring 1½ cups water to a boil. Stir in barley. Reduce heat; cover and simmer 45 minutes, stirring occasionally. Drain.

2. Bring ¼ cup water to a boil. Add mixed vegetables. Bring to a boil again, then remove from heat and drain. Set aside.

3. In 1-quart saucepan, melt margarine. Add garlic; cook 1 minute. Stir in flour, salt, dry mustard and pepper; blend well. Whisk in remaining ½ cup water and milk to smooth consistency; cook over medium heat until sauce thickens. Remove from heat; add mushrooms, ½ cup cheese, parsley, barley and vegetables. Mix well.

4. Peel pears, if desired. Cut into halves; remove seeds, keeping shells intact. Arrange pear halves in 10-inch baking dish or pan. Mound equal portions barley-vegetable mixture into pear halves. Sprinkle with remaining ¼ cup cheese. Bake in preheated 350°F oven 20 minutes or until cheese melts and barley-vegetable mixture is heated through.   *Makes 6 servings*

Favorite recipe from **North Dakota Barley Council**

Raspberry Eggnog

½ cup sugar
2 tablespoons cornstarch
4 cups skim milk, divided
2 eggs, beaten
1 package (12 ounces) frozen raspberries, thawed
1 teaspoon vanilla
6 to 9 drops red food coloring
 Ground nutmeg

1. Combine sugar and cornstarch in large saucepan; stir in 2 cups milk. Bring to a boil over low heat, stirring constantly. Continue boiling 1 minute or until thickened, stirring constantly. Whisk small amount of hot milk mixture into eggs in small bowl. Whisk egg mixture back into hot milk mixture in saucepan. Cook over low heat 1 minute. Strain; cool.

2. Place raspberries in food processor or blender; process until smooth. Strain; discard seeds. Stir raspberry purée into milk mixture; stir in remaining 2 cups milk and vanilla. Add red food coloring, one drop at a time, until eggnog is desired shade. Cover; refrigerate until cold or ready to serve. Sprinkle each serving with nutmeg. Garnish with mint sprigs and raspberries, if desired.   *Makes 12 (½-cup) servings*

Pixel

QUICK
MEAL

1 large onion, thinly sliced
1 tablespoon olive oil
2 teaspoons dried oregano leaves
1 clove garlic, minced
½ teaspoon ground cumin
2 cans (about 14 ounces each) chicken broth
1 package (10 ounces) frozen corn
1 to 2 cans (4 ounces each) chopped green chiles, undrained
1 can (2¼ ounces) sliced black olives, drained
¾ pound boneless skinless chicken breasts

Raspberry Eggnog

Combine onion, oil, oregano, garlic and cumin in Dutch oven. Cover and cook over medium heat about 6 minutes or until onion is tender, stirring occasionally.

Stir broth, corn, chiles with liquid and olives into onion mixture. Cover and bring to a boil over high heat.

While soup is cooking, cut chicken into thin strips. Add to soup. Reduce heat to medium-low; cover and cook 3 to 4 minutes or until chicken is cooked through.   *Makes 6 servings*

Prep and cook time: 20 minutes

Party Cheese Wreath

- **2 packages (8 ounces each) PHILADELPHIA BRAND® Cream Cheese,* softened**
- **1 package (8 ounces) KRAFT® Natural Shredded Sharp Cheddar Cheese**
- **1 tablespoon finely chopped onion**
- **1 tablespoon chopped red bell pepper**
- **2 teaspoons Worcestershire sauce**
- **1 teaspoon lemon juice**
- **Dash ground red pepper**

*May also use PHILADELPHIA BRAND® Neufchâtel Cheese, ⅓ Less Fat Than Cream Cheese or PHILADELPHIA BRAND® FREE® Fat Free Cream Cheese.

• Beat cream cheese and Cheddar cheese with electric mixer at medium speed until well blended. Add onion, bell pepper, Worcestershire sauce, lemon juice and red pepper; mix well. Refrigerate several hours or overnight.

• Place drinking glass in center of serving platter. Drop rounded tablespoonfuls of mixture to form ring around glass, just touching outer edge of glass; smooth with spatula. Remove glass. Garnish with chopped fresh parsley and additional chopped red bell pepper. Serve with crackers.   *Makes 2 cups*

Roasted Pepper and Avocado Salad

- **2 red bell peppers**
- **2 orange bell peppers**
- **2 yellow bell peppers**
- **2 ripe avocados, halved, pitted and peeled**
- **3 shallots, thinly sliced**
- **¼ cup FILIPPO BERIO® Extra Virgin Olive Oil**
- **1 clove garlic, crushed**
- **Finely grated peel and juice of 1 lemon**
- **Salt and freshly ground black pepper**

Place bell peppers on baking sheet. Broil, 4 to 5 inches from heat, 5 minutes on each side or until entire surface of each bell pepper is blistered and blackened slightly. Place bell peppers in paper bag. Close bag; cool 15 to 20 minutes. Cut around cores of bell peppers; twist and remove. Cut bell peppers lengthwise into halves. Peel off skin with paring knife; rinse under cold water to remove seeds. Slice bell peppers into ½-inch-thick strips; place in shallow dish. Cut avocados into ¼-inch-thick slices; add to bell peppers. Sprinkle with shallots.

In small bowl, whisk together olive oil, garlic, lemon peel and juice. Pour over bell pepper mixture. Cover; refrigerate at least 1 hour before serving. Season to taste with salt and black pepper.   *Makes 6 servings*

✦ MENU SUGGESTION ✦

Your friends will celebrate if you ring in the New Year together with this elegant dinner menu.

Roasted Red Pepper and Avocado Salad
Scallops with Linguine and Spinach (page 31)
Eggnog Cheesecake (page 47)

↣ ENTREES & SIDES ↢

Chicken Enchiladas

1¾ cups fat free sour cream
½ cup chopped green onions
⅓ cup minced fresh cilantro
1 tablespoon minced fresh jalapeño chili pepper
1 teaspoon ground cumin
1 tablespoon vegetable oil
12 ounces boneless, skinless chicken breasts, cut into 3×1-inch strips
1 teaspoon minced garlic
8 flour tortillas (8 inches)
1 cup (4 ounces) shredded ALPINE LACE® Reduced Fat Cheddar Cheese
1 cup bottled chunky salsa (medium or hot)
1 small ripe tomato, chopped
Sprigs of cilantro (optional)

Preheat the oven to 350°F. Spray a 13×9×3-inch baking dish with nonstick cooking spray.

In small bowl, mix together the sour cream, green onions, cilantro, jalapeño pepper and cumin. Spray a large nonstick skillet with the cooking spray, pour in the oil and heat over medium-high heat. Add the chicken and garlic and sauté for 4 minutes or until the juices run clear when the chicken is pierced with a fork.

Divide the chicken strips among the 8 tortillas, placing them down the center of the tortillas. Top with the sour cream mixture, then roll them up and place them, seam side down, in the baking dish.

Sprinkle with the cheese, cover with foil and bake for 30 minutes or until bubbly. Spoon the salsa in a strip down the center and sprinkle the salsa with the tomato. Garnish with the sprigs of cilantro, if you wish. Serve hot!   *Makes 8 servings*

Nutrients per Serving (1 enchilada):

Calories	247	Cholesterol	33 mg
Fat	6 g		

Countdown Casserole

1 jar (8 ounces) pasteurized processed cheese spread
¾ cup milk
2 cups (12 ounces) cubed cooked roast beef
1 bag (16 ounces) frozen vegetable combination (broccoli, corn, red pepper), thawed and drained
4 cups frozen hash brown potatoes, thawed
1 can (2.8 ounces) FRENCH'S® French Fried Onions, divided
½ teaspoon seasoned salt
¼ teaspoon black pepper
½ cup (2 ounces) shredded Cheddar cheese

Preheat oven to 375°. Spoon cheese spread into 8×12-inch baking dish; place in oven just until cheese melts, about 5 minutes. Using fork, stir milk into melted cheese until well blended. Stir in beef, vegetables, potatoes, *½ can* French Fried Onions and the seasonings. Bake, covered, at 375° for 30 minutes or until heated through. Top with Cheddar cheese and sprinkle remaining onions down center. Bake, uncovered, 3 minutes or until onions are golden brown.   *Makes 4 to 6 servings*

Microwave Directions: In an 8×12-inch microwave-safe dish, combine cheese spread and milk. Cook, covered, on HIGH 3 minutes; stir. Add ingredients as above. Cook, covered, 14 minutes or until heated through. Stir beef mixture halfway through cooking time. Top with Cheddar cheese and remaining onions as above. Cook, uncovered, 1 minute or until cheese melts. Let stand 5 minutes.

Italian Sausage Supper

  1 pound mild Italian sausage, casings removed
  1 cup chopped onion
  3 medium zucchini, sliced (about 1½ cups)
  ⅔ cup (6-ounce can) CONTADINA® Tomato Paste
  1 cup water
  1 teaspoon dried basil leaves, crushed
  ½ teaspoon salt
  3 cups cooked rice
  1 cup (4 ounces) shredded mozzarella cheese
  ¼ cup (1 ounce) grated Romano cheese

In large skillet, brown sausage with onion, stirring to break up sausage; drain, reserving 1 tablespoon drippings. Spoon sausage mixture into greased 2-quart casserole dish. Add zucchini to skillet; sauté for 5 minutes or until crisp-tender. In medium bowl, combine tomato paste, water, basil and salt. Stir in rice. Spoon over sausage mixture. Arrange zucchini slices on top; sprinkle with mozzarella and Romano cheeses. Cover. Bake in preheated 350°F oven for 20 minutes.   *Makes 6 servings*

Chunky Chicken Chili

  1 tablespoon vegetable oil
  1 pound boneless chicken breast, cut into pieces
  1 cup chopped onion
  ½ cup chopped celery
  ½ cup chopped carrot
  2 cloves garlic, minced
  1 can (27 ounces) FRANK'S or SNOWFLOSS
      Original Style Diced Tomatoes, undrained
  1 can (15½ ounces) dark red kidney beans,
      drained
  1 can (8 ounces) tomato sauce
  1 cup MISSISSIPPI BARBECUE SAUCE
  3 teaspoons chili powder
  ½ teaspoon ground cumin
  1 green bell pepper, chopped

1. In large saucepan heat oil. Add chicken, onion, celery, carrot and garlic. Cook and stir over high heat until chicken is no longer pink.

2. Stir in diced tomatoes, kidney beans, tomato sauce, barbecue sauce, chili powder and cumin.

3. Bring to a boil; reduce heat to low. Simmer, uncovered, 30 minutes, stirring occasionally.

4. Add green pepper and allow to heat through before serving.   *Makes 4 to 6 servings*

Simple Supper Sauté

  1 cup USA lentils
  2 cups water
  3 cloves garlic, minced
  ½ teaspoon dried oregano
  1 large onion, sliced
  2 medium zucchini, sliced
  2 tablespoons oil
  1 cup corn kernels *or* 1 can (11 ounces) corn,
      drained
  2 tablespoons chopped fresh basil

Rinse lentils. Place in medium saucepan with water, garlic and oregano. Heat to boiling. Reduce heat to simmer. Cover and simmer until lentils are tender, about 18 minutes. Drain.

In large skillet, sauté onion and zucchini in hot oil until tender, about 10 minutes. Stir in corn and lentils and heat through. Sprinkle with basil just before serving.   *Makes 4 servings*

Favorite recipe from **USA Dry Pea & Lentil Council**

Asparagus Wreath

1 pound fresh asparagus, cleaned and steamed
1 tablespoon butter or margarine
1 teaspoon lemon juice
6 thin slices pepperoni, finely chopped
¼ cup seasoned dry bread crumbs
    Pimiento strips for garnish

Arrange asparagus spears in glass ring mold or make wreath of spears on warm, round serving platter.

Melt butter and lemon juice in small saucepan over medium heat; pour over asparagus. Combine chopped pepperoni and bread crumbs in small bowl; sprinkle over asparagus. Garnish, if desired. Serve immediately.

Makes 4 side-dish servings

Funky Buffalo-Style Chicken Pizza

2 large prebaked pizza crust shells (12 inches each)
1 cup prepared pizza sauce or barbecue sauce
½ cup thinly sliced celery
3 cups sliced cooked chicken*
6 tablespoons FRANK'S® REDHOT® Original Cayenne Pepper Sauce
2 tablespoons butter or margarine, melted
2 cups (8 ounces) shredded mozzarella cheese
⅔ cup (3 ounces) Gorgonzola or blue cheese, crumbled

*To cook chicken, grill 1 pound boneless skinless chicken over hot coals 10 minutes or until no longer pink in center, turning once.

Asparagus Wreath

Place pizza shells on disposable foil pizza pans or on heavy-duty foil. Spread shells with pizza sauce and sprinkle with celery, dividing evenly. Place chicken in large bowl. Add RedHot® sauce and butter; toss well to coat evenly. Arrange chicken evenly on top of pizzas. Sprinkle with the cheeses.

Place pizzas on grid. Cook** pizzas over medium-high coals 15 minutes or until crust is crispy and cheese melts. To serve, cut into wedges.   *Makes 8 servings*

**Or, bake in 400°F oven 15 minutes.

✦ FOOD FOR THOUGHT ✦

"A good cook is like a sorceress who dispenses happiness."

Elsa Schiaperelli

Beef 'n' Broccoli

½ cup A.1.® Steak Sauce
¼ cup soy sauce
2 cloves garlic, crushed
1 pound top round steak, thinly sliced
1 bag (16 ounces) frozen broccoli, red bell peppers, bamboo shoots and mushrooms, thawed*
Hot cooked rice (optional)

*1 bag (16 ounces) frozen broccoli cuts, thawed, may be substituted.

In small bowl, combine steak sauce, soy sauce and garlic. Pour marinade over steak in nonmetal dish. Cover; refrigerate 1 hour, stirring occasionally.

Remove steak from marinade; reserve marinade. In large lightly oiled skillet, over medium-high heat, stir-fry steak 3 to 4 minutes or until steak is no longer pink. Remove steak with slotted spoon; keep warm.

In same skillet, heat vegetables and reserved marinade to a boil; reduce heat to low. Cover; simmer for 2 to 3 minutes. Stir in steak. Serve over rice, if desired.
    Makes 4 servings

Nutrients per Serving:

Calories	209	Cholesterol	65 mg
Fat	4 g	Sodium	166 mg

Creamy Chicken Florentine

8 ounces uncooked fusilli
1 box (10 ounces) frozen chopped spinach
1 package (8 ounces) cream cheese
½ cup canned chicken broth
½ teaspoon dried Italian seasoning
¼ teaspoon salt
¼ teaspoon black pepper
    Dash hot pepper sauce
1 can (10 ounces) premium chunk white chicken in water, drained
1 tablespoon lemon juice

Cook pasta according to package directions; drain. While pasta is cooking, remove outer wrapping from spinach, leaving spinach in box. Microwave spinach at HIGH 3 minutes or until thawed. Drain in colander; cool slightly. Squeeze spinach to remove excess moisture. Set aside.

Combine cream cheese, broth, Italian seasoning, salt, black pepper and hot pepper sauce in microwavable 2-quart casserole. Cover and microwave at HIGH 2 to 3 minutes; whisk until smooth and blended.

Add spinach, chicken and lemon juice. Microwave at HIGH 2 to 3 minutes or until hot, stirring after 1 minute. Combine pasta and spinach mixture in large bowl; toss until blended.   *Makes 4 servings*

Prep and cook time: 20 minutes

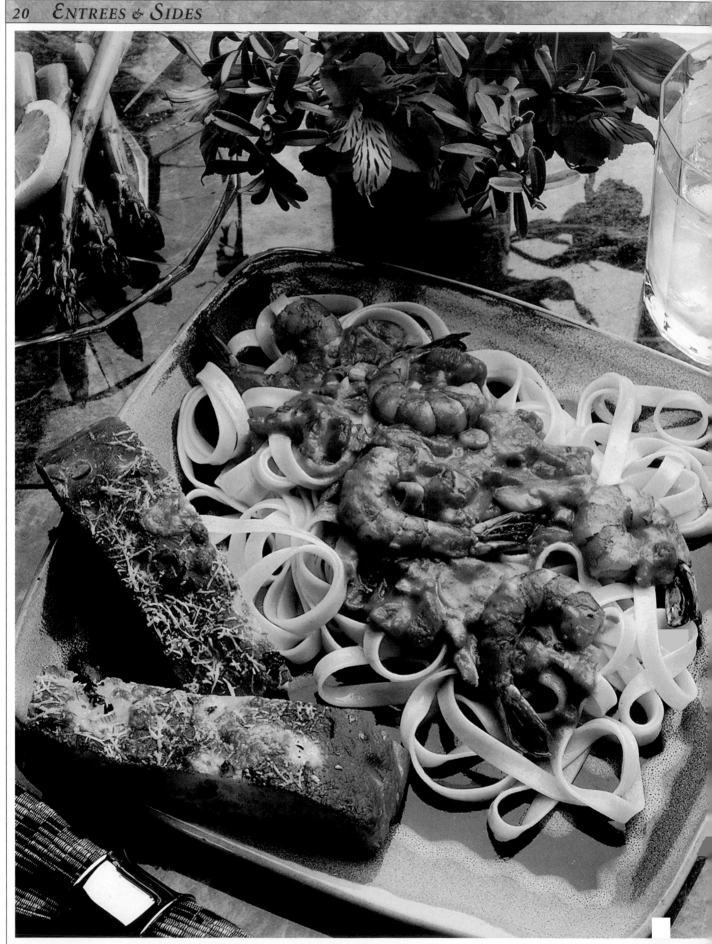

Milano Shrimp Fettucine

- 4 ounces uncooked egg or spinach fettucine
- ½ pound raw medium shrimp, shelled and deveined
- 1 clove garlic, minced
- 1 tablespoon olive oil
- 1 can (14½ ounces) DEL MONTE® Pasta Style Chunky Tomatoes
- ½ cup whipping cream
- ¼ cup sliced green onions

Cook pasta according to package directions; drain. In large skillet, cook shrimp and garlic in oil over medium-high heat until shrimp are pink and opaque. Stir in tomatoes; simmer, uncovered, 5 minutes. Blend in cream and green onions; heat through. *Do not boil.* Serve over hot pasta. *Makes 3 to 4 servings*

BEL PAESE® and Vegetable Casserole

- ½ small head cauliflower, cut into small flowerettes
- ½ pound broccoli, cut into medium-sized pieces
- 2 large carrots, cut into medium-sized pieces
- 2 red potatoes, cut into quarters
- ½ fennel bulb, cut up
- 1 clove garlic, minced
- 2 tablespoons butter
- 1 tablespoon all-purpose flour
- ½ teaspoon salt
- 1¼ cups milk
- 2 cups (8 ounces) shredded BEL PAESE® semi-soft cheese
- 2 egg yolks, beaten
  Black pepper

Preheat oven to 350°F. Grease 2-quart casserole; set aside. In Dutch oven, cook cauliflower, broccoli, carrots, potatoes and fennel in enough boiling water to cover for about 7 minutes. Drain; let cool. Arrange vegetables in prepared casserole dish; sprinkle with garlic. In small saucepan, melt butter. Stir in flour and salt. Blend in milk. Cook over medium-low heat until thick and bubbly, stirring constantly. Stir in cheese until melted. Remove from heat. Blend egg yolks into cheese sauce. Pour over vegetables. Sprinkle with pepper. Bake until hot, 20 to 25 minutes.

Makes 4 servings

Cheese & Chili Pepper Bread

- 4½ to 5 cups all-purpose flour, divided
- 2 cups (8 ounces) shredded Cheddar cheese
- 1 cup cornmeal
- 2 packages RED STAR® Active Dry Yeast or QUICK•RISE™ Yeast
- 2 tablespoons sugar
- 2 teaspoons salt
- 1¾ cups water
- ½ cup vegetable shortening
- 2 eggs
- 1 can (3 ounces) chopped green chili peppers, well drained
  Additional cornmeal

Preheat oven to 375°F.

In large bowl, combine 2½ cups flour, cheese, cornmeal, yeast, sugar and salt; mix well. Heat water and shortening until very warm (120° to 130°F; shortening does not need to melt). Add to flour mixture. Add eggs. Blend at low speed of electric mixer until moistened. Beat at medium speed 3 minutes. By hand, gradually stir in chilies and enough remaining flour to make a stiff batter. Cover; let rise in warm place about 30 minutes (15 minutes for QUICK•RISE™ Yeast).

Grease two 1½-quart casseroles and sprinkle with cornmeal. Spoon batter evenly into casseroles. Cover; let rise in warm place about 30 minutes (15 minutes for QUICK•RISE™ Yeast). Bake at 375°F 35 to 40 minutes or until golden brown. Remove from casseroles; serve warm or cold.

Makes 2 loaves bread

Variation: Batter may also be baked in 2 greased 8×4-inch bread pans.

Jamaican Pork Skillet

- 1 tablespoon vegetable oil
- 4 well-trimmed center cut pork chops, cut ½ inch thick
- ¾ teaspoon blackened or Cajun seasoning mix
- ¼ teaspoon ground allspice
- 1 cup chunky salsa, divided
- 1 can (15 ounces) black beans, drained and rinsed
- 1 can (about 8 ounces) whole kernel corn, drained *or* 1 cup thawed frozen whole kernel corn
- 1 tablespoon fresh lime juice

Heat oil in large deep skillet over medium-high heat until hot. Sprinkle both sides of pork chops with blackened seasoning mix and allspice; cook 2 minutes per side or until browned.

Pour ½ cup salsa over pork chops; reduce heat to medium. Cover and simmer about 12 minutes or until pork is no longer pink.

While pork chops are simmering, combine beans, corn, remaining ½ cup salsa and lime juice in medium bowl; mix well. Serve bean mixture with pork chops.

Makes 4 servings

Chicken-Cucumber Stir Fry

- 2 whole broiler-fryer chicken breasts, halved, boned, skinned, cut into bite-size pieces
- ¼ cup water
- ¼ cup dry sherry
- ¼ cup soy sauce
- 2 tablespoons dark corn syrup
- 1 tablespoon vinegar
- 4 teaspoons cornstarch
- ¼ teaspoon crushed red pepper
- ⅛ teaspoon ground ginger
- 3 tablespoons vegetable oil
- ½ pound fresh mushrooms, sliced
- 1 bunch green onions, cut into 2-inch pieces
- 1 can (8 ounces) water chestnuts, drained, sliced
- 2 cloves garlic, minced
- 1 cucumber, halved lengthwise, seeded, cut into thin 2-inch strips
- 12 cherry tomatoes, halved

In medium bowl, mix together water, sherry, soy sauce, corn syrup, vinegar, cornstarch, red pepper and ginger; set aside. Heat oil in wok or large skillet over medium-high heat. Add chicken; stir-fry 3 to 4 minutes or until chicken is lightly browned. Add mushrooms, green onions, water chestnuts and garlic; stir-fry 3 minutes. Add cucumber and stir-fry about 1 minute or until vegetables are crisp-tender. Add soy mixture and cook, stirring, until sauce thickens. Add cherry tomatoes and heat through.

Makes 4 servings

Favorite recipe from **Delmarva Poultry Industry, Inc.**

Hot and Spicy Onion Beef

- 2 tablespoons soy sauce, divided
- 1 tablespoon cornstarch, divided
- ¾ pound flank steak, thinly sliced across the grain
- 2 tablespoons dry sherry
- 1 teaspoon Oriental sesame oil
- 1 teaspoon chili paste (optional)
- 2 tablespoons vegetable oil
- 1 large onion (12 to 14 ounces), sliced vertically
- 1 teaspoon minced garlic
  Dried whole red chili peppers to taste
- 1 tablespoon water

Combine 1 tablespoon soy sauce and 1 teaspoon cornstarch in medium bowl. Add beef; stir to coat. Let stand 30 minutes. Combine remaining 1 tablespoon soy sauce, the sherry, sesame oil and chili paste in small bowl; set aside. Heat wok or large skillet over high heat. Add vegetable oil, swirling to coat sides. Add onion, garlic and chili peppers; cook and stir until onion is tender. Add beef; stir-fry 2 minutes or until lightly browned. Add soy sauce mixture and mix well. Combine remaining 2 teaspoons cornstarch and the water; mix into onion mixture. Cook and stir until sauce boils and thickens. *Makes about 4 servings*

Favorite recipe from **National Onion Association**

Apricot Carrot Bread

1¾ cups all-purpose flour
1 teaspoon baking powder
¼ teaspoon baking soda
¼ teaspoon salt
½ cup granulated sugar
½ cup finely shredded carrots
½ cup MOTT'S® Natural Apple Sauce
1 egg, beaten lightly
2 tablespoons vegetable oil
⅓ cup dried apricots, snipped into small bits
½ cup powdered sugar
2 teaspoons MOTT'S® Apple Juice

1. Preheat oven to 350°F. Spray 8×4-inch loaf pan with nonstick cooking spray.

2. In large bowl, combine flour, baking powder, baking soda and salt.

3. In small bowl, combine granulated sugar, carrots, applesauce, egg and oil.

4. Stir applesauce mixture into flour mixture just until moistened. (Batter will be thick.) Fold in apricots. Spread batter in prepared pan.

5. Bake 45 to 50 minutes or until toothpick inserted in center comes out clean. Cool in pan 10 minutes. Invert onto wire rack; turn right side up and cool completely. For best flavor, wrap loaf in plastic wrap or foil; store at room temperature overnight.

6. Just before serving, in small bowl, combine powdered sugar and apple juice until smooth. Drizzle over top of loaf. *Makes 12 servings*

Mustard Chicken & Vegetables

¼ cup FRENCH'S® Dijon or Classic Yellow® Mustard
¼ cup vegetable oil
1 tablespoon red wine vinegar
½ teaspoon dried oregano, crumbled
¼ teaspoon pepper
¼ teaspoon salt
2 pounds chicken pieces, fat trimmed
1 can (10¾ ounces) condensed cream of chicken soup
½ cup milk
2 cups (8 ounces) fusilli or rotini, cooked in unsalted water and drained
1 cup *each* zucchini and yellow squash, cut into 1-inch chunks
1 can (2.8 ounces) FRENCH'S® French Fried Onions, divided
1 medium tomato, cut into wedges

Preheat oven to 375°. In large bowl, combine mustard, oil, vinegar and seasonings; mix well. Toss chicken in mustard sauce until coated. Reserve remaining mustard sauce. Arrange chicken in 9×13-inch baking dish. Bake, uncovered, at 375° for 30 minutes. Stir soup, milk, hot pasta, squash and ½ *can* French Fried Onions into remaining mustard sauce. Spoon pasta mixture into baking dish, placing it under and around chicken. Bake, uncovered, 15 to 20 minutes or until chicken is done. Top pasta mixture with tomato wedges and top chicken with remaining onions; bake, uncovered, 3 minutes or until onions are golden brown. *Makes 4 to 6 servings*

Microwave Directions: Prepare mustard sauce as above; add chicken and toss until coated. Reserve remaining mustard sauce. In 8×12-inch microwave-safe dish, arrange chicken with meatiest parts toward edges of dish. Cook, uncovered, on HIGH 10 minutes. Rearrange chicken. Prepare pasta mixture and add to chicken as above. Cook, uncovered, 15 to 17 minutes or until chicken and vegetables are done. Stir vegetables and pasta and rotate dish halfway through cooking time. Top with tomato wedges and remaining onions as above; cook, uncovered, 1 minute. Let stand 5 minutes.

Angel Hair Carbonara

Angel Hair Carbonara

⅔ cup milk

2 tablespoons margarine or butter

1 package (4.8 ounces) PASTA RONI™ Angel Hair Pasta with Herbs

2 cups chopped cooked pork or ham

1 package (10 ounces) frozen peas

¼ cup sliced green onions

1. In round 3-quart microwavable glass casserole, combine 1½ cups water, milk and margarine. Microwave, uncovered, on HIGH (100% power) 4 to 5 minutes or until boiling.

2. Gradually add pasta, stirring constantly. Separate pasta with fork, if needed.

3. Stir in contents of seasoning packet.

4. Microwave, uncovered, on HIGH 4 minutes, stirring gently after 2 minutes. Separate pasta with fork, if needed. Stir in pork, frozen peas and onions. Microwave, uncovered, 2 to 3 minutes. Sauce will be thin but will thicken upon standing.

5. Let stand 3 minutes or until to desired consistency. Stir before serving.   *Makes 4 servings*

Honey Sweet Potato Biscuits

2 cups all-purpose flour
1 tablespoon baking powder
½ teaspoon salt
¼ cup vegetable shortening
¾ cup mashed cooked sweet potato (1 large sweet potato baked until tender, peeled and mashed)
⅓ cup honey
1 tablespoon grated orange peel
1 tablespoon grated lemon peel
½ cup milk (about)

Combine flour, baking powder and salt in large bowl. Cut in shortening until mixture resembles size of small peas. Add sweet potato, honey and orange and lemon peels; mix well. Add enough milk to make soft, but not sticky, dough. Knead 3 or 4 times on lightly floured surface. Pat dough to 1-inch thickness and cut into 2¼-inch rounds. Place on ungreased baking sheet.

Bake in preheated 400°F oven 15 to 18 minutes or until lightly browned. Serve warm.

Makes 10 biscuits

Favorite recipe from **National Honey Board**

> ## ⁖ COOK'S TIP ⁖
>
> If honey crystallizes, place the container in a pan of hot water and gently stir the honey until it liquefies. You can also remove the lid and microwave the honey at HIGH for 20 to 60 seconds.

Savory Pork & Apple Stir-Fry

1 package (7.2 ounces) RICE-A-RONI® Rice Pilaf
1⅓ cups apple juice or apple cider, divided
1 pound boneless pork loin, pork tenderloin or skinless, boneless chicken breast halves
1 teaspoon paprika
1 teaspoon dried thyme leaves
½ teaspoon ground sage or poultry seasoning
½ teaspoon salt (optional)
2 tablespoons margarine or butter
2 medium apples, cored, sliced
1 teaspoon cornstarch
⅓ cup coarsely chopped walnuts

1. Prepare Rice-A-Roni mix as package directs, substituting 1 cup water and 1 cup apple juice for water in directions.

2. While Rice-A-Roni is simmering, cut pork into 1½×¼-inch strips. Combine seasonings; toss with meat.

3. In second large skillet, melt margarine over medium heat. Stir-fry meat 3 to 4 minutes or just until pork is no longer pink.

4. Add apples; stir-fry 2 to 3 minutes or until apples are almost tender. Add combined remaining ⅓ cup apple juice and cornstarch. Stir-fry 1 to 2 minutes or until thickened to form glaze. Stir in nuts.

5. Serve rice topped with pork mixture.

Makes 4 servings

Prep and cook time: 25 minutes

Hot Mediterranean Chicken Salad

4 cups chicken broth
6 boneless skinless chicken breast halves
⅓ cup FILIPPO BERIO® Extra Virgin Olive Oil
1 medium onion, cut into thin strips
1 clove garlic, crushed
1 tablespoon chopped fresh oregano *or*
    1½ teaspoons dried oregano leaves
1 cup cooked small green beans
1 cup quartered cherry tomatoes
¾ cup pitted ripe olives
2 teaspoons grated lemon peel
1 to 2 tablespoons white wine vinegar
    Juice of 1 lemon
    Salt and freshly ground black pepper
6 cups finely shredded lettuce
    Additional lemon juice
    Chopped fresh parsley

In large saucepan or Dutch oven, bring chicken broth to a boil over high heat. Add chicken. Cover; reduce heat to low and simmer about 20 minutes or until chicken is no longer pink in center. Drain; let cool slightly. Coarsely chop.

In large skillet, heat olive oil over medium heat until hot. Add onion and garlic; cook and stir 5 minutes. Sprinkle with oregano; cook and stir an additional 5 to 10 minutes or until onion is almost transparent. Add green beans, tomatoes, olives and lemon peel; cook and stir until heated through. Add chicken. Season to taste with vinegar, juice of 1 lemon, salt and pepper. Heat briefly.

In large bowl, toss lettuce with additional lemon juice. Season to taste with salt and pepper. Divide equally among 6 plates. Spoon hot chicken salad over lettuce; garnish with parsley.

Makes 6 servings

Low Fat Pumpkin Bread

1 cup prepared prune butter
1 cup packed brown sugar
1 cup granulated sugar
1 cup egg substitute
1 cup canned solid pack pumpkin
2⅔ cups all-purpose flour
2 teaspoons baking powder
1 teaspoon baking soda
1 teaspoon ground cinnamon
½ teaspoon salt
½ teaspoon ground cloves
¼ teaspoon ground ginger
¼ teaspoon ground nutmeg

Preheat oven to 350°F. Coat two 8½×4½×2¾-inch loaf pans with vegetable cooking spray. In mixer bowl, beat prune butter with sugars until well blended. Beat in egg substitute and pumpkin just until blended. In medium bowl, combine flour, baking powder, baking soda, cinnamon, salt, cloves, ginger and nutmeg; stir into prune butter mixture until well blended. Spoon batter into prepared pans, dividing equally. Bake in center of oven 1 hour until pick inserted into centers comes out clean. Cool in pans 10 minutes; remove from pans to wire racks to cool completely. Serve with fat-free cream cheese, if desired.

Makes 2 loaves (16 slices per loaf)

Nutrients per Serving (1 slice):

Calories	106	Cholesterol	0 mg
Fat	1 g	Sodium	97 mg

Favorite recipe from **California Prune Board**

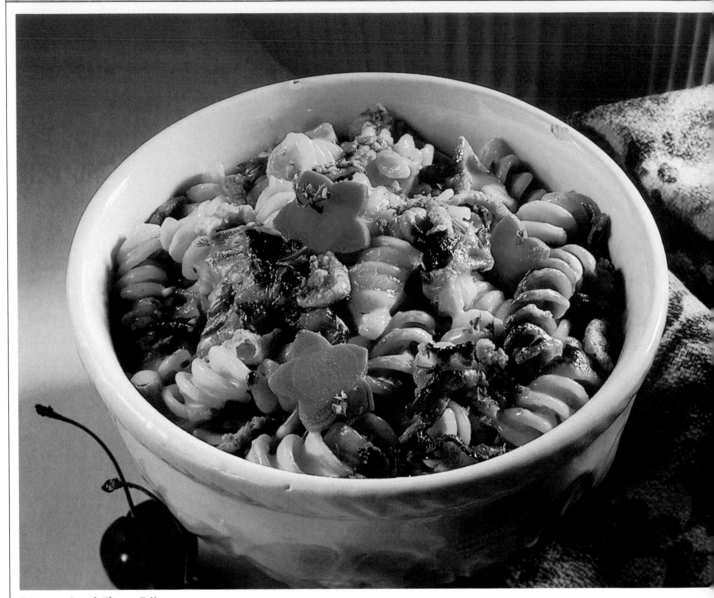

Macaroni and Cheese Dijon

Macaroni and Cheese Dijon

1¼ cups milk

12 ounces pasteurized process Cheddar cheese spread, cubed

½ cup GREY POUPON® Dijon Mustard

⅓ cup sliced green onions

6 slices bacon, cooked and crumbled

⅛ teaspoon ground red pepper

12 ounces tri-color rotelle or spiral-shaped pasta, cooked

1 can (2.8 ounces) French fried onion rings

In medium saucepan, over low heat, heat milk, cheese and mustard until cheese melts and mixture is smooth. Stir in green onions, bacon and pepper; remove from heat.

In large bowl, combine hot pasta and cheese mixture, tossing until well coated; spoon into greased 2-quart casserole. Cover; bake at 350°F for 15 to 20 minutes. Uncover and stir; top with onion rings. Bake, uncovered, for 5 minutes more. Let stand 10 minutes before serving. Garnish as desired.

Makes 6 servings

Broccoli & Cheddar Noodle Casserole

3 tablespoons margarine or butter, divided
2 cups chopped onions
4 cups broccoli flowerets
1¾ cups (14½-ounce can) CONTADINA® Stewed Tomatoes and juice
⅔ cup (6-ounce can) CONTADINA® Tomato Paste
1 package (1.5 ounces) spaghetti sauce seasoning mix
2 cups water
1 teaspoon garlic salt
6 cups (12-ounce package) dry wide egg noodles, cooked, drained
1½ cups (6 ounces) shredded Cheddar cheese
½ cup CONTADINA® Seasoned Bread Crumbs

In 5-quart saucepan, melt 2 tablespoons margarine; sauté onions until tender. Stir in broccoli, tomatoes and juice, tomato paste, seasoning mix, water, and garlic salt. Bring to a boil. Reduce heat; simmer, uncovered, for 10 minutes, stirring occasionally. Stir in cooked noodles. In 13×9×2-inch baking dish, layer half of the noodle mixture. Sprinkle with cheese. Layer with remaining noodle mixture. Melt remaining 1 tablespoon margarine; stir in crumbs. Sprinkle over casserole; cover and bake in preheated 350°F oven 20 minutes. Uncover; bake 5 minutes.

Makes 6 servings

Scallops with Linguine and Spinach

2 to 3 tablespoons olive oil
1½ cups finely chopped onion
1 cup slivered red bell pepper
2 tablespoons minced garlic
⅛ to ¼ teaspoon cayenne pepper
1 tablespoon grated lemon zest
⅓ cup fresh lemon juice
1 tablespoon brown sugar
1 teaspoon salt
1 teaspoon black pepper
¾ pound uncooked linguine
1 package (10 ounces) frozen chopped spinach, thawed and drained
1½ pounds scallops, cooked and kept warm
⅓ cup crumbled feta cheese

Heat oil in 12-inch heavy skillet on medium-low heat. Add onion, bell pepper, garlic and cayenne; cook until vegetables are tender, about 10 minutes. Add lemon zest, lemon juice, brown sugar, salt and black pepper; heat 1 minute.

While preparing onion mixture, bring a large pot of water to a boil; salt to taste. Add pasta; cook until tender, 8 to 10 minutes. About 1 minute before pasta is done, add spinach. Drain pasta and spinach and place in a large, warmed serving bowl. Add onion mixture and toss to coat. Taste and adjust seasonings. Add cooked scallops to pasta and sprinkle with feta cheese.

Makes 4 servings

Favorite recipe from **National Fisheries Institute**

Kielbasa & Chicken Gumbo

 6 slices bacon
 1 pound BOB EVANS FARMS® Kielbasa Sausage, cut into 1-inch pieces
 ½ pound boneless skinless chicken breasts, cut into 1-inch chunks
 ¼ cup all-purpose flour
 1 can (12 ounces) tomato juice
 1 cup water
 1 can (28 ounces) whole tomatoes, undrained
 2 cubes chicken bouillon
 1 can (8 ounces) tomato sauce
 1½ cups sliced fresh okra *or* 1 package (10 ounces) frozen cut okra, thawed
 1 medium onion, coarsely chopped
 1 medium green bell pepper, coarsely chopped
 2 bay leaves
 ½ teaspoon salt
 ½ teaspoon ground red pepper
 ⅛ teaspoon ground allspice
 1 pound uncooked medium shrimp, peeled
 Hot cooked rice (optional)

Cook bacon in large Dutch oven over medium-high heat until crisp. Remove bacon; drain on paper towel and crumble. Set aside. Cook and stir kielbasa and chicken in drippings over medium heat until chicken is lightly browned. Remove kielbasa and chicken; set aside. Drain off all but 3 tablespoons drippings from Dutch oven. Add flour to drippings; cook over medium heat 12 to 15 minutes or until reddish-brown, stirring constantly. Gradually stir in tomato juice and water until smooth. Add tomatoes with juice and bouillon, stirring well to break up tomatoes. Add reserved kielbasa, chicken, tomato sauce, okra, onion, green pepper, bay leaves, salt, red pepper and allspice; mix well. Bring to a boil over high heat. Reduce heat to low; simmer, covered, 1 hour, stirring occasionally. Add shrimp and simmer, covered, 10 minutes more or until shrimp turn pink and opaque. Remove and discard bay leaves. Stir in reserved bacon. Serve hot over rice, if desired. Refrigerate leftovers.

Makes 10 servings

✦ MENU SUGGESTION ✦

Who could resist sharing this wonderful Valentine's Day dinner?

Fruited Pork Loin
BEL PAESE® and Vegetable Casserole (page 21)
Chocolate and Raspberry Cream Torte (page 47)

Fruited Pork Loin

 1 cup dried apricot halves
 ½ cup dry sherry
 1 center cut pork rib or loin roast (3 to 5 pounds), backbone cracked
 1 cup KARO® Light or Dark Corn Syrup
 1 tablespoon grated orange peel
 ½ cup orange juice
 ¼ cup soy sauce

In small saucepan, combine apricots and sherry. Cover and cook over medium heat, stirring occasionally, until liquid is absorbed. Trim excess fat from surface of roast. Cut deep slits in meat directly over rib bones; insert 3 or 4 apricots in each slit. Place roast, bone-side down, on rack in roasting pan.

Roast in 325°F oven 1 to 2 hours* or until meat thermometer registers 160°F. Meanwhile, prepare glaze. In small saucepan, stir corn syrup, orange peel, orange juice and soy sauce. Bring to boil; reduce heat and simmer 5 minutes. Set aside half of glaze to serve with pork loin. Brush pork loin frequently with remaining glaze during last 30 minutes of roasting. Serve with reserved glaze. *Makes 6 to 10 servings*

*Roast pork loin at 325°F for 20 to 25 minutes per pound.

California Walnut Noodles

DRESSING
½ cup plain nonfat yogurt
½ cup orange juice
3 tablespoons balsamic vinegar or wine vinegar
2 tablespoons brown sugar
2 teaspoons sesame oil
1½ teaspoons grated fresh ginger *or* ½ teaspoon ground ginger
½ teaspoon crushed red pepper (optional)
2 cloves garlic, minced
   Salt to taste (optional)

NOODLES
12 ounces uncooked spaghetti or linguine
2 cups cooked, diced skinless chicken breasts
1 red or green bell pepper, halved, seeded and thinly sliced
1 cucumber, halved, seeded and thinly sliced
½ cup chopped green onions
2 teaspoons minced jalapeño pepper or other hot chili pepper
2 tablespoons chopped cilantro (optional)
⅔ cup Savory California Walnut Sprinkles (recipe follows)

For dressing, whisk together yogurt, orange juice, vinegar, sugar, oil, ginger, crushed red pepper, garlic and salt in large bowl. Set aside.

Cook pasta according to package directions. Drain and rinse well; drain. Toss pasta and ¾ cup dressing in large bowl. Combine chicken, bell pepper, cucumber, green onions, jalapeño pepper and cilantro with remaining dressing. Arrange pasta on large platter or in shallow bowl. Spoon chicken mixture down center. Just before serving, top each serving with one quarter of walnut sprinkles.   *Makes 4 servings*

Savory California Walnut Sprinkles

4 ounces (1 cup) chopped California walnuts
½ cup fresh white bread crumbs
1 tablespoon paprika
¼ teaspoon cayenne pepper
¼ teaspoon salt (optional)

Preheat oven to 325°F. In food processor, process walnuts until finely ground; transfer to small bowl. Add bread crumbs; stir to combine. Spread mixture in even layer on ungreased baking sheet. Bake 15 minutes, stirring frequently, until mixture is golden brown and crisp. Stir in paprika, cayenne pepper and salt. Cool to room temperature.   *Makes 1¼ cups*

Favorite recipe from **Walnut Marketing Board**

SPAM™ Lasagna

6 uncooked lasagna noodles
3½ cups chunky spaghetti sauce, divided
2 teaspoons dried basil leaves
1 can (12 ounces) SPAM® Luncheon Meat, thinly sliced, divided
2 cups (8 ounces) shredded mozzarella cheese, divided
⅓ cup grated Parmesan cheese

Heat oven to 350°F. Cook lasagna noodles according to package directions. In large bowl, combine spaghetti sauce and basil. In 9-inch square baking pan, spread ½ cup spaghetti sauce. Top with 3 lasagna noodles, cutting and overlapping noodles to fit, ½ of the SPAM® and ½ of the mozzarella cheese. Spread 1½ cups spaghetti sauce over mozzarella cheese. Repeat layers, ending with spaghetti sauce. Top with Parmesan cheese. Bake 45 to 50 minutes or until thoroughly heated.   *Makes 6 servings*

Speedy Beef & Bean Burritos

8 flour tortillas (7 inches)
1 pound ground beef
1 cup chopped onion
1 teaspoon bottled minced garlic
1 can (15 ounces) black beans, drained and rinsed
1 cup spicy thick and chunky salsa
2 teaspoons ground cumin
1 bunch cilantro
2 cups (8 ounces) shredded cojack or Monterey Jack cheese

Wrap tortillas in aluminum foil; place in oven. Turn temperature to 350°F; heat tortillas 15 minutes.

While tortillas are warming, prepare burrito filling. Combine meat, onion and garlic in large skillet; cook over medium-high heat until meat is no longer pink, breaking meat apart with wooden spoon. Pour off drippings.

Stir beans, salsa and cumin into meat mixture; reduce heat to medium. Cover and simmer 10 minutes, stirring once.

While filling is simmering, chop enough cilantro to measure ¼ cup. Stir into filling. Spoon filling down centers of warm tortillas; top with cheese. Roll up and serve immediately.   *Makes 4 servings*

Prep and cook time: 20 minutes

⊹ FOOD FOR THOUGHT ⊹

"We may live without poetry, music and art;
We may live without conscience, and live
without heart;
We may live without friends; we may live
without books;
But civilized man cannot live without cooks."

Owen Meredith

Stuffed Chicken Breasts à la Francaise

6 boneless, skinless chicken breast halves, with pockets (6 ounces each)
6 ounces (1 carton) ALPINE LACE® Fat Free Cream Cheese with Garlic & Herbs
½ cup finely chopped green onions (tops only)
2 teaspoons snipped fresh rosemary leaves *or* ¾ teaspoon dried rosemary
½ cup all-purpose flour
1 teaspoon freshly ground black pepper
⅓ cup low sodium chicken broth
⅓ cup dry white wine or low sodium chicken broth
8 sprigs fresh rosemary, about 3 inches long (optional)

1. Preheat the oven to 350°F. Spray a 13×9×2-inch baking dish with nonstick cooking spray. Rinse the chicken and pat dry with paper towels. In a medium-size bowl, mix the cream cheese with the green onions and rosemary until well blended. Stuff the pockets of the chicken breasts with this mixture.

2. On a piece of wax paper, blend the flour and pepper. Roll each chicken breast in the seasoned flour, then arrange in the baking dish. Pour over the broth and the wine.

3. Cover the dish tightly with foil and bake for 30 minutes. Uncover and bake 10 minutes more or until the juices run clear when the thickest piece of chicken is pierced with a fork.

4. Transfer the chicken to a serving platter and garnish each with a sprig of rosemary, if you wish.
Makes 6 servings

Homespun Turkey 'n' Vegetables

1 package (9 ounces) frozen cut green beans,
    thawed and drained
1 can (14 ounces) sliced carrots, drained
1 can (2.8 ounces) FRENCH'S® French Fried
    Onions, divided
1 can (16 ounces) whole potatoes, drained
1 can (10¾ ounces) condensed cream of celery
    soup
¼ cup milk
1 tablespoon FRENCH'S® Classic Yellow®
    Mustard
¼ teaspoon garlic powder
1 pound uncooked turkey breast slices

Preheat oven to 375°. In 8×12-inch baking dish,
combine green beans, carrots and ½ *can* French Fried
Onions. Slice potatoes into halves; arrange as many
halves as will fit, cut-side down, around edges of
baking dish. Combine any remaining potatoes with
vegetables in dish. In medium bowl, combine soup,
milk, mustard and garlic powder; pour *half* the soup
mixture over vegetables. Overlap turkey slices on
vegetables. Pour remaining soup mixture over turkey
and potatoes. Bake, covered, at 375° for 40 minutes or
until turkey is done. Top turkey with remaining
onions; bake, uncovered, 3 minutes or until onions are
golden brown.   *Makes 4 servings*

Anadama Bread

7¾ to 8¼ cups all-purpose flour, divided
2 packages (¼ ounce each) active dry yeast
1½ teaspoons salt
2¾ cups water
¾ cup molasses
¼ cup butter or margarine
1¼ cups yellow cornmeal

Combine 4 cups flour, yeast and salt in large bowl; set
aside. Combine water, molasses and butter in medium
saucepan. Heat over low heat until mixture is 120° to
130°F. (Butter does not need to melt completely.)

Gradually beat water mixture into flour mixture with
electric mixer at low speed. Increase speed to medium;
beat 2 minutes, scraping down side of bowl once. Beat
in cornmeal and 2 cups flour at low speed. Increase
speed to medium; beat 2 minutes, scraping down side
of bowl once. Stir in enough additional flour, about
1¾ cups, with wooden spoon to make soft dough.
Turn out dough onto floured surface; flatten slightly.
Knead dough 8 to 10 minutes or until smooth and
elastic, adding remaining ½ cup flour to prevent
sticking, if necessary. Shape dough into ball; place in
large greased bowl. Turn dough over so that top is
greased. Cover with towel; let rise in warm place about
1 hour or until doubled in bulk.

Punch down dough. Knead dough on well-floured
surface 1 minute. Cut dough into halves. Cover with
towel; let rest 10 minutes. Grease 2 (1½-quart) soufflé
or casserole dishes or 2 (9×5-inch) loaf pans. For
soufflé dishes, shape each half of dough into a ball;
place in prepared pans. For loaf pans, roll out one half
of dough into 12×8-inch rectangle with well-floured
rolling pin. Starting with one 8-inch side, roll up
dough jelly-roll style. Pinch seam and ends to seal.
Place loaf, seam side down, in prepared pan, tucking
ends under. Repeat with remaining dough. Cover
loaves with towel. Let rise in warm place about 40
minutes or until doubled in bulk.

Preheat oven to 375°F. Bake 35 to 40 minutes or until
loaves are browned and sound hollow when tapped.
Immediately remove from dishes or pans; cool on wire
racks.   *Makes 2 loaves*

Anadama Bread

✦ DESSERTS ✦

White Chocolate Bavarian Christmas Tree

INGREDIENTS
- 1 cup half-and-half
- 2 teaspoons vanilla
- 2 envelopes unflavored gelatin
- 6 eggs, separated*
- 12 ounces high-quality white or semisweet chocolate
- 1 teaspoon cream of tartar
- 1½ cups whipping cream, whipped
- Decorations: spearmint candy leaves, red cinnamon candies, red candy-coated licorice pieces, green miniature jaw breakers

SUPPLIES
- 1 tree mold or other decorative mold (8 cup)

*Use only grade A clean, uncracked eggs.

1. Combine half-and-half and vanilla in medium saucepan. Sprinkle gelatin over mixture; let stand 1 minute. Stir over low heat until gelatin is completely dissolved.

2. Beat egg yolks in small bowl. Stir about ½ cup gelatin mixture into egg yolks; return egg yolk mixture to saucepan. Cook over low heat, stirring constantly, until thick enough to coat the back of a spoon.

3. Melt chocolate in top of double boiler over hot, not boiling, water, stirring constantly. Stir gelatin mixture into chocolate. Remove from heat; cool to room temperature.

4. Beat egg whites and cream of tartar until stiff peaks form. Gently fold cooled chocolate mixture into beaten egg whites. Fold in whipped cream.

5. Spoon mixture into 8-cup tree or other decorative mold. Refrigerate until set, 8 hours or overnight.

6. To unmold, pull chocolate mixture from edge of mold with moistened fingers. Or, run small metal spatula or pointed knife dipped in warm water around edge of mold. Dip bottom of mold briefly in warm water. Place serving plate on top of mold. Invert mold and plate and shake to loosen chocolate mixture. Gently remove mold. Decorate with candies as shown in photo.   *Makes 12 to 14 servings*

✦ MENU SUGGESTION ✦

When you gather the family together for this Christmas menu, you'll be creating memories that will last a lifetime.

Orange-Berry Salad (page 10)
Asparagus Wreath (page 18)
Beef Tenderloin
Wild Rice
White Chocolate Bavarian Christmas Tree

White Chocolate Bavarian Christmas Tree

Cherry, Almond & Chocolate Breakfast Wreath

    1 cup cold water
    1 cup dry sweet or sour cherries
 ½ cup sugar, divided
 ¼ cup warm water (105° to 115°F)
    1 package active dry yeast
 ½ cup plus 1 tablespoon milk, divided
    3 tablespoons butter or margarine, cut into pieces
    2 eggs, divided
    1 tablespoon grated lemon peel
 ½ teaspoon salt
 ½ teaspoon almond extract
2½ to 2¾ cups all-purpose flour
 ½ cup canned almond filling (about 12 ounces)
 ¾ cup semisweet chocolate chips
    Almond Glaze (recipe follows)

Grease large bowl and large baking sheet. Set aside. Combine 1 cup water, cherries and ¼ cup sugar in small saucepan. Bring to a boil over high heat, stirring constantly. Cover saucepan; remove from heat. Set aside.

Pour ¼ cup warm water into large bowl. Sprinkle yeast over water. Let stand 5 minutes. Stir to dissolve.

Meanwhile heat ½ cup milk and butter in medium saucepan over high heat until milk bubbles around edge of saucepan, stirring constantly (butter does not need to melt completely). Remove saucepan from heat; stir occasionally until milk is warm to touch.

Add milk mixture to yeast mixture. Stir in remaining ¼ cup sugar, 1 egg, lemon peel, salt and almond extract until well blended. Add 2¼ cups flour; stir until dough forms sticky ball. Stir in enough remaining flour until soft dough forms.

Place dough on lightly floured surface. Knead dough 5 minutes or until smooth and elastic. Shape dough into ball; place in prepared bowl, turning dough to grease. Cover bowl with plastic wrap; let rise in warm place 1 to 2 hours or until dough doubles in bulk.

Preheat oven to 350°F. Punch down dough. Turn out onto lightly floured surface. Knead 10 to 12 times or until smooth. Shape into 10-inch-long log; flatten slightly.

Roll out dough into 18×8-inch rectangle. Trim ½-inch-thick strip of dough from short ends of rectangle; set aside for decorating wreath.

Starting ½ inch from long edge that is furthest from you, spread almond filling evenly over dough. Sprinkle cherries and chocolate evenly over filling. Beginning at long edge nearest you, roll up dough jelly-roll style. Pinch seam along length to seal.

Place on prepared baking sheet, curving into 8-inch circle. Pinch ends together.

Cut dough at 1½-inch intervals to within ¾ inch of center with sharp knife. Gently lift each section and turn on its side, overlapping slices.

Beat remaining egg and remaining 1 tablespoon milk in small bowl until well blended. Brush lightly over wreath.

To decorate wreath, cut 1 reserved dough strip into 15 or 18 pieces. Roll pieces into balls; place on wreath in clusters of three. Roll remaining dough strip into 12-inch-long log; shape into bow. Place bow on wreath. Brush berries and bow with egg mixture.

Bake 30 minutes or until wreath is golden brown. (If outer edge browns more rapidly than inner edge of circle, cover outer edge with heavy-duty foil. Bake until inner edge is golden brown.) Cool on baking sheet 5 minutes. Remove from pan to wire rack. Cool completely. Prepare Almond Glaze; drizzle over wreath. Store at room temperature up to 1 week.

Makes 1 wreath

Almond Glaze

 ½ cup powdered sugar, sifted
    2 teaspoons milk
 ¼ teaspoon almond extract

Combine all ingredients in small bowl; add additional milk until just thickened.   *Makes about ¼ cup*

Cherry, Almond & Chocolate Breakfast Wreath

Praline Pecans & Cranberries

3½ cups pecan halves
¼ cup light corn syrup
¼ cup packed light brown sugar
2 tablespoons butter or margarine
1 teaspoon vanilla
¼ teaspoon baking soda
1½ cups dried cranberries or cherries

Preheat oven to 250°F. Grease 13×9-inch baking pan. Cover large baking sheet with heavy-duty foil. Set aside.

Spread pecans in single layer in prepared baking pan.

Combine corn syrup, sugar and butter in 2-cup glass measure or small microwavable bowl. Microwave at HIGH 1 minute. Stir. Microwave 30 seconds to 1 minute or until boiling rapidly. Stir in vanilla and baking soda until well blended. Drizzle evenly over pecans; stir with wooden spoon until evenly coated.

Bake 1 hour, stirring with wooden spoon after each 20 minutes of baking. Immediately transfer mixture to prepared baking sheet, spreading pecans evenly over foil with lightly greased spatula.

Cool completely. Break pecans apart with wooden spoon. Combine pecans and cranberries in large bowl.

Store in airtight container at room temperature up to 2 weeks.   *Makes about 5 cups*

Hidden Treasure

Hidden Treasures

⅔ BUTTER FLAVOR* CRISCO® Stick or ⅔ cup
　 BUTTER FLAVOR CRISCO all-vegetable
　 shortening
¾ cup sugar
1 egg
1 tablespoon milk
1 teaspoon vanilla
1¾ cups all-purpose flour
1 teaspoon baking powder
½ teaspoon salt
½ teaspoon baking soda
48 maraschino cherries, well drained on paper
　 towels

WHITE DIPPING CHOCOLATE
　 1 cup white melting chocolate
　 2 tablespoons BUTTER FLAVOR CRISCO Stick or
　　 2 tablespoons BUTTER FLAVOR CRISCO all-
　　 vegetable shortening

DARK DIPPING CHOCOLATE
　 1 cup semisweet chocolate chips
　 2 tablespoons BUTTER FLAVOR CRISCO Stick or
　　 2 tablespoons BUTTER FLAVOR CRISCO all-
　　 vegetable shortening
　 Finely chopped pecans
　 Slivered white chocolate

*Butter Flavor Crisco is artificially flavored.

1. Preheat oven to 350°F. Cream shortening, sugar, egg, milk and vanilla in large bowl at medium speed of electric mixer until well blended.

2. Combine flour, baking powder, salt and baking soda. Beat into creamed mixture at low speed. Divide into 48 equal pieces.

3. Press dough into very thin layer around well-drained cherries. Place 2 inches apart on ungreased baking sheet.

4. Bake 10 minutes. Cool 1 minute on baking sheet. Remove to wire rack to cool completely.

5. For dipping chocolate, place chocolate of choice and shortening in glass measuring cup. Microwave at 50% (MEDIUM). Stir after 1 minute. Repeat until smooth (or melt on range top in small saucepan on very low heat).

6. Drop one cookie at a time into chocolate. Use fork to turn. Cover completely with chocolate.** Lift cookie out of chocolate with fork. Allow excess to drip off. Place on waxed paper-lined baking sheet.

7. Sprinkle chopped pecans on top of white chocolate cookies before chocolate sets. Sprinkle white chocolate on dark chocolate cookies before chocolate sets. Chill in refrigerator to set chocolate.

Makes about 4 dozen cookies

**If chocolate becomes too firm, reheat in microwave or on range top.

Chocolate-Dipped Almond Horns

　 1 can SOLO® Almond Paste
　 3 egg whites
½ cup superfine sugar
½ teaspoon almond extract
¼ cup plus 2 tablespoons all-purpose flour
½ cup sliced almonds
　 5 squares (1 ounce each) semisweet chocolate,
　　 melted and cooled

Preheat oven to 350°F. Grease 2 cookie sheets; set aside. Break almond paste into small pieces and place in medium bowl or container of food processor. Add egg whites, sugar and almond extract. Beat with electric mixer or process until mixture is very smooth. Add flour and beat or process until blended.

Spoon almond mixture into pastry bag fitted with ½-inch (#8) plain tip. Pipe mixture into 5- or 6-inch crescent shapes on prepared cookie sheets about 1½ inches apart. Sprinkle with sliced almonds.

Bake 13 to 15 minutes or until edges are golden. Cool on cookie sheets on wire racks 2 minutes. Remove from cookie sheets and cool completely on wire racks. Dip ends of cookies in melted chocolate and place on sheet of foil. Let stand until chocolate is set.

Makes about 16 cookies

Chocolate and Raspberry Cream Torte

6 tablespoons extra light corn oil spread
1 cup sugar
1 cup skim milk
1 tablespoon white vinegar
½ teaspoon vanilla extract
1¼ cups all-purpose flour
⅓ cup HERSHEY'S Cocoa or HERSHEY'S
    European Style Cocoa
1 teaspoon baking soda
¼ cup red raspberry jam
    Raspberry Cream (recipe follows)

Heat oven to 350°F. Spray 15½×10½×1-inch jelly-roll pan with vegetable cooking spray. In medium saucepan over low heat, melt corn oil spread; stir in sugar. Remove from heat; stir in milk, vinegar and vanilla. In small bowl, stir together flour, cocoa and baking soda; add gradually to sugar mixture, stirring with whisk until well blended. Pour into prepared pan.

Bake 16 to 18 minutes or until wooden pick inserted in center comes out clean. Cool 10 minutes; remove from pan to wire rack. Cool completely. To assemble, cut cake crosswise into four pieces. Place one piece on serving plate; spread 1 tablespoon jam over top. Carefully spread a scant ¾ cup Raspberry Cream over jam. Repeat procedure with remaining cake layers, jam and Raspberry Cream, ending with plain layer on top. Spread remaining 1 tablespoon jam over top. Spoon or pipe remaining Raspberry Cream over jam. Refrigerate torte until ready to serve. Garnish as desired. Cover; refrigerate leftover torte.

Makes 14 servings

RASPBERRY CREAM: Thaw and thoroughly drain 1 package (10 ounces) frozen red raspberries. In blender container, place raspberries. Cover; blend until smooth. Strain in sieve; discard seeds. In small mixer bowl, prepare 1 envelope (1.3 ounces) dry whipped topping mix as directed on package, using ½ cup cold skim milk, omitting vanilla and adding 2 to 3 drops red food color, if desired. Fold in puréed raspberries.

Nutrients per Serving:

Calories	170	Cholesterol	0 mg
Fat	3 g	Sodium	100 mg

Eggnog Cheesecake

CRUST
2 cups vanilla wafer cookie crumbs
6 tablespoons butter or margarine, melted
½ teaspoon ground nutmeg

FILLING
4 packages (8 ounces each) PHILADELPHIA
    BRAND® Cream Cheese, softened
1 cup sugar
3 tablespoons all-purpose flour
3 tablespoons rum
1 teaspoon vanilla
2 eggs
1 cup whipping cream
4 egg yolks

• Heat oven to 325°F.

• To prepare Crust, mix together crumbs, butter and nutmeg; press onto bottom and 1½ inches up side of 9-inch springform pan. Bake 10 minutes.

• To prepare Filling, beat cream cheese, sugar, flour, rum and vanilla with electric mixer at medium speed until well blended. Add eggs, 1 at a time, mixing at low speed after each addition, just until blended. Blend in whipping cream and egg yolks; pour into crust.

• Bake 1 hour and 10 minutes to 1 hour and 15 minutes or until center is almost set. Run knife or metal spatula around rim of pan to loosen cake; cool before removing rim of pan. Refrigerate 4 hours or overnight. Garnish with thawed COOL WHIP® Whipped Topping and ground nutmeg.

Makes 12 servings

Chocolate Steamed Pudding

1½ squares (1 ounce) unsweetened chocolate
1 tablespoon butter
1 cup sugar
2 eggs
½ teaspoon vanilla
¾ cup hot coffee
1½ cups all-purpose flour
1½ teaspoons baking powder
¼ teaspoon salt
Ellie's Mom's Sauce (recipe follows)

Preheat oven to 350°F. Melt chocolate with butter in small saucepan over very low heat. Remove from heat and cool. Combine sugar, eggs and vanilla in large bowl; beat well. Blend in coffee. Sift together dry ingredients in separate large bowl. Add to sugar mixture; mix well. Blend chocolate mixture into sugar mixture. Divide batter evenly among 8 buttered (6-ounce) custard cups. Cover each tightly with aluminum foil. Place cups in pan with at least 1-inch sides; fill with ½ inch very hot water. Cover pan tightly with aluminum foil. Bake 45 minutes. Cool; unmold. Serve warm with Ellie's Mom's Sauce.

Makes 8 servings

Ellie's Mom's Sauce

1¼ cups sifted powdered sugar
5 tablespoons butter, melted
1 egg
¾ teaspoon vanilla
⅛ teaspoon salt
½ cup whipping cream

Combine all ingredients except whipping cream in small bowl; mix well. Beat cream in medium bowl until thickened. Fold sugar mixture into whipped cream until combined.

Favorite recipe from **Wisconsin Milk Marketing Board**

Pfeffernüsse

3½ cups all-purpose flour
2 teaspoons baking powder
1½ teaspoons ground cinnamon
1 teaspoon ground ginger
½ teaspoon baking soda
½ teaspoon salt
½ teaspoon ground cloves
½ teaspoon ground cardamom
¼ teaspoon freshly ground black pepper
1 cup butter, softened
1 cup granulated sugar
¼ cup dark molasses
1 egg
Powdered sugar

Grease cookie sheets. Place flour, baking powder, cinnamon, ginger, baking soda, salt, cloves, cardamom and pepper in large bowl; stir to combine. Beat butter and sugar in large bowl with electric mixer at medium speed until light and fluffy. Beat in molasses and egg. Gradually add flour mixture. Beat at low speed until dough forms. Form into a disc; wrap in plastic wrap and refrigerate until firm. Preheat oven to 350°F. Roll dough into 1-inch balls. Place 2 inches apart on prepared cookie sheets. Bake 12 to 14 minutes or until golden brown. Remove to wire racks; dust with sifted powdered sugar. Cool completely.

Makes about 5 dozen cookies

Candy Cane & Wreath Ornaments

  1 cup sugar
  ½ cup shortening
  ½ cup butter or margarine
  1 teaspoon salt
  1 egg
  2 teaspoons vanilla
2½ cups all-purpose flour
  ½ teaspoon almond extract
  ¼ teaspoon liquid green food coloring
  ¼ teaspoon peppermint extract
  ½ teaspoon liquid red food coloring, divided
    Decorator Frosting (recipe follows)
    Assorted red candies
    Ribbon

Beat sugar, shortening, butter and salt in large bowl with electric mixer at medium speed until light and fluffy, scraping down side of bowl once. Beat in egg and vanilla until well blended. Beat in flour at low speed until soft dough forms, scraping down side of bowl once.

Remove half of dough from bowl. Set aside. Divide remaining dough evenly between 2 medium bowls. Stir almond extract and green food coloring into one medium bowl with wooden spoon until well blended.

Stir peppermint extract and ¼ teaspoon red food coloring into remaining medium bowl until well blended.

Place level teaspoonfuls of each dough on large baking sheet. Cover; refrigerate 15 minutes or until slightly firm.

Preheat oven to 375°F. Place 1 teaspoon red dough, 1 teaspoon green dough and 2 teaspoons uncolored dough on lightly floured surface. Roll out each portion into 6- to 7-inch rope with lightly floured hands.

Place 1 green rope next to 1 uncolored rope and 1 red rope next to remaining uncolored rope. Twist each pair of ropes together 7 or 8 times; place on *ungreased* baking sheet.

Shape red and uncolored rope into candy cane and green and uncolored rope into wreath. Repeat with remaining dough.

Bake 7 to 9 minutes or until cookies are firm. *Do not allow to brown.* Transfer cookies with spatula to wire racks; cool completely.

Prepare Decorator Frosting. Tint half of frosting with remaining ¼ teaspoon red liquid food coloring. Spoon frostings into piping bags fitted with writing tips.

Pipe cluster of berries onto wreaths with red frosting. Glue candies onto wreaths with white frosting. Let stand 1 hour or until icing is set. Tie ribbon loops or bows onto each cookie for hanging.

Makes about 4 dozen cookies

Decorator Frosting

  ¾ cup butter, softened
4½ cups powdered sugar, sifted
  3 tablespoons water
  1 teaspoon vanilla
  ¼ teaspoon lemon extract

Beat butter in medium bowl with electric mixer at medium speed until smooth. Add 2 cups sugar. Beat at medium speed until light and fluffy. Add water and extracts. Beat at low speed until well blended, scraping down side of bowl once. Beat in remaining 2½ cups sugar until mixture is creamy.

⊰ COOK'S TIP ⊱

To prevent cracking, do not overmix cheesecake batter. Beat just until the mixture is blended.

Peppermint Stick Cheesecake

2 packages (8 ounces each) PHILADELPHIA BRAND® Cream Cheese, softened

½ cup sugar

½ teaspoon vanilla

2 eggs

¾ cup finely crushed peppermint candy, divided

1 ready to use graham cracker pie crust (6 ounces or 9 inch)

MIX cream cheese, sugar and vanilla at medium speed with electric mixer until well blended. Add eggs; mix until blended. Stir in ½ cup of the peppermint candy.

POUR into crust. Sprinkle with remaining ¼ cup peppermint candy.

BAKE at 350°F, 40 minutes or until center is almost set. Cool. Refrigerate 3 hours or overnight. Garnish with COOL WHIP Whipped Topping and crushed peppermint candy.   *Makes 8 servings*

Variation: For **Confetti Sprinkles,** omit peppermint candy. Stir 3 tablespoons multicolored sprinkles into batter. Top with additional 2 tablespoons sprinkles before baking.

Peppermint Stick Cheesecake

Smucker's® Crimson Ribbon Bars

6 tablespoons butter or margarine, softened
½ cup firmly packed brown sugar
1 teaspoon vanilla
½ cup all-purpose flour
¼ teaspoon baking soda
1½ cups rolled oats
1 cup chopped walnuts
½ cup chopped figs
⅓ cup SMUCKER'S® Red Raspberry Preserves

Preheat oven to 375°F. Combine butter, brown sugar and vanilla; beat until well blended. Add flour and baking soda; mix well. Stir in oats and walnuts. Reserve ¾ cup oat mixture for topping. Press remaining oat mixture into 8-inch square baking pan coated with nonstick cooking spray. Combine figs and preserves; spread over oat mixture leaving ½-inch border. Sprinkle with reserved oat mixture; press lightly.

Bake 25 to 30 minutes or until golden brown. Cool in pan; cut into bars. *Makes 20 bars*

Triple Layer Fudge

Chocolate Fudge (recipe follows)
Peanut Butter Fudge (recipe follows)
White Fudge (recipe follows)

1. Grease 13×9-inch baking pan. Set aside. Prepare Chocolate Fudge. Immediately spread into prepared pan with lightly greased rubber spatula.

2. Immediately prepare Peanut Butter Fudge; spread evenly over Chocolate Fudge with lightly greased rubber spatula.

3. Immediately prepare White Fudge; spread evenly over Peanut Butter Fudge with lightly greased spatula.

4. If desired, to marble fudge, swirl knife through all layers, lifting and turning fudge with each swirl.

5. Cover fudge with plastic wrap. Refrigerate 2 hours or until firm. Cut into 1-inch squares. Store tightly covered in refrigerator up to 3 weeks.
Makes about 10 dozen pieces

Chocolate Fudge

1½ cups granulated sugar
1 can (5 ounces) evaporated milk
2 tablespoons butter or margarine
¼ teaspoon salt
1½ cups miniature marshmallows
1 cup (6 ounces) semisweet chocolate chips
1½ teaspoons vanilla

1. Combine sugar, milk, butter and salt in medium saucepan. Bring to a boil over medium heat, stirring constantly with wooden spoon. Boil 5 minutes, stirring constantly.

2. Remove saucepan from heat. Stir in marshmallows with wooden spoon until melted and mixture is well blended.

3. Add chocolate chips and vanilla. Stir until mixture is smooth. Stir mixture 6 minutes or until slightly thickened.

Peanut Butter Fudge

Reduce granulated sugar to ¾ cup; *add* ¾ cup packed light brown sugar. *Omit* butter and chocolate. Prepare as directed for Chocolate Fudge in Steps 1 and 2. *Stir* ½ cup creamy peanut butter into mixture; continue as directed in Step 3.

White Fudge

Substitute white chocolate chips for semisweet chocolate chips. Prepare as directed for Chocolate Fudge.

Black Forest Chocolate Fudge Cake

        2 cups cake flour
        1 cup unsweetened cocoa powder
        1 teaspoon baking powder
     ½ teaspoon salt
    1½ cups packed brown sugar
        2 eggs
        1 egg white
        1 cup prepared prune butter
     ¾ cup nonfat milk
        4 teaspoons vanilla
        1 cup boiling water
        2 tablespoons instant espresso coffee powder
        2 teaspoons baking soda
        2 cups frozen pitted unsweetened dark sweet
            cherries, coarsely chopped, thawed and well
            drained
     ½ cup chopped toasted walnuts
        Mocha Glaze (recipe follows)
        Chocolate Drizzle (optional, recipe follows)
        Fresh cherries or frozen cherries, thawed
        Mint sprigs, for garnish

Preheat oven to 350°F. Coat 12- to 16-cup Bundt or other tube pan with vegetable cooking spray. In large bowl, combine flour, cocoa, baking powder and salt; mix in brown sugar. In medium bowl, whisk eggs, egg white, prune butter, milk and vanilla. In 2-cup measure, combine boiling water, espresso powder and baking soda. Stir prune butter and water mixtures into flour mixture; mix just until blended. Pour half the batter into prepared pan; sprinkle cherries and walnuts evenly over batter. Top with remaining batter. Bake in center of oven about 45 minutes until pick inserted into center comes out clean. Cool in pan on wire rack 15 minutes; remove from pan. Cool completely on wire rack. Prepare Mocha Glaze. Spoon over cake, allowing glaze to run down sides. Prepare Chocolate Drizzle, if desired. Drizzle over glaze. Fill cake center with fresh cherries and garnish with mint sprigs.   *Makes 16 servings*

MOCHA GLAZE: Place 1 cup powdered sugar in small bowl. Dissolve ⅛ teaspoon instant espresso coffee powder in 4 teaspoons water. Stir into sugar until smooth, adding 1 teaspoon water, if needed, for desired consistency.

CHOCOLATE DRIZZLE: In top of double boiler or bowl set over simmering water, melt 2 tablespoons semisweet chocolate chips. Stir in 2 teaspoons hot water until blended. Cool until desired consistency.

Favorite recipe from **California Prune Board**

Snow Covered Almond Crescents

        1 cup (2 sticks) margarine or butter, softened
     ¾ cup powdered sugar
     ½ teaspoon almond extract *or* 2 teaspoons vanilla
    1¾ cups all-purpose flour
     ¼ teaspoon salt (optional)
        1 cup QUAKER® Oats (quick or old fashioned, uncooked)
     ½ cup finely chopped almonds
        Powdered sugar

Preheat oven to 325°F. Beat margarine, sugar and almond extract until well blended. Add flour and salt, if desired; mix until well blended. Stir in oats and almonds. Using level measuring tablespoonfuls, shape dough into crescents. Bake on ungreased cookie sheet 14 to 17 minutes or until bottoms are light golden brown. Remove to wire rack. Sift additional powdered sugar generously over warm cookies. Cool completely. Store tightly covered.   *Makes about 3 dozen cookies*

Spring

"I know there will be spring; as surely as the birds know it when they see above the snow two tiny, quivering green leaves. Spring cannot fail us."

Olive Schreiner

Spiced Orange Chicken with Lentils (page 69)

✦ *STARTERS* ✦

Quesadillas

  4 flour tortillas (8 inch)
  ¾ cup (3 ounces) shredded ALPINE LACE®
      American Flavor Pasteurized Process Cheese
      Product with Jalapeño Peppers, divided
  ⅓ cup finely chopped green onions, divided
  2 tablespoons minced fresh cilantro *or* ¼ cup
      minced fresh parsley, divided
  1 small avocado, peeled, seeded and thinly sliced
      lengthwise (optional)
  ½ cup chunky salsa

1. Preheat the oven to 350°F. Arrange 2 tortillas on a baking sheet. Top each tortilla with half the cheese, half the green onions and half the cilantro. Cover each with a second tortilla, pressing down lightly with your hands.

2. Bake for 10 minutes or until the cheese melts and the tortillas are crisp. Cut each quesadilla into 6 wedges. Garnish each wedge with a slice of avocado, if you wish, and a spoonful of salsa.

Makes 12 appetizer servings

Nutrients per Serving (1 wedge):

Calories	59	Total Fat	2 g
Calories from fat	18	Cholesterol	5 mg

Mediterranean Greek Salad

  ½ cup olive oil
  ⅓ cup red wine vinegar
  2 teaspoons chopped fresh oregano *or* ¾ teaspoon
      dried oregano
  1 teaspoon LAWRY'S® Seasoned Salt
  1 teaspoon LAWRY'S® Garlic Powder with Parsley
  3 medium cucumbers, peeled and chopped
  3 to 4 medium tomatoes, seeded and coarsely
      chopped
  1 medium onion, thinly sliced and separated into
      rings
  1 can (6 ounces) Greek or ripe olives, drained,
      pitted
  1 cup (4 ounces) crumbled feta cheese

In container with stopper or lid, combine oil, vinegar, oregano and seasonings. Cover; shake well. Set aside. In medium bowl, combine cucumbers, tomatoes, onion, olives and cheese; mix lightly. Shake dressing. Add to salad; toss lightly to coat. Refrigerate 30 minutes.

Makes 8 servings

Mini Vegetable Quiches

2 cups cut-up vegetables (bell peppers, broccoli, zucchini and/or carrots)
2 tablespoons chopped green onions
2 tablespoons FLEISCHMANN'S® Margarine
4 flour tortillas (8 inches), each cut into 8 triangles
1 cup EGG BEATERS® Healthy Real Egg Product
1 cup skim milk
½ teaspoon dried basil leaves

In medium nonstick skillet, over medium-high heat, sauté vegetables and green onions in margarine until tender.

Arrange 4 tortilla pieces in each of 8 (6-ounce) greased custard cups or ramekins, placing points of tortilla pieces at center of bottom of cup and pressing lightly to form shape of cup. Divide vegetable mixture evenly among cups. In small bowl, combine Egg Beaters, milk and basil. Pour evenly over vegetable mixture. Place cups on baking sheet. Bake at 375°F for 20 to 25 minutes or until puffed and knife inserted into centers comes out clean. Let stand 5 minutes before serving.   *Makes 8 servings*

Nutrients per Serving:

Calories	122	Cholesterol	1 mg
Fat	4 g	Sodium	198 mg

California Apricot Fruit Salad

2 cups sliced pitted fresh California apricots
1½ cups sliced fresh strawberries
1½ cups sliced peeled kiwi
¼ cup California apricot nectar
¼ cup flaked coconut, lightly toasted
1 tablespoon finely chopped fresh mint

Combine apricots, strawberries, kiwi, nectar, coconut and mint in medium bowl; refrigerate. Serve as a salad or thread onto wooden skewers for fresh fruit kabobs.
                                    Makes 5 servings

Favorite recipe from **California Apricot Advisory Board**

⊹ COOK'S TIP ⊹

When herbs are dried, their oils become more pungent. As a general rule, when substituting dried herbs for fresh, use 1 teaspoon dried herbs for 1 tablespoon chopped fresh herbs.

Seafood Louis

⅓ cup mayonnaise
⅓ cup chili sauce
3 tablespoons finely chopped green bell pepper
1½ tablespoons chopped green onion
2 teaspoons lemon juice
¾ teaspoon Worcestershire sauce
⅛ teaspoon black pepper
4 large lettuce leaves
3 cups shredded lettuce leaves, divided
1 pound flake-style surimi seafood
1 medium tomato, cut into 8 wedges
2 hard-cooked eggs, quartered
16 pitted ripe olives
8 lemon wedges

To prepare dressing, combine mayonnaise, chili sauce, bell pepper, onion, lemon juice, Worcestershire sauce and black pepper in medium bowl; mix well.

To serve, line 4 serving plates each with lettuce leaf. Arrange ¾ cup shredded lettuce over each leaf. Divide surimi evenly among plates, spooning into center of plate. Arrange tomato, eggs, olives and lemon around the edges of the plates. Serve with dressing.
                                    Makes 4 servings

Favorite recipe from **Surimi Seafood Education Center**

Crudités with Creamy Cheese Dip

CREAMY CHEESE DIP

12 ounces (2 cartons) ALPINE LACE® Fat Free
   Cream Cheese with Garlic & Herbs
⅔ cup nonfat mayonnaise dressing
⅓ cup finely chopped red onion
 1 tablespoon whole-grain Dijon mustard
½ teaspoon freshly ground black pepper
¼ teaspoon curry powder
   Red onion rings (optional)

CRUDITÉS

Assorted fresh vegetables (your choices!): bell
   pepper strips (green, red and yellow), broccoli
   florets, peeled baby carrots, celery sticks,
   whole green beans, mushroom slices, snow
   peas, yellow squash circles, zucchini circles,
   unpeeled red potato chunks, cherry tomatoes,
   cucumber rounds

1. To make the Creamy Cheese Dip: In a medium-size bowl, using an electric mixer set on high speed, beat the cream cheese until smooth. Stir in the remaining dip ingredients except onion rings. Place in a small serving bowl, cover with plastic wrap and chill.

2. To prepare the Crudités: Half-fill a large saucepan with water and bring to a boil over high heat. Add the bell pepper, broccoli, carrots, celery, beans, mushrooms, peas, yellow squash and zucchini, one at a time, and blanch for 15 to 30 seconds or just until their color brightens *(Do not overcook!)* Remove the vegetables with a slotted spoon, immediately plunge them into cold water, then drain well. Cook the potatoes in the same water for 15 minutes or until tender.

3. Arrange the blanched vegetables, potatoes, tomatoes and cucumbers in a circle on a large platter, leaving space in the center for the bowl of dip. Cover with plastic wrap and chill. To serve: uncover, garnish with the onion rings and place the bowl of dip in the center.   *Makes 2 cups dip*

Nutrients per Serving (1 tablespoon dip):

Calories	17	Total Fat	0 g
Calories from fat	<1	Cholesterol	2 mg

Ravioli Soup

8 ounces sweet Italian sausage, casing removed
1 clove garlic, crushed
2 cans (13¾ ounces each) COLLEGE INN® Lower
   Sodium Chicken Broth
2 cups water
1 package (9 ounces) frozen miniature
   cheese-filled ravioli
1 can (15 ounces) garbanzo beans, drained
1 can (14½ ounces) stewed tomatoes
⅓ cup GREY POUPON® Dijon Mustard
½ teaspoon dried oregano leaves
¼ teaspoon coarsely ground black pepper
1 cup torn fresh spinach leaves
   Grated Parmesan cheese

In 4-quart heavy pot, over medium heat, brown sausage and cook garlic until tender, stirring to break up sausage, about 5 minutes. Pour off excess fat; remove sausage mixture from pot and set aside.

In same pot, over medium-high heat, heat chicken broth and water to a boil. Add ravioli; cook for 4 to 5 minutes or until tender. Stir in beans, stewed tomatoes, sausage mixture, mustard, oregano and pepper; heat through. Stir in spinach and cook until wilted, about 1 minute. Serve topped with Parmesan cheese.   *Makes 8 servings*

⇥ Entrees & Sides ⇤

Stuffed Shells Florentine

LOW FAT

1 cup (about 4 ounces) coarsely chopped mushrooms
½ cup chopped onion
1 clove garlic, minced
1 teaspoon Italian seasoning
¼ teaspoon ground black pepper
1 tablespoon FLEISCHMANN'S® Margarine
1 container (16 ounces) fat-free cottage cheese
1 package (10 ounces) frozen chopped spinach, thawed and well drained
½ cup EGG BEATERS® Healthy Real Egg Product
24 jumbo pasta shells, cooked in unsalted water and drained
1 jar (15¼ ounces) reduced-sodium spaghetti sauce, divided

In large skillet, over medium-high heat, sauté mushrooms, onion, garlic, Italian seasoning and pepper in margarine until tender. Remove from heat; stir in cottage cheese, spinach and Egg Beaters. Spoon mixture into shells.

Spread ½ cup spaghetti sauce in bottom of 13×9×2-inch baking dish; arrange shells over sauce. Top with remaining sauce; cover. Bake at 350°F for 35 minutes or until hot.   *Makes 8 servings*

Nutrients per Serving:

Calories	229	Cholesterol	3 mg
Fat	5 g	Sodium	549 mg

Grilled Chicken Caesar Salad

½ cup olive oil
¼ cup GREY POUPON® COUNTRY DIJON Mustard
2 tablespoons lemon juice
2 teaspoons Worcestershire sauce
1 teaspoon grated lemon peel
1 clove garlic, minced
½ teaspoon sugar
¼ teaspoon coarsely ground black pepper
1 pound boneless, skinless chicken breasts
5 cups torn romaine lettuce
1 cup sliced mushrooms
1 cup cherry tomato halves
½ cup prepared seasoned croutons
1 tablespoon grated Parmesan cheese

In small bowl, whisk together oil, mustard, lemon juice, Worcestershire sauce, lemon peel, garlic, sugar and pepper. In nonmetal bowl, pour ¼ cup mustard dressing over chicken breasts, turning to coat. Cover and chill at least 1 hour. Chill remaining dressing until serving time.

Remove chicken from marinade; discard marinade. Grill or broil chicken breasts for 10 to 15 minutes or until done, turning once. Diagonally slice chicken breasts into strips.

In large bowl, combine lettuce, chicken, mushrooms, tomatoes and croutons. Toss with reserved dressing; sprinkle with Parmesan cheese and serve.

Makes 6 servings

Stuffed Shells Florentine

Braised Chicken with Artichokes

1 jar (4 ounces) marinated artichoke hearts,
    undrained
1 jar (2 ounces) chopped pimiento, drained
⅔ cup white wine
3 tablespoons honey mustard
¼ teaspoon salt
¼ teaspoon pepper
8 ounces uncooked wide egg noodles
¾ cup herb-seasoned stuffing mix, crushed
4 boneless skinless chicken breast halves
    (4 ounces each)
1 tablespoon olive oil
2 tablespoons chopped fresh parsley

Drain artichoke marinade into small skillet. Set artichokes aside in bowl. Add pimiento, wine, mustard, salt and pepper to small skillet; bring to a boil. Cook over high heat 3 minutes. Pour mixture over artichokes; refrigerate, covered, at least 45 minutes.

Cook noodles according to package directions; drain. While pasta is cooking, place stuffing mix in large resealable plastic food storage bag. Add chicken; seal bag and toss to coat chicken.

Heat oil in large skillet over medium-high heat until hot. Remove chicken from bag; shake off excess stuffing mix. Cook chicken 3 minutes per side or until browned. Add artichoke mixture. Bring to a boil. Reduce heat to low. Simmer, covered, 10 minutes or until chicken is no longer pink in center. Serve chicken mixture over cooked noodles; sprinkle with parsley.

Makes 4 servings

Honey of a Whole Wheat Bread (for bread machines)

1–POUND LOAF
1½ teaspoons RED STAR® Active Dry Yeast
1⅓ cups bread flour
⅔ cup whole wheat flour
1½ teaspoons salt
2 teaspoons butter, cut in small pieces
2 tablespoons honey (80°F)
¼ cup milk (80°F)
¼ cup water (80°F)
1 large egg, at room temperature

1½–POUND LOAF
2¼ teaspoons RED STAR® Active Dry Yeast
2 cups bread flour
1 cup whole wheat flour
2 teaspoons salt
1 tablespoon butter, cut in small pieces
¼ cup honey (80°F)
½ cup milk (80°F)
¼ cup water (80°F)
1 large egg, at room temperature

Place ingredients into the pan in the order specified by the bread machine owner's manual. Set the bread machine on the basic/standard bread-making setting; select the medium or normal baking cycle. Cool bread to room temperature before slicing.

Makes 1 loaf

⬦ MENU SUGGESTION ⬦

This creative menu gives Easter a new twist.

**Barbecued Leg of Lamb with
Cucumber Yogurt Dip (page 78)
Honey of a Whole Wheat Bread
Marinated Vegetables (page 70)
Lemon Pudding Soufflés (page 99)**

Mediterranean Pita Pizza

Mediterranean Pita Pizzas

    2 tablespoons olive or vegetable oil
2½ cups (8 ounces) diced, peeled eggplant
    1 cup sliced zucchini
    1 cup sliced fresh mushrooms
    ¼ cup chopped green bell pepper
    ¼ cup chopped onion
    1 clove garlic, minced
    1 cup (half of 15-ounce can) CONTADINA® Pizza
        Sauce
    ½ cup sliced pitted ripe olives, drained
    ¼ teaspoon salt
    ⅛ teaspoon cayenne pepper
    6 (6-inch) pita breads
1½ cups (6 ounces) shredded mozzarella or fontina
        cheese

In large skillet, heat oil. Add eggplant, zucchini, mushrooms, bell pepper, onion and garlic; sauté for 4 to 5 minutes or until vegetables are tender. Stir in pizza sauce, olives, salt and cayenne pepper; simmer for 5 minutes, stirring occasionally. Toast both sides of pita bread under broiler. Spoon *½ cup* vegetable mixture onto each pita bread; top with cheese. Broil 6 to 8 inches from heat for 2 to 3 minutes or until cheese is melted.   *Makes 6 servings*

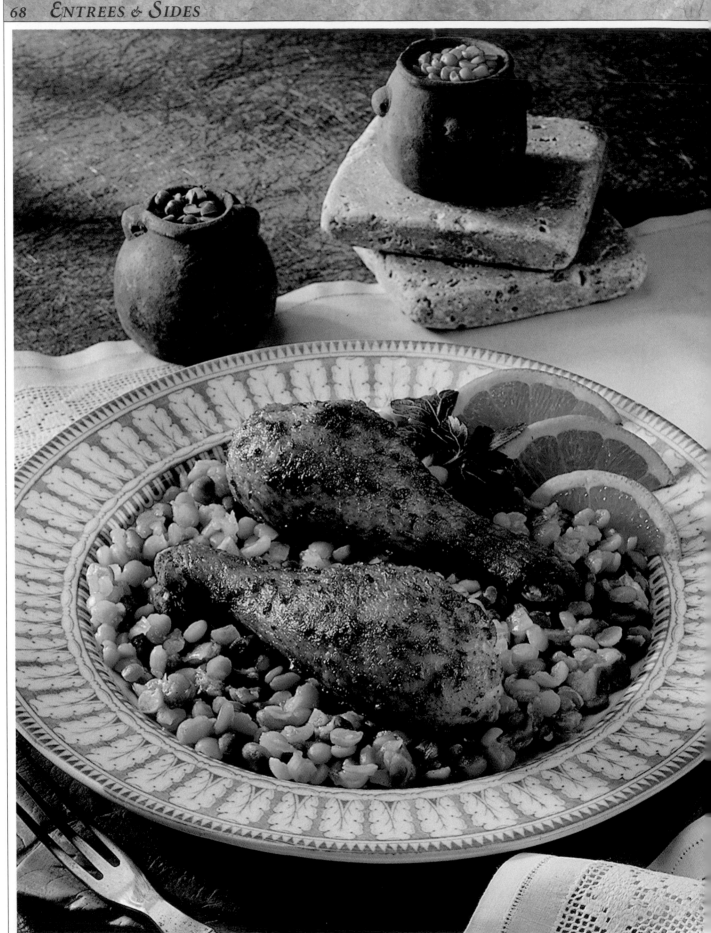

Spiced Orange Chicken with Lentils

    3 tablespoons all-purpose flour
    1 teaspoon ground coriander
    1 teaspoon ground cumin
    ½ teaspoon salt
    ½ teaspoon dried mixed herbs (thyme, marjoram
        and rosemary)
    ¼ teaspoon freshly ground black pepper
    8 chicken drumsticks
    2 tablespoons FILIPPO BERIO® Olive Oil,
        divided
      Finely grated peel and juice of 1 orange
    1 large onion, finely chopped
    2 cloves garlic, minced
  2½ cups chicken broth
    8 ounces dried lentils (about 1¼ cups), rinsed and
        drained
      Additional salt and freshly ground black pepper
    1 to 2 tablespoons honey
      Orange wedges and chopped fresh parsley
        (optional)

In small brown paper bag or plastic food storage bag, combine flour, coriander, cumin, salt, dried herbs and ¼ teaspoon pepper; shake until well mixed. Place 1 chicken drumstick at a time into flour mixture; shake well to coat evenly. In large skillet, heat 1 tablespoon olive oil over medium-high heat until hot. Add drumsticks; cook 5 minutes or until brown, turning occasionally. Stir orange peel and juice into skillet. Cover; reduce heat to low and simmer 20 minutes or until chicken is no longer pink in center and juices run clear.

Meanwhile, in another large skillet, heat remaining 1 tablespoon olive oil over medium heat until hot. Add onion and garlic; cook and stir 5 minutes or until onion is softened. Add chicken broth and lentils; bring to a boil. Cover; reduce heat to low and simmer 20 minutes or until lentils are tender and broth is absorbed. Season to taste with additional salt and pepper. Arrange lentils on serving plate; place drumsticks on top. Stir honey into chicken juices remaining in skillet. Heat through, stirring occasionally. Spoon over chicken and lentils. Garnish with orange wedges and parsley, if desired.

Makes 4 servings

Thai Beef Salad

DRESSING
    1 cup prepared olive oil vinaigrette salad dressing
    ⅓ cup FRANK'S® REDHOT® Original Cayenne
        Pepper Sauce
    3 tablespoons chopped peeled fresh ginger
    3 tablespoons sugar
    3 cloves garlic, chopped
    2 teaspoons FRENCH'S® Worcestershire Sauce
    1 cup packed fresh mint or basil leaves, coarsely
        chopped

SALAD
    1 flank steak (about 1½ pounds)
    6 cups washed and torn mixed salad greens
    1 cup sliced peeled cucumber
    ⅓ cup chopped peanuts

Place Dressing ingredients in blender or food processor. Cover and process until smooth. Reserve *1 cup* Dressing. Place steak in large resealable plastic food storage bag. Pour remaining Dressing over steak. Seal bag and marinate in refrigerator 30 minutes.

Place steak on grid, reserving marinade. Grill over hot coals about 15 minutes for medium-rare, basting frequently with marinade. Let steak stand 5 minutes. To serve, slice steak diagonally and arrange on top of salad greens and cucumber. Sprinkle with nuts and drizzle with reserved Dressing. Serve warm. Garnish as desired.

Makes 6 servings

Marinated Vegetables

2 cups broccoli flowerettes
2 cups cauliflower flowerettes
8 ounces fresh green beans, cut into 2-inch pieces
2 cups diagonally sliced carrots
1 cup cherry tomatoes, halved
½ cup chopped red onion
⅓ cup GREY POUPON® COUNTRY DIJON
    Mustard
⅓ cup olive oil
¼ cup REGINA® Red Wine Vinegar
1 teaspoon sugar
1 teaspoon dried oregano leaves
¼ teaspoon coarsely ground black pepper
⅓ cup oil-packed sundried tomato strips

In large heavy pot, steam broccoli, cauliflower, green beans and carrots until tender-crisp. Rinse vegetables in cold water and drain well; place in large serving bowl. Stir in cherry tomatoes and onion.

In small bowl, whisk mustard, oil, vinegar, sugar, oregano and pepper; stir in sundried tomatoes. Pour dressing over vegetables, tossing to coat well. Chill for at least 2 hours before serving, stirring occasionally. Garnish as desired.   *Makes 6 servings*

Vegetarian White Bean Chili with Waffles

1 tablespoon butter or margarine
1 tablespoon all-purpose flour
1 cup evaporated skimmed milk
1 to 2 tablespoons chili powder
1 teaspoon dried basil leaves
¼ teaspoon ground nutmeg
1 package (10 ounces) frozen mixed vegetables,
    thawed and drained
1 can (16 ounces) cannellini or other white beans,
    drained
1 cup (4 ounces) shredded JARLSBERG or
    NOKKELOST cheese
   Warm waffles
½ cup finely chopped green onions

Melt butter in large skillet or saucepan over medium-high heat. Stir in flour using wooden spoon. Gradually whisk in milk until smooth consistency. Stir in chili powder, basil and nutmeg. Stir in mixed vegetables, beans and cheese.

Ladle over warm waffles and top with chopped green onions, if desired.   *Makes 6 servings*

Favorite recipe from **Norseland, Inc.**

Beef & Vegetable Fried Rice

1 pound lean ground beef
2 cloves garlic, crushed
1 teaspoon grated fresh gingerroot *or* ¼ teaspoon
    ground ginger
2 tablespoons water
1 red bell pepper, cut into ½-inch pieces
1 package (6 ounces) frozen pea pods
3 cups cooked rice, cold
3 tablespoons soy sauce
2 teaspoons dark sesame oil
¼ cup thinly sliced green onions

1. In large nonstick skillet, brown ground beef, garlic and ginger over medium heat 8 to 10 minutes or until beef is no longer pink, breaking beef up into ¾-inch crumbles. Remove with slotted spoon; pour off drippings.

2. In same skillet, heat water over medium-high heat until hot. Add bell pepper and pea pods; cook 3 minutes or until bell pepper is crisp-tender, stirring occasionally. Add rice, soy sauce and sesame oil; mix well. Return beef to skillet; heat through, about 5 minutes. Stir in green onions before serving.
          Makes 4 servings

Favorite recipe from **National Cattlemen's Beef Association**

Penne Primavera with Sundried Tomato Sauce

- 4 cups assorted cut-up vegetables (zucchini, eggplant, peppers, mushrooms)
- ½ cup GREY POUPON® Dijon Mustard, divided
- 1 tablespoon olive oil
- 1 jar (7 ounces) sundried tomato strips in oil, drained
- 1 clove garlic, minced
- 2 cups light cream or half-and-half
- 1 tablespoon chopped fresh basil leaves
- 1 pound penne pasta, cooked
  Grated Parmesan cheese, optional

In large bowl, combine vegetables, 2 tablespoons mustard and oil. Place vegetables on broiler pan; broil for 8 to 10 minutes or until golden and tender, stirring occasionally.

In medium saucepan, over medium heat, sauté tomato strips and garlic for 2 minutes. Reduce heat to low and stir in cream, remaining mustard and basil; heat through.*

In large serving bowl, combine hot cooked pasta, vegetables and cream sauce, tossing to coat well. Serve immediately with Parmesan cheese and garnish if desired. *Makes 6 servings*

*If sauce thickens upon standing before tossing with pasta, thin with additional light cream or half-and-half.

Bacon & Potato Frittata

- 2 cups frozen O'Brien-style potatoes with onions and peppers
- 3 tablespoons butter or margarine
- 5 eggs
- ½ cup canned real bacon pieces
- ¼ cup half-and-half or milk
- ⅛ teaspoon salt
- ⅛ teaspoon pepper

Preheat broiler. Place potatoes in microwavable medium bowl; microwave at HIGH 1 minute. Melt butter in large ovenproof skillet over medium-high heat. Swirl butter up side of pan. Add potatoes; cook 3 minutes, stirring occasionally.

Beat eggs in medium bowl. Add bacon, half-and-half, salt and pepper; mix well. Pour egg mixture into skillet; reduce heat to medium. Stir gently to incorporate potatoes. Cover and cook 6 minutes or until eggs are set at edges (top will still be wet).

Transfer skillet to broiler. Broil 4 inches from heat about 1 to 2 minutes or until center is set and frittata is golden brown. Cut into wedges.

Makes 4 servings

Prep and cook time: 20 minutes

✧ FOOD FOR THOUGHT ✧

"The pleasures of the table—that lovely old-fashioned phrase—depict food as an art form, as a delightful part of civilized life. In spite of food fads, fitness programs, and health concerns, we must never lose sight of a beautifully conceived meal."

Julia Child

Curried Tuna Salad

 3 cups hot cooked rice (about 1 cup uncooked)
½ cup frozen peas
 1 to 2 cans (6⅛ ounces each) tuna packed in water, drained, flaked
¾ cup chopped celery
¼ cup sliced green onions
 1 tablespoon drained capers (optional)
¼ cup lemon juice
 2 tablespoons olive oil
¼ teaspoon curry powder
¼ teaspoon hot pepper sauce
   Shredded romaine lettuce
 2 medium tomatoes, cut into wedges, for garnish

Combine hot rice and peas in large bowl; toss lightly. Add tuna, celery, onions and capers. Combine lemon juice, oil, curry powder and pepper sauce in small jar with lid. Pour over rice mixture; toss lightly. Cover and chill 30 minutes. Serve on shredded lettuce and garnish with tomato wedges. *Makes 6 servings*

Favorite recipe from **USA Rice Council**

Curried Tuna Salad

Golden Apple-Salmon Pasta

8 ounces salmon, thawed if necessary, cut into
   ¾-inch chunks*
2 tablespoons butter or margarine, divided
1 cup sliced mushrooms
¾ cup diagonally sliced asparagus**
¼ cup chopped onion
¼ teaspoon oregano, crushed
⅛ teaspoon salt
⅛ teaspoon black pepper
⅓ cup half-and-half
1 Golden Delicious apple, cored and diced
4 ounces fettuccine noodles or spaghetti, cooked
   and drained
   Grated Parmesan cheese

*8 ounces tiny pink shrimp can be substituted for salmon.

**½ cup thawed frozen peas can be substituted for asparagus. Add peas with apple.

Sauté salmon in 1 tablespoon butter 5 minutes or until barely cooked; remove from skillet. Sauté mushrooms, asparagus and onion in remaining 1 tablespoon butter 2 minutes. Add seasonings and half-and-half; cook and stir on high heat 1 minute. Add apple and salmon; cook and stir 30 seconds or until vegetables are tender and salmon flakes easily when tested with fork. Serve over hot fettuccine. Sprinkle with Parmesan cheese.   *Makes 2 or 3 servings*

Favorite recipe from **Washington Apple Commission**

Peppered Beef Rib Roast

1½ tablespoons black peppercorns
1 boneless beef rib roast (2½ to 3 pounds), well
   trimmed
¼ cup Dijon-style mustard
2 cloves garlic, minced
¾ cup sour cream
2 tablespoons prepared horseradish
1 tablespoon balsamic vinegar
½ teaspoon sugar

Prepare grill with rectangular metal or foil drip pan. Bank briquets on either side of drip pan for indirect cooking. Meanwhile, place peppercorns in heavy, small resealable plastic food storage bag. Squeeze out excess air; seal bag tightly. Using flat side of meat mallet or rolling pin, pound peppercorns until cracked. Pat roast dry with paper towels. Combine mustard and garlic in small bowl; spread with spatula over top and sides of roast. Sprinkle cracked pepper over mustard mixture.

Insert meat thermometer into center of thickest part of roast. Place roast, pepper side up, on grid directly over drip pan. Grill, covered, over medium coals 60 to 70 minutes or until thermometer registers 150°F for medium-rare or to desired doneness, adding 4 to 9 briquets to both sides of the fire after 45 minutes to maintain medium coals. Meanwhile, combine sour cream, horseradish, vinegar and sugar in small bowl; mix well. Cover; refrigerate until serving. Transfer roast to carving board; tent with foil. Let stand 5 to 10 minutes before carving. Serve with horseradish sauce.
Makes 6 to 8 servings

Vegetarian Burgers

½ cup A.1.® Steak Sauce, divided
¼ cup plain yogurt
⅔ cup slivered almonds
⅔ cup salted peanuts
⅔ cup sunflower kernels
½ cup chopped green bell pepper
¼ cup chopped onion
1 clove garlic, minced
1 tablespoon red wine vinegar
4 pita breads (5 inches), halved
4 lettuce leaves
4 tomato slices

In small bowl, combine ¼ cup steak sauce and yogurt; set aside.

In food processor or blender, process almonds, peanuts, sunflower kernels, green pepper, onion and garlic until coarsely chopped. With motor running, slowly add remaining steak sauce and vinegar until blended; shape mixture into 4 patties.

Grill burgers over medium heat for 1½ minutes on each side or until heated through, turning once. Split open top edge of each pita bread. Layer lettuce, burger, tomato slice and 2 tablespoons prepared sauce in each pita bread half. Serve immediately.

Makes 4 servings

Good-for-You Zucchini Bread

⅔ cup pitted prunes
3 tablespoons water
1 cup sugar
½ cup orange juice
1 teaspoon grated orange peel
2 cups grated zucchini
1½ cups all-purpose flour
1½ cups whole wheat flour
2 teaspoons pumpkin pie spice
1 teaspoon baking powder
1 teaspoon baking soda
¼ teaspoon salt
¼ cup plain low-fat yogurt, divided

Preheat oven to 350°F. Coat 9×5-inch loaf pan with nonstick cooking spray; set aside. Combine prunes and water in food processor or blender; process until smooth. Combine prune mixture, sugar, orange juice and orange peel in large bowl; mix well. Stir in zucchini.

Combine flours, pumpkin pie spice, baking powder, baking soda and salt in medium bowl. Stir half of flour mixture into zucchini mixture, then stir in half of yogurt. Repeat with remaining flour mixture and yogurt; stir just until blended. Pour batter into prepared pan.

Bake 1 hour and 15 minutes or until wooden toothpick inserted in center comes out clean. Cool in pan 10 minutes. Remove from pan; cool completely on wire rack. For best flavor, wrap bread in plastic and store overnight before serving.   *Makes 1 loaf*

Provençal Chicken Sandwiches

½ pound sliced deli chicken breast, cut into ½-inch-wide strips
½ cup sliced roasted red peppers
½ cup sliced red onion
¼ cup sliced pitted ripe olives
1 tablespoon extra-virgin olive oil
1 tablespoon red wine vinegar
½ teaspoon salt
¼ teaspoon black pepper
Fresh parsley
4 submarine or hoagie sandwich rolls

Combine chicken, roasted peppers, onion and olives in medium bowl. Whisk together oil, vinegar, salt and black pepper in small bowl. Pour over chicken mixture; toss until coated. Cover and refrigerate at least 1 hour or up to 2 days.

To complete recipe, chop enough parsley to measure 2 tablespoons. Stir into chicken mixture. Cut rolls in half; fill with chicken mixture. Serve immediately.

Makes 4 servings

Vegetarian Burger

Barbecued Leg of Lamb with Cucumber Yogurt Dip

1 leg of lamb (5 to 6 pounds), bone removed and butterflied
1 onion, thinly sliced
½ cup dry white wine
½ cup FILIPPO BERIO® Olive Oil
¼ cup lemon juice
2 cloves garlic, thinly sliced
1 tablespoon dried oregano leaves
1 bay leaf
Salt and freshly ground black pepper
Cucumber Yogurt Dip (recipe follows)
Pita bread wedges
2 lemons, cut into wedges

Place lamb in large shallow glass dish. In medium bowl, combine onion, wine, olive oil, lemon juice, garlic, oregano and bay leaf. Pour marinade over lamb; turn to coat both sides. Cover; marinate in refrigerator 3 to 4 hours or overnight, turning occasionally. Remove lamb, reserving marinade.

Brush barbecue grid with additional olive oil. Grill lamb, on covered grill, over hot coals 20 minutes, basting occasionally with reserved marinade. Turn with tongs. Grill an additional 20 minutes or until desired doneness is reached. Transfer lamb to warm serving platter. Carve into thin slices; season to taste with salt and pepper. Serve with Cucumber Yogurt Dip, pita bread and lemon wedges.

Makes 6 to 8 servings

Cucumber Yogurt Dip

2 containers (8 ounces each) plain yogurt without gelatin
1 large cucumber, peeled
2 tablespoons FILIPPO BERIO® Olive Oil
1 tablespoon white vinegar
2 cloves garlic, minced
Salt and white pepper

Line large plastic colander or sieve with large piece of double thickness cheesecloth or large coffee filter. Place colander over deep bowl. Spoon yogurt into colander; cover with waxed paper. Refrigerate until liquid no longer drains from yogurt, about 24 hours. Remove yogurt; place in medium bowl. Discard liquid.

Cut cucumber into quarters; remove seeds. Finely chop cucumber; drain on paper towels. Stir cucumber, olive oil, vinegar and garlic into yogurt. Season to taste with salt and pepper. Cover; refrigerate at least 1 hour before serving.

Makes about 2 cups

Honey Mustard Steaks with Grilled Onion

4 boneless beef top loin steaks, cut 1 inch thick
⅓ cup coarse-grain Dijon-style mustard
1 tablespoon chopped parsley
1 tablespoon plus 1½ teaspoons honey
1 tablespoon cider vinegar
1 tablespoon water
¼ teaspoon hot pepper sauce
⅛ teaspoon coarsely ground black pepper
1 large red onion, sliced ½ inch thick

Combine mustard, parsley, honey, vinegar, water, hot pepper sauce and pepper. Place beef steaks and onion on grid over medium coals; brush both with mustard mixture. Grill 9 to 12 minutes for rare (140°F) to medium (160°F), turning once and brushing with mustard mixture.

Makes 4 servings

Prep and cook time: 30 minutes

Favorite recipe from **North Dakota Beef Commission**

→ COOK'S TIP ←

When substituting glass bakeware in recipes that call for baking pans, reduce oven temperature by 25°F.

Vegetable Strata

  2 slices white bread, cubed
¼ cup shredded reduced-fat Swiss cheese
½ cup sliced carrots
½ cup sliced mushrooms
¼ cup chopped onion
  1 clove garlic, crushed
  1 teaspoon FLEISCHMANN'S® Margarine
½ cup chopped tomato
½ cup snow peas
  1 cup EGG BEATERS® Healthy Real Egg Product
¾ cup skim milk

Place bread cubes evenly into bottom of greased 1½-quart casserole dish. Sprinkle with cheese; set aside.

In medium nonstick skillet, over medium heat, sauté carrots, mushrooms, onion and garlic in margarine until tender. Stir in tomato and snow peas; cook 1 to 2 minutes more. Spoon over cheese. In small bowl, combine Egg Beaters and milk; pour over vegetable mixture. Bake at 375°F for 45 to 50 minutes or until knife inserted in center comes out clean. Let stand 10 minutes before serving.   *Makes 6 servings*

Spinach-Stuffed Chicken Breasts

  2 boneless skinless chicken breasts (8 ounces each), halved
  5 ounces frozen chopped spinach, thawed, well drained
  2 tablespoons freshly grated Parmesan cheese
  1 teaspoon grated lemon peel
¼ teaspoon black pepper
    Nonstick cooking spray
  1 cup thinly sliced mushrooms
  6 slices (2 ounces) thinly sliced low fat turkey-ham
  1 cup white grape juice

Preheat oven to 350°F. Pound chicken breasts to ¼-inch thickness with flat side of meat mallet or chef's knife. Combine spinach, Parmesan, lemon peel and pepper in large bowl.

Spray small nonstick skillet with cooking spray; add mushrooms. Cook and stir over medium heat 3 to 4 minutes or until tender. Arrange 1½ slices turkey-ham over each chicken breast half. Spread each with ¼ of the spinach mixture. Top each with mushrooms. Beginning with longer side, roll chicken tightly. Tie with kitchen string.

Place stuffed chicken breasts in 9-inch square baking pan, seam side down. Lightly spray chicken with cooking spray. Pour grape juice over top. Bake 30 minutes or until chicken is no longer pink. Remove string; cut chicken rolls into ½-inch diagonal slices. Arrange on plate. Pour pan juices over chicken. Garnish as desired.   *Makes 4 servings*

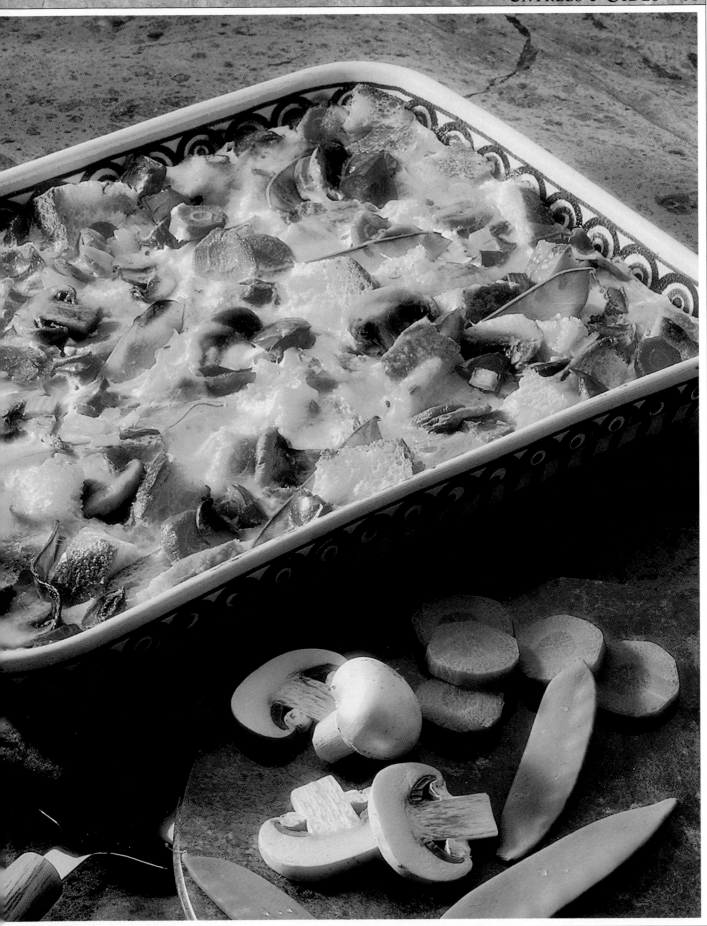

SPAM™, Pasta & Spinach Salad

DRESSING
- ⅓ cup thawed frozen orange juice concentrate
- ¼ cup plain yogurt
- 1 tablespoon olive oil
- 1 teaspoon packed brown sugar
- ⅛ teaspoon ground nutmeg
- ⅛ teaspoon black pepper

SALAD
- 6 ounces uncooked bow tie pasta or elbow macaroni
- 6 cups torn fresh spinach
- 1 can (12 ounces) SPAM® Luncheon Meat, cut into 2-inch strips
- 1 cup sliced celery
- 1 orange, peeled, sectioned, sections cut in half
- ½ cup thinly sliced red onion rings

In small bowl using wire whisk or fork, whisk together all dressing ingredients; set aside. Cook pasta according to package directions; drain. In large bowl, combine all salad ingredients; toss gently. Pour dressing over salad; toss gently. Serve immediately.

Makes 6 servings

Chicken and Tomatoes in Red Pepper Cream

- 9 ounces refrigerated angel hair pasta
- 1 jar (7 ounces) roasted red peppers, drained
- ⅓ cup half-and-half
- 2 teaspoons Dijon mustard
- 1 teaspoon salt
- 12 sundried tomatoes packed in oil, drained
- 1 tablespoon olive oil
- 4 boneless skinless chicken breast halves (about 1 pound)
- Grated Parmesan cheese

Cook pasta according to package directions; drain. While the pasta is cooking, combine red peppers, half-and-half, mustard and salt in food processor or blender; cover and process until smooth. Set aside.

Rinse tomatoes in warm water; drain and pat dry. Cut into halves. Heat olive oil in large skillet over medium-high heat until hot. Add chicken and tomatoes. Cook chicken, uncovered, 3 minutes per side.

Add red pepper mixture. Simmer 3 minutes or until sauce thickens slightly and chicken is no longer pink in center. Season to taste with black pepper. Serve chicken and sauce over pasta. Sprinkle with Parmesan cheese.

Makes 4 servings

Prep and cook time: 15 minutes

Grilled Country Dijon Vegetables

- ⅓ cup GREY POUPON® COUNTRY DIJON Mustard
- ⅓ cup olive oil
- ¼ cup balsamic vinegar
- ¼ cup chopped parsley
- 2 tablespoons chopped chives
- 1 tablespoon minced garlic
- 4 baby eggplants
- 2 Spanish onions
- 2 medium zucchini
- 2 medium yellow squash
- 2 roasted red peppers, cut into strips

In bowl, whisk mustard, oil, vinegar, parsley, chives and garlic until blended; set aside.

Cut eggplant and onions crosswise into 4 slices each; cut zucchini and yellow squash into 8 slices each. Grill vegetables, basting with ¾ cup mustard mixture. Grill onions for about 6 to 8 minutes and remaining vegetables for 2 to 3 minutes. To serve, arrange vegetables on serving platter; top with pepper strips and drizzle with remaining mustard mixture.

Makes 6 to 8 servings

→ MENU SUGGESTION ←

*Enjoy these no-fuss **Memorial Day** party-pleasers while relaxing in the backyard with family and friends.*

Mediterranean Greek Salad (page 58)
Southern Barbecue Sandwich
Cole Slaw
Blonde Brickle Brownies (page 96)

Pasta Primavera

2 tablespoons butter or margarine
1 medium onion, finely chopped
1 clove garlic, minced
¾ pound asparagus, cut diagonally into 1½-inch pieces
½ pound fresh mushrooms, sliced
1 medium zucchini, sliced
1 carrot, sliced
1 cup half-and-half or light cream
½ cup chicken broth
1 tablespoon all-purpose flour
2 teaspoons dried basil leaves, crushed
1 pound uncooked fettuccine
¾ cup (3 ounces) SARGENTO® Fancy Shredded Parmesan & Romano Cheese

In large skillet over medium heat, melt butter. Add onion and garlic; cook and stir until onion is tender. Add asparagus, mushrooms, zucchini and carrot; cook, stirring constantly, 2 minutes. *Increase heat to high.* Combine half-and-half, broth, flour and basil in small bowl; add to skillet. Bring mixture to a boil. Boil, stirring occasionally, until thickened.

Meanwhile, cook fettuccine according to package directions; drain. In serving bowl, place hot fettuccine, sauce and Parmesan & Romano Cheese; toss gently.

Makes 8 servings

Southern Barbecue Sandwiches

1 pound boneless sirloin or flank steak*
¾ cup FRENCH'S® Worcestershire Sauce, divided
½ cup ketchup
½ cup light molasses
¼ cup FRENCH'S® Classic Yellow® Mustard
2 tablespoons FRANK'S® REDHOT® Original Cayenne Pepper Sauce
½ teaspoon hickory salt
4 sandwich buns, split

*You may substitute 1 pound pork tenderloin for the steak. Cook pork until meat is juicy and barely pink in center *or* substitute leftover sliced steak for the grilled steak. Stir into sauce and heat through.

Place steak in large resealable plastic food storage bag. Pour ½ *cup* Worcestershire over steak. Seal bag and marinate meat in refrigerator 20 minutes.

To prepare barbecue sauce, combine ketchup, molasses, remaining ¼ *cup* Worcestershire, mustard, RedHot® sauce and hickory salt in medium saucepan. Bring to a boil over high heat. Reduce heat to low. Cook 5 minutes until slightly thickened, stirring occasionally. Set aside.

Place steak on grid, discarding marinade. Grill over hot coals 15 minutes, turning once. Remove steak from grid; let stand 5 minutes. Cut steak diagonally into thin slices. Stir steak into barbecue sauce. Cook until heated through, stirring often. Serve steak and sauce in sandwich buns. Garnish as desired.

Makes 4 servings

Scrumptious SPAM™ Spring Chili

Nonstick cooking spray
4 cloves garlic, minced
2 green bell peppers, cut into strips
1 cup sliced green onions
3 jars (4.25 ounces) CHI-CHI'S® Diced Green
     Chilies
2 jalapeño peppers, seeded and minced
2 teaspoons dried oregano leaves
2 teaspoons ground cumin
2 cans (15 ounces) cannellini beans or kidney
     beans
2 cans (10¾ ounces) condensed chicken broth,
     undiluted
1 can (12 ounces) SPAM® Luncheon Meat, cubed

In large saucepan coated with cooking spray, sauté garlic over medium heat 1 minute. Add bell peppers, green onions, chilies, jalapeños, oregano and cumin; sauté 5 minutes. Stir in beans and broth. Bring to a boil. Cover. Reduce heat and simmer 10 minutes. Stir in SPAM®. Simmer 2 minutes.

Makes 4 to 6 servings

Garden Omelet

3 teaspoons butter or margarine, divided
⅓ cup chopped onion
⅓ cup chopped red bell pepper
½ cup sliced mushrooms
½ teaspoon dried basil leaves
4 eggs, beaten
1 tablespoon milk
¼ teaspoon black pepper
   Dash salt
½ cup (2 ounces) shredded Swiss cheese

Melt 1 teaspoon butter in large nonstick skillet over medium heat. Cook and stir onion and bell pepper 2 to 3 minutes or until onion is tender. Add mushrooms and basil; cook and stir 3 to 5 minutes more. Remove vegetables from skillet and keep warm.

Whisk together eggs, milk, black pepper and salt in medium bowl. Melt remaining 2 teaspoons butter in same skillet over medium heat; rotate pan to coat bottom. Pour egg mixture into skillet. Cook over medium heat; as eggs begin to set, gently lift edges of omelet with spatula and tilt skillet so that uncooked portion flows underneath.

When eggs are fully cooked, spoon vegetable mixture over half of omelet. Sprinkle with cheese. Loosen omelet with spatula and fold in half. Transfer to warm serving plate.   *Makes 2 servings*

Linguine with Asparagus and Asiago

1 pound fresh asparagus, cut into 1-inch pieces
16 ounces uncooked linguine, broken into halves
1 tablespoon butter or margarine
1 cup (4 ounces) shredded Asiago or grated
     Parmesan cheese
½ cup sour cream
½ cup pitted black olive slices

Place 3 quarts of water in Dutch oven; cover and bring to a boil over high heat.

Drop asparagus into boiling water; boil 1 to 2 minutes or until crisp-tender. Remove with slotted spoon; rinse under cold water. Drain.

Add linguine to boiling water; cook according to package directions until al dente. Drain.

Combine linguine and butter in large bowl; toss gently until butter is melted. Add asparagus, cheese, sour cream and olives; toss gently until linguine is coated and cheese is melted. Season to taste with salt and pepper. Serve immediately.   *Makes 4 servings*

Prep and cook time: 30 minutes

Quick Skillet Rice Gratin

2 tablespoons olive oil
1 onion, chopped
2 cloves garlic, minced
2 medium carrots, peeled and chopped
1 teaspoon dried thyme leaves
2 cups uncooked instant white rice
1 can (15½ ounces) kidney beans, rinsed and
    drained
1 teaspoon salt
⅓ cup grated Parmesan cheese

Heat oil in large skillet over medium-high heat until hot. Add onion and garlic; cook and stir 2 minutes. Add carrots and thyme; cook and stir 4 minutes more.

Add rice, 2 cups water, beans and salt; season to taste with black pepper. Stir well. Bring to a boil. Reduce heat to low. Sprinkle with cheese. Cover and simmer 5 minutes or until cheese is melted and all liquid is evaporated. *Makes 4 to 6 servings*

Prep and cook time: 15 minutes

Quick Skillet Rice Gratin

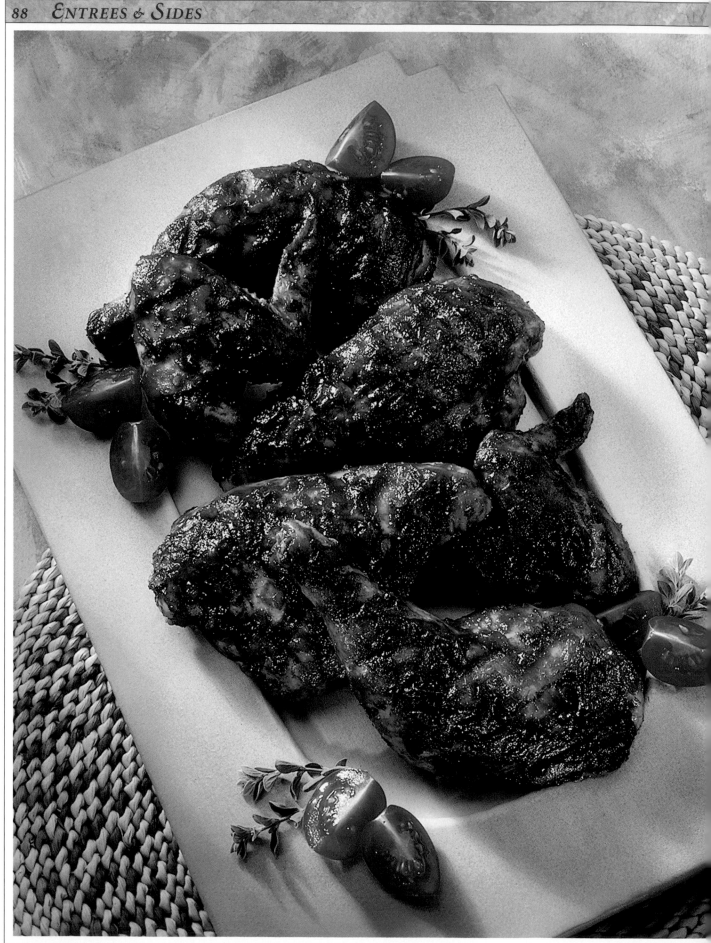

Hot 'n' Spicy Chicken Barbecue

½ cup A.1.® Steak Sauce
½ cup tomato sauce
¼ cup finely chopped onion
2 tablespoons cider vinegar
2 tablespoons maple syrup
1 tablespoon vegetable oil
2 teaspoons chili powder
½ teaspoon crushed red pepper flakes
1 chicken (3 pounds), cut up

In medium saucepan, combine Steak Sauce, tomato sauce, onion, vinegar, maple syrup, oil, chili powder and red pepper flakes. Over medium heat, heat mixture to a boil; reduce heat. Simmer 5 to 7 minutes or until mixture thickens; cool.

Grill chicken over medium heat 30 to 40 minutes or until chicken is no longer pink, turning and basting frequently with prepared sauce. Serve hot.

Makes 4 servings

⟶ FOOD FOR THOUGHT ⟵

"It's odd how large a part food plays in memories of childhood. There are grown men and women who still shudder at the sight of spinach, or turn away with loathing from stewed prunes and tapioca... Luckily, however, it's the good tastes one remembers first."

Caroline Lejeune

Border Black Bean Chicken Salad

¼ cup olive oil, divided
1½ pounds boneless skinless chicken breasts,
     cut into 2-inch strips
1 clove garlic, minced
½ jalapeño pepper, seeded and finely chopped
1¼ teaspoons salt, divided
4 cups torn romaine lettuce
1 can (15 to 16 ounces) black beans, drained
     and rinsed
1 cup peeled and seeded cucumber cubes
1 cup red bell pepper strips
1 cup chopped tomato
½ cup chopped red onion
⅓ cup tomato juice
2 tablespoons fresh lime juice
½ teaspoon ground cumin
½ cup chopped pecans, toasted
     Fresh parsley, for garnish

Heat 2 tablespoons oil in large skillet over medium heat until hot. Add chicken; stir-fry 2 minutes or until no longer pink in center. Add garlic, jalapeño and ¾ teaspoon salt; stir-fry 30 seconds. Combine chicken mixture, lettuce, beans, cucumber, red pepper, tomato and onion in large salad bowl. Combine tomato juice, lime juice, remaining 2 tablespoons oil, cumin and remaining ½ teaspoon salt in small jar with lid; shake well. Add to skillet; heat over medium heat until slightly warm. Pour warm dressing over chicken mixture; toss to coat. Sprinkle with pecans. Garnish with parsley. Serve immediately.   *Makes 4 servings*

Favorite recipe from **National Broiler Council**

Hot 'n' Spicy Chicken Barbecue

Tortellini with Three-Cheese Tuna Sauce

1 pound uncooked cheese-filled spinach or egg tortellini
2 green onions, thinly sliced
1 clove garlic, minced
1 tablespoon butter or margarine
1 cup low-fat ricotta cheese
½ cup low-fat milk
1 can (9 ounces) STARKIST® Tuna, drained and broken into chunks
½ cup (2 ounces) shredded low-fat mozzarella cheese
¼ cup grated Parmesan or Romano cheese
2 tablespoons chopped fresh basil *or* 2 teaspoons dried basil leaves, crushed
1 teaspoon grated lemon peel
Fresh tomato wedges, red peppers and basil leaves for garnish (optional)

In large saucepan, cook tortellini in boiling salted water according to package directions. When tortellini are almost done, in separate large saucepan, cook and stir onions and garlic in butter 2 minutes. Whisk in ricotta and milk. Add tuna, mozzarella and Parmesan cheeses, basil and lemon peel. Cook over medium-low heat until mixture is heated through and cheeses are melted.

Drain pasta; add to sauce. Toss well to coat; garnish if desired. Serve immediately. *Makes 4 to 5 servings*

Chicken Marengo

2 tablespoons olive or vegetable oil
2½ to 3 pounds skinless chicken pieces for frying *or* 1½ pounds (about 6) boneless, skinless chicken breast halves
½ cup chopped onion
½ cup chopped green bell pepper
½ cup sliced fresh mushrooms
1 clove garlic, minced
1¾ cups (14.5-ounce can) CONTADINA® Recipe Ready Diced Tomatoes, undrained
⅔ cup (6-ounce can) CONTADINA® Tomato Paste
½ cup dry red wine
½ cup chicken broth
1 teaspoon Italian herb seasoning
½ teaspoon salt
⅛ teaspoon ground black pepper

In large skillet, heat oil. Add chicken; cook until browned on all sides. Remove chicken from skillet, reserving any drippings in skillet. Add onion, bell pepper, mushrooms and garlic to skillet; sauté for 5 minutes. Add tomatoes and juice, tomato paste, wine, broth, Italian seasoning, salt and black pepper. Return chicken to skillet. Bring to a boil. Reduce heat to low; cover. Cook for 30 to 40 minutes or until chicken is no longer pink in center. Serve over hot cooked rice or pasta, if desired. *Makes 6 servings*

Note: *Red wine may be omitted. Increase chicken broth to 1 cup.*

Tortellini with Three-Cheese Tuna Sauce

Sausage & Pasta Primavera

4 ounces uncooked spaghetti
12 ounces fully-cooked beef knockwurst or beef
      polish sausage links, cut diagonally into
      ½-inch-thick slices
½ pound fresh asparagus,* trimmed, cut
      diagonally into 1-inch pieces
1 medium onion, cut lengthwise into thin wedges
¼ cup water
1 clove garlic, minced
2 medium tomatoes, coarsely chopped
2 tablespoons finely chopped fresh basil *or*
      1½ teaspoons dried basil leaves
2 tablespoons grated Parmesan cheese (optional)

*Or, use 1 package (10 ounces) frozen cut asparagus for fresh asparagus. Use as directed.

1. Cook spaghetti according to package directions. Drain; keep warm.

2. Meanwhile, combine beef knockwurst, asparagus, onion, water and garlic in large skillet. Cook over medium-high heat 5 to 7 minutes or until asparagus is crisp-tender, stirring occasionally. Add spaghetti, tomatoes and basil; toss lightly. Cook 2 minutes or until heated through.

3. Serve with cheese, if desired.

Makes 4 (2-cup) servings

Favorite recipe from **National Cattlemen's Beef Association**

⊹ COOK'S TIP ⊹

When entertaining frequently, keep notes with the menu listing any preparation problems encountered, costs and suggested improvements. This will make it easy to reuse the menu with another group of guests. Just be sure to include the guest list to avoid repetition!

Easy Spinach-Zucchini Pie

1 to 2 medium zucchini (each about 8 inches long)
   Hot water
2 packages (10 ounces each) frozen chopped
      spinach, thawed and well drained
½ cup sour cream
1 package (3 ounces) cream cheese, softened
¼ cup (1 ounce) grated Parmesan cheese
3 tablespoons dry bread crumbs
1 egg, slightly beaten
½ teaspoon garlic salt
½ teaspoon dried basil, crumbled
1 can (2.8 ounces) FRENCH'S® French Fried
      Onions
½ cup (2 ounces) shredded Cheddar cheese

Preheat oven to 375°. Using sharp knife, trim off 1 side of zucchini to form a straight edge. Starting at straight edge, cut zucchini lengthwise into eight thin strips (about ⅛ inch thick). Place zucchini strips in shallow dish filled with hot water about 3 minutes to soften; drain. In large bowl, using fork, thoroughly combine spinach, sour cream, cream cheese, Parmesan cheese, bread crumbs, egg, seasonings and ⅔ can French Fried Onions. Line bottom and side of 9-inch pie plate or quiche dish with zucchini strips, allowing 3 inches of each strip to hang over edge. Spoon spinach mixture evenly into pie plate. Fold zucchini strips over spinach mixture, tucking ends into center of mixture. Cover pie plate with foil. Bake, covered, at 375° for 40 minutes or until zucchini is tender. Top center of pie with cheese and remaining onions; bake, uncovered, 3 minutes or until onions are golden brown.

Makes 6 to 8 servings

Microwave Directions: Cut zucchini into strips as above. Place zucchini strips in shallow microwave-safe dish and cook, covered, on HIGH 2 minutes or until softened; drain. Prepare spinach mixture as above. Line 9-inch microwave-safe pie plate with zucchini strips and fill as above. Cook, covered, 12 to 14 minutes or until zucchini is tender. Rotate dish halfway through cooking time. Top center of pie with cheese and remaining onions; cook, uncovered, 1 minute or until cheese melts. Let stand 5 minutes.

⇥ DESSERTS ⇤

Cappuccino Cake

½ cup (3 ounces) semisweet chocolate chips
½ cup chopped hazelnuts, walnuts or pecans
1 package (18.25 ounces) yellow cake mix
¼ cup instant espresso coffee powder
2 teaspoons ground cinnamon
1¼ cups water
3 large eggs
⅓ cup FILIPPO BERIO® Pure or Extra Light
    Tasting Olive Oil
   Powdered sugar
1 container (15 ounces) ricotta cheese
2 teaspoons granulated sugar
   Additional ground cinnamon

Preheat oven to 325°F. Grease 10-inch (12-cup) Bundt pan or 10-inch tube pan with olive oil. Sprinkle lightly with flour.

In small bowl, combine chocolate chips and hazelnuts. Spoon evenly into bottom of prepared pan.

In large bowl, combine cake mix, coffee powder and 2 teaspoons cinnamon. Add water, eggs and olive oil. Beat with electric mixer at low speed until dry ingredients are moistened. Beat at medium speed 2 minutes. Pour batter over topping in pan.

Bake 60 minutes or until toothpick inserted in center comes out clean. Cool on wire rack 15 minutes. Remove from pan. Place cake, fluted side up, on serving plate. Cool completely. Sprinkle with powdered sugar.

In medium bowl, combine ricotta cheese and granulated sugar. Sprinkle with cinnamon. Serve alongside slices of cake. Serve cake with cappuccino, espresso or your favorite coffee, if desired.

Makes 12 to 16 servings

Chocolate Espresso Brownies

4 squares (1 ounce each) unsweetened chocolate
1 cup sugar
¼ cup prepared prune butter
3 egg whites
1 to 2 tablespoons instant espresso coffee powder
1 teaspoon baking powder
1 teaspoon salt
1 teaspoon vanilla
½ cup all-purpose flour
   Powdered sugar (optional)

Preheat oven to 350°F. Coat 8-inch square baking pan with vegetable cooking spray. In small heavy saucepan, melt chocolate over very low heat, stirring until melted and smooth. Remove from heat; cool. In mixer bowl, beat chocolate and remaining ingredients except flour and powdered sugar at medium speed until well blended; mix in flour. Spread batter evenly in prepared pan. Bake in center of oven about 30 minutes until pick inserted into center comes out clean. Cool completely in pan on wire rack. Dust with powdered sugar. Cut into 1⅓-inch squares.

Makes 36 brownies

Favorite recipe from **California Prune Board**

Blonde Brickle Brownies

Blonde Brickle Brownies

1⅓ cups all-purpose flour
½ teaspoon baking powder
¼ teaspoon salt
2 eggs, room temperature
½ cup granulated sugar
½ cup packed brown sugar
⅓ cup butter or margarine, melted
1 teaspoon vanilla
¼ teaspoon almond extract
1 package (7.5 ounces) BITS 'O BRICKLE®, divided
½ cup chopped pecans (optional)

Preheat oven to 350°F. Grease 8-inch square baking pan. Combine flour, baking powder and salt; set aside. Beat eggs well. Gradually add granulated and brown sugars; beat until thick and creamy. Add butter, vanilla and almond extract. Gently stir in flour mixture until moistened. Fold in ⅔ cup of the Bits 'O Brickle® and nuts. Pour into prepared pan.

Bake 30 minutes. Remove from oven and immediately sprinkle remaining Bits 'O Brickle® over top. Cool completely in pan on wire rack before cutting.

Makes 16 generous bars

Oatmeal Scotchies

1¼ cups all-purpose flour
1 teaspoon baking soda
½ teaspoon salt
½ teaspoon ground cinnamon
1 cup (2 sticks) butter or margarine, softened
¾ cup granulated sugar
¾ cup firmly packed brown sugar
2 eggs
1 teaspoon vanilla extract *or* grated rind of
    1 orange
3 cups quick or old-fashioned oats, uncooked
1⅔ cups (12-ounce package) NESTLÉ® TOLL
    HOUSE® Butterscotch Flavored Morsels

COMBINE flour, baking soda, salt and cinnamon in
small bowl; set aside. Beat butter, granulated sugar,
brown sugar, eggs and vanilla in large mixing bowl.
Gradually beat in flour mixture. Stir in oats and
morsels. Drop dough by rounded tablespoons onto
ungreased cookie sheets.

BAKE in preheated 375°F oven 7 to 8 minutes for
chewy cookies; 9 to 10 minutes for crisp cookies. Let
cool on cookie sheets 2 minutes. Remove from cookie
sheets; cool completely on wire racks.

Makes about 4 dozen bars

Variation: For **Oatmeal Scotchie Pan Cookies,**
SPREAD dough into greased 15½×10½-inch jelly-roll
pan. Bake in preheated 375°F oven 18 to 22 minutes or
until very lightly browned. Cool completely on wire
rack.   *Makes about 35 bars*

Chocolate Chip Cheesecake

2 packages (8 ounces each) PHILADELPHIA
    BRAND® Cream Cheese, softened
½ cup sugar
½ teaspoon vanilla
2 eggs
¾ cup mini semisweet chocolate chips, divided
1 ready to use graham cracker or chocolate-
    flavored pie crust (6 ounces or 9 inch)

MIX cream cheese, sugar and vanilla at medium speed
with electric mixer until well blended. Add eggs; mix
until blended. Stir in ½ cup of the chips.

POUR into crust. Sprinkle with remaining ¼ cup
chips.

BAKE at 350°F, 40 minutes or until center is almost
set. Cool. Refrigerate 3 hours or overnight.

Makes 8 servings

Prep time: 10 minutes
Cooking time: 40 minutes

Variation: For **Peanut Butter Chocolate Chip,** beat
⅓ cup peanut butter in with cream cheese.

Variation: For **Banana Chocolate Chip,** beat ½ cup
mashed ripe banana in with cream cheese.

⊹ MENU SUGGESTION ⊹

*On Mother's Day, give Mom a break from
the kitchen by preparing this easy and
enticing meal for her.*

Mixed Green Salad
Braised Chicken with Artichokes (page 66)
Chocolate Chip Cheesecake

Lemon Pudding Soufflés

1 cup sugar, divided
¼ cup all-purpose flour
⅛ teaspoon salt
¼ cup prepared prune butter
1 egg yolk
⅓ cup fresh lemon juice
   Grated peel of 1 lemon
1 cup nonfat milk
4 egg whites
   Powdered sugar
   Lemon peel, for garnish

Preheat oven to 350°F. Coat eight 5-ounce custard cups with vegetable cooking spray. In mixer bowl, beat ¾ cup sugar, flour and salt until blended. Beat in prune butter until well blended. Add egg yolk, lemon juice and lemon peel; mix well. Add milk; mix until well blended. In another mixer bowl, with clean beaters, beat egg whites until soft peaks form. Gradually beat in the remaining ¼ cup sugar until stiff peaks form. Mix one fourth of egg white mixture into lemon mixture; fold in the remaining egg white mixture. Spoon batter into prepared custard cups, dividing equally. Set cups in shallow pan and add ½ inch boiling water to pan. Bake in center of oven 45 to 50 minutes until puffy, set and browned. Cool 10 minutes. Dust with powdered sugar and garnish with lemon peel. Serve hot. *Makes 8 servings*

Favorite recipe from **California Prune Board**

Banana Caramel Shortcake

1½ cups all-purpose flour
⅓ cup sugar
2 teaspoons baking powder
½ teaspoon baking soda
½ teaspoon salt
½ teaspoon ground nutmeg
3 tablespoons prepared prune butter
1 tablespoon cold butter or margarine
1 container (8 ounces) plain nonfat yogurt
4 ripe bananas, sliced
1 cup prepared fat-free caramel sauce
1 cup low-fat nondairy whipped topping
   Additional low-fat nondairy whipped topping (optional)
8 teaspoons toasted slivered almonds

Preheat oven to 400°F. Coat baking sheet with vegetable cooking spray. In large bowl, mix flour, sugar, baking powder, baking soda, salt and nutmeg. Cut in prune butter and butter with pastry blender until mixture resembles coarse crumbs. Mix in yogurt just until blended. Spoon onto baking sheet in 8 equal mounds. Bake in center of oven about 20 minutes until lightly browned and springy to the touch. Remove from baking sheet to wire rack to cool. To serve, cut each shortcake horizontally into halves; place each bottom half on serving plate. Cover each with 1/16 of banana slices, 1 tablespoon caramel sauce, 2 tablespoons whipped topping, shortcake half, 1/16 of banana slices and 1 tablespoon caramel sauce. Dollop with 2 tablespoons whipped topping, if desired. Sprinkle with 1 teaspoon almonds. *Makes 8 servings*

Favorite recipe from **California Prune Board**

Banana Caramel Shortcake

Killer Brownies

½ cup hazelnuts or unblanched almonds
¾ cup butter or margarine
2 cups sugar
¾ cup cocoa powder
3 eggs, slightly beaten
2 teaspoons vanilla
1 cup all-purpose flour
1½ cups fresh or thawed frozen raspberries
    White Chocolate Ganache (recipe follows)
    Chocolate Ganache (recipe follows)
3 to 4 tablespoons raspberry jam

Preheat oven to 350°F. To remove skins from nuts, spread nuts in single layer on baking sheet. Bake 10 to 12 minutes or until skins begin to flake off; let cool slightly. Wrap hazelnuts in heavy kitchen towel; rub against towel to remove as much of the skins as possible.

Place hazelnuts in food processor. Process using on/off pulsing action until finely chopped. Set aside.

Lightly grease 2 (8-inch) square baking pans. Line bottoms of pans with foil; lightly grease foil. Set aside.

Melt butter in medium saucepan over medium heat; remove from heat. Stir in sugar and cocoa powder until well blended. Stir in eggs and vanilla until smooth. Stir in flour just until blended. Pour batter evenly into prepared pans. Place raspberries on top of batter, pressing gently into batter. Bake 15 to 20 minutes or until center is just set. *Do not overbake.* Cool brownies completely in pans on wire rack.

Run knife around edges of pans to loosen brownies from sides. Hold wire rack over top of 1 pan; invert to release brownie. Remove foil; discard. Lay cutting board or plate over brownie; invert brownie.

Prepare White Chocolate Ganache and Chocolate Ganache. Reserve 2 tablespoons White Chocolate Ganache; spread remaining White Chocolate Ganache evenly on brownie. Spread raspberry jam on top of ganache.

Unmold remaining brownie. Place flat-side down on bottom layer, pressing gently to seal. Spread Chocolate Ganache evenly on top layer. Drizzle reserved 2 tablespoons White Chocolate Ganache over top with spoon. Sprinkle with hazelnuts. Cut into 16 squares.
Makes 16 brownies

White Chocolate Ganache

1 cup (6 ounces) white chocolate chips or chopped white chocolate, divided
3 tablespoons whipping cream
½ teaspoon almond extract

Combine ½ cup chocolate and whipping cream in medium saucepan. Heat over medium heat until chocolate is half melted, stirring occasionally.

Remove saucepan from heat. Stir in remaining ½ cup chocolate and almond extract until mixture is smooth. Keep warm (ganache is semi-firm at room temperature).
Makes ¾ cup

Chocolate Ganache

2 tablespoons whipping cream
1 tablespoon butter
½ cup (2 ounces) semisweet chocolate chips or chopped semisweet chocolate
½ teaspoon vanilla

Combine whipping cream and butter in small saucepan. Heat over medium heat until mixture boils, stirring frequently. Remove saucepan from heat. Stir in chocolate and vanilla until mixture is smooth, returning to heat for 20 to 30 second intervals as needed to melt chocolate. Keep warm (ganache is semi-firm at room temperature).
Makes ¾ cup

⤖ COOK'S TIP ⬿

To measure flour accurately, first stir to aerate the flour. Next, spoon the flour into the appropriate dry measure until overflowing. With a straight-edged metal spatula, sweep across the top of the measure to level the flour.

Summer

"Summer afternoon—summer afternoon; to me those have always been the two most beautiful words in the English language."

Edith Wharton

Country Glazed Ribs (page 112)

→ STARTERS ←

Cool Italian Tomato Soup

1¾ cups (14½-ounce can) CONTADINA® Pasta
    Ready Chunky Tomatoes with Crushed Red
    Pepper, undrained
2 cups tomato juice
½ cup half-and-half
2 tablespoons lemon juice
1 large cucumber, peeled, diced (about 2 cups)
1 medium green bell pepper, diced (about ½ cup)
    Chopped fresh basil (optional)
    Croutons (optional)

In blender container, place tomatoes with juice,
tomato juice, half-and-half and lemon juice; blend
until smooth. Pour into large bowl or soup tureen; stir
in cucumber and bell pepper. Sprinkle with basil and
croutons just before serving, if desired.

Makes 6 cups

Herbed Tomato Cucumber Salad

½ cup MIRACLE WHIP® FREE® Nonfat Dressing
1 cucumber, peeled, seeded and chopped
⅓ cup finely chopped red onion
⅓ cup finely chopped fresh basil
¼ teaspoon salt
3 tomatoes, sliced

MIX dressing, cucumber, onion, basil and salt until
well blended; refrigerate. Spoon over tomatoes.

Makes 6 servings

Chicken Kabobs with Thai Dipping Sauce

1 pound boneless skinless chicken breasts, cut
    into 1-inch cubes
1 small cucumber, seeded and cut into small
    chunks
1 cup cherry tomatoes
2 green onions, cut into 1-inch pieces
⅔ cup teriyaki baste & glaze sauce
⅓ cup FRANK'S® REDHOT® Original Cayenne
    Pepper Sauce
⅓ cup peanut butter
3 tablespoons frozen orange juice concentrate,
    undiluted
2 cloves garlic, minced

Thread chicken, cucumber, tomatoes and onions
alternately onto metal skewers; set aside.

To prepare Thai Dipping Sauce, combine teriyaki baste
& glaze sauce, RedHot® sauce, peanut butter, orange
juice concentrate and garlic; mix well. Reserve ⅔ *cup*
sauce for dipping.

Brush skewers with some of remaining sauce. Place
skewers on oiled grid. Grill over hot coals 10 minutes
or until chicken is no longer pink in center, turning
and basting often with remaining sauce. Serve skewers
with Thai Dipping Sauce. Garnish as desired.

Makes 6 appetizer servings

Chicken Kabobs with Thai Dipping Sauce

Albacore and White Bean Salad with Orange Dressing

- 2 cans (15 ounces each) Great Northern beans, rinsed and drained
- 3 hard-cooked eggs, chopped
- ⅓ cup chopped green onions, including tops
- ⅓ cup chopped red onion
- ¾ teaspoon salt
- ⅓ cup bottled Italian dressing
- 1 tablespoon frozen orange juice concentrate, thawed
- 2 teaspoons grated orange peel
- ½ to 1 teaspoon crushed red pepper
- 1 can (6 ounces) STARKIST® Solid White Tuna, drained and chunked
- 2 chopped plum tomatoes, drained
  Quartered orange slices and chives, for garnish

In large bowl, combine beans, eggs, onions and salt. In glass measuring cup, blend dressing, orange juice concentrate, orange peel and crushed red pepper. Add to salad in bowl.

Chill several hours or overnight. Just before serving, gently toss in tuna and tomatoes. Garnish with orange slices and chives. *Makes 6 servings*

Albacore and White Bean Salad with Orange Dressing

Gazpacho

6 large ripe tomatoes (about 3 pounds), chopped, divided
1½ cups tomato juice, divided
1 clove garlic
2 tablespoons lime juice
2 tablespoons olive oil
1 tablespoon white wine vinegar
1 teaspoon sugar
½ to 1 teaspoon salt
½ teaspoon dried oregano leaves
6 green onions, thinly sliced
¼ cup finely chopped celery
¼ cup finely chopped, seeded, unpeeled cucumber
1 or 2 fresh jalapeño chili peppers,* seeded and minced
Prepared croutons
1 cup diced avocado
1 red or green bell pepper, seeded and chopped
2 tablespoons fresh cilantro
Lime wedges (optional)
Sour cream (optional)

*Jalapeño peppers can sting and irritate the skin; wear rubber gloves when handling peppers and do not touch eyes.

Seed and finely chop 1 tomato; set aside. Coarsely chop remaining 5 tomatoes. Process half of coarsely chopped tomatoes, ¾ cup tomato juice and garlic in blender or food processor until smooth. Press through sieve into large bowl; discard seeds. Repeat with remaining coarsely chopped tomatoes and ¾ cup tomato juice.

Whisk lime juice, oil, vinegar, sugar, salt and oregano into tomato mixture. Stir in finely chopped tomato, onions, celery, cucumber and chili peppers. Cover; refrigerate at least 4 hours or up to 24 hours to blend flavors.

Stir soup; ladle into chilled bowls. Add croutons, avocado, bell pepper, cilantro, lime wedges and sour cream according to taste. *Makes 2 servings*

✦ MENU SUGGESTION ✦

This spectacular Fourth of July menu is bursting with flavor.

Albacore and White Bean Salad with Orange Dressing
America's Favorite Cheddar Beef Burgers (page 117)
Wisconsin Ricotta Tart with Kiwi and Raspberry Sauce (page 140)

Fresh Tomato Pasta Andrew

1 pound fresh tomatoes, cut into wedges
1 cup packed fresh basil leaves
2 cloves garlic, chopped
2 tablespoons olive oil
8 ounces Camenzola cheese *or* 6 ounces ripe Brie plus 2 ounces Stilton cheese, each cut into small pieces
Salt and white pepper to taste
4 ounces uncooked angel hair, vermicelli or other thin pasta, cooked, drained, kept warm
Grated Parmesan cheese

Place tomatoes, basil, garlic and oil in food processor or blender; process using on/off pulsing action until coarsely chopped. Combine tomato mixture and Camenzola cheese in large bowl. Season to taste with salt and white pepper. Add pasta; toss gently until cheese melts. Serve with Parmesan cheese. Garnish as desired. *Makes 6 appetizer servings*

Favorite recipe from **California Tomato Board**

Kielbasa Tomato Salad

1 pound BOB EVANS FARMS® Kielbasa Sausage
1 pound tomatoes, cut into wedges
1 large red onion, chopped
1 red bell pepper, chopped
1 yellow bell pepper, chopped
3 green onions with tops, cut into ½-inch pieces
½ cup chopped fresh parsley
⅓ cup balsamic vinegar
2 teaspoons salt
1 teaspoon chopped fresh rosemary
1 teaspoon chopped fresh thyme
1 teaspoon black pepper
½ cup olive oil
  Fresh rosemary sprig (optional)

Cut sausage into ½-inch rounds; place in medium skillet. Cook over medium heat until browned, turning occasionally. Transfer sausage to large glass bowl. Add tomatoes, red onion, bell peppers and green onions to sausage; toss lightly. Combine parsley, vinegar, salt, rosemary, thyme and black pepper in small bowl. Whisk in oil gradually until well blended. Pour over sausage mixture; cover and refrigerate 2 hours or until chilled. Garnish with rosemary sprig, if desired. Serve cold. Refrigerate leftovers.

Makes 8 side-dish servings

Panzanella (Italian Bread Salad)

QUICK MEAL

4 ounces day-old Italian bread, cubed
4 plum tomatoes, chopped
3 tablespoons extra-virgin olive oil
2 tablespoons red wine vinegar
¼ cup chopped fresh basil
1 clove garlic, minced
½ teaspoon salt

Combine bread cubes and tomatoes in medium serving bowl.

Whisk together oil, vinegar, basil, garlic and salt in small bowl. Pour over bread mixture; toss until well mixed. *Makes 6 servings*

Prep time: 10 minutes

SPAM™ Tostada Salad

8 flour tortillas (7 inches)
1 tablespoon vegetable oil
1 can (12 ounces) SPAM® Luncheon Meat, cut into ½-inch strips
1 onion, cut into wedges
4 cups torn romaine lettuce
2 tomatoes, chopped
1 can (2¼ ounces) sliced ripe olives, drained
1 cup (4 ounces) shredded Monterey Jack cheese
  CHI-CHI'S® Salsa

In large skillet over medium-high heat, cook tortillas in hot oil 2 to 3 minutes or until crisp; set aside. In same skillet, cook SPAM® and onion 7 to 10 minutes or until SPAM® is browned. Meanwhile, toss together lettuce, tomatoes, olives and cheese. Place SPAM® mixture on top of tortillas. Top with lettuce mixture. Serve with salsa. *Makes 4 servings*

Basil Jicama Fruit Salad

1 cup red California seedless grapes
1 cup green California seedless grapes
1 cup cubed cantaloupe, honeydew melon or mango
1 cup fresh pineapple chunks
1 orange, peeled, sliced and quartered
1 nectarine, cubed
½ cup halved strawberries
½ cup julienned jicama
¼ cup orange juice
1 tablespoon chopped fresh basil *or* 1 teaspoon dried basil, crushed
  Orange-flavored yogurt, optional
  Basil sprigs, optional

Combine all ingredients except yogurt and basil; mix gently. Serve with dollop of yogurt and garnish with sprigs of basil, if desired. *Makes 6 servings*

Favorite recipe from **California Table Grape Commission**

Basil Jicama Fruit Salad

Entrees & Sides

Oriental Chicken and Spinach Salad

⅓ cup peanut oil
¼ cup honey
¼ cup soy sauce
2 teaspoons Worcestershire sauce
1 teaspoon Oriental sesame oil
3 boneless chicken breast halves (about 12 ounces)
1 cup baby carrots
3 cups coarsely chopped bok choy (stems and leaves)
3 cups fresh spinach, torn into bite-size pieces
1 cup bean sprouts
¼ cup dry roasted peanuts

To prepare dressing, combine peanut oil, honey, soy sauce, Worcestershire sauce and sesame oil in small bowl with wire whisk until well blended.

Slice chicken breasts into 2×1/2-inch strips. Cut carrots crosswise into ¼-inch-thick slices. Heat 2 tablespoons dressing in large nonstick skillet over medium heat. Add chicken and carrots; cook and stir about 5 minutes or until chicken is cooked through. Remove from skillet and let cool.

Heat another 2 tablespoons dressing in same skillet. Add bok choy; cook and stir about 1 minute or just until wilted.

Place spinach on individual plates. Arrange bok choy over spinach. Top with chicken, carrots and bean sprouts. Sprinkle with peanuts; serve with remaining dressing. *Makes 4 servings*

Prep and cook time: 19 minutes

Skillet Shrimp with Rotelle

3 tablespoons FILIPPO BERIO® Olive Oil
1 medium onion, chopped
2 cloves garlic, minced
2 cups uncooked rotelle or other curly pasta
3 cups chicken broth
1 cup asparagus tips
¾ pound raw medium shrimp, shelled and deveined
¾ cup halved cherry tomatoes
¼ cup pitted ripe olives
1 teaspoon dried oregano leaves
1 teaspoon dried basil leaves
Salt and freshly ground black pepper

In large skillet, heat olive oil over medium heat until hot. Add onion and garlic; cook and stir 4 to 6 minutes or until onion is softened but not brown. Add pasta; stir to coat pasta with oil. Increase heat to high; pour in chicken broth. Bring to a boil. Reduce heat to medium-high; cook, stirring occasionally, 12 to 14 minutes or until pasta is al dente (tender but still firm). Add asparagus. Cook, stirring frequently, 2 to 3 minutes or until asparagus is tender-crisp. Add shrimp, tomatoes, olives, oregano and basil. Cook, stirring frequently, 3 minutes or until liquid is almost completely absorbed and shrimp are opaque (*do not overcook shrimp*). Season to taste with salt and pepper.

Makes 4 to 6 servings

Skillet Shrimp with Rotelle

Country Glazed Ribs

3 to 4 pounds pork baby back ribs, cut into
    3- to 4-rib portions
½ cup FRENCH'S® Deli Brown Mustard
½ cup packed brown sugar
½ cup finely chopped onion
¼ cup FRENCH'S® Worcestershire Sauce
¼ cup cider vinegar
1 tablespoon mustard seeds
1 teaspoon ground allspice
    Honey Mustard Dip (recipe follows)

Place ribs in large shallow glass baking pan or
resealable plastic food storage bag. To prepare
marinade, combine mustard, sugar, onion,
Worcestershire, vinegar, mustard seeds and allspice in
small bowl; mix well. Pour over ribs, turning to coat
all sides. Cover and marinate in refrigerator 1 hour or
overnight.

Place ribs on grid, reserving marinade. Grill over
medium coals 45 minutes or until ribs are barely pink
near bone, turning and basting frequently with
marinade. (Do not baste during last 10 minutes of
cooking.) Serve with Honey Mustard Dip. Garnish as
desired. *Makes 4 to 6 servings*

Honey Mustard Dip

½ cup FRENCH'S® Deli Brown Mustard
½ cup honey

Combine mustard and honey in small bowl; mix well.
Makes 1 cup

Grilled Tuna Niçoise

4 tuna steaks, 1 inch thick (about 1½ pounds)
2 tablespoons FRENCH'S® Worcestershire Sauce
2 tablespoons olive oil

NIÇOISE DRESSING
½ cup prepared olive oil vinaigrette salad dressing
¼ cup FRENCH'S® Dijon Mustard
¼ cup sour cream
1 tablespoon capers, drained
2 cloves garlic, minced

SALAD
6 cups washed and torn mixed gourmet baby
    lettuce leaves
8 small (12 ounces) red potatoes, cooked and
    sliced
2 ripe tomatoes, cut into wedges
1 small seedless cucumber, sliced
½ pound green beans, cooked until tender
½ cup oil-cured black olives

Place tuna steaks on large platter. Combine
Worcestershire and oil in cup; brush on both sides of
steaks.

Place steaks on oiled grid. Grill over hot coals 10
minutes or until fish is opaque, but still feels
somewhat soft in center,* turning once. Remove from
grill.

To prepare Niçoise Dressing, combine salad dressing,
mustard, sour cream, capers and garlic in small bowl;
mix well. To serve, arrange lettuce, tuna steaks,
potatoes, tomatoes, cucumber, beans and olives on
individual salad plates, dividing evenly. Serve with
Niçoise Dressing. *Makes 4 servings*

Prep Time: 30 minutes
Cook Time: 10 minutes

*Tip: Potatoes and green beans cook easily in microwave.
Place sliced potatoes and beans in 3-quart microwave-
safe baking dish. Pour 1 cup water over vegetables. Cover
and microwave on HIGH 12 minutes or until vegetables
are tender, stirring once. Drain and cool.*

*Tuna becomes dry and tough if overcooked. Watch carefully
while grilling.

Tex-Mex Chops

    4 boneless pork loin chops, about 1 pound
    1 teaspoon vegetable oil
1½ cups bottled salsa, chunky style
    1 can (4 ounces) diced green chilies
 ½ teaspoon ground cumin
 ¼ cup (1 ounce) shredded Cheddar cheese

Heat oil in nonstick pan over medium-high heat.
Brown chops on one side, about 2 minutes. Turn
chops over. Add salsa, chilies and cumin to skillet; mix
well. Lower heat, cover and barely simmer for 8
minutes. Uncover; top each chop with 1 tablespoon
cheese. Cover and simmer an additional 2 to 3
minutes, until cheese melts. Serve immediately.

Makes 4 servings

Prep and cook time: 15 minutes

Favorite recipe from **National Pork Producers Council**

Teriyaki Trout

    4 whole trout (about 2 pounds)
 ¾ cup LAWRY'S® Teriyaki Marinade with
        Pineapple Juice
 ½ cup sliced green onions
    2 medium lemons, sliced
        Chopped fresh parsley (optional)

Pierce skin of trout several times with fork. Brush the
inside and outside of each trout with Teriyaki
Marinade with Pineapple Juice; stuff with green
onions and lemon slices. Place in shallow glass dish.
Pour all but ¼ cup Teriyaki Marinade with Pineapple
Juice over trout; cover dish. Marinate in refrigerator at
least 30 minutes. Heat grill for medium-hot coals.
Remove trout, reserving marinade. Place trout in oiled
hinged wire grill basket; brush with reserved
marinade. Grill, 4 to 5 inches from heat source, 10
minutes or until trout flakes easily with fork, turning
and brushing occasionally with reserved ¼ cup
Teriyaki Marinade with Pineapple Juice. Sprinkle with
parsley, if desired.   *Makes 4 servings*

Grilled Stuffed Eggplant

    4 baby eggplant (1½ pounds)*
    2 tablespoons olive oil
    4 ounces small mushrooms, wiped clean and
        quartered (about 1 cup)
 ½ cup finely chopped green and/or red bell pepper
    2 cloves garlic, minced
    1 cup chunky-style salsa
    1 can (2.8 ounces) FRENCH'S® French Fried
        Onions, divided
    2 tablespoons crumbled goat cheese
    1 tablespoon grated Parmesan cheese

*You may substitute 2 medium eggplant (1½ pounds) for the baby
eggplant. Cut eggplant in half lengthwise; proceed as directed.

Cut lengthwise slice ½ inch from top of each eggplant;
discard. Using a spoon or melon baller, scoop out pulp
leaving ¼-inch shell. Set aside eggplant shells. Finely
chop pulp.

Heat oil in large skillet over high heat. Add eggplant
pulp and mushrooms; cook about 5 minutes or until
liquid is evaporated, stirring often. Add pepper and
garlic; cook and stir until pepper is tender. Stir in
salsa. Bring to a boil. Reduce heat to medium. Cook
and stir 2 minutes. Stir in *1 cup* French Fried Onions.
Spoon filling into shells, mounding slightly. Sprinkle
remaining French Fried Onions and cheeses on top.

Place eggplant on oiled grid. Grill over medium coals
15 minutes or until eggplant shells are tender. Serve
warm.   *Makes 4 side-dish servings*

America's Favorite Cheddar Beef Burgers

1 pound ground beef
⅓ cup A.1.® Steak Sauce, divided
1 medium onion, cut into strips
1 medium green or red bell pepper, cut into strips
1 tablespoon margarine
4 ounces Cheddar cheese, sliced
4 hamburger rolls
4 tomato slices

In medium bowl, combine ground beef and 3 tablespoons steak sauce; shape mixture into 4 patties. Set aside.

In medium skillet, over medium heat, cook onion and pepper in margarine until tender, stirring occasionally. Stir in remaining steak sauce; keep warm.

Grill burgers over medium heat for 4 minutes on each side or to desired doneness. When almost done, top with cheese; grill until cheese melts. Spoon 2 tablespoons onion mixture onto each roll bottom; top each with burger, tomato slice, some of remaining onion mixture and roll top. Serve immediately.

Makes 4 servings

⇾ COOK'S TIP ⇽

Freezer burn, which is indicated by dry white or gray patches on the surface of frozen foods, is caused by improper wrapping. Food that is freezer burned is perfectly safe to eat. Just trim off and discard the affected areas because they will have an unpleasant flavor and texture.

Scallops with Vermicelli

1 pound bay scallops
2 tablespoons fresh lemon juice
2 tablespoons chopped fresh parsley
2 tablespoons olive oil
2 tablespoons butter, divided
1 medium onion, chopped
1 clove garlic, minced
1½ cups canned Italian tomatoes, undrained and chopped
2 tablespoons chopped fresh basil *or* ½ teaspoon dried basil leaves
¼ teaspoon dried oregano leaves
¼ teaspoon dried thyme leaves
2 tablespoons heavy cream
Dash ground nutmeg
12 ounces uncooked vermicelli, cooked and drained

Rinse scallops. Combine scallops, lemon juice and parsley in glass bowl. Cover; marinate in refrigerator while preparing sauce.

Heat oil and 1 tablespoon butter in large skillet over medium-high heat. Add onion and garlic; cook and stir until onion is tender. Add tomatoes with juice, basil, oregano and thyme. Reduce heat to low. Cover; simmer 30 minutes, stirring occasionally.

Drain scallops; discard marinade. Heat remaining 1 tablespoon butter in separate large skillet over medium heat. Add scallops; cook and stir about 2 minutes or until scallops are opaque. Stir in cream, nutmeg and tomato sauce mixture.

Pour sauce over vermicelli in large serving bowl; toss gently to coat. Garnish as desired.

Makes 4 servings

Favorite recipe from **New Jersey Department of Agriculture**

→ MENU SUGGESTION ←

*Prepare this **Graduation Party** buffet in advance so you can spend more time with your guests.*

Garden Party Pasta Salad
Grilled Rosemary Chicken* (page 118)
Chocolate Cake

*Grill chicken one day before party. Refrigerate and serve cold.

Grilled Rosemary Chicken

2 tablespoons lemon juice
2 tablespoons olive oil
2 cloves garlic, minced
2 tablespoons minced fresh rosemary
¼ teaspoon salt
4 boneless skinless chicken breasts

Whisk together lemon juice, oil, garlic, rosemary and salt in small bowl. Pour into shallow glass dish. Add chicken, turning to coat both sides with lemon juice mixture. Cover and marinate in refrigerator 15 minutes, turning chicken once.

Grill chicken over medium-hot coals 5 to 6 minutes per side or until chicken is no longer pink in center.
Makes 4 servings

Garden Party Pasta Salad

1 package (16 ounces) uncooked multicolor rotini
1 package (8 ounces) refrigerated tricolor tortellini
2½ cups cauliflowerets or broccoli flowerets
1 cup diced carrots
1 cup diced green bell pepper
1 cup sliced ripe olives
1 cup frozen green peas
½ cup chopped green onions
1 tablespoon dried oregano
1 tablespoon dried basil
1 jar (26 ounces) NEWMAN'S OWN® Diavolo Sauce
¾ cup NEWMAN'S OWN® Olive Oil & Vinegar Salad Dressing

Cook pastas according to package directions; drain.

Mix together pastas, cauliflower, carrots, green pepper, olives, peas and green onions in large salad bowl.

Sprinkle oregano and basil over pasta mixture. Add NEWMAN'S OWN® Diavolo Sauce and Olive Oil & Vinegar Salad Dressing; toss and refrigerate at least 3 hours.
Makes 15 to 20 side-dish servings

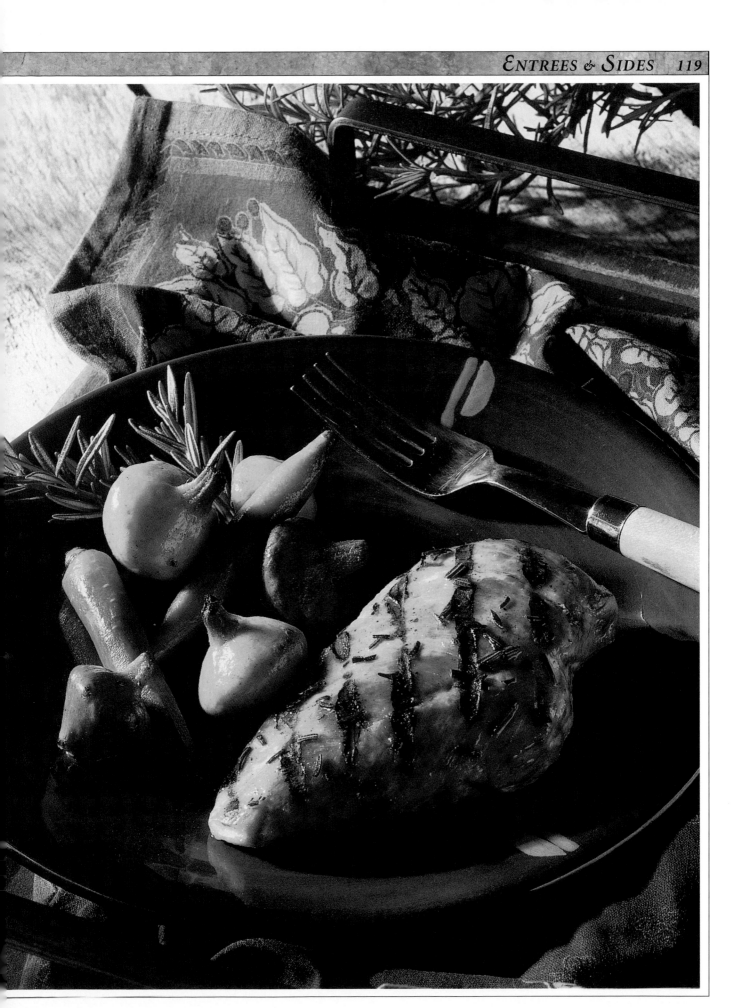

Barbecued Pork Loin

2 teaspoons LAWRY'S® Seasoned Salt
1 boneless pork loin (3 to 3½ pounds)
1 cup orange juice
¼ cup soy sauce
1 teaspoon LAWRY'S® Garlic Powder with Parsley
½ teaspoon LAWRY'S® Seasoned Pepper
   Vegetable oil

Sprinkle Seasoned Salt onto all sides of meat. In large resealable plastic bag or shallow glass baking dish, place meat; let stand 10 to 15 minutes. Combine orange juice, soy sauce, Garlic Powder with Parsley and Seasoned Pepper; pour over meat. Seal bag or cover dish. Marinate in refrigerator at least 2 hours or overnight, turning occasionally. Heat grill for medium coals; brush grid with vegetable oil. Remove meat, reserving marinade. Grill, 4 to 5 inches from heat, 30 minutes or until internal meat temperature reaches 170°F, turning and brushing frequently with reserved marinade. Remove meat from grill; let stand about 10 minutes before thinly slicing. Meanwhile, in small saucepan, bring remaining marinade to a boil; boil 1 minute. *Makes 6 servings*

Conventional Directions: Marinate meat as directed. Remove meat, reserving marinade. Place meat in shallow roasting pan; brush with reserved marinade. Bake, uncovered, in 350°F oven 1 hour or until internal temperature reaches 170°F, brushing frequently with remaining marinade. Discard any unused marinade.

Presentation: Serve sliced meat with extra heated marinade poured over top. Garnish with fresh herb sprigs. Serve with steamed vegetables.

Lemon-Garlic Chicken & Rice

4 skinless, boneless chicken breast halves
1 teaspoon paprika
   Salt and pepper (optional)
2 tablespoons margarine or butter
2 cloves garlic, minced
1 package (6.9 ounces) RICE-A-RONI® Chicken Flavor
2 tablespoons lemon juice
1 cup chopped red or green bell pepper
½ teaspoon grated lemon peel

1. Sprinkle chicken with paprika, salt and pepper.

2. In large skillet, melt margarine over medium-high heat. Add chicken and garlic; cook 2 minutes on each side or until browned. Remove from skillet; set aside, reserving drippings. Keep warm.

3. In same skillet, sauté rice-vermicelli mix in reserved drippings over medium heat until vermicelli is golden brown. Stir in 2¼ cups water, lemon juice and contents of seasoning packet. Top rice with chicken; bring to a boil over high heat.

4. Cover; reduce heat. Simmer 10 minutes. Stir in red pepper and lemon peel.

5. Cover; continue to simmer 10 minutes or until liquid is absorbed, rice is tender and chicken is no longer pink inside. *Makes 4 servings*

Albacore Stir-Fry

Albacore Stir-Fry

  3 tablespoons vegetable oil
½ cup sliced onion
  1 clove garlic, minced or pressed
  1 bag (16 ounces) frozen Oriental vegetables,
      thawed and drained*
  1 can (12 ounces) STARKIST® Solid White Tuna,
      drained and chunked
  3 tablespoons soy sauce
  1 tablespoon lemon juice
  1 tablespoon water
  1 teaspoon sugar
  2 cups hot cooked rice

*May use 4 cups fresh vegetables such as carrots, snow peas,
broccoli, bell peppers, mushrooms, celery and bean sprouts.

In wok or large skillet, heat oil over medium-high
heat; cook and stir onion and garlic until onion is soft.
Add vegetables; cook about 3 to 4 minutes or until
crisp-tender. Add tuna, soy sauce, lemon juice, water
and sugar. Cook 1 more minute; serve over rice.

Makes 4 servings

Falafel

¾ **cup sliced green onions**
½ **cup sliced celery**
2 **cloves garlic, minced**
1 **can (15 ounces) garbanzo beans, drained**
1 **can (15 ounces) pinto beans, rinsed and drained**
1 **egg**
2 **tablespoons flour**
2 **teaspoons lemon juice**
½ **teaspoon salt**
½ **teaspoon ground cumin**
¼ **teaspoon pepper**
2 **cans (15 ounces each) whole tomatoes, drained, coarsely chopped**
½ **cup chopped cucumber**
2 **teaspoons sliced pitted ripe olives**
1 **cup plain nonfat yogurt**
½ **teaspoon dried mint leaves**
4 **pita breads, cut into halves**

Heat small skillet; spray with nonstick cooking spray. Cook and stir onions, celery and garlic until tender; remove from heat. Process beans in food processor until smooth. Combine bean mixture, egg, flour, juice, salt, cumin and pepper in large bowl; stir in cooked vegetables. Form mixture into eight patties. Heat large skillet; spray with cooking spray. Cook patties over medium-low heat until lightly browned, about 5 minutes per side.

Combine tomatoes, cucumber and olives in small bowl. Combine yogurt and mint in separate small bowl. Serve falafel with pita breads; serve with tomato and yogurt mixtures. *Makes 8 servings*

Favorite recipe from **Canned Food Information Council**

Tomato, Basil & Broccoli Chicken

4 **skinless, boneless chicken breast halves**
  Salt and pepper (optional)
2 **tablespoons margarine or butter**
1 **package (6.9 ounces) RICE-A-RONI® Chicken Flavor**
1 **teaspoon dried basil leaves**
2 **cups broccoli flowerets**
1 **medium tomato, seeded, chopped**
1 **cup (4 ounces) shredded mozzarella cheese**

1. Sprinkle chicken with salt and pepper, if desired.

2. In large skillet, melt margarine over medium-high heat. Add chicken; cook 2 minutes on each side or until browned. Remove from skillet; set aside, reserving drippings. Keep warm.

3. In same skillet, sauté rice-vermicelli mix in reserved drippings over medium heat until vermicelli is golden brown. Stir in 2½ cups water, contents of seasoning packet and basil. Place chicken over rice mixture; bring to a boil over high heat.

4. Cover; reduce heat. Simmer 15 minutes. Top with broccoli and tomato.

5. Cover; continue to simmer 5 minutes or until liquid is absorbed and chicken is no longer pink in center. Sprinkle with cheese. Cover; let stand a few minutes before serving. *Makes 4 servings*

Nutrients per Serving:

Calories	460	Cholesterol	90 mg
Fat	14 g	Sodium	975 mg

Green Beans and Tomatoes Provençal

    1 pound fresh green beans, trimmed
    ¼ cup FILIPPO BERIO® Olive Oil
    1 clove garlic, crushed
      Salt and freshly ground black pepper
    3 shallots, sliced
    3 tomatoes, cored and cut crosswise in half
    ¼ cup dry bread crumbs
    2 tablespoons chopped fresh Italian parsley
    1 tablespoon chopped fresh thyme *or* 1 teaspoon
      dried thyme leaves
      Additional fresh Italian parsley (optional)

Preheat oven to 400°F. Steam green beans 6 minutes; place in 13×9-inch dish. In small bowl, combine olive oil and garlic; drizzle 1 tablespoon olive oil mixture over beans. Season to taste with salt and pepper.

In large nonstick skillet, heat remaining olive oil mixture over medium heat until hot. Add shallots; cook and stir 2 minutes. Add tomatoes; cook 1 minute, turning halfway through cooking time.

Place tomatoes, cut side up, and shallots on top of beans. In small bowl, combine bread crumbs, 2 tablespoons parsley and thyme. Sprinkle over top of tomatoes and beans. Drizzle with oil remaining in skillet. Bake 15 to 20 minutes or until golden brown. Garnish with additional parsley, if desired.

Makes 6 servings

✦ MENU SUGGESTION ✦

Delight Dad with a fantastic Father's Day barbecue.

Dad's Favorite Turkey Kabobs
Savory Grilled Potatoes in Foil (page 130)
Creamy Cappuccino Frozen Dessert (page 140)

Dad's Favorite Turkey Kabobs

    3 ears corn, cut into 1-inch pieces
    2 medium zucchini, cut into ¾-inch pieces
    2 red bell peppers, cut into 1-inch cubes
    2 Turkey Tenderloins (about 1 pound), cut into
      1-inch cubes
    ⅓ cup reduced-calorie Italian salad dressing
      Additional reduced-calorie Italian salad
      dressing

In medium saucepan over high heat, blanch corn in boiling water about 1 to 2 minutes. Remove corn from saucepan and plunge into cold water.

In large glass bowl, place corn, zucchini, peppers, turkey and ⅓ cup dressing; cover and refrigerate 1 to 2 hours.

Drain turkey and vegetables, discarding marinade. Alternately thread turkey cubes and vegetables on 8 metal skewers, leaving ½-inch space between turkey and vegetables.

On outdoor charcoal grill, cook kabobs 18 to 20 minutes, brushing with additional dressing. Turn skewers after first 10 minutes.

Makes 4 servings, 8 kabobs

Nutrients per Serving (2 kabobs):

Calories	218	Cholesterol	70 mg
Fat	4 g	Sodium	381 mg

Favorite recipe from **National Turkey Federation**

Green Beans and Tomato Provençal

Shrimp & Asparagus Fettuccine

12 ounces uncooked fettuccine
1 box (10 ounces) BIRDS EYE® frozen Asparagus Cuts*
1 tablespoon vegetable oil
1 package (16 ounces) frozen, uncooked cocktail-size shrimp
1 jar (12 ounces) prepared alfredo sauce
1 jar (4 ounces) sliced pimiento, drained

*Or, substitute 1½ cups BIRDS EYE® frozen Green Peas or 1 package BIRDS EYE® frozen Broccoli Cuts.

• Cook pasta according to package directions, adding asparagus to water 8 minutes before pasta is done. Drain; keep warm.

• Meanwhile, heat oil in large skillet over medium-high heat. Add shrimp; cover and cook 3 minutes or until shrimp turn pink. Drain excess liquid, leaving shrimp and about 2 tablespoons liquid in skillet. Reduce heat to low. Stir in alfredo sauce and pimiento. Cover; cook 5 minutes. *Do not boil.*

• Toss fettuccine and asparagus with shrimp mixture.

Makes about 4 servings

15-Minute Summer Pasta Toss

8 ounces uncooked spaghetti, broken in half
½ cup KRAFT® House Italian with Olive Oil Blend Dressing
2 large tomatoes, seeded and chopped
2 cups cubed LOUIS RICH® Hickory Smoked Turkey Breast
1 cup (4 ounces) KRAFT® 100% Grated Parmesan Cheese

• Cook spaghetti according to package directions; drain. Keep warm.

• In same pan used to cook spaghetti, heat dressing over medium heat. Add warm spaghetti; toss until well coated.

• Add tomatoes, turkey and Parmesan cheese; toss lightly. Garnish as desired.

Makes 6 servings

Prep and cook time: 15 minutes

☙ COOK'S TIP ☙

The veins of large and jumbo shrimp are gritty; they must always be removed. The veins of medium and small shrimp are not gritty and need not be removed unless a more elegant presentation is desired.

Southwestern Lamb Grill

      1 rack of American lamb, 8 ribs
      3 tablespoons stone ground mustard
      1 tablespoon Worcestershire sauce
    ½ teaspoon crushed red pepper
      2 cloves garlic, minced

Trim all visible fat from rack. Stir together remaining ingredients in small bowl. Spread on outside of lamb. (If desired, for maximum flavor, cover and marinate in refrigerator up to 2 days.)

Prepare grill. Place lamb on grid. Grill 6 to 8 inches over hot coals until thermometer registers 140°F for rare or 150°F for medium-rare, turning frequently.

Makes 2 servings

Conventional Directions: Prepare lamb as directed. Place lamb on rack over broiler pan. Roast in preheated 325°F oven until meat thermometer registers 140°F for rare or 150°F for medium-rare.

Serving suggestion: Slice red or green bell peppers, zucchini, chili peppers and corn to desired size; brush with mixture of oil and chopped fresh cilantro. Grill 6 to 8 inches over hot coals until tender.

Favorite recipe from **American Lamb Council**

Pesto Dijon Pizza

    ½ cup chopped parsley*
    ⅓ cup GREY POUPON® Dijon Mustard
    ¼ cup Planters® Walnuts, chopped*
      1 tablespoon olive oil*
      2 tablespoons grated Parmesan cheese,* divided
    1½ teaspoons dried basil leaves,* divided
      2 packages (8 ounces each) small prepared pizza crusts
      4 ounces thinly sliced deli baked ham
      3 plum tomatoes, sliced
      1 cup (4 ounces) shredded mozzarella cheese

*1 container (7 ounces) prepared pesto sauce may be substituted for parsley, walnuts, olive oil, 1 tablespoon Parmesan cheese and 1 teaspoon basil. Stir mustard into prepared pesto sauce.

In small bowl, combine parsley, mustard, walnuts, oil, 1 tablespoon Parmesan cheese and 1 teaspoon basil. Divide mixture and spread evenly onto each pizza crust. Top each crust with 2 ounces ham, tomato slices and mozzarella cheese. Sprinkle with remaining Parmesan cheese and basil. Place on baking sheet. Bake at 450°F for 8 to 10 minutes or until cheese melts. Cut into wedges; serve warm.

Makes 4 servings

Chicken Tikka (Tandoori-Style Grilled Chicken)

      2 chickens (3 pounds each), cut up
      1 pint nonfat yogurt
    ½ cup FRANK'S® REDHOT® Original Cayenne Pepper Sauce
      1 tablespoon grated peeled fresh ginger
      3 cloves garlic, minced
      1 tablespoon paprika
      1 tablespoon cumin seeds, crushed *or* 1½ teaspoons ground cumin
      2 teaspoons salt
      1 teaspoon ground coriander

Remove skin and visible fat from chicken pieces. Rinse with cold water and pat dry. Randomly poke chicken all over with the tip of sharp knife. Place chicken in resealable plastic food storage bags or large glass bowl. Combine yogurt, RedHot® sauce, ginger, garlic, paprika, cumin, salt and coriander in small bowl; mix well. Pour over chicken pieces, turning pieces to coat evenly. Seal bags or cover bowl and marinate in refrigerator 1 hour or overnight.

Place chicken on oiled grid, reserving marinade. Grill over medium coals 45 minutes or until chicken is no longer pink near bone and juices run clear, turning and basting often with marinade. (Do not baste during last 10 minutes of cooking.) Discard any remaining marinade. Serve warm.

Makes 6 to 8 servings

Savory Grilled Potatoes in Foil

½ cup MIRACLE WHIP® Salad Dressing
3 garlic cloves, minced
½ teaspoon paprika
¼ teaspoon salt
¼ teaspoon pepper
3 baking potatoes, cut into ¼-inch slices
1 large onion, sliced

• Mix salad dressing and seasonings in large bowl until well blended. Stir in potatoes and onions to coat.

• Divide potato mixture evenly among six 12-inch square pieces of heavy-duty foil. Seal each to form packet.

• Place foil packets on grill over medium-hot coals (coals will have slight glow). Grill, covered, 25 to 30 minutes or until potatoes are tender.

Makes 6 side-dish servings

Vegetable Sauté

2 tablespoons olive oil
6 cups assorted cut-up vegetables, such as broccoli flowerets, green beans, cauliflowerets, sugar snap peas, bell pepper strips, diagonally sliced carrots, mushrooms, onions, yellow squash and zucchini
1 envelope GOOD SEASONS® Italian Salad Dressing Mix
2 tablespoons red wine vinegar

HEAT oil in large skillet on medium-high heat. Add vegetables; cook and stir until tender-crisp.

STIR in salad dressing mix and vinegar; cook and stir until heated. Garnish with chopped fresh parsley, if desired. *Makes 4 to 6 servings*

Lamb-Asparagus Stir-Fry

12 ounces boneless lean American lamb, leg or shoulder, cut into ⅛-inch strips
2 teaspoons cornstarch
⅛ teaspoon ground ginger
1 tablespoon reduced-sodium soy sauce
1 cup reduced-sodium chicken broth
1 tablespoon oil
1 clove garlic, minced
4 cups asparagus, trimmed and cut diagonally into ¾-inch pieces
1 large onion, cut into ⅛-inch strips (about 1 cup)
½ cup thinly sliced carrots
Hot cooked rice or ramen noodles (optional)
¼ cup slivered almonds or peanuts (optional)

Mix cornstarch and ginger. Gradually add soy sauce and broth, blending well. Set aside. Heat oil over medium-high heat in large skillet or wok. Add garlic and lamb strips; stir-fry until lamb is slightly pink. Remove lamb from skillet. Add asparagus, onion and carrots to skillet; stir-fry until crisp-tender, 3 to 5 minutes. Return lamb to skillet. Stir broth mixture; gradually add to lamb mixture, stirring constantly. Continue cooking until lamb mixture is glazed and thoroughly heated. Serve over rice, if desired. Top with nuts, if desired. *Makes 4 servings*

Prep Time: 15 minutes
Cook Time: 15 minutes

Favorite recipe from **American Lamb Council**

Smoked Turkey & Artichoke Salad with Hearts of Palm

½ cup MIRACLE WHIP® Salad Dressing
⅓ cup KRAFT® House Italian Dressing
½ teaspoon coarse grind pepper
¼ teaspoon dried tarragon leaves, crushed
3 cups cubed LOUIS RICH® Hickory Smoked Breast of Turkey
1 can (14 ounces) artichoke hearts, drained, quartered
⅓ cup *each* chopped green, red and yellow bell peppers
1 can (14 ounces) hearts of palm, drained
1 pint cherry tomatoes

• Mix dressings and seasonings until well blended.

• Stir in turkey, artichokes and peppers; refrigerate. Serve with hearts of palm and tomatoes.

Makes 6 cups

Prep time: 20 minutes plus refrigerating

Quick Chicken Marinara

1 tablespoon olive oil
2 boneless skinless chicken breast halves (about ¾ pound), cut into strips
1 yellow or green pepper, cut into strips
1 package (15 ounces) DI GIORNO® Marinara Sauce
1 package (9 ounces) DI GIORNO® Spinach Fettuccine, cooked, drained

HEAT oil in skillet on medium-high heat. Add chicken and pepper; cook and stir 3 minutes.

STIR in sauce. Cook on medium heat 3 to 5 minutes or until chicken is cooked through. Serve over hot fettuccine. Top with DI GIORNO® 100% Shredded Parmesan Cheese, if desired.   *Makes 3 to 4 servings*

Savory Grilled Tournedos

⅓ cup A.1.® Steak Sauce
¼ cup ketchup
¼ cup orange marmalade
2 tablespoons lemon juice
2 tablespoons minced onion
1 clove garlic, crushed
8 slices bacon (about 5 ounces)
8 (4-ounce) beef tenderloin steaks (tournedos), about 1 inch thick
Mushroom halves, radishes and parsley sprigs for garnish

In small bowl, blend steak sauce, ketchup, marmalade, lemon juice, onion and garlic; set aside.

Wrap a bacon slice around edge of each steak; secure with string or wooden toothpick. Grill steaks over medium-high heat for 10 minutes or to desired doneness, turning occasionally and brushing often with ½ cup prepared sauce. Remove string or toothpicks; serve steaks with remaining sauce. Garnish with mushrooms, radishes and parsley if desired.

Makes 8 servings

Smoked Turkey & Artichoke Salad with Hearts of Palm

Rice Crust Pizza

Rice Crust (recipe follows)
1 jar (15 to 16 ounces) pizza sauce
2 teaspoons Italian seasoning
Choice of toppings: turkey sausage, bell pepper, black olives, mushrooms and hot pepper sauce to taste
2 cups (8 ounces) mozzarella cheese, shredded

Prepare Rice Crust as directed below.

Combine pizza sauce and Italian seasoning in a small bowl and mix well. Spoon sauce over crust, up to 1 inch from edge. Cover with toppings of your choice and mozzarella cheese. Bake at 450°F until cheese melts, about 10 minutes. Cut into wedges and serve.

Makes 8 servings

Rice Crust

1 bag SUCCESS® Rice
Vegetable cooking spray
2 eggs, well beaten
1 cup (4 ounces) shredded mozzarella cheese
¼ cup onion, finely chopped
1 teaspoon salt

Prepare rice according to package directions.

Preheat oven to 400°F. Lightly spray 12-inch pizza pan with cooking spray and set aside. Combine eggs, rice, cheese, onion and salt in medium bowl and mix well. With back of spoon, press mixture evenly onto bottom and sides of pan. Bake 20 minutes or until lightly browned. Remove from oven.

Salisbury Steaks with Mushroom-Wine Sauce

1 pound lean ground sirloin
¾ teaspoon garlic salt or seasoned salt
¼ teaspoon pepper
2 tablespoons butter or margarine
1 package (8 ounces) sliced button mushrooms or 2 packages (4 ounces each) sliced exotic mushrooms
2 tablespoons sweet vermouth or ruby port wine
1 jar (12 ounces) *or* 1 can (10½ ounces) beef gravy

Heat large heavy nonstick skillet over medium-high heat 3 minutes or until hot. Meanwhile, combine ground beef, garlic salt and pepper; mix well. Shape mixture into four ¼-inch-thick oval patties.

Place patties in skillet as they are formed; cook 3 minutes per side or until browned. Transfer to plate; keep warm. Pour off any drippings.

Melt butter in skillet; add mushrooms and cook 2 minutes, stirring occasionally. Add vermouth; cook 1 minute. Add gravy; mix well.

Return meat to skillet; simmer uncovered over medium heat 3 minutes for medium or until desired doneness, turning meat and stirring sauce once.

Makes 4 servings

Prep and cook time: 20 minutes

Grilled Beef with Two Sauces

1 boneless beef sirloin steak (1 pound)

ROASTED GARLIC SAUCE
¾ cup mayonnaise*
¼ cup Roasted Garlic Purée (recipe follows)
¼ cup GREY POUPON® Dijon Mustard
1 tablespoon lemon juice
2 tablespoons chopped parsley

SUNDRIED TOMATO SAUCE
¾ cup chopped roasted red peppers
½ cup sundried tomatoes,** chopped
3 tablespoons GREY POUPON® Dijon Mustard
2 tablespoons chopped parsley
2 to 3 tablespoons olive oil
¼ teaspoon crushed red pepper flakes

*Lowfat mayonnaise may be substituted for regular mayonnaise.

**If sundried tomatoes are very dry, soften in warm water for 15 minutes. Drain before using.

Grill beef over medium heat to desired doneness and chill.

For Roasted Garlic Sauce, in medium bowl, blend all ingredients. Chill at least 1 hour to blend flavors.

For Sundried Tomato Sauce, in medium bowl, combine roasted red peppers, sundried tomatoes, mustard and parsley. Slowly add oil as needed to bind. Add red pepper flakes. Chill at least 1 hour to blend flavors. Bring to room temperature before serving.

To serve, slice beef and arrange on 4 serving plates. Spoon about 2 tablespoons of each sauce onto each plate. Serve with sliced tomatoes and cooled steamed asparagus; garnish as desired.   *Makes 4 servings*

ROASTED GARLIC PURÉE: Remove excess papery outside of 1 head garlic and separate into cloves. Place in 8×8×2-inch baking pan. Add 2 to 3 tablespoons olive oil and 1 cup chicken broth. Bake at 350°F for 25 to 30 minutes or until garlic is soft. Cool and squeeze garlic pulp from skins; discard liquid in pan.

→ FOOD FOR THOUGHT ←

"Eating is not merely a natural pleasure. Eating well gives a spectacular joy to life and contributes immensely to goodwill and happy companionship. It is of great importance to the morale."

Elsa Schiaperelli

Amigo Pita Pocket Sandwiches

1 pound ground turkey
1 can (7 ounces) whole kernel corn, drained
1 can (6 ounces) tomato paste
½ cup water
½ cup chopped green bell pepper
1 package (1 ounce) LAWRY'S® Taco Spices & Seasonings
8 pita breads
Curly lettuce leaves
Shredded Cheddar cheese

In large nonstick skillet, cook ground turkey until no longer pink; drain fat. Add corn, tomato paste, water, green pepper and taco seasoning; blend well. Bring to a boil; reduce heat and simmer, uncovered, 15 minutes. Cut off top quarter of pita breads and open to form pockets. Line each with lettuce leaves. Spoon about ½ cup filling into each pita bread and top with cheese.   *Makes 8 servings*

Jamaican Pork Chops with Tropical Fruit Salsa

⅔ cup prepared Italian salad dressing
⅓ cup FRANK'S® REDHOT® Original Cayenne
    Pepper Sauce
⅓ cup lime juice
2 tablespoons brown sugar
2 teaspoons dried thyme leaves
1 teaspoon ground allspice
½ teaspoon ground nutmeg
½ teaspoon ground cinnamon
6 loin pork chops, cut 1 inch thick (about
    2½ pounds)
Tropical Fruit Salsa (recipe follows)

Place salad dressing, RedHot® sauce, lime juice, sugar and seasonings in blender or food processor. Cover and process until smooth. Reserve ½ cup dressing mixture for Tropical Fruit Salsa. Place pork chops in large resealable plastic food storage bag. Pour remaining dressing mixture over chops. Seal bag and marinate in refrigerator 1 hour.

Place chops on grid, reserving dressing mixture. Grill over medium coals 30 minutes or until pork is juicy and barely pink in center, turning and basting frequently with dressing mixture. (Do not baste during last 5 minutes of cooking.) Serve chops with Tropical Fruit Salsa. Garnish as desired.

Makes 6 servings

Tropical Fruit Salsa

1 cup finely chopped fresh pineapple
1 ripe mango, peeled, seeded and finely chopped
2 tablespoons finely chopped red onion
1 tablespoon minced fresh cilantro leaves

Combine pineapple, mango, onion, cilantro and reserved ½ cup dressing mixture in small bowl. Refrigerate until chilled.

Makes about 2½ cups

Carrot-Artichoke Sauté

1 tablespoon butter
2 small carrots, diagonally cut into thin slices
1 clove garlic, minced
½ teaspoon dried basil leaves, dill weed or
    tarragon leaves
1 small red bell pepper, cut into thin strips
1 medium yellow squash, cut into matchsticks
4 jarred artichoke hearts, drained and rinsed, cut
    into quarters
1½ teaspoons lemon juice

Melt butter in large skillet over medium heat. Add carrots, garlic and basil; cook and stir 2 minutes. Add bell pepper; cook and stir 2 minutes. Add yellow squash and artichokes; cook and stir 3 minutes.

Add lemon juice; cook and stir 1 minute. Add salt and pepper to taste.

Makes 2 servings

Prep and cook time: 20 minutes

Beijing Chicken

3 pounds frying chicken pieces
½ cup KIKKOMAN® Teriyaki Marinade & Sauce
1 tablespoon dry sherry
2 teaspoons minced fresh ginger root
½ teaspoon fennel seed, crushed
½ teaspoon grated orange peel
½ teaspoon honey

Rinse chicken under cold water; pat dry with paper towels. Combine teriyaki sauce, sherry, ginger, fennel, orange peel and honey; pour over chicken in large plastic food storage bag. Press air out of bag; close top securely. Refrigerate 8 hours or overnight, turning bag over occasionally. Reserving marinade, remove chicken; place on grill 5 to 7 inches from hot coals. Cook 30 to 40 minutes, or until chicken is no longer pink in center, turning over and basting occasionally with reserved marinade. (Or, place chicken on rack of broiler pan. Broil 5 to 7 inches from heat 40 minutes, or until chicken is no longer pink in center, turning over and brushing occasionally with reserved marinade.)

Makes 4 servings

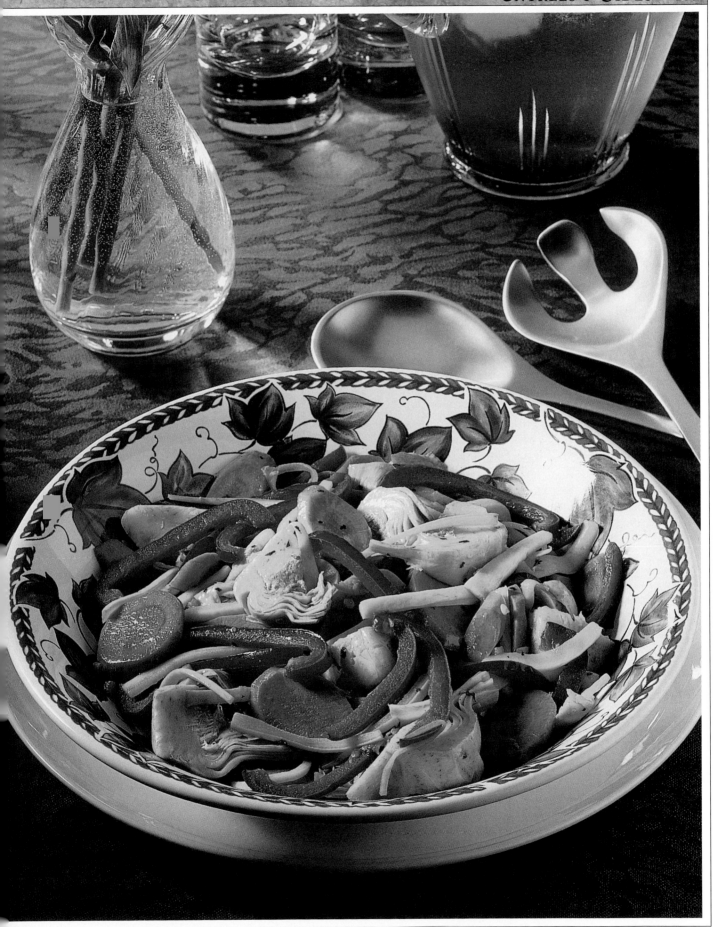

~ DESSERTS ~

Fabulous Fondue

    1 cup semisweet chocolate chips
    ¼ cup milk
    2 to 3 tablespoons chopped pecans or walnuts
    1 large banana, sliced
    2 medium apples, sliced
    2 medium oranges, peeled and cut into segments

1. Heat chocolate chips in small saucepan over very low heat until melted and smooth. Stir in milk and pecans; cook 1 minute.

2. Pour fondue into serving dish; serve immediately with fruit for dipping.   *Makes 6 servings*

Prep and cook time: 15 minutes

Wisconsin Ricotta Tart with Kiwi and Raspberry Sauce

    ⅓ cup all-purpose flour
    ⅓ cup packed brown sugar
    3 tablespoons butter
    1 cup flaked coconut
    ½ cup chopped pecans or macadamia nuts
    2 cups (16 ounces) Wisconsin ricotta cheese
    ½ cup powdered sugar
    1 teaspoon vanilla
    1 teaspoon grated lime peel
    1 package (10 ounces) frozen raspberries, thawed
    1 kiwi

Preheat oven to 350°F. Combine flour and brown sugar; cut in butter until mixture resembles coarse crumbs. Stir in coconut and nuts. Press into 10-inch tart pan or pie plate. Bake crust 15 minutes. Remove from oven and cool. Combine cheese, powdered sugar, vanilla and lime peel in food processor or blender; process until smooth. Spoon mixture into prepared crust. Refrigerate 1 hour. Before serving, place

raspberries in food processor or blender; process until sauce forms. Cut kiwi into slices and arrange in circle on top of tart. Drizzle tart with ½ of the raspberry sauce. Serve with remaining sauce.

Makes 8 to 10 servings

Favorite recipe from **Wisconsin Milk Marketing Board**

Creamy Cappuccino Frozen Dessert

DESSERT
    1 package (8 ounces) cream cheese, softened
    1 can (14 ounces) sweetened condensed milk
    ½ cup chocolate-flavored syrup
    1 tablespoon instant coffee powder
    1 tablespoon hot water
    1½ cups frozen whipped topping, thawed
    1 prepared chocolate crumb crust (6 ounces)
    ¼ cup chopped pecans, toasted

TOPPING
    Additional chocolate-flavored syrup

For Dessert, beat cream cheese in large mixing bowl on medium speed of electric mixer for 2 to 3 minutes or until fluffy. Add sweetened condensed milk and ½ cup syrup; beat on low speed until well blended.

Dissolve coffee powder in hot water in small bowl. Slowly stir into cream cheese mixture. Fold in whipped topping; spoon mixture into crust. Sprinkle with pecans. Cover and freeze overnight.

To complete recipe, let dessert stand in refrigerator 10 to 15 minutes before serving. Cut into wedges. For Topping, drizzle with additional syrup.

Makes 16 servings

Creamy Cappuccino Frozen Dessert

Lemon Crème Bars

LOW FAT

CRUST

2 cups sifted all-purpose flour
¾ cup sifted confectioners' sugar
1 teaspoon grated lemon rind
½ cup unsalted butter, at room temperature
2 tablespoons cold water

LEMON FILLING

½ cup egg substitute *or* 2 large eggs
1¾ cups granulated sugar
¾ cup (3 ounces) shredded ALPINE LACE®
   Reduced Sodium Muenster Cheese
1½ cups sifted all-purpose flour
1 tablespoon baking powder
⅔ cup fresh lemon juice
1 teaspoon grated lemon rind
¼ cup slivered almonds (optional)
3 tablespoons sifted confectioners' sugar
   Additional grated lemon rind (optional)

1. To make the Crust: Preheat the oven to 350°F and butter a 13×9×2-inch baking pan. In a medium-size bowl, mix the flour, confectioners' sugar and lemon rind, then work in the butter with your fingers until coarse crumbs form. Add the water and continue mixing until a dough forms. Press evenly onto the bottom of the baking pan and bake for 10 minutes.

2. While the crust is baking, make the Lemon Filling: In a medium-size bowl, whisk the egg substitute (or whole eggs) until light yellow. Whisk in the granulated sugar, cheese, flour, baking powder, lemon juice and lemon rind until well blended. Pour the egg mixture over the hot crust and sprinkle with the almonds, if you wish. Return to the oven and bake 25 minutes longer or until the filling is set.

3. Cool in the pan on a wire rack for 10 minutes, then cut into 36 (2×1½-inch) bars. Cool on wire racks. Dust with confectioners' sugar. Garnish with additional lemon rind, if you wish. Refrigerate in an airtight container.   *Makes 3 dozen bars*

Nutrients per Serving (1 bar):

Calories	105	Total Fat	3 g
Calories from Fat	33	Cholesterol	9 mg

→ MENU SUGGESTION ←

Every day is a picnic when you pack this lunch in your basket.

Beijing Chicken* (page 138)
Fresh Fruit Kabobs
German Potato Salad
Lemon Crème Bars

*Grill chicken one day before party.
Refrigerate and serve cold.

Rich Chocolate Pudding

QUICK MEAL

⅔ cup sugar
¼ cup unsweetened cocoa
3 tablespoons cornstarch
2 cups milk
1 egg
½ teaspoon vanilla
1 tablespoon butter or margarine

1. Combine sugar, cocoa and cornstarch in medium saucepan; whisk in milk. Cook over medium-high heat, stirring frequently, until mixture boils. Boil 1 minute, stirring constantly.

2. Beat egg in small bowl. Whisk about ½ cup hot milk mixture into egg; whisk egg mixture back into saucepan. Cook over medium heat 2 minutes, stirring constantly.

3. Remove pudding from heat; stir in vanilla and butter. Pour into serving dishes. Serve warm or cover and refrigerate until ready to serve.

Makes 4 servings

Prep and cook time: 18 minutes

Variation: For Rich Mocha Pudding, add 1 to 1½ teaspoons instant coffee crystals to sugar mixture in Step 1.

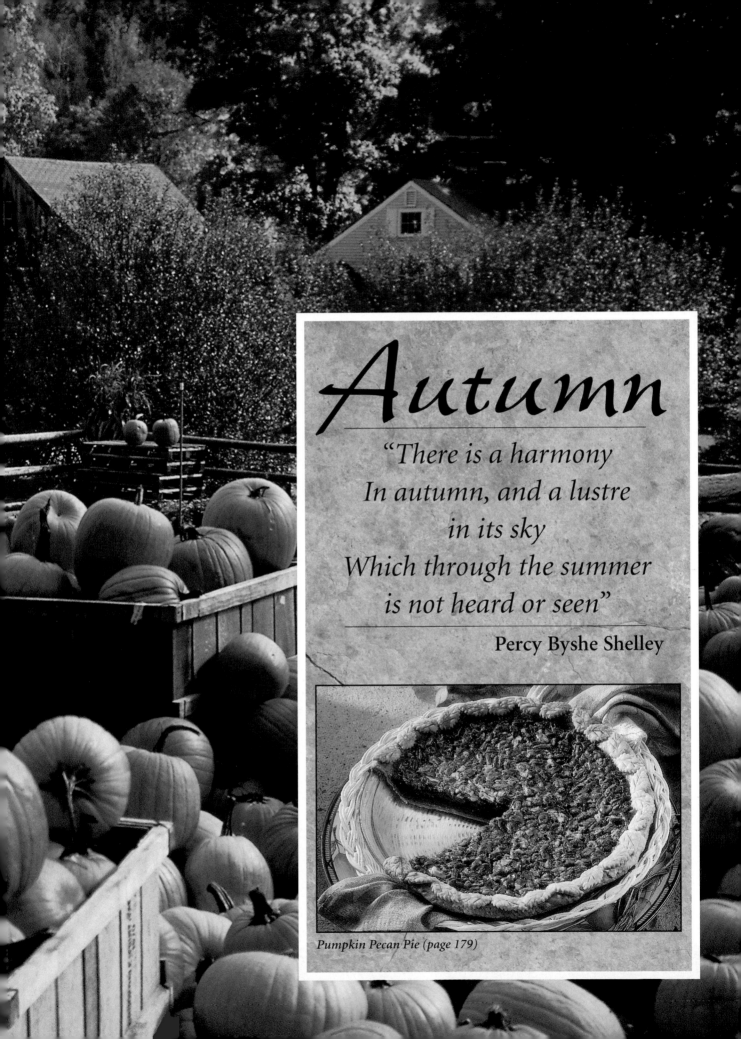

Autumn

"There is a harmony
In autumn, and a lustre
in its sky
Which through the summer
is not heard or seen"

Percy Byshe Shelley

Pumpkin Pecan Pie (page 179)

→ STARTERS ←

Baked Brie

½ pound Brie cheese, rind removed
¼ cup chopped pecans
¼ cup KARO® Dark Corn Syrup

Preheat oven to 350°F. Place cheese in shallow oven-safe serving dish. Top with pecans and corn syrup. Bake 8 to 10 minutes or until cheese is almost melted. Serve warm with plain crackers or melba toast.

Makes about 8 servings

Ristafel Salad

1 bag SUCCESS® Brown Rice
1 bag SUCCESS® Rice
12 ounces cooked deveined peeled shrimp
¾ cup chopped green onions
¾ cup chopped bell red peppers
¾ cup currants
¾ cup mango chutney
2 tablespoons lime juice
2 tablespoons low-sodium soy sauce
2 teaspoons peanut oil
1 teaspoon curry powder
1 teaspoon ground ginger
½ teaspoon crushed red pepper flakes
   Lettuce leaves
   Chopped peanuts

Prepare rice according to package directions. Combine cooked, cooled rice with shrimp, green onions, red peppers and currants.

In food processor, combine chutney, lime juice, soy sauce, peanut oil, curry powder, ginger and red pepper flakes. Process until smooth. Pour over rice mixture. Toss gently. Refrigerate.

Serve over lettuce leaves and top with chopped peanuts.

Makes 8 servings

Chili Soup Jarlsberg

2 tablespoons vegetable oil
1 pound beef round steak, cubed
2 cans (14½ ounces each) beef broth
1 can (15 ounces) dark red kidney beans, rinsed and drained
1 can (14½ ounces) tomatoes, chopped, undrained
1 medium green bell pepper, chopped
1 medium red bell pepper, chopped
1 large onion, chopped
1 large clove garlic, minced
3¼ teaspoons chili powder, divided
¼ teaspoon ground cumin
1½ cups (6 ounces) shredded JARLSBERG or JARLSBERG LITE™ cheese, divided
¼ cup butter or margarine, softened
1 small clove garlic, minced
12 KAVLI® Norwegian Thick-Style Crispbreads

Heat oil in large, deep saucepan over medium-high heat. Add beef and cook until browned. Add beef broth; bring to a boil over high heat. Reduce heat to low. Cover and simmer 1 hour. Add beans, tomatoes, bell peppers, onion, 1 large clove garlic, 3 teaspoons chili powder and cumin. Simmer, covered, 30 minutes. Gradually blend in ½ cup cheese. Heat just until cheese is melted.

Blend butter, garlic and remaining ¼ teaspoon chili powder in small bowl. Spread on crispbreads; arrange on cookie sheet. Bake in preheated 375°F oven about 3 to 5 minutes or until butter is melted. Sprinkle with ½ cup cheese. Bake just until cheese is melted.

Ladle soup into bowls. Garnish with remaining ½ cup cheese. Serve with crispbreads.   *Makes 6 servings*

Potato Skins with Cheddar Melt

LOW FAT

4 medium-size Idaho baking potatoes (about 2 pounds)
4 slices lean turkey bacon
2 tablespoons vegetable oil
2 cups (8 ounces) shredded ALPINE LACE® Reduced Fat Cheddar Cheese
¼ cup fat free sour cream
2 tablespoons finely chopped chives or green onions
1 tablespoon minced jalapeño pepper

1. Place a piece of foil on the bottom rack of the oven and preheat the oven to 425°F. Scrub the potatoes well and pierce the skins a few times with a sharp knife. Place the potatoes directly on the middle oven rack and bake for 1 hour or until soft.

2. Meanwhile, in a small skillet, cook the bacon over medium heat until crisp. Drain on paper towels, then crumble the bacon.

3. Using a serrated knife, cut the potatoes in half lengthwise. With a small spoon, scoop out the pulp, leaving a ¼-inch-thick shell. (Save the potato pulp for another use.) Cut the skins into appetizer-size triangles.

4. Place the skins on a baking sheet; brush the insides with the oil and bake for 15 minutes or until crisp.

5. Remove the skins from the oven, sprinkle with the cheese and return to the oven for 5 minutes or until the cheese melts. Top the skins with the sour cream, then sprinkle with the chives, jalapeño pepper and bacon.   *Makes about 24 appetizers*

Nutrients per Serving (1 appetizer):

Calories	58	Total Fat	3 g
Calories from Fat	28	Cholesterol	7 mg

✦ MENU SUGGESTION ✦

Greet the cool days of autumn with this sensational Labor Day menu.

Potato Skins with Cheddar Melt
Chicken and Vegetable Ragoût (page 164)
Caramel-Layered Brownies (page 176)

Spinach, Bacon and Mushroom Salad

1 large bunch (12 ounces) fresh spinach leaves, washed, drained and torn
¾ cup sliced fresh mushrooms
4 slices bacon, cooked and crumbled
¾ cup croutons
4 hard-cooked eggs, finely chopped
    Black pepper
¾ cup prepared HIDDEN VALLEY RANCH® Original Ranch® salad dressing

In medium salad bowl, combine spinach, mushrooms and bacon; toss. Top with croutons and eggs; season with pepper to taste. Pour salad dressing over all.
                    Makes 6 servings

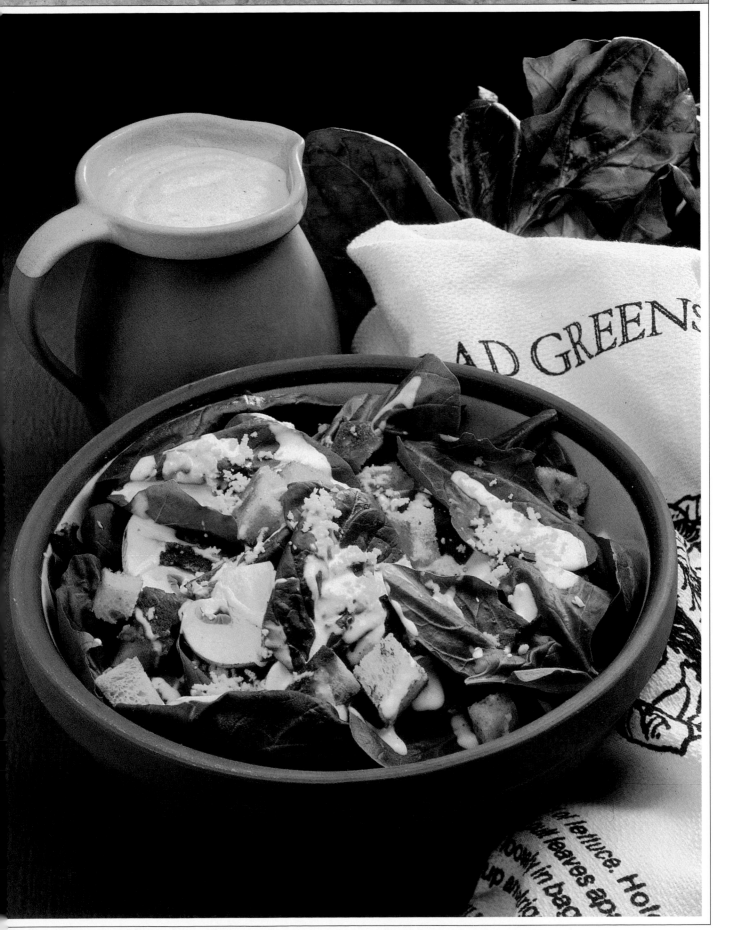

→ ENTREES & SIDES ←

Lasagne Roll-Ups

1 pound mild Italian sausage, casings removed
½ cup chopped onion
1 clove garlic, minced
1⅓ cups (12-ounce can) CONTADINA® Tomato Paste
1⅔ cups water
1 teaspoon dried oregano leaves, crushed
½ teaspoon dried basil leaves, crushed
1 egg
1 package (10 ounces) frozen chopped spinach, thawed, squeezed dry
2 cups (15-ounce container) ricotta cheese
1½ cups (6 ounces) shredded mozzarella cheese, divided
1 cup (4 ounces) grated Parmesan cheese
½ teaspoon salt
¼ teaspoon ground black pepper
8 dry lasagne noodles, cooked, drained, kept warm

In large skillet, crumble sausage. Add onion and garlic; cook until sausage is no longer pink. Drain. Stir in tomato paste, water, oregano and basil; cover. Bring to a boil. Reduce heat to low; simmer, uncovered, for 20 minutes. In medium bowl, beat egg lightly. Add spinach, ricotta cheese, *1 cup* mozzarella cheese, Parmesan cheese, salt and pepper. Spread about *½ cup* cheese mixture onto each noodle; roll up. Place, seam side down, in 12×7½-inch baking dish. Pour sauce over rolls; top with *remaining* mozzarella cheese. Bake in preheated 350°F oven for 30 to 40 minutes or until heated through. *Makes 8 servings*

Golden Apple Buttermilk Bread

1½ cups unsifted all-purpose flour
1 cup whole wheat flour
½ cup natural bran cereal
1 teaspoon baking soda
½ teaspoon baking powder
¼ teaspoon ground ginger
1⅓ cups buttermilk
¾ cup sugar
¼ cup vegetable oil
1 large egg
1 teaspoon grated orange peel
1 cup chopped Golden Delicious apples

1. Heat oven to 350°F. Grease 9×5-inch loaf pan. In medium bowl, combine flours, bran, baking soda, baking powder and ginger. In large bowl, beat together buttermilk, sugar, oil, egg and orange peel.

2. Add flour mixture to buttermilk mixture, stirring just until combined. Fold in apples. Spread batter in prepared pan and bake 45 to 50 minutes or until wooden toothpick inserted in center comes out clean. Cool bread in pan 10 minutes. Remove from pan and cool on wire rack. *Makes 1 loaf (8 servings)*

Favorite recipe from **Washington Apple Commission**

Superb Fillet of Sole & Vegetables

1 can (10¾ ounces) condensed cream of celery
    soup
½ cup milk
1 cup (4 ounces) shredded Swiss cheese, divided
½ teaspoon dried basil, crumbled
¼ teaspoon seasoned salt
¼ teaspoon pepper
1 package (10 ounces) frozen baby carrots, thawed
    and drained
1 package (10 ounces) frozen asparagus cuts,
    thawed and drained
1 can (2.8 ounces) FRENCH'S® French Fried
    Onions, divided
1 pound unbreaded sole fillets, thawed if frozen

Preheat oven to 375°. In small bowl, combine soup, milk, *½ cup* cheese and the seasonings; set aside. In 8×12-inch baking dish, combine carrots, asparagus and *½ can* French Fried Onions. Roll up fish fillets. (If fillets are wide, fold in half lengthwise before rolling.) Place fish rolls upright along center of vegetable mixture. Pour soup mixture over fish and vegetables. Bake, covered, at 375° for 30 minutes or until fish flakes easily with fork. Stir vegetables; top fish with remaining cheese and onions. Bake, uncovered, 3 minutes or until onions are golden brown. *Makes 3 to 4 servings*

Microwave Directions: Prepare soup mixture as above; set aside. In 8×12-inch microwave-safe dish, combine vegetables as above. Roll up fish fillets as above; place upright around edges of dish. Pour soup mixture over fish and vegetables. Cook, covered, on HIGH 14 to 16 minutes or until fish flakes easily with fork. Stir vegetables and rotate dish halfway through cooking time. Top fish with remaining cheese and onions; cook, uncovered, 1 minute or until cheese melts. Let stand 5 minutes.

Mexican Beef Stir-Fry

1 pound beef flank steak
2 tablespoons vegetable oil
1 teaspoon ground cumin
1 teaspoon dried oregano leaves
1 clove garlic, crushed
1 red or green bell pepper, cut into thin strips
1 medium onion, cut into thin wedges
1 to 2 jalapeño peppers,* thinly sliced
3 cups thinly sliced lettuce

*Remove seeds and membrane if milder flavor is desired.

Cut beef steak into ⅛-inch-thick strips. Combine oil, cumin, oregano and garlic. Reserve half of oil mixture; heat remaining oil mixture in large nonstick skillet over medium-high heat. Add bell pepper, onion and jalapeño peppers; stir-fry 2 to 3 minutes or until crisp-tender. Remove from skillet and set aside. In same skillet, stir-fry beef strips (one half at a time) in reserved oil mixture 1 to 2 minutes. Return vegetables to skillet and heat through. Serve beef mixture over lettuce. *Makes 4 servings*

Prep time: 25 minutes

Favorite recipe from **North Dakota Beef Commission**

Roast Turkey with Fresh Herb Stuffing

  4 cups cubed fresh herb- or garlic-flavored
     bread sticks
  1 turkey (8 to 10 pounds)
  1 tablespoon margarine
  1½ cups sliced brown mushrooms
  1 cup chopped onion
  ⅔ cup chopped celery
  ¼ cup chopped fresh parsley
  2 tablespoons chopped fresh tarragon
  1 tablespoon chopped fresh thyme
  ¼ teaspoon pepper
  ¼ cup chicken broth

Preheat oven to 350°F. Place cubed bread sticks on nonstick baking sheet. Bake 20 minutes to dry.

Remove giblets from turkey. Rinse turkey and cavities; pat dry with paper towels. Melt margarine in large nonstick skillet. Add mushrooms, onion and celery. Cook and stir 5 minutes or until onion is soft and golden; remove from heat. Add parsley, tarragon, thyme, pepper and bread cubes; stir until blended. Gently mix chicken broth into bread cube mixture. Fill turkey cavities with stuffing.

Spray roasting pan with nonstick cooking spray. Place turkey, breast side up, in roasting pan. Bake in 350°F oven 3 hours or until meat thermometer inserted in thigh registers 180°F and juices run clear.

Transfer turkey to serving platter. Cover loosely with foil; let stand 20 minutes. Remove and discard skin. Slice turkey and serve with herb stuffing. Garnish with grapes and fresh sage, if desired.

Makes 10 servings

Pasta with Roasted Peppers and Broccoli

  1 pound mostaccioli, ziti or other medium-sized
     pasta, uncooked
  2 tablespoons vegetable oil
  ½ teaspoon crushed red pepper
  1 pound (6 cups) broccoli flowerettes
  2 jars (6 ounces each) roasted peppers or whole
     pimientos, drained and diced
     Salt and black pepper
  ¼ cup grated Parmesan cheese

Cook pasta according to package directions; drain well.

Heat oil and crushed red pepper in large skillet over medium heat 2 minutes. Add broccoli; sauté 2 to 3 minutes. Add ½ cup water; cover. Cook broccoli about 3 minutes or until crisp-tender.

Toss pasta with diced peppers. Season to taste with salt and black pepper. Pour broccoli mixture over pasta; sprinkle with Parmesan cheese just before serving.

Makes 6 servings

Favorite recipe from **National Pasta Association**

Chicken Phyllo Wraps

Vegetable cooking spray
1 pound ground chicken
1 cup chopped fresh mushrooms
1 medium onion, chopped
3 cups cooked rice (cooked without salt and fat)
1 cup nonfat low-salt ricotta cheese
1 package (10 ounces) chopped spinach, thawed and well drained
1 can (2¼ ounces) sliced black olives, drained
¼ cup pine nuts, toasted*
2 cloves garlic, minced
1 teaspoon ground oregano
1 teaspoon lemon pepper
12 phyllo dough sheets

*To toast nuts, place on baking sheet. Bake at 350°F 5 to 7 minutes or until lightly browned.

Coat large skillet with cooking spray; heat over medium-high heat until hot. Add chicken, mushrooms, and onion; cook and stir 2 to 4 minutes or until chicken is no longer pink and vegetables are tender. Reduce heat to medium. Add rice, ricotta cheese, spinach, olives, nuts, garlic, oregano, and lemon pepper; cook and stir 3 to 4 minutes until well blended and thoroughly heated. Working with 1 phyllo sheet at a time, spray 1 sheet with cooking spray; fold sheet in half lengthwise. Place ¾ to 1 cup rice mixture on one end of phyllo strip. Fold left bottom corner over mixture, forming a triangle. Continue folding back and forth into triangle at end of strip. Repeat with remaining phyllo sheets and rice mixture. Place triangles, seam side down, on baking sheets coated with cooking spray. Coat top of each triangle with cooking spray. Bake at 400°F 15 to 20 minutes or until golden brown. Serve immediately.

Makes 12 servings

Nutrients per Serving:

Calories	219	Cholesterol	27 mg
Fat	6 g	Sodium	224 mg

Favorite recipe from **USA Rice Council**

Szechuan Vegetable Lo Mein

2 cans (about 14 ounces each) vegetable or chicken broth
2 teaspoons bottled minced garlic
1 teaspoon bottled minced fresh ginger *or* ½ teaspoon ground ginger
¼ teaspoon red pepper flakes
1 package (5 ounces) Oriental curly noodles or 5 ounces angel hair pasta, broken into halves
1 package (16 ounces) frozen vegetable medley, such as broccoli, carrots, water chestnuts and red bell peppers
3 tablespoons soy sauce
1 tablespoon Oriental sesame oil
¼ cup thinly sliced green onion tops

Combine broth, garlic, ginger and red pepper flakes in large deep skillet. Cover and bring to a boil over high heat.

Add noodles and vegetables to skillet; cover and return to a boil. Reduce heat to medium-low; simmer, uncovered, 5 to 6 minutes or until noodles and vegetables are tender, stirring occasionally.

Stir soy sauce and sesame oil into broth mixture; cook 3 minutes. Stir in green onions; ladle into bowls.

Makes 4 servings

Prep and cook time: 20 minutes

Thai Noodles with Peanut Sauce

2 packages (3 ounces each) Oriental flavor instant ramen noodles
2 cups BIRDS EYE® frozen Farm Fresh Mixtures Broccoli, Carrots and Water Chestnuts
⅓ cup hot water
¼ cup creamy peanut butter
1 teaspoon sugar
⅛ to ¼ teaspoon crushed red pepper

• Reserve seasoning packets from noodles.

• Bring 4 cups water to a boil in large saucepan. Add noodles and vegetables. Cook 3 minutes, stirring occasionally; drain.

• Meanwhile, whisk together hot water, peanut butter, sugar, red pepper and contents of reserved seasoning packets in large bowl until blended.

• Add noodles and vegetables; toss to coat evenly. Serve warm.   *Makes about 4 servings*

Vegetable Chili

Vegetable Chili

½ cup instant minced onion
1 tablespoon instant minced garlic
3½ cups water, divided
¾ cup uncooked bulgur
1 cup orange juice
2 tablespoons vegetable oil
2 cups coarsely chopped red bell peppers
⅓ cup chili powder
2 tablespoons ground cumin
2 tablespoons dried oregano leaves
1½ tablespoons dried thyme leaves
¼ teaspoon ground red pepper
¼ teaspoon ground cinnamon
1 can (28 ounces) Italian plum tomatoes, undrained, chopped
1½ teaspoons salt
2 cups sliced zucchini
1 can (19 ounces) chick-peas, rinsed and drained
1 can (16 ounces) red kidney beans, rinsed and drained
1 package (10 ounces) frozen cut green beans, thawed, drained
1 package (10 ounces) frozen corn, thawed, drained

Combine onion, garlic and ½ cup water in small bowl; let stand 10 minutes to soften. Combine bulgur and orange juice in medium bowl; set aside 15 minutes or until juice is absorbed.

Heat oil in large saucepan or Dutch oven until hot; add bell peppers and reserved onion mixture. Cook and stir occasionally 5 minutes or until vegetables are crisp-tender. Stir in chili powder, cumin, oregano, thyme, ground red pepper and cinnamon. Cook and stir 1 minute or until spices are fragrant. Add tomatoes, salt, remaining 3 cups water and reserved bulgur; bring to a boil. Cover; reduce heat and simmer 25 minutes or until thickened. Stir in zucchini, chick-peas, kidney beans, green beans and corn; simmer 5 minutes or until vegetables are crisp-tender.

Makes about 8 servings

Favorite recipe from **American Spice Trade Association**

Apple Cheddar Muffins

2 cups sifted all-purpose flour
1 tablespoon baking powder
⅓ cup sugar
½ teaspoon salt
¼ teaspoon ground nutmeg
½ cup egg substitute or 2 large eggs
¾ cup 2% low fat milk
¼ cup unsalted butter, melted
1 cup grated, cored, peeled baking apples, such as Granny Smith, Rome Beauty or Winesap
¾ cup (3 ounces) shredded ALPINE LACE® Fat Free Pasteurized Process Skim Milk Cheese Product—For Cheddar Lovers

Preheat the oven to 400°F. Spray 12 regular-size muffin cups with nonstick cooking spray.

In a large bowl, sift together the flour, baking powder, sugar, salt and nutmeg. In a small bowl, whisk the egg substitute (or the whole eggs) with the milk and butter until blended. Using a wooden spoon, make a hole in the center of the flour mixture, then pour in the egg mixture all at once. Stir just until the flour disappears. *(Avoid overmixing!)* Fold in the apples and cheese. Spoon the batter into the muffin cups until three-fourths full.

Bake the muffins for 20 to 25 minutes or until golden brown. Cool the muffins in the pan on a wire rack for 5 minutes, then lift them out with a spatula. They're delicious when served hot with honey!

Makes 12 muffins

Nutrients per Serving (1 muffin):

Calories	165	Cholesterol	13 mg
Fat	5 g		

Easy Chicken Couscous

  2 tablespoons olive oil
  1 onion, chopped
  1 pound chicken tenders
1½ cups (10 ounces) uncooked couscous
  ½ teaspoon salt
  1 can (14½ ounces) diced tomatoes with roasted
      garlic, undrained
  1 can (15½ ounces) chick-peas, drained and
      rinsed
  ¼ teaspoon ground cinnamon
  ¼ teaspoon ground cumin
  1 cup frozen peas
  ¼ teaspoon hot pepper sauce

Heat oil in large skillet over medium-high heat until
hot. Add onion; cook and stir 3 minutes or until
translucent. Add chicken tenders; cook and stir 5
minutes.

While chicken is cooking, bring 2½ cups water to a
boil in medium saucepan. Add couscous and salt;
cover and remove from heat. Let stand 10 minutes.

While couscous is standing, add tomatoes, chick-peas,
cinnamon and cumin to chicken mixture; mix well.
Reduce heat to medium-low. Cover and cook 5
minutes, stirring occasionally. Add peas and hot
pepper sauce; mix well. Cover and cook 5 minutes
more or until chicken is no longer pink in center.
Fluff couscous with fork. Serve chicken mixture
with couscous. *Makes 6 servings*

Rigatoni with Four Cheeses

 12 ounces uncooked rigatoni
  3 cups milk
  1 tablespoon chopped carrot
  1 tablespoon chopped celery
  1 tablespoon chopped onion
  1 tablespoon parsley sprigs
  ½ bay leaf
  ¼ teaspoon black peppercorns
  ¼ teaspoon hot pepper sauce
     Dash ground nutmeg
  ¼ cup butter
  ¼ cup all-purpose flour
  ½ cup grated Wisconsin Parmesan cheese
  ¼ cup grated Wisconsin Romano cheese
1½ cups (6 ounces) shredded Wisconsin Cheddar
      cheese
1½ cups (6 ounces) shredded Wisconsin mozzarella
      cheese
  ¼ teaspoon chili powder

Cook rigatoni according to package directions. Drain
and keep warm.

Combine milk, carrot, celery, onion, parsley, bay leaf,
peppercorns, hot pepper sauce and nutmeg in large
saucepan. Bring to a boil. Reduce heat to low; simmer
10 minutes. Strain; reserve liquid.

Preheat oven to 350°F. Melt butter in medium
saucepan over medium heat. Stir in flour. Gradually
stir in reserved liquid. Cook, stirring constantly, until
thickened. Remove from heat. Add Parmesan and
Romano cheeses; stir until blended. Pour into large
bowl. Add rigatoni; toss gently to coat. Combine
shredded cheeses in medium bowl. Place half the
rotini mixture in greased 2-quart casserole; sprinkle
with cheese mixture. Top with remaining rotini
mixture. Sprinkle with chili powder. Bake 25 minutes
or until bubbly. Garnish as desired.

Makes 6 servings

Favorite recipe from **Wisconsin Milk Marketing Board**

Rosy Potato and Pepper Gratin

3 tablespoons extra virgin olive oil
1 tablespoon fresh thyme leaves *or* 1 teaspoon
    dried thyme
½ teaspoon salt
½ teaspoon freshly ground black pepper
3 pounds unpeeled red-skinned potatoes, sliced
    ¼ inch thick (4 cups)
2 cups thin strips yellow onion
2 cups thin strips red bell pepper
3 cups (12 ounces) shredded ALPINE LACE® Fat
    Free Pasteurized Process Skim Milk Cheese
    Product—For Mozzarella Lovers
¼ cup low sodium chicken broth
¼ cup white wine or chicken broth
    Sprigs of fresh thyme (optional)

Preheat the oven to 375°F. Spray a 13×9×3-inch baking dish with nonstick cooking spray. In a cup, mix the oil, thyme, salt and black pepper.

Half-fill a large saucepan with water and bring to a boil over high heat. Add the potatoes, cover, remove from the heat and let stand for 10 minutes. Drain the potatoes well and transfer them to a large bowl. Drizzle with the oil mixture.

Line the bottom of the baking dish with a third of the potatoes. Layer with half of the onions, half of the bell pepper strips and a third of the cheese. Repeat layers beginning with the potatoes, then top with the remaining third of the potatoes and cheese.

In a measuring cup, combine the chicken broth and wine. Pour evenly over the gratin. Cover with foil and bake for 20 minutes. Remove the foil and bake for 30 minutes or until the potatoes are tender and the top is golden brown. Garnish with the thyme sprigs, if you wish.   *Makes 8 servings*

Nutrients per Serving:

Calories	289	Cholesterol	5 mg
Fat	5 g		

Chicken with Walnuts

1 cup uncooked instant rice
½ cup chicken broth
¼ cup Chinese plum sauce
2 tablespoons soy sauce
2 teaspoons cornstarch
2 tablespoons vegetable oil, divided
3 cups frozen bell peppers and onions
1 pound boneless skinless chicken breasts, cut
    into ¼-inch slices
1 clove garlic, minced
1 cup walnut halves

Cook rice according to package directions. Set aside. Combine broth, plum sauce, soy sauce and cornstarch; set aside.

Heat 1 tablespoon oil in wok or large skillet over medium-high heat until hot. Add frozen peppers and onions; stir-fry 3 minutes or until crisp-tender. Remove vegetables from wok. Drain; discard liquid.

Heat remaining 1 tablespoon oil in wok until hot. Add chicken and garlic; stir-fry 3 minutes or until chicken is no longer pink in center.

Stir broth mixture; add to wok. Cook and stir 1 minute or until sauce thickens. Stir in vegetables and walnuts; cook 1 minute more. Serve with rice.
                      Makes 4 servings

Prep and cook time: 19 minutes

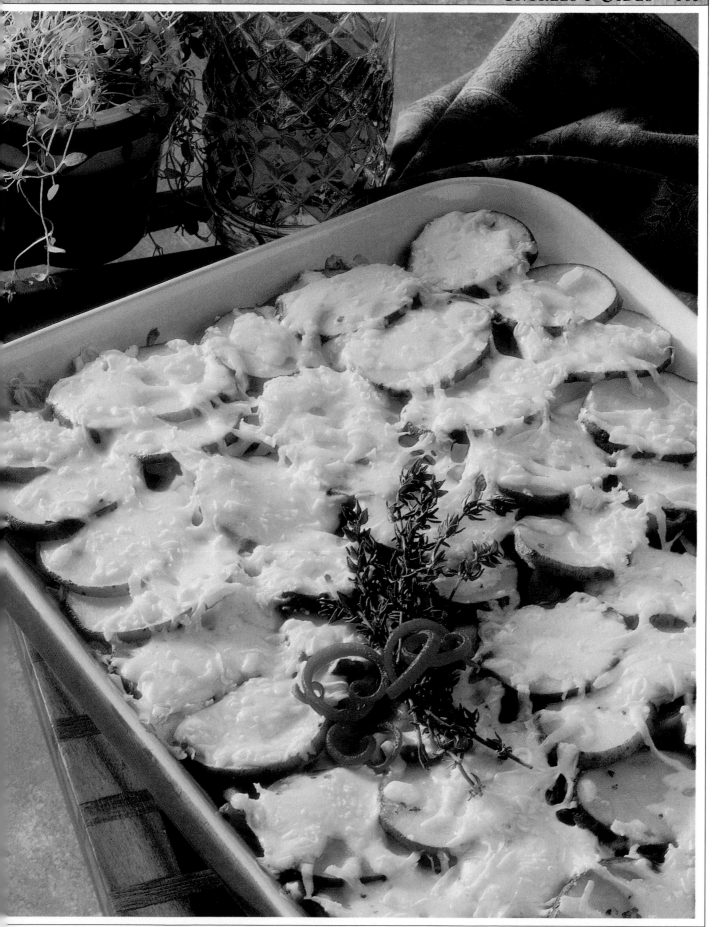

Pumpkin Harvest Bread

1½ cups all-purpose flour
½ cup cornmeal
1½ teaspoons baking powder
1 teaspoon baking soda
2 teaspoons ground cinnamon
½ teaspoon ground nutmeg
¼ teaspoon salt
1 cup LIBBY'S® Solid Pack Pumpkin
2 eggs
½ cup granulated sugar
½ cup packed brown sugar
¼ cup vegetable oil
¼ cup applesauce
½ cup raisins

Combine flour, cornmeal, baking powder, baking soda, cinnamon, nutmeg and salt in medium bowl. Beat pumpkin, eggs, granulated sugar, brown sugar, oil and applesauce in large mixer bowl. Beat in flour mixture just until blended. Stir in raisins.

Spoon into greased and floured 9×5-inch loaf pan. Bake in preheated 350°F oven for 50 to 55 minutes or until wooden pick inserted in center comes out clean. Cool in pan for 5 to 10 minutes. Remove to wire rack to cool completely.   *Makes 18 servings*

Baked Vegetables en Croûte

Salt
3 cups finely chopped peeled eggplant
3 tablespoons vegetable oil
½ cup chopped onion
¼ cup minced celery
1 clove garlic, minced
1 cup mushroom, sliced
1½ cups shredded carrots (about 3 medium)
¾ cup (3 ounces) shredded Monterey Jack cheese
3 tablespoons chopped fresh parsley
½ teaspoon dried oregano leaves, crumbled
Black pepper
1 sheet frozen puff pastry, thawed
Chopped fresh chives for garnish

1. Sprinkle salt uniformly over eggplant; let drain on paper towels 30 minutes. Pat dry with additional paper towels.

2. Heat oil in large skillet over medium-high heat. Add eggplant, onion, celery and garlic; cook over medium heat 4 minutes. Add mushrooms; continue cooking 4 to 5 minutes or until mushrooms are tender. Remove from heat; stir in carrots, cheese, parsley and oregano. Season with salt and pepper to taste; set aside.

3. Preheat oven to 400°F. Roll out pastry to 14-inch square. Place pastry on large ungreased baking sheet. Spread vegetable mixture over half of pastry to within ½ inch of outer edges; fold pastry over vegetables. Press edges together; seal with fork. Bake 20 to 25 minutes or until puffed and golden brown. Cut crosswise to serve. Serve warm, sprinkled with chives.
Makes 4 to 5 servings

Chicken and Vegetable Ragoût

2 tablespoons olive or vegetable oil
½ cup chopped onion
3 cloves garlic, minced
1 pound (about 4) boneless, skinless chicken breast halves, cut into ½-inch pieces
1 cup water or chicken broth
1¾ cups (14.5-ounce can) CONTADINA® Recipe Ready Diced Tomatoes, undrained
⅔ cup (6-ounce can) CONTADINA® Italian-Style Tomato Paste
1 cup sliced peeled carrots
1 cup halved zucchini slices
1 cup red or green bell pepper strips
1 teaspoon Italian herb seasoning
½ teaspoon salt
⅛ teaspoon ground black pepper

In large skillet, heat oil. Add onion and garlic; sauté for 2 to 3 minutes or until onion is tender. Add chicken; cook until browned, stirring frequently. Add water, tomatoes and juice, tomato paste and carrots; cover. Bring to a boil. Reduce heat to low; simmer for 10 minutes, stirring occasionally. Add zucchini, bell pepper, Italian seasoning, salt and black pepper; cover. Simmer for 15 to 20 minutes or until chicken is no longer pink in center and vegetables are tender. Serve over hot cooked rice or pasta, if desired.
Makes 6 servings

Pumpkin Harvest Bread

Cheese and Bean Quesadillas

1 can (15 ounces) pinto beans, rinsed and drained
½ cup salsa
1 teaspoon chili powder
4 flour tortillas (10 inches)
1 cup (4 ounces) shredded Monterey Jack cheese
¼ cup chopped fresh cilantro
¼ cup sour cream
    Fresh cilantro leaves (optional)

Place beans in medium saucepan. Mash beans with potato masher or fork. Stir in salsa and chili powder. Cook and stir over medium heat until bubbly. Reduce heat to low. Simmer 5 minutes, adding more salsa if mixture becomes dry.

Spray griddle with nonstick cooking spray. Heat over medium heat until hot. Brush 1 tortilla lightly on both sides with water. Heat on griddle until lightly browned. Turn over tortilla. Spread with half of bean mixture; sprinkle with ½ cup cheese and 2 tablespoons cilantro. Top with a second tortilla and press lightly. Brush top of tortilla with water. Carefully turn quesadilla to brown second side. Remove from heat; repeat with remaining tortillas.

Cut each quesadilla into 6 wedges. Serve with sour cream. Garnish with cilantro leaves, if desired.

Makes 6 servings

Aztec Chili Salad

1 pound ground beef
1 package (1.48 ounces) LAWRY'S® Spices & Seasonings for Chili
½ cup water
1 can (15¼ ounces) kidney beans, undrained
1 can (14½ ounces) whole peeled tomatoes, cut up, undrained
½ cup sour cream
3 tablespoons mayonnaise
1 fresh medium tomato, diced
¼ cup chopped fresh cilantro
½ teaspoon LAWRY'S® Seasoned Pepper
1 head lettuce
1 red bell pepper, sliced
¼ cup sliced green onions
1½ cups (6 ounces) shredded Cheddar cheese
¼ cup sliced ripe olives

In large skillet, brown beef until crumbly; drain fat. Stir in Spices & Seasonings for Chili, water, beans and canned tomatoes with liquid; blend well. Bring to a boil; reduce heat and simmer, uncovered, 10 minutes. For dressing, in blender or food processor, blend sour cream, mayonnaise, fresh tomato, cilantro and Seasoned Pepper. Refrigerate until chilled. On 6 individual plates, layer lettuce leaves, chili meat, bell pepper, onions, cheese and olives. Drizzle with chilled dressing.   *Makes 6 servings*

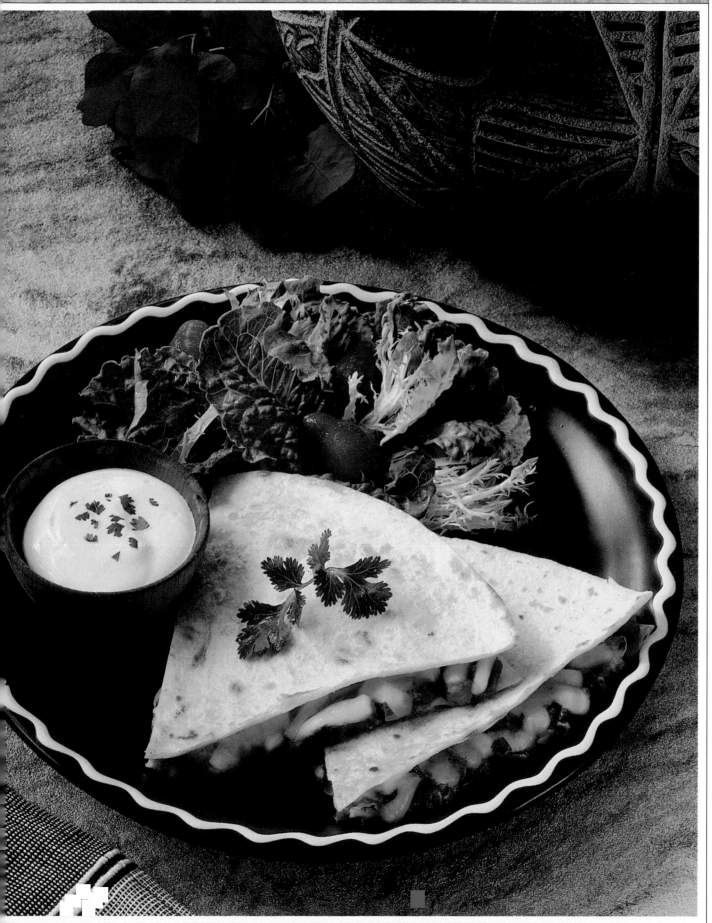

Oatmeal Apple Cranberry Scones

   2 cups all-purpose flour
   1 cup uncooked rolled oats
   1/3 cup sugar
   2 teaspoons baking powder
   1/2 teaspoon salt
   1/2 teaspoon baking soda
   1/2 teaspoon ground cinnamon
   3/4 cup MOTT'S® Natural Apple Sauce, divided
   2 tablespoons margarine
   1/2 cup coarsely chopped cranberries
   1/2 cup chopped peeled apple
   1/4 cup skim milk
   1/4 cup plus 2 tablespoons honey, divided

1. Preheat oven to 425°F. Spray baking sheet with nonstick cooking spray.

2. In large bowl, combine flour, oats, sugar, baking powder, salt, baking soda and cinnamon. Add 1/2 cup applesauce and margarine; cut in with pastry blender or fork until mixture resembles coarse crumbs. Stir in cranberries and apple.

3. In small bowl, combine milk and 1/4 cup honey. Add milk mixture to flour mixture; stir together until dough forms a ball.

4. Turn out dough onto well-floured surface; knead 10 to 12 times. Pat dough into 8-inch circle. Place on prepared baking sheet. Use tip of knife to score dough into 12 wedges.

5. In another small bowl, combine remaining 1/4 cup applesauce and 2 tablespoons honey. Brush mixture over top of dough.

6. Bake 12 to 15 minutes or until lightly browned. Immediately remove from baking sheet; cool on wire rack 10 minutes. Serve warm or cool completely. Cut into 12 wedges.   *Makes 12 servings*

Pasta with Onions and Goat Cheese

   2 teaspoons olive oil
   4 cups thinly sliced sweet onions
   3/4 cup (3 ounces) goat cheese
   1/4 cup skim milk
   6 ounces uncooked baby bow tie or other small
       pasta
   1 clove garlic, minced
   2 tablespoons dry white wine or fat-free
       reduced-sodium chicken broth
   1 1/2 teaspoons chopped fresh sage *or* 1/2 teaspoon
       dried sage leaves
   1/2 teaspoon salt
   1/4 teaspoon pepper
   2 tablespoons chopped toasted walnuts

Heat oil in large nonstick skillet over medium heat. Add onions; cook slowly until golden and caramelized, about 20 to 25 minutes, stirring occasionally.

Combine goat cheese and milk in small bowl; stir until well blended. Set aside.

Cook pasta according to package directions, omitting salt. Drain and set aside.

Add garlic to onions in skillet; cook until softened, about 3 minutes. Add wine, sage, salt and pepper; cook until moisture has evaporated. Remove from heat; add pasta and goat cheese mixture, stirring to melt cheese. Sprinkle with walnuts.   *Makes 8 (1/2-cup) servings*

Nutrients per Serving:

Calories	150	Total Fat	5 g
Calories from Fat	45	Cholesterol	9 mg

Kahlúa® Stir-Fry Chicken

1½ pounds boneless skinless chicken, cut into
        ½-inch pieces
  2 tablespoons beaten egg
  ¼ cup plus 2 tablespoons vegetable oil, divided
  2 tablespoons plus 1 teaspoon cornstarch, divided
  ½ cup water chestnuts, sliced
  6 asparagus tips, fresh or frozen
  1 green bell pepper, cut into ½-inch strips
  4 ounces mushrooms, sliced
  4 ounces snow peas
  3 tablespoons KAHLÚA®
  1 cup cashews
  3 green onions, chopped

Coat chicken in mixture of egg, 2 tablespoons oil and
2 tablespoons cornstarch. Heat remaining ¼ cup oil in
wok or skillet. Add chicken. Cook until golden brown;
remove and drain well. Remove all but 2 tablespoons
oil from wok; heat. Add all vegetables except green
onions. Stir fry 3 to 5 minutes. Combine Kahlúa® and
remaining 1 teaspoon cornstarch; add to vegetables.
Bring to a boil, then simmer to thicken slightly. Add
chicken and cashews; heat thoroughly. Remove to
serving platter. Garnish with green onions.

Makes 4 to 6 servings

California Turkey Chili

1¼ cups chopped onion
  1 cup chopped green bell pepper
  2 cloves garlic, minced
  3 tablespoons vegetable oil
  1 can (28 ounces) kidney beans, drained
  1 can (28 ounces) stewed tomatoes, undrained
  1 cup red wine or water
  3 cups cubed cooked California-grown turkey
  1 tablespoon chili powder
  1 tablespoon chopped cilantro *or* 1 teaspoon
        dried coriander
  1 teaspoon crushed red pepper
  ½ teaspoon salt
     Shredded Cheddar cheese (optional)
     Additional chopped onion (optional)
     Chopped cilantro (optional)

Cook and stir onion, green pepper, garlic and oil in
large saucepan over high heat until tender. Add beans,
tomatoes with liquid, wine, turkey, chili powder,
cilantro, red pepper and salt. Cover; simmer 25
minutes or until heated through. Top with cheese,
onion or cilantro, if desired.   *Makes 6 servings*

Favorite recipe from **California Poultry Industry Federation**

Meat and Potato Stir-Fry

  1 tablespoon vegetable oil
  1 large baking potato, peeled and cut into ½-inch
        cubes
  2 medium carrots, peeled and thinly sliced
  1 medium onion, halved and sliced
  ⅔ cup beef broth
  1 teaspoon salt, divided
  1 pound lean ground round beef
  1 large clove garlic, minced
  1 tablespoon dried parsley flakes
  1 teaspoon paprika
  ½ teaspoon ground cinnamon
  ½ teaspoon ground cumin
  ¼ teaspoon pepper

Heat oil in a wok or large skillet over medium-high
heat until hot. Add potato, carrots and onion; cook
and stir 3 minutes. Stir in broth and ½ teaspoon salt.
Reduce heat to medium. Cover and cook 6 to 7
minutes more or until potato is tender, stirring once
or twice. Remove vegetables from wok; set aside. Wipe
out wok with paper towel.

Heat wok over medium-high heat until hot. Add beef
and garlic; stir-fry 3 minutes or until meat is no longer
pink. Add parsley, paprika, cinnamon, cumin,
remaining ½ teaspoon salt and pepper; cook and stir 1
minute. Add vegetables; heat through.

Makes 4 servings

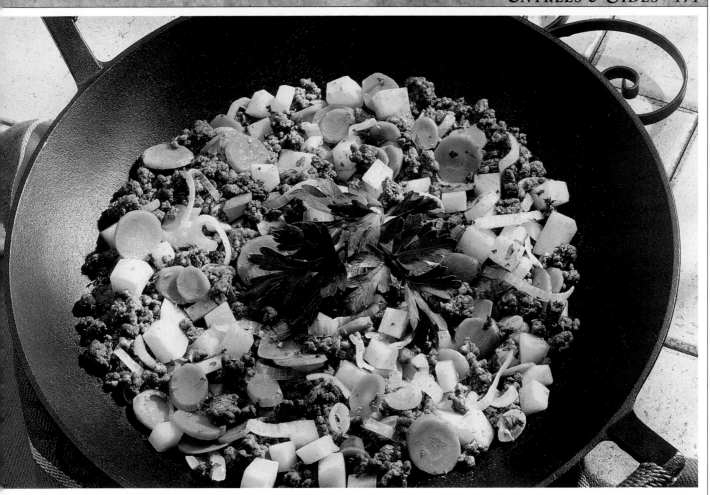

Meat and Potato Stir-Fry

Turkey Roulade

1½ **pounds (10 slices) uncooked boneless turkey breast**

2 **cups (15-ounce container) ricotta cheese**

1½ **cups (6 ounces) shredded mozzarella cheese, divided**

1 **package (10 ounces) frozen chopped spinach, thawed, squeezed dry**

½ **teaspoon garlic salt**

1 **tablespoon olive or vegetable oil**

½ **cup chopped onion**

2 **cloves garlic, minced**

1¾ **cups (14.5-ounce can) CONTADINA® Recipe Ready Diced Tomatoes, undrained**

⅔ **cup (6-ounce can) CONTADINA® Tomato Paste**

1 **cup chicken broth**

1 **teaspoon Italian herb seasoning**

1 **teaspoon salt**

¼ **teaspoon ground black pepper**

Pound turkey slices between 2 pieces of plastic wrap to ⅛-inch thickness. In medium bowl, combine ricotta cheese, *1 cup* mozzarella cheese, spinach and garlic salt. Spread *⅓ cup* cheese mixture onto each turkey slice; roll up. Secure with toothpicks. Place rolls in greased 13×9-inch baking dish. In large skillet, heat oil. Add onion and garlic; sauté for 2 minutes. Add tomatoes and juice, tomato paste, broth, Italian seasoning, salt and pepper. Bring to a boil. Reduce heat to low; simmer, uncovered, for 10 minutes. Spoon sauce over rolls; cover. Bake in preheated 425°F oven for 20 to 25 minutes or until turkey is done. Sprinkle with *remaining* mozzarella cheese. Bake for 5 minutes or until cheese is melted. *Makes 10 servings*

Fish Françoise

LOW FAT

- 1 can (14½ ounces) DEL MONTE® FreshCut™ Diced Tomatoes, undrained
- 1 tablespoon lemon juice
- 2 cloves garlic, minced
- ½ teaspoon dried tarragon leaves, crushed
- ⅛ teaspoon black pepper
- 3 tablespoons whipping cream
  Vegetable oil
- 1½ pounds firm white fish (such as halibut or cod)
  Lemon wedges

Preheat broiler; position rack 4 inches from heat. In large saucepan, combine tomatoes with liquid, lemon juice, garlic, tarragon and pepper. Cook, uncovered, over medium-high heat about 10 minutes or until liquid has evaporated. Add cream. Cook over low heat 5 minutes or until very thick; set aside. Brush broiler pan with oil. Arrange fish on pan; season with salt and additional pepper, if desired. Broil fish 3 to 4 minutes per side or until fish flakes easily with fork. Spread tomato mixture over top of fish. Broil 1 minute. Serve immediately with lemon wedges. *Makes 4 servings*

Nutrients per Serving:

Calories	301	Cholesterol	85 mg
Fat	9 g	Sodium	253 mg

Fish Françoise

Quick Tamale Casserole

- 1½ pounds ground beef
- ¾ cup sliced green onions
- 1 can (4 ounces) chopped green chiles, drained and divided
- 1 can (10¾ ounces) tomato soup
- ¾ cup mild salsa
- 1 can (16 ounces) corn, drained
- 1 can (2¼ ounces) chopped pitted black olives (optional)
- 1 tablespoon Worcestershire sauce
- 1 teaspoon chili powder
- ¼ teaspoon garlic powder
- 4 slices (¾ ounce each) American cheese, halved
- 4 corn muffins, cut into ½-inch cubes
  Mexican Sour Cream Topping (recipe follows) (optional)

Preheat oven to 350°F. Heat medium skillet over medium heat. Add beef and onions; cook until beef is no longer pink. Reserve 2 tablespoons chiles for Mexican Sour Cream Topping, if desired. Stir in remaining chiles, tomato soup, salsa, corn, olives, Worcestershire sauce, chili powder and garlic powder until well blended. Place in 2-quart casserole. Top with cheese. Spread muffin cubes evenly over cheese. Bake at 350°F 5 to 10 minutes or until cheese is melted. Serve with Mexican Sour Cream Topping, if desired. *Makes 6 servings*

Mexican Sour Cream Topping

- 1 cup sour cream
- 2 tablespoons chopped green chiles, reserved from casserole (optional)
- 2 teaspoons chopped jalapeño peppers (optional)
- 2 teaspoons lime juice

Combine ingredients in small bowl; mix well.

DESSERTS

Marble Cheesecake

HERSHEY®S Chocolate Crumb Crust (recipe follows)
3 packages (8 ounces each) cream cheese, softened
1 cup sugar, divided
½ cup dairy sour cream
2½ teaspoons vanilla extract, divided
3 tablespoons all-purpose flour
3 eggs
¼ cup HERSHEY®S Cocoa
1 tablespoon vegetable oil

Prepare HERSHEY®S Chocolate Crumb Crust. Heat oven to 450°F. In large mixer bowl on medium speed of electric mixer, beat cream cheese, ¾ cup sugar, sour cream and 2 teaspoons vanilla until smooth. Gradually add flour, beating well. Add eggs, one at a time, beating well after each addition.

In medium bowl, stir together cocoa and remaining ¼ cup sugar. Add oil, remaining ½ teaspoon vanilla and 1½ cups cream cheese mixture; blend well. Spoon plain and chocolate batters alternately into prepared crust, ending with spoonfuls of chocolate batter; gently swirl with knife for marbled effect. Bake 10 minutes. *Without opening oven door, reduce temperature to 250°F;* continue baking 30 minutes. *Turn off oven; without opening door,* leave cheesecake in oven 30 minutes. Remove from oven to wire rack. With knife, immediately loosen cheesecake from side of pan; cool completely. Refrigerate several hours or overnight; remove side of pan. Cover; refrigerate leftover cheesecake.   *Makes 10 to 12 servings*

HERSHEY'S Chocolate Crumb Crust

1¼ cups vanilla wafer crumbs (about 40 wafers)
⅓ cup powdered sugar
⅓ cup HERSHEY®S Cocoa
¼ cup (½ stick) butter or margarine, melted

Heat oven to 350°F. In medium bowl, stir together crumbs, powdered sugar and cocoa; blend in butter. Press mixture onto bottom and ½ inch up side of 9-inch springform pan. Bake 8 minutes; cool completely.

Orange Pumpkin Tart

1½ cups all-purpose flour
1 cup QUAKER® Oats (quick or old fashioned, uncooked), divided
1 cup plus 2 tablespoons sugar, divided
¾ cup (1½ sticks) margarine
2 tablespoons water
1 can (16 ounces) pumpkin (1¾ cups)
1 egg white
1 teaspoon pumpkin pie spice
½ cup powdered sugar
2 teaspoons orange juice
½ teaspoon grated orange peel

Preheat oven to 400°F. Combine flour, ¾ cup oats and ½ cup sugar; cut in margarine until crumbly. Reserve ¾ cup oat mixture. Mix remaining oat mixture with water until dough is moistened. Divide into halves. Press one half onto baking pan to form 12×5-inch tart. Repeat step, using remaining dough half and another baking pan. Combine pumpkin, egg white, ½ cup sugar and pumpkin pie spice. Spread evenly over tarts. Top tarts with combined remaining ¼ cup oats, remaining 2 tablespoons sugar and reserved oat mixture. Bake 25 minutes or until golden. Cool. Drizzle with combined remaining ingredients. Refrigerate leftovers.   *Makes 12 servings*

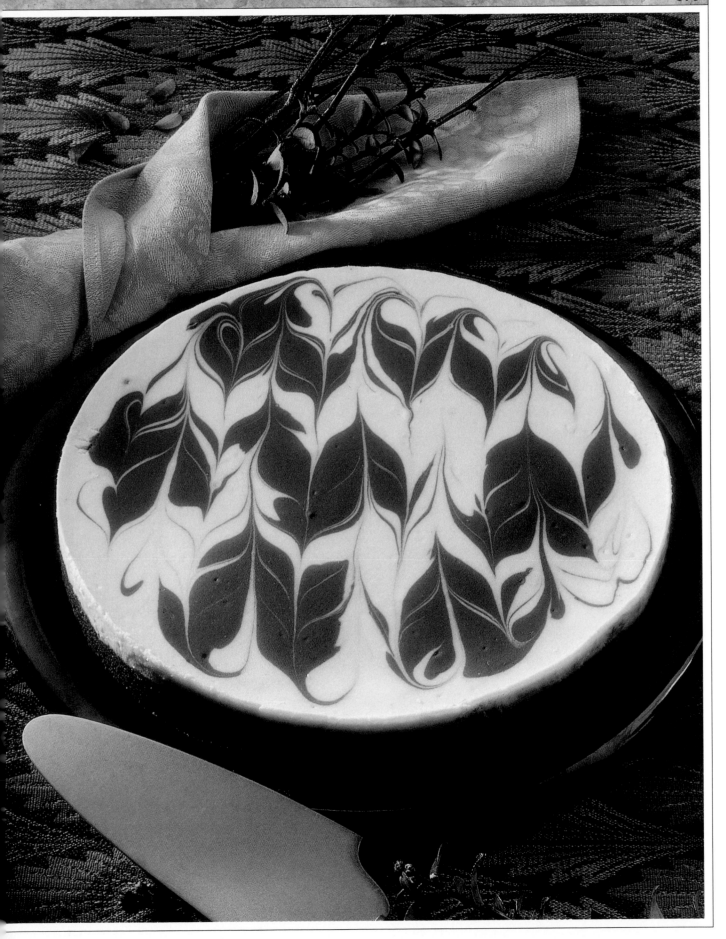

Mocha Marble Pound Cake

2 cups all-purpose flour
2 teaspoons baking powder
1 teaspoon baking soda
½ teaspoon salt
1 cup sugar
¼ cup FLEISCHMANN'S® Margarine, softened
1 teaspoon vanilla extract
½ cup EGG BEATERS® Healthy Real Egg Product
1 container (8 ounces) low-fat coffee yogurt
¼ cup unsweetened cocoa
    Mocha Yogurt Glaze (recipe follows)

In small bowl, combine flour, baking powder, baking soda and salt; set aside.

In large bowl, with electric mixer at medium speed, beat sugar, margarine and vanilla until creamy. Add Egg Beaters; beat until smooth. With mixer at low speed, add yogurt alternately with flour mixture, beating well after each addition. Remove half of batter to medium bowl. Add cocoa to batter remaining in large bowl; beat until blended. Alternately spoon coffee and chocolate batters into greased 9×5×3-inch loaf pan. With knife, cut through batters to create marbled effect.

Bake at 325°F for 60 to 65 minutes or until toothpick inserted in center comes out clean. Cool in pan on wire rack for 10 minutes. Remove from pan; cool completely on wire rack. Frost with Mocha Yogurt Glaze.   *Makes 16 servings*

MOCHA YOGURT GLAZE: In small bowl, combine ½ cup powdered sugar, 1 tablespoon unsweetened cocoa and 1 tablespoon low-fat coffee yogurt until smooth; add more yogurt if necessary to make spreading consistency.

Nutrients per Serving:

Calories	159	Cholesterol	1 mg
Fat	3 g	Sodium	215 mg

Caramel-Layered Brownies

4 squares BAKER'S® Unsweetened Chocolate
¾ cup (1½ sticks) margarine or butter
2 cups sugar
3 eggs
1 teaspoon vanilla
1 cup all-purpose flour
1 cup BAKER'S® Semi-Sweet Real Chocolate Chips
1½ cups coarsely chopped nuts
1 bag (14 ounces) caramels
⅓ cup evaporated milk

HEAT oven to 350°F.

MICROWAVE chocolate and margarine in large microwavable bowl on HIGH 2 minutes or until margarine is melted.* Stir until chocolate is completely melted.

STIR in sugar. Mix in eggs and vanilla. Stir in flour. Remove 1 cup batter; set aside. Spread remaining batter into greased 13×9-inch pan. Sprinkle with chocolate chips and 1 cup of the nuts.

MICROWAVE caramels and milk in same bowl on HIGH 4 minutes, stirring after 2 minutes. Stir until caramels are completely melted. Spoon over chips and nuts, spreading to edges of pan. Gently spread reserved batter over caramel mixture. Sprinkle with the remaining ½ cup nuts. BAKE 40 minutes or until toothpick inserted into center comes out with fudgy crumbs. Do not overbake. Cool in pan; cut into squares.   *Makes 24 brownies*

*__*Top of Stove Preparation:__* Melt chocolate and butter in heavy saucepan over very low heat, stirring constantly, until just melted. Continue as above.

Pumpkin Pecan Pie

3 eggs, divided
1 cup canned solid pack pumpkin
1 cup sugar, divided
$\frac{1}{2}$ teaspoon cinnamon
$\frac{1}{4}$ teaspoon ground ginger
$\frac{1}{8}$ teaspoon ground cloves
1 frozen deep dish pie crust* (9 inches)
$\frac{2}{3}$ cup KARO® Light or Dark Corn Syrup
2 tablespoons MAZOLA® margarine or butter, melted
1 teaspoon vanilla
1 cup coarsely chopped pecans or walnuts

*Do not thaw crust.

Place cookie sheet in oven; preheat oven to 350°F. In small bowl, combine 1 egg, pumpkin, $\frac{1}{3}$ cup sugar, cinnamon, ginger and cloves. Spread evenly in bottom of frozen pie crust. In medium bowl, slightly beat remaining 2 eggs. Stir in corn syrup, remaining $\frac{2}{3}$ cup sugar, margarine and vanilla until blended. Stir in pecans; carefully spoon over pumpkin mixture.

Bake on cookie sheet 50 to 60 minutes or until filling is set around edge. Cool completely on wire rack.

Makes 8 servings

→ COOK'S TIP ←

To easily dice dried fruit, first spray your knife or kitchen scissors with nonstick cooking spray to prevent the fruit from sticking to the blade.

Apricot-Pecan Tassies

BASE
1 cup all-purpose flour
$\frac{1}{2}$ cup butter, cut into pieces
6 tablespoons reduced-calorie cream cheese

FILLING
$\frac{3}{4}$ cup firmly packed light brown sugar
1 egg, lightly beaten
1 tablespoon butter, softened
$\frac{1}{2}$ teaspoon vanilla
$\frac{1}{4}$ teaspoon salt
$\frac{2}{3}$ cup (about 4 ounces) California dried apricot halves, diced
$\frac{1}{3}$ cup chopped pecans

For base, in food processor, combine flour, $\frac{1}{2}$ cup butter and cream cheese; process until mixture forms large ball. Wrap dough in plastic wrap and chill 15 minutes.

For filling, combine brown sugar, egg, 1 tablespoon butter, vanilla and salt in bowl until smooth. Stir in apricots and nuts.

Preheat oven to 325°F. Shape dough into 2 dozen 1-inch balls and place in paper-lined or greased miniature muffin cups. Press dough on bottom and up side of each cup; fill each with 1 teaspoon apricot-pecan filling. Bake 25 minutes or until golden and filling sets. Cool and remove from cups. Cookies can be wrapped tightly in plastic and frozen up to six weeks.

Makes 2 dozen cookies

Favorite recipe from **California Apricot Advisory Board**

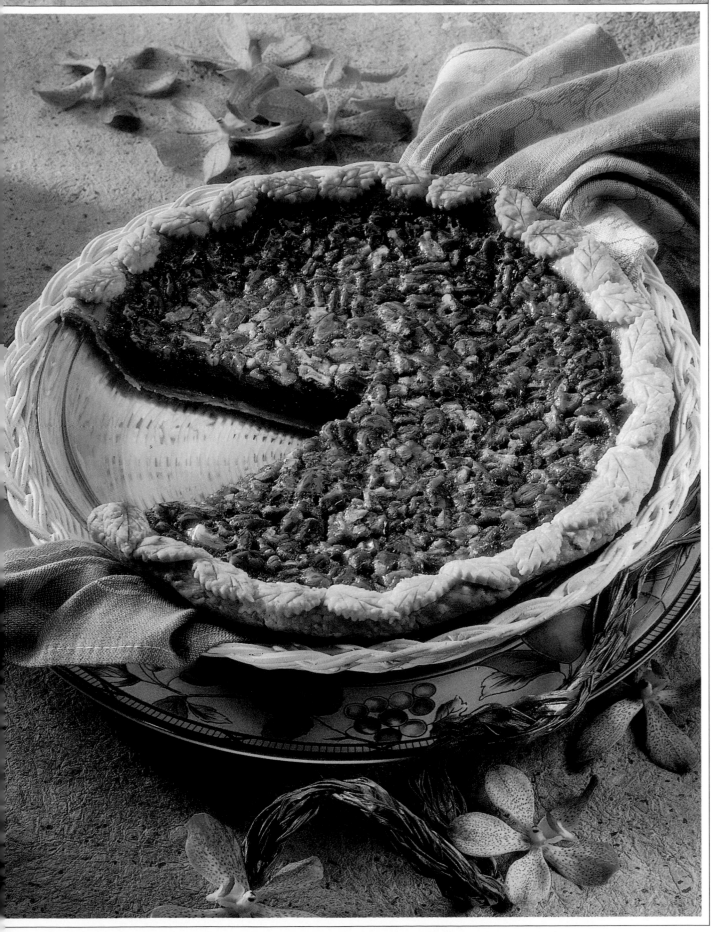

→ MENU SUGGESTION ←

All the neighborhood kids will haunt your Halloween party if the dessert table contains these out-of-this-world treats.

Turtle Caramel Apples
Apricot-Pecan Tassies (page 178)
Choco-Caramel Delights (page 183)

Amaretto Cheesecake Tart

CRUST
- ¾ **cup amaretti cookie crumbs**
- ¾ **cup zwieback crumbs**
- 1 **tablespoon sugar**
- ¼ **cup prune butter**

FILLING
- 1 **carton (16 ounces) nonfat cottage cheese**
- 4 **ounces fat-free cream cheese, softened**
- 2 **eggs**
- 2 **tablespoons almond-flavored liqueur**

TOPPING & GLAZE
- 2 **oranges, peeled and sliced into rounds**
- 1 **kiwifruit, peeled and sliced into rounds**
- 2 **tablespoons apple jelly, melted**
  Fresh raspberries, orange peel and mint leaves, for garnish

Preheat oven to 325°F. To prepare crust, in medium bowl, combine crumbs and sugar. Cut in prune butter with pastry blender until mixture resembles coarse crumbs. Press onto bottom and side of 9-inch tart pan with removable bottom. To prepare filling, process cottage cheese and cream cheese in food processor 3 to 5 minutes or until smooth. Add eggs and liqueur; process until blended. Pour into prepared crust. Bake in center of oven 30 minutes until filling is set. Cool on wire rack; refrigerate until completely chilled. Arrange oranges and kiwifruit on top of filling. Brush fruit with jelly. Garnish with raspberries, orange peel and mint. Cut into wedges. *Makes 10 servings*

Favorite recipe from **California Prune Board**

Turtle Caramel Apples

- 4 **large Golden Delicious apples**
- 2 **jars (3½ ounces each) macadamia nuts or pecans**
- 1 **package (14 ounces) caramels**
- 1 **bittersweet or semisweet chocolate candy bar (about 2 ounces), broken into small pieces**

EQUIPMENT:
  Craft sticks

Line 13×9-inch baking pan with waxed paper; set aside.

Wash and dry apples completely. Remove stems. Insert craft sticks into centers of apples.

Place nuts in food processor. Process using on/off pulsing action until coarsely chopped. Place nuts in medium bowl. Set aside.

Combine caramels and 2 tablespoons water in small saucepan. Simmer over low heat until caramels melt and mixture is smooth, stirring frequently with wooden spoon.

Immediately dip apples, one at a time, into caramel to cover completely. Scrape excess caramel from bottom of apple into saucepan.

Immediately roll apples in nuts to lightly coat, pressing nuts with fingers. Place apples, stick-side up, on prepared baking sheet. Let stand 20 minutes or until caramel is set.

Place chocolate in small resealable plastic freezer bag; seal bag. Microwave at MEDIUM (50% power) 1 minute. Turn bag over; microwave at MEDIUM 1 more minute or until melted. Knead bag until chocolate is smooth. Cut off very tiny corner of bag; pipe or drizzle chocolate decoratively onto apples. Let apples stand 30 minutes or until chocolate is set.

Store loosely covered in refrigerator up to 3 days. Let stand at room temperature 15 minutes before serving.
Makes 4 apples

Turtle Caramel Apples

Heavenly Cheesecake

½ **cup graham cracker crumbs**

4 **packages (8 ounces each) PHILADELPHIA BRAND® Neufchâtel Cheese, ⅓ Less Fat Than Cream Cheese or PHILADELPHIA BRAND® FREE® Fat Free Cream Cheese, softened**

1 **cup sugar**

¼ **teaspoon almond extract** *or* **1 teaspoon vanilla**

2 **eggs**

3 **egg whites**

• Heat oven to 325°F.

• Lightly grease bottom of 9-inch springform pan. Sprinkle with crumbs.

• Beat Neufchâtel cheese, sugar and extract at medium speed with electric mixer until well blended. Add eggs and egg whites, 1 at a time, mixing at low speed after each addition, just until blended. Pour into pan.

• Bake 45 to 50 minutes or until center is almost set. Run knife or metal spatula around rim of pan to loosen cake; cool before removing rim of pan. Refrigerate 4 hours or overnight.

• Garnish with raspberries, strawberries or blueberries and mint leaves. *Makes 12 servings*

Choco-Caramel Delights

Choco-Caramel Delights

⅔ cup sugar
½ cup butter or margarine, softened
1 egg, separated
2 tablespoons milk
1 teaspoon vanilla extract
1 cup all-purpose flour
⅓ cup HERSHEY'S Cocoa
¼ teaspoon salt
1 cup finely chopped pecans
  Caramel Filling (recipe follows)
½ cup HERSHEY'S Semi-Sweet Chocolate Chips
1 teaspoon shortening*

*Do not use butter, margarine or oil.

In small mixer bowl, beat sugar, butter, egg yolk, milk and vanilla until blended. Stir together flour, cocoa and salt; blend into butter mixture. Chill dough at least 1 hour or until firm enough to handle.

Preheat oven to 350°F. Lightly grease cookie sheets. Slightly beat egg white. Shape dough into 1-inch balls. Dip each ball into egg white; roll in pecans to coat. Place 1 inch apart on prepared cookie sheet. Press thumb gently in center of each ball.

Bake 10 to 12 minutes or until set. While cookies bake, prepare Caramel Filling. Press center of each cookie again with thumb to make indentation. Immediately spoon about ½ teaspoon Caramel Filling in center of each cookie. Carefully remove to wire racks to cool completely.

In small microwave-safe bowl combine chocolate chips and shortening. Microwave at HIGH 1 minute or until softened; stir. Allow to stand several minutes to finish melting; stir until smooth. Place waxed paper under wire racks with cookies. Drizzle chocolate mixture over top of cookies.

Makes about 2 dozen cookies

CARAMEL FILLING: In small saucepan, combine 14 unwrapped light caramels and 3 tablespoons whipping cream. Cook over low heat, stirring frequently, until caramels are melted and mixture is smooth.

Almond Rice Madeleines

  Vegetable oil cooking spray
1 cup whole blanched almonds, lightly toasted
1½ cups sugar
¾ cup flaked coconut
3 cups cooked rice, chilled
3 egg whites
  Fresh raspberries (optional)
  Frozen nondairy whipped topping, thawed (optional)
  Powdered sugar (optional)

Preheat oven to 350°F. Coat madeleine pans* with vegetable oil cooking spray. Place almonds in food processor fitted with knife blade; process until finely ground. Add sugar and coconut to processor; process until coconut is finely minced. Add rice; pulse to blend. Add egg whites; pulse to blend. Spoon mixture evenly into madeleine pans, filling to tops.

Bake 25 to 30 minutes or until lightly browned. Cool completely in pans on wire rack. Cover and refrigerate 2 hours or until serving time. Run a sharp knife around each madeleine shell and gently remove from pan. Invert onto serving plates; serve with raspberries and whipped topping, if desired. Sprinkle with powdered sugar, if desired.

Makes about 3 dozen madeleines

*You may substitute miniature muffin pans for madeleine pans, if desired.

Favorite recipe from **USA Rice Council**

Mini Morsel Pound Cake

3 cups all-purpose flour
1 teaspoon baking powder
½ teaspoon salt
2 cups granulated sugar
1 cup (2 sticks) butter or margarine, softened
1 tablespoon vanilla extract
4 eggs
¾ cup milk
2 cups (12-ounce package) NESTLÉ® TOLL
    HOUSE® Semi-Sweet Chocolate Mini Morsels
Powdered sugar

COMBINE flour, baking powder and salt in small bowl. Beat sugar, butter and vanilla in large mixer bowl until blended. Beat in eggs one at a time, beating well after each addition. Gradually beat in flour mixture alternately with milk. Stir in morsels. Pour into greased and floured 10-inch bundt pan or two greased and floured 9×5-inch loaf pans.

BAKE in preheated 325°F oven for 1 hour 5 minutes to 1 hour 15 minutes or until wooden pick inserted in cake comes out clean. Cool in pan on wire rack for 15 minutes. Remove from pan; serve warm or cool completely on wire rack. Sprinkle with powdered sugar before serving.   *Makes 16 servings*

COOK'S TIP

There are so many types of apples available that it can be confusing to choose the right one for a particular recipe. For baking, reliable choices include Golden Delicious, Granny Smith, Jonathan and Winesap apples.

Baked Apple Crisp

LOW FAT

8 cups unpeeled, thinly sliced apples (about 8 medium)
2 tablespoons granulated sugar
4½ teaspoons lemon juice
4 teaspoons ground cinnamon, divided
1½ cups MOTT'S® Natural Apple Sauce
1 cup uncooked rolled oats
½ cup firmly packed light brown sugar
⅓ cup all-purpose flour
⅓ cup evaporated skim milk
¼ cup nonfat dry milk powder
1 cup vanilla nonfat yogurt

1. Preheat oven to 350°F. Spray 2-quart casserole dish with nonstick cooking spray.

2. In large bowl, toss apple slices with granulated sugar, lemon juice and 2 teaspoons cinnamon. Spoon into prepared dish. Spread applesauce evenly over apple mixture.

3. In medium bowl, combine oats, brown sugar, flour, evaporated milk, dry milk powder and remaining 2 teaspoons cinnamon. Spread over apple sauce.

4. Bake 35 to 40 minutes or until lightly browned and bubbly. Cool slightly; serve warm. Top each serving with dollop of yogurt.   *Makes 12 servings*

Nutrients per Serving:

Calories	185	Cholesterol	0 mg
Fat	2 g	Sodium	35 mg

Baked Apple Crisp

✦ Acknowledgments ✦

Alpine Lace Brands, Inc.

American Lamb Council

American Spice Trade Association

Best Foods, a Division of CPC International Inc.

Birds Eye

Bob Evans Farms®

California Apricot Advisory Board

California Poultry Industry Federation

California Prune Board

California Table Grape Commission

California Tomato Board

Canned Food Information Council

Cucina Classica Italiana, Inc.

Delmarva Poultry Industry, Inc.

Del Monte Corporation

Filippo Berio Olive Oil

The Fremont Company, Makers of Frank's & SnowFloss Kraut and Tomato Products

Golden Grain/Mission Pasta

Hershey Foods Corporation

Hormel Foods Corporation

The HVR Company

Kahlúa® Liqueur

Kikkoman International Inc.

Kraft Foods, Inc.

Lawry's® Foods, Inc.

Leaf®, Inc.

MOTT'S® Inc., a division of Cadbury Beverages Inc.

Nabisco, Inc.

National Broiler Council

National Cattlemen's Beef Association

National Fisheries Institute

National Honey Board

National Onion Association

National Pasta Association

National Pork Producers Council

National Turkey Federation

Nestlé Food Company

New Jersey Department of Agriculture

Newman's Own, Inc.

Norseland, Inc.

North Dakota Barley Council

North Dakota Beef Commission

The Procter & Gamble Company

The Quaker® Oatmeal Kitchen

Reckitt & Colman Inc.

RED STAR® Yeast & Products, A Division of Universal Foods Corporation

Riviana Foods Inc.

Sargento Foods Inc.®

The J.M. Smucker Company

Sokol & Company

StarKist Seafood Company

Surimi Seafood Education Center

USA Dry Pea & Lentil Council

USA Rice Council

Walnut Marketing Board

Washington Apple Commission

Wisconsin Milk Marketing Board

✦ INDEX ✦

A

Albacore and White Bean Salad with
  Orange Dressing, 106
Albacore Stir-Fry, 122
Almond Glaze, 42
Almond Rice Madeleines, 183
Amaretto Cheesecake Tart, 180
America's Favorite Cheddar Beef
  Burgers, 116
Amigo Pita Pocket Sandwiches, 136
Anadama Bread, 38
Angel Hair Carbonara, 25
Appetizers
  Baked Brie, 146
  Barley Mounds in Avocado Pears, 10
  Chicken Kabobs with Thai Dipping
    Sauce, 104
  Crudités with Creamy Cheese Dip, 62
  Fresh Tomato Pasta Andrew, 107
  Mini Vegetable Quiches, 60
  Party Cheese Wreath, 13
  Potato Skins with Cheddar Melt, 148
  Quesadillas, 58
Apple Cheddar Muffins, 159
Apricot Carrot Bread, 24
Apricot-Pecan Tassies, 178
Asparagus Wreath, 18
Aztec Chili Salad, 166

B

Bacon & Potato Frittata, 72
Baked Apple Crisp, 184
Baked Brie, 146
Baked Vegetables en Croûte, 164
Banana Caramel Shortcake, 99
Barbecued Leg of Lamb with Cucumber
  Yogurt Dip, 78
Barbecued Pork Loin, 120
Barley Mounds in Avocado Pears, 10
Basil Jicama Fruit Salad, 108
Beans & Legumes
  Albacore and White Bean Salad with
    Orange Dressing, 106
  Aztec Chili Salad, 166
  Border Black Bean Chicken Salad, 89
  California Turkey Chili, 170

Beans & Legumes *(continued)*
  Cheese and Bean Quesadillas, 166
  Chili Soup Jarlsberg, 146
  Chunky Chicken Chili, 16
  Falafel, 123
  Green Beans and Tomatoes
    Provençal, 125
  Quick Skillet Rice Gratin, 87
  Scrumptious SPAM™ Spring Chili, 86
  Simple Supper Sauté, 16
  Speedy Beef & Bean Burritos, 36
  Spiced Orange Chicken with
    Lentils, 69
  Vegetable Chili, 159
  Vegetarian White Bean Chili with
    Waffles, 70
Beef
  America's Favorite Cheddar Beef
    Burgers, 116
  Aztec Chili Salad, 166
  Beef & Vegetable Fried Rice, 70
  Beef 'n' Broccoli, 19
  Chili Soup Jarlsberg, 146
  Countdown Casserole, 14
  Grilled Beef with Two Sauces, 136
  Honey Mustard Steaks with Grilled
    Onion, 78
  Hot and Spicy Onion Beef, 22
  Meat and Potato Stir-Fry, 170
  Mexican Beef Stir-Fry, 152
  Peppered Beef Rib Roast, 75
  Quick Tamale Casserole, 173
  Salisbury Steaks with Mushroom-
    Wine Sauce, 134
  Savory Grilled Tournedos, 132
  Southern Barbecue Sandwiches, 84
  Speedy Beef & Bean Burritos, 36
  Thai Beef Salad, 69
Beijing Chicken, 138
BEL PAESE® and Vegetable Casserole,
  21
Black Forest Chocolate Fudge Cake, 54
Blonde Brickle Brownies, 96
Border Black Bean Chicken Salad, 89
Braised Chicken with Artichokes, 66
Breads
  Anadama Bread, 38
  Apple Cheddar Muffins, 159
  Apricot Carrot Bread, 24
  Cheese & Chili Pepper Bread, 21

Breads *(continued)*
  Cherry, Almond & Chocolate
    Breakfast Wreath, 42
  Golden Apple Buttermilk Bread, 151
  Good-for-You Zucchini Bread, 77
  Honey of a Whole Wheat Bread, 6
  Honey Sweet Potato Biscuits, 26
  Low Fat Pumpkin Bread, 28
  Oatmeal Apple Cranberry
    Scones, 168
  Pumpkin Harvest Bread, 164
Broccoli & Cheddar Noodle
  Casserole, 31

C

Cakes
  Banana Caramel Shortcake, 99
  Black Forest Chocolate Fudge
    Cake, 54
  Cappuccino Cake, 94
  Chocolate and Raspberry Cream
    Torte, 47
  Chocolate Chip Cheesecake, 97
  Eggnog Cheesecake, 47
  Heavenly Cheesecake, 182
  Marble Cheesecake, 174
  Mini Morsel Pound Cake, 184
  Mocha Marble Pound Cake, 176
  Peppermint Stick Cheesecake, 51
California Apricot Fruit Salad, 60
California Turkey Chili, 170
California Walnut Noodles, 34
Candy Cane & Wreath Ornaments, 50
Cappuccino Cake, 94
Caramel-Layered Brownies, 176
Carrot-Artichoke Sauté, 138
Casseroles
  BEL PAESE® and Vegetable Casserole,
    21
  Broccoli & Cheddar Noodle
    Casserole, 31
  Countdown Casserole, 14
  Italian Sausage Supper, 16
  Mustard Chicken & Vegetables, 24
  Quick Tamale Casserole, 173
Cheese and Bean Quesadillas, 166
Cheese & Chili Pepper Bread, 21

METRIC CONVERSION CHART

VOLUME MEASUREMENTS (dry)

$1/8$ teaspoon = 0.5 mL
$1/4$ teaspoon = 1 mL
$1/2$ teaspoon = 2 mL
$3/4$ teaspoon = 4 mL
1 teaspoon = 5 mL
1 tablespoon = 15 mL
2 tablespoons = 30 mL
$1/4$ cup = 60 mL
$1/3$ cup = 75 mL
$1/2$ cup = 125 mL
$2/3$ cup = 150 mL
$3/4$ cup = 175 mL
1 cup = 250 mL
2 cups = 1 pint = 500 mL
3 cups = 750 mL
4 cups = 1 quart = 1 L

VOLUME MEASUREMENTS (fluid)

1 fluid ounce (2 tablespoons) = 30 mL
4 fluid ounces ($1/2$ cup) = 125 mL
8 fluid ounces (1 cup) = 250 mL
12 fluid ounces ($1 1/2$ cups) = 375 mL
16 fluid ounces (2 cups) = 500 mL

WEIGHTS (mass)

$1/2$ ounce = 15 g
1 ounce = 30 g
3 ounces = 90 g
4 ounces = 120 g
8 ounces = 225 g
10 ounces = 285 g
12 ounces = 360 g
16 ounces = 1 pound = 450 g

DIMENSIONS

$1/16$ inch = 2 mm
$1/8$ inch = 3 mm
$1/4$ inch = 6 mm
$1/2$ inch = 1.5 cm
$3/4$ inch = 2 cm
1 inch = 2.5 cm

OVEN TEMPERATURES

250°F = 120°C
275°F = 140°C
300°F = 150°C
325°F = 160°C
350°F = 180°C
375°F = 190°C
400°F = 200°C
425°F = 220°C
450°F = 230°C

BAKING PAN SIZES

Utensil	Size in Inches/Quarts	Metric Volume	Size in Centimeters
Baking or Cake Pan (square or rectangular)	$8 \times 8 \times 2$	2 L	$20 \times 20 \times 5$
	$9 \times 9 \times 2$	2.5 L	$22 \times 22 \times 5$
	$12 \times 8 \times 2$	3 L	$30 \times 20 \times 5$
	$13 \times 9 \times 2$	3.5 L	$33 \times 23 \times 5$
Loaf Pan	$8 \times 4 \times 3$	1.5 L	$20 \times 10 \times 7$
	$9 \times 5 \times 3$	2 L	$23 \times 13 \times 7$
Round Layer Cake Pan	$8 \times 1 1/2$	1.2 L	20×4
	$9 \times 1 1/2$	1.5 L	23×4
Pie Plate	$8 \times 1 1/4$	750 mL	20×3
	$9 \times 1 1/4$	1 L	23×3
Baking Dish or Casserole	1 quart	1 L	—
	$1 1/2$ quart	1.5 L	—
	2 quart	2 L	—

Woodpeckers of North America

Woodpeckers of North America

FRANCES BACKHOUSE

FIREFLY BOOKS

A FIREFLY BOOK

Published by Firefly Books Ltd. 2005

First printing

Publisher Cataloging-in-Publication Data (U.S.)

Backhouse, Frances.
    Woodpeckers of North America / Frances Backhouse.
[224] p. : col. photos. ;   cm.
Includes bibliographical references and index.
Summary: An examination of the biology and environment of all 28 species of the
North American woodpecker.
ISBN 1-55407-046-5
1. Woodpeckers – North America. I. Title.
598/.72 dc22   QL696.P56B335   2005

Library and Archives Canada Cataloguing in Publication

Backhouse, Frances
        Woodpeckers of North America / Frances Backhouse. – 1st ed.
Includes bibliographical references and index.
ISBN 1-55407-046-5
        1. Woodpeckers–North America. I. Title.
QL696.P56B32 2005   598.7'2'097   C2005-901192-0

Published in the United States by
Firefly Books (U.S.) Inc.
P.O. Box 1338, Ellicott Station
Buffalo, New York 14205

Published in Canada by
Firefly Books Ltd.
66 Leek Crescent
Richmond Hill, Ontario L4B 1H1

Cover and interior design by Sara Battersby and Sari Naworynski
Illustrations: Imagineering Media Services Inc.
Maps reprinted with permission from the Cornell Lab of Ornithology's *Birds of North
America Online*, www.birds.cornell.edu/bna

Printed in China

*The publisher gratefully acknowledges the financial support for our publishing program by
the Canada Council for the Arts, the Ontario Arts Council and the Government of Canada
through the Book Publishing Industry Development Program.*

Table of Contents

Introduction

Nature's Map

Most field guides to the birds of North America limit their geographic reach to Canada and the United States. Although convenient, this practice warrants reconsideration. After all, political borders mean nothing to our winged neighbors. As far as the gila woodpecker is concerned, the saguaro desert of Arizona is little different from the saguaro desert of Sonora, Mexico. The same goes for other species with international citizenship. From an ecosystem perspective, the continent is bigger than just two countries.

Having decided that this book should reflect ecological reality, I was faced with the dilemma of where to draw the line. Through the Isthmus of Panama, following the lead of the American Ornithologists' Union? Along Mexico's southern border, in keeping with various governmental alliances and trade agreements? Somewhere across the middle of Mexico? After much deliberation I concluded that, when it comes to woodpeckers, the latter approach makes the most sense.

During the 19th century, zoogeographers developed the concept of partitioning the terrestrial portions of the planet into faunal regions – vast areas characterized by their distinctive animal life. This system is still widely used today, in a modified form that recognizes eight biogeographical realms instead of the original six faunal regions. In simple terms, Canada, the continental United States and northern Mexico are assigned to the Nearctic realm (along with Greenland and Bermuda), while southern Mexico joins Central and South America and the Caribbean islands in the Neotropical realm. Although debate continues as to the exact boundary between the two realms, the least complicated interpretation uses the tropic of Cancer (the latitudinal line 23°27° north of the equator) as the reference line. I have done the same.

There will be those who quibble with this demarcation, saying it inappropriately includes species that are primarily thought of as Central or South American residents, such as the golden-olive or pale-billed woodpecker. Others will question why the line was not drawn farther south to encompass the ranges of species that share some affinities with northern relatives, one obvious example being Strickland's woodpecker, a Mexican endemic that was only recently designated as distinct from the Arizona woodpecker. The truth is, there is no one incontestable definition of North America. What really matters is that we move beyond an outdated allegiance to political boundaries and try to see the map as nature would draw it.

Golden pollen dusts the face of a foraging gila woodpecker as he probes deep into a saguaro cactus flower.

Chapter 1

What Is a Woodpecker?

Woodpeckers are among the most ancient of all birds. A 25-million-year-old fossil leg bone from Germany, a feather trapped in Caribbean amber that dates back at least 24 million years, and cavities in 40- to 50-million-year-old petrified wood from Arizona and Wyoming offer tantalizing clues as to when woodpeckers first diverged from their less specialized ancestors. The question of where this happened remains shrouded in mystery. The Americas, Asia and Africa have each been proposed by different experts as the home of the earliest woodpeckers.

Today, members of the Picidae or woodpecker family (often referred to as picids) are found on every continent except Australia and Antarctica and inhabit many of the world's major islands, the most notable omissions being New Zealand, New Guinea, the Oceania island chain in the South Pacific, Hawaii, Madagascar, Greenland and Iceland. This large family is divided into three subfamilies: the Jynginae or wrynecks, represented by two species; the Picumninae or piculets, with 31 species; and the Picinae, also known as the true woodpeckers, with 183 species. No wrynecks or piculets reside in North America.

All of the true woodpeckers are hole-nesters with the ability to excavate their own cavities, generally in trees or tree substitutes such as columnar cacti or telephone poles. As a result, to a greater or lesser extent the Picinae subfamily has a number of distinctive morphological (structural) features: a long, stiff tail for bracing against tree trunks; short legs and long toes to assist in climbing vertical surfaces; a head built to withstand repeated hammering against hard surfaces; a long, straight bill designed for chopping into wood, removing bark or probing into crevices; a long, extensible tongue with a barbed end, able to reach deep into narrow openings and extract hidden prey; and nostrils covered with feathers to keep them free of wood debris. These attributes (described in more detail in Chapter 2) are displayed most completely by the most highly specialized tree excavators.

The first part of a species' scientific name indicates the genus (plural: genera) to which it belongs. The second part completes its unique species identification. Worldwide there are 24 genera within the Picinae subfamily. The true woodpeckers are represented by seven genera in North America – *Picoides, Melanerpes, Sphyrapicus, Colaptes, Piculus, Dryocopus* and *Campephilus* – which together include 28 species. Because members of the same genus are more closely related to each other than to other woodpeckers, they typically share

A red head patch clearly marks this downy woodpecker as a male.

certain physical characteristics, including body size and plumage patterns, as well as behavioral traits such as feeding habits.

Woodpeckers that belong to the same genus often wear similar "sexual badges," the red (or in a few cases, yellow) head markings that differentiate adult males and females of most species. Only three North American woodpecker species – the red-headed woodpecker, Lewis's woodpecker and the red-breasted sapsucker – are sexually monochromatic, meaning that males and females cannot be distinguished by their plumage colors and patterns. All other North American woodpeckers are dichromatic, meaning that adult males and females have different plumage. Males of these latter species invariably display more conspicuous sexual badges than their female counterparts. The females may have no equivalent markings or their badges may be a smaller or less prominent version of the male's. Sexual size differences are not pronounced in most woodpecker species.

The genus *Picoides* is the largest in North America, with nine species: the American three-toed, Arizona, black-backed, downy, hairy, ladder-backed, Nuttall's, red-cockaded and white-headed woodpeckers. Sometimes collectively referred to as pied woodpeckers because of their mixed black-and-white plumage (brown-and-white in the case of the Arizona woodpecker), these are small to medium-sized woodpeckers. Their sexual badges are red – except for those of the American three-toed and black-backed woodpeckers, whose males sport yellow caps – and are worn on the forehead, crown or nape. In this genus the males tend to be slightly heavier than females and have proportionally longer bills and shorter tails, though these differences are not generally obvious in the field. The *Picoides* woodpeckers have straight, chisel-tipped bills and are largely insectivorous.

The six North American members of the genus *Melanerpes* are the acorn, gila, golden-fronted, Lewis's, red-bellied and red-headed woodpeckers. (The range of western Mexico's golden-cheeked woodpecker extends north of the tropic of Cancer by such a narrow margin that it has not been included here.) Within this genus there is much variation in appearance from one species to the next, but most are visually striking. The red-headed and Lewis's woodpeckers are sexually monochromatic, while males and females of the other *Melanerpes* woodpeckers are differentiated by the amount of red on their heads. In some of these species the males are notably heavier and longer-billed than females, while in others the difference is less pronounced. Fruits, nuts and seeds figure prominently in the dietary regime of all members of this genus, either seasonally or year-round. These woodpeckers often attract attention with their raucous voices.

Closely related to the *Melanerpes* woodpeckers are the four species of the genus *Sphyrapicus*. Commonly known as the red-breasted, red-naped, Williamson's and yellow-bellied sapsuckers, these birds are named for their practice of tapping live trees for sap. Dependence on this seasonal food source makes the sapsuckers the most migratory of all North American woodpeckers.

Lewis's woodpecker is one of the few North American species with no markings that separate males from females.

The plumage of all four species features white wing patches and a white rump, as well as some yellow on the belly. Williamson's sapsucker has the distinction of being the most sexually dichromatic woodpecker in the world: adult males and females are barely recognizable as members of the same species. Red-breasted sapsuckers are sexually monochromatic and the other two sapsuckers display only subtle differences between the sexes, with males generally having more red on their throats. There are no appreciable sexual differences in weight or body measurements in any of these species.

The genus *Colaptes* has only two North American representatives, the gilded flicker and the northern flicker, which at times have been regarded as a single species. The flickers are the least arboreal of all North American woodpeckers, foraging primarily on the ground. Their terrestrial habits are reflected in several characteristics: mostly camouflage-brown plumage; less rigid tail feathers and less specialized skull structure compared to more arboreal woodpeckers; large feet with well-developed claws; and a long, curved, pointed bill that is ideally suited for digging into ant nests but less efficient for hewing wood. Although they spend much of their time on the ground, gilded and northern flickers nest in trees or cacti. Two other members of the genus *Colaptes* – the Andean and campo flickers of South America – have entirely abandoned the arboreal lifestyle, excavating their nest cavities in the earth, as has the appropriately named ground woodpecker of South Africa. The sexual badges of the gilded and northern flickers are the male's red or black malar stripes, popularly known as mustache stripes. Sexual size differences are minimal, but males are generally slightly larger than females.

The *Colaptes* flickers, especially those that live in Central and South America, are closely related to members of the largely Neotropical genus *Piculus*. Only two *Piculus* species have ranges that reach as far north as northern Mexico: the gray-crowned woodpecker, along the country's western flank, and the golden-olive woodpecker, on the eastern side. These woodpeckers have sharply pointed, slightly curved bills. Although they are mainly arboreal in their habits, they have well-developed claws like those of more terrestrial species and their tails are only moderately adapted for bracing. The body plumage of the gray-crowned and golden-olive woodpeckers is predominantly green, and males are distinguished by their red mustache stripes. Members of this genus tend to be less animated than many other woodpeckers and are easily overlooked by observers, which contributes to the scarcity of recorded information about their behavior and ecology.

The genus *Dryocopus* includes two species found in North America. The pileated woodpecker resides only in the United States and Canada. The lineated woodpecker is a primarily Neotropical species whose range extends into parts of northern Mexico. Wood-dwelling ants dominate the diet of these powerful excavators, which have long, straight bills with a chisel-shaped tip, and long, sturdy tail feathers. Their large size and brilliant red head crests separate these two black-and-white-bodied woodpeckers from all the other North

American species except the members of the next genus. Males have red mustache stripes, as well as more red on the crown than females; they are also heavier and longer-billed than the females.

The genus *Campephilus* comprises a group of large, spectacularly crested woodpeckers with predominantly black backs. The males generally have more extensive areas of red on the head and are heavier, longer-billed and shorter-tailed than the females. Long, straight, chisel-tipped bills and long, stiff tails contribute to their impressive bark-stripping and wood-excavating capabilities, used for gaining access to the hefty beetle larvae that are their primary prey. When climbing or gripping tree trunks, these woodpeckers turn all four of the long toes on each foot forward to help support the heavy weight of their bodies. Historically, North America was home to three *Campephilus* species, including the pale-billed woodpecker, whose range extends from northern Mexico to Panama. One of the three – the imperial woodpecker – is now almost certainly extinct, and until recently the ivory-billed woodpecker was generally believed to have met the same fate. In April 2005 the unexpected rediscovery of this species in eastern Arkansas was announced with great fanfare. The fact that at least one male survived into the 21st century offers new hope for the ivory-billed woodpecker, but the species' existence remains tenuous at best.

Besides having the dubious distinction of being the first, and so far only, member of the Picidae family to have been driven to extinction, the imperial woodpecker was also the largest of its kind worldwide. Some imperial woodpeckers reportedly weighed more than 1.5 pounds (about 700 g) – a hundred times heavier than the smallest piculet. The ivory-billed woodpecker held the number three position globally, weighing in at about 1 pound (450 g), just behind the 1.2-pound (563 g) great slaty woodpecker of southeast Asia. The other woodpeckers in the worldwide top seven are Eurasia's black woodpecker (10.1–13.3 ounces / 285–378 g); the magellanic woodpecker of southern South America (9.7–12.8 ounces / 276–363 g); the white-bellied woodpecker, a species that varies widely in size in different parts of its eastern and southern Asian range (5.5–12.2 ounces / 156–347 g); and the pileated woodpecker (8.5–12 ounces / 240–341 g).

Since most bird enthusiasts will never have an opportunity to feel the weight of a woodpecker in their hands, it is perhaps more meaningful to compare the size of different species in terms of length, which is conventionally measured from the tip of the bill to the end of the tail. At about 22 to 24 inches (56–61 cm) long, imperial woodpeckers were comparable in size to common ravens. In contrast, North America's most diminutive woodpecker, the 6- to 6.7-inch-long (15–17 cm) downy, is roughly sparrow-sized.

Once you become familiar with their key identifying characteristics, woodpeckers are easy to tell apart from other birds. From a distance they can often

White wing patches flash into view as a male golden-fronted woodpecker takes flight.

be recognized by their distinctive undulating flying pattern, which is known as flap-bounding. This rising and falling flight path is caused by regular alteration between flapping phases, which carry the bird upward, and non-flapping, or bounding, phases in which the wings are pulled into the body and the momentum is downward. In contrast to continuous flapping, this mode of travel reduces the energy expended to get from one place to another.

Most small and medium-sized woodpeckers primarily use flap-bounding flight. Flap-bounding is also characteristic of the *Dryocopus* and *Campephilus* woodpeckers, but it is not uncommon for these large woodpeckers to fly with strong, uninterrupted wing beats, resulting in a more direct and level flight path. Lewis's woodpecker is an anomaly, rarely using flap-bounding flight. Instead these agile birds generally combine periods of continuous flapping with prolonged glides.

At closer range only a few North American species are likely to be confused with woodpeckers, and a few minutes of observation will usually provide enough clues to set the record straight. Kingfishers are sometimes mistaken for woodpeckers because of their prominent pointed bills and hole-nesting behavior. However, they excavate their nest cavities in earthen banks along shorelines, not in trees. Kingfishers also make frequent plunges into water to capture fish, a behavior that is completely foreign to woodpeckers.

Sharp-billed nuthatches can be distinguished from woodpeckers by their short, square-ended tails, which are not used to provide support. Nuthatches foraging on tree trunks typically travel headfirst down the trunk, a style of locomotion never undertaken by woodpeckers. But don't be surprised if you see certain woodpeckers, most notably the ladder-backed and Nuttall's, engaging in other nuthatch-like foraging behavior, such as hanging upside down from twigs. Nuthatches, along with chickadees, are the only North American birds other than woodpeckers that are capable of excavating nest cavities in trees, but both are weak excavators that can only dig into wood that has been thoroughly softened by decay. They often take advantage of natural cavities, such as those that develop in knotholes, or use old woodpecker cavities when they are available.

Brown creepers, with their stiff, pointed tail feathers and long, thin bills, are also candidates for mistaken identification. Like woodpeckers, these small birds ascend trees headfirst, but they can be distinguished by their strongly downcurved bills. Although brown creepers are occasional hole-nesters, they do not excavate their own cavities. Usually their hammock-style nests are hidden behind loose patches of bark.

Despite the superficial similarities between these other birds and woodpeckers, none of them are more than remotely related to the picids. Morphological studies, DNA analysis and other research have produced convincing evidence that the birds with the closest kinship to the Picidae are the honeyguides of Africa and Asia, which belong to the family Indicatoridae. Together with the Neotropical barbets (Capitonidae) and the toucans and aracaris (Ramphastidae), the Indicatoridae are believed to have descended from a common ancestor. Based on this evidence it is thought that the woodpecker lineage most likely branched off from the others 50 to 53 million years ago. Every one of the highly specialized and uniquely adapted woodpecker species we know today has many millennia of evolutionary history behind it.

Chapter 2

Anatomy

The Spanish word for woodpecker, *carpintero*, recognizes these birds as the master carpenters of the avian world. Although they do not saw planks or nail together two-by-fours, their aptitude for creating cozy, secure wooden havens in trees makes them worthy of this title. A handful of other bird species are capable of enlarging natural tree cavities or excavating holes in decay-softened wood. Some, including nuthatches and chickadees, use their bills to whittle and chip, while parrots and others bite and tear. But woodpeckers surpass them all with their ability to hew sound wood and tunnel deep inside tree trunks. Aside from the three fully terrestrial woodpecker species (none of which live in North America), even the weakest excavators among the *carpinteros* have the basic tools for constructing elegantly designed arboreal dwellings that are coveted by their more poorly equipped neighbors. Most woodpecker species also use their excavating abilities to obtain at least some of their food.

Head

A woodpecker that is highly specialized for excavating – such as the black-backed or pileated – has a straight, broad-based bill that is laterally compressed near the tip, giving it a chisel shape. The beveled cutting edges of this flattened tip self-sharpen as the continuously and rapidly growing horny sheath is worn away by the friction of beak against wood. Longitudinal ridges add extra strength. Woodpecker bills that are less specialized for excavating trees become more curved, narrower at the base and more pointed at the tip, like those of the flickers.

It's all very well to possess such a powerful tool, but how does its owner use it effectively without harming itself? One occupational hazard is exposure to the wood dust and chips that every strike of the bill sends flying straight into the excavator's face. Woodpeckers' nostrils are protected by special tufts of feathers, but for clear vision the eyes must remain exposed. Lacking safety glasses, a woodpecker copes in the only way it can – by tightly closing its eyes as its head lunges forward and not opening them again until after the impact.

More sophisticated measures are needed to insure against brain damage, whiplash and other injuries commonly linked with head-on collisions. When a woodpecker delivers a typical hard blow to a tree trunk, its bill strikes at a speed of 20 to 23 feet (6–7 m) per second. For pileated woodpeckers, the resulting

Wood chips fly as a red-headed woodpecker excavates a new nest cavity.

deceleration impact force has been measured at 600 to 1,500 Gs. (By comparison, the deceleration impact in a survivable car crash rarely exceeds 100 Gs.) The strikes are rapid – yellow-bellied sapsuckers excavating nest cavities have been clocked at 100 to 300 strikes per minute – and many hours of every day may be spent drilling for food or constructing cavities. All of which raises the question of how these birds avoid concussion or, at the very least, severe headaches. This enigma has made it into the esteemed pages of the medical journal *The Lancet*, where four physicians wrote in 1976 that "those who have seen the effects of even a limited degree of head-banging in patients . . . will wonder why the countryside is not littered with dazed and dying woodpeckers." The doctors concluded that understanding the woodpecker's brain protection mechanisms "could be of basic importance for [human] head injury and its prevention" through the improved design of crash helmets and military headgear.

Upper mandible

Cross-section of a northern flicker skull. The frontal bones slope gradually instead of bulging out over the base of the bill.

Frontal bones

Upper mandible

Cross-section of a blackbacked woodpecker skull. Bony struts provide reinforcement in the space formed by the bulging of the frontal bones and at the base of the bill.

By human standards, woodpeckers have small brains relative to their body size. The lower mass-to-surface ratio of the woodpecker's brain means that the force of any cranial impact is distributed over a greater area, reducing the risk of injury by 50 to 100 times compared to that faced by humans in an equivalent situation. In this regard, woodpeckers are similar to most other birds. What sets them apart is a series of modifications to the basic avian model. One important adaptation is that the frontal bones of the skull project out over the base of the upper mandible (the upper half of the beak), creating a forehead profile that is more rounded than sloping. Like most birds, woodpeckers can move their upper mandible independent of the lower mandible or the braincase. This mobility produces a wide gape that is useful for capturing prey and manipulating food. However, it also means that the upper mandible could be forced upward when the bill strikes hard against a surface, an action that could have severe consequences. The skull's frontal bulge limits such unintended movement. The more excavating a species does, the more its frontal bones project; bony struts within this hollow pocket provide reinforcement.

Equally critical is the role of the protractor muscles that attach near the base of the upper mandible. In woodpeckers that engage in strenuous excavating, these muscles are considerably larger than in most other birds. They contract before and during the moment of impact, absorbing shock impulses and holding the bill steady.

A red-bellied woodpecker perches beside his newly constructed nest hole.

Frame-by-frame analysis of laboratory films of excavating woodpeckers has shown that a line drawn along the length of the bill is essentially perpendicular to the tree surface at the point of contact. Straight blows prevent shearing injuries to the brain that could be produced by rotating the head during impact. As well, the woodpecker head is shaped so that the force of the bill striking a surface is transmitted in a plane that runs below the braincase. This keeps direct shock waves from reaching the bird's vulnerable gray matter.

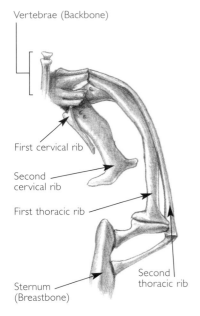

Vertebrae (Backbone)

First cervical rib

Second cervical rib

First thoracic rib

Sternum (Breastbone)

Second thoracic rib

Head-on view of the right side of a hairy woodpecker's rib cage showing the first four ribs. The second cervical and first thoracic ribs are wider than those of non-excavating birds like the wryneck. These modified ribs support the enlarged neck muscles required for excavating.

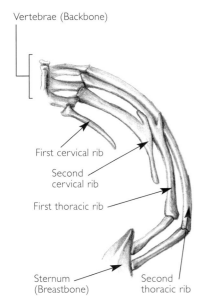

Vertebrae (Backbone)

First cervical rib

Second cervical rib

First thoracic rib

Sternum (Breastbone)

Second thoracic rib

Head-on view of the right side of a wryneck's rib cage showing the first four ribs. Although wrynecks are related to true woodpeckers, they lack anatomical adaptations for excavating, including modification of the ribs.

Several special features give woodpecker ears extra protection against mechanical shock. The columella is a rod-like bone in the middle ear that picks up sound vibrations from the eardrum and transmits them to the membranous window of the inner ear. In woodpeckers the columella is fortified by two basal plates instead of the single plate common to other birds. As well, the window in the woodpecker inner ear is less than half the size of this structure in other birds, and the membrane is thicker than usual at one end.

Another reinforcement for the woodpecker skull is a thickened interorbital septum – the bony wall between the two eye sockets. Some bird species have such large eyes that this wall is incomplete, with one or more openings in it. In woodpeckers the interorbital septum is well developed and is entire or has only small openings.

The black-backed and American three-toed woodpeckers can be considered the poster-birds for all these modifications of the head that prevent frequent and vigorous excavators from knocking themselves silly. They are among the North American picids with the most robust skulls and the greatest development of features to protect the brain and other vulnerable areas of the head. They also have the most specialized ribs, an adaptation that prevents excavating from becoming, quite literally, a pain in the neck.

Ribs

The woodpecker rib cage is formed by six pairs of thoracic ribs, which attach to the sternum (breastbone) in front and to the spinal column behind, plus two pairs of cervical ribs – shorter bones that are connected to neck vertebrae at the back and are unattached in front. (To picture this it may help to recall your Thanksgiving turkey after it has been picked clean.) Counting from head to tail, the second cervical and the first thoracic ribs of woodpeckers are conspicuously broader than those of other birds. For a long time, nobody knew why.

In the 1970s Smithsonian Institution researcher Virginia C. Kirby tackled this puzzle. She began by measuring rib width (relative to body size) on the skeletons of 89 woodpecker species from around the world and by gathering information about woodpecker foraging techniques, which she rated according to the amount of stress they placed on the base of the neck. She determined that excavating and bark-scaling are the most neck-stressing foraging modes and that gleaning and probing are the least.

Then Kirby ranked 61 of the species in order of relative rib-width and compared her results to the frequency with which they used various foraging modes. The comparison revealed a clear relationship between the two: the more a woodpecker relies on neck-stressing foraging modes, the greater the broadening of its second cervical and first thoracic ribs. The northern flicker, which mostly digs for ants in the ground, was among the species with the least-modified ribs. Williamson's sapsucker, which captures most of its insect prey by gleaning from tree surfaces but uses its bill to drill sap wells, landed near the

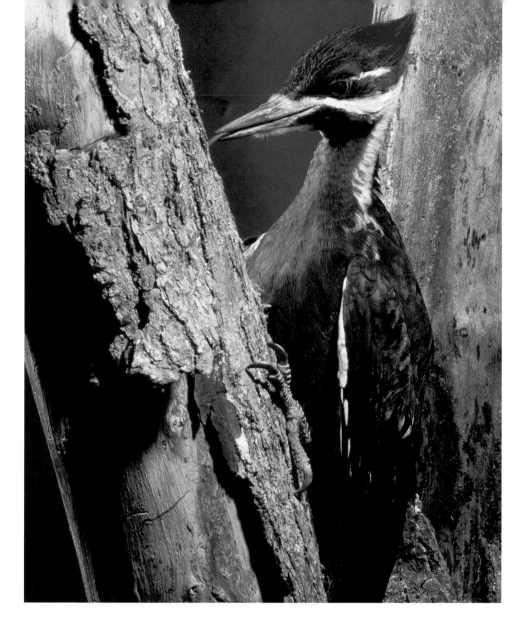

A long tongue and powerful bill allow pileated woodpeckers, like this male, to reach prey that are inaccessible to other insect-eating birds.

middle of the flock. And topping the list were the American three-toed, black-backed and ivory-billed woodpeckers – all experts in bark removal and excavation to gain access to tunneling beetle larvae.

But how do wider ribs help relieve neck stress? Kirby found the answer to this question through careful study of the muscles that connect the woodpecker's first three ribs to the base of the neck. She discovered that these muscles provide the strength needed to pull the neck forward and down as the bill strikes and to stabilize the neck against the force of the blow. Hard-impact foraging modes require highly developed neck muscles, an adaptation that is possible only if the ribs are modified to provide solid attachment points for those muscles.

Tongue

The bone and muscular adaptations that contribute to the excavating prowess of woodpeckers are matched by the equally innovative design of the tongue. Woodpecker tongues are slender, cylindrical, maneuverable and, in many

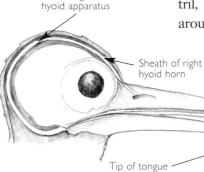

End of right horn of hyoid apparatus fully retracted within its sheath

Tip of tongue

Cross-section of a woodpecker skull showing the tongue in its retracted position. The right horn of the hyoid apparatus extends into the base of the upper half of the bill.

End of right horn of hyoid apparatus

Sheath of right hyoid horn

Tip of tongue

Cross-section of a woodpecker skull showing the tongue in its extended position. The hyoid apparatus moves within the sheath.

species, exceptionally long and protrusible. The longest-tongued woodpeckers in North America, the flickers, can extend their tongues more than 1.6 inches (4 cm) beyond the tip of the bill.

Woodpecker tongues, like those of all birds, are rigidly supported by a complex of cartilage and thin, flexible hyoid bones. The hyoid apparatus, as it is called, extends to the tip of the tongue. In the area of the throat, the hyoid apparatus splits into two branches, referred to as horns, each surrounded by a sheath of muscle and connective tissue. From the fork in the Y, the horns curl under the base of the jaw and wrap some distance around the skull, then rejoin. The muscles that extend and retract the tongue attach to the horns. When these muscles contract, the hyoid horns slide forward in their sheathing and thrust out the tongue.

How far a bird can extend its tongue depends on the length of its hyoid horns. The short-tongued sapsuckers have rather abbreviated hyoid horns, which reach only to the back of the skull. Many woodpeckers have tongues of intermediate length, supported by a hyoid apparatus that extends up over the skull and ends between the eyes or toward the base of the upper mandible.

The woodpeckers that have the most protrusible tongues have greatly elongated hyoid horns. The anatomical challenge of how to find room for these structures is met in one of two ways. Either the horns extend into the right nostril, as exemplified by the northern and gilded flickers, or they coil partway around the right eye socket, as in the hairy woodpecker, whose hyoid horns are almost three inches (7 cm) long. The latter solution is characteristic of woodpeckers that are relatively strong excavators, because the heavy reinforcement of their bills leaves no room in the nasal cavity for the horns. The strongest excavators avoid the problem of accommodating extremely long hyoid horns by having intermediate-length tongues.

Despite the great length of their tongues, woodpeckers can dart them in and out extremely rapidly. One of the hairy woodpeckers that biologist Lawrence Kilham kept in captivity for research purposes regularly joined him when he ate lunch in the aviary. As he sat in his chair she foraged over his body, beginning at his shoes and moving up his pant legs and jacket to his lunch plate. Sometimes she pecked a few hard blows, but mostly she explored buttonholes and other openings with her tongue. He noted that her tongue flicking against his bare skin felt like "a fine electric buzzer or . . . a jet of air."

The tip of the woodpecker tongue is highly touch-sensitive, allowing its owner to feel for prey hidden in deep holes and crevices. The tongue's pointed tip and stiff, backward-pointing barbs impale the quarry and hold it fast as it is drawn out. The arrangement, type and number of barbs on the tongue vary from species to species. The golden-olive woodpecker, for example, has rows of single, loosely spaced barbs that are restricted to the extreme tip of its tongue. Pale-billed and golden-fronted woodpeckers have denser, brush-like rows of variously sized barbs over a larger portion of the end of the tongue.

Many woodpeckers also have large salivary glands that secrete sticky saliva, coating the end of the tongue with this adhesive substance every time the tongue is extended, a particularly useful adaptation for capturing small prey that cannot be speared. Well-developed salivary glands are characteristic of species that feed extensively on ants, including northern and gilded flickers and lineated, pileated, gray-crowned and golden-olive woodpeckers. Besides producing the sticky substance that traps prey, the glands may also help neutralize the formic acid found in ants.

The tongue of ground-foraging species such as flickers is typically deployed as a glue-stick rather than as a spear, so it generally has shorter and thinner barbs and is more rounded than pointed at the tip. Sapsucker tongues are shorter and less protrusible than those of other woodpeckers and are tipped with stiff, brush-like hairs that help in lapping up liquid food. Acorn woodpeckers, which feed heavily on sap at certain times of the year, have similarly equipped tongues.

Tail

Adaptations of the tail and lower limbs help woodpeckers resist gravity and work with ease on vertical tree surfaces. The ability to move confidently and efficiently in a vertical plane gives woodpeckers access to a wealth of feeding opportunities that most birds cannot exploit. Of the nearly 10,000 bird species in the world, fewer than a hundred species outside the Picidae family can forage proficiently on tree trunks. Within this exclusive club, the woodpeckers are by far the best adapted to take advantage of the abundance of insect prey hidden beneath tight layers of bark and deep inside the wood of trees. Most non-woodpeckers are restricted to gleaning prey from bark surfaces or probing under loose bark (except for the nuthatches, which have limited excavating capabilities).

The gravitational force acting upon a woodpecker as it clings to a tree trunk can be divided into two components: an outward force tending to pull it away from the tree, and a stronger, largely downward force. These forces are opposed by the combined action of tail and feet. To understand how they function, imagine a telephone repairman climbing a pole. The woodpecker's tail, with assistance from the middle two toes of each foot, serves the same purpose as the climbing spurs attached to the man's boots: counteracting the downward pull of gravity. The strap that encircles the pole and the man's waist, supporting him when he leans back, corresponds to the woodpecker's toes (particularly the outer ones), which grasp the trunk and prevent the bird from tumbling backward. Without his special equipment, the repairman might still be able to climb the pole, but it would be a tiring and dangerous undertaking. Similarly, woodpeckers are not the only birds that can maneuver on vertical surfaces, but their anatomical specializations afford them an unparalleled level of proficiency.

The woodpecker tail works as an effective prop because of modifications to both its skeletal structure and its long flight feathers, which are called retrices. Woodpeckers have six pairs of retrices, though the outermost pair are much

Woodpecker tail. The two central feathers are the longest and have pointed tips.

smaller than the rest and are not always evident. The two central feathers are the longest and have pointed tips. Woodpecker retrices are generally stiff, with rigid, reinforced shafts and strong barbs. In species that frequently use their tails as props, the central pair of feathers is particularly sturdy. The ends of the tail feathers are slightly curved toward the front to increase the area of contact and the amount of support they give when pressed against a tree trunk. This camber is most evident in the strong excavators. Woodpeckers that are mainly terrestrial or do little arboreal excavating have flatter tails.

Because the tail is so important to woodpeckers, during the annual adult molt they do not replace their retrices in the usual order. In other bird species the most common tail molt pattern is from the middle outward. The tail molt of woodpeckers begins with the second-innermost pair of feathers and proceeds outward. The central pair is replaced last and only after the newly regenerated feathers on either side are big enough to temporarily serve as the main supports.

Constant abrasion against tree bark and other rough surfaces causes woodpecker tail feathers to become quite tattered from one molt to the next. Having black retrices is an advantage for woodpeckers because melanins – the granular pigments that produce black coloring (as well as dull yellows, reds and browns) – make the feathers more resistant to wear.

Pelvic bones

Pygostyle

Tarsus

Rear half of a woodpecker skeleton. The last six vertebrae in the spinal column are fused to form the pygostyle.

The tail feathers and the muscles that move them are attached to the pygostyle, a plowshare-shaped bone formed by the fusion of the last six vertebrae in a bird's spinal column. The size of this bone is directly related to the degree of development of the tail muscles. Birds that use the tail as a prop when climbing or clinging to vertical surfaces have a large pygostyle; those that use it for less demanding functions, such as balancing, have a smaller version. Not surprisingly, the birds with the largest pygostyles are woodpeckers, especially those that spend much of their lives climbing trees and bracing themselves as they hammer with their bills. A study that compared nine North American picids found a predictable increase in pygostyle size from the northern flicker and the largely aerial-foraging Lewis's woodpecker through to the black-backed and American three-toed woodpeckers.

Feet

Unlike the pole-climbing repairman's simple gear, the woodpecker's equipment is highly sophisticated, particularly the feet, which are involved in resisting both the downward and outward forces of gravity. This complex action is achieved by a unique arrangement of the toes.

The basic avian foot has four digits, and bird feet are categorized according to which way the toes point. The toe that is counted as number one (roughly equivalent to the human big toe) is called the hallux; in some bird species it is absent. The anisodactyl feet of crows and other passerines (perching birds) are characterized by a backward-pointing hallux, with the other three toes pointing forward. Woodpeckers have zygodactyl feet – or so you may have read. However, this is an oversimplification based on inadequate observation and the use of traditional terminology.

The term zygodactyl comes from the Greek words for yoke (*zugon*) and finger (*daktulos*) and refers to a yoke-like arrangement of the toes, with the second and third toes pointing forward and the first and fourth pointing backward. The only true woodpeckers that have precisely this type of foot are the flickers, which share this ancestral trait with the wrynecks and piculets. The rest of the woodpeckers have only part-time zygodactyl feet, but were erroneously assigned to the zygodactyl category for two reasons. One reason is that the original system of foot-type categories was based on the assumption that the direction a bird's toes point is a permanent characteristic. This is true for most birds, but woodpeckers (other than flickers) are in a minority group of species that have more versatile feet; they can alter the direction of some of their toes as required. The other reason for the error is that early ornithologists paid far more attention to inert museum skins than to living birds carrying out their normal activities. They failed to realize the important difference between the position of a dead woodpecker's toes – which generally settle into a zygodactyl arrangement – and the movements of the functioning foot on a live individual.

All woodpeckers, even the most specialized climbers, hold their toes in the zygodactyl position when they hop on the ground. They also commonly use this arrangement for perching on horizontal limbs. But the zygodactyl foot is not particularly well designed for clambering up tree trunks. The superior tree-climbing and vertical clinging abilities of the woodpeckers come from their unique ability to rearrange their toes. What they have are ectropodactyl – or "turning-out-of the-way-toe" – feet, so named because the fourth toe is not locked into a backward-pointing direction, but can also be rotated to the side or, in some species, forward.

The word ectropodactyl was coined by Waldron DeWitt Miller of the American Museum of Natural History. Miller was one of the first people to recognize the uniqueness of the woodpecker foot, though he focused mostly on a single species, the ivory-billed woodpecker. Unfortunately Miller's research on the ectropodactyl foot languished in an unpublished manuscript for three decades after his death in 1929. It finally saw the light of day again in a

All woodpeckers hold their toes in the zygodactyl position (two toes forward, two backward) when perching on horizontal branches.

posthumous collaboration with Harvard University professor Walter J. Bock, who refined it by identifying three variations on the ectropodactyl theme.

The most common version of the ectropodactyl foot features a somewhat elongated fourth toe, which is turned more or less straight out to the side when the bird is climbing or clinging. The claws of these laterally directed fourth toes grip the trunk and together act like a pincer, drawing the bird toward the tree and counteracting the outward force of gravity. (Remember the pole-climber's waist strap?) The second and third toes point consistently forward, just as in the zygodactyl arrangement, and may be spread apart in a wide V. (On a vertical surface, forward-directed toes actually point upward, which means that when their claws grip the tree they offer effective resistance to the downward gravitational pull, just like the repairman's spurs.) The hallux is reduced in length and largely without function in climbing and clinging mode. It tends to be cramped beneath the leg, sometimes lying on its side with its claw not hooked into the tree.

When climbing or clinging to trees, woodpeckers with the most common form of ectropodactyl foot can extend the fourth toe straight out to the side. The first toe (hallux) makes little or no contribution to holding the woodpecker in place.

Eight woodpecker species, including the black-backed and American three-toed woodpeckers, have the second type of ectropodactyl foot, which resembles the first type except that the hallux is completely eliminated. The loss of the first toe allows these woodpeckers to assume a stance that maximizes their striking force when excavating.

Black-backed and American three-toed woodpeckers have an ectropodactyl foot with no hallux. This modification allows lower body movements during excavation that intensify the impact force with which the bill strikes the tree.

The third type of ectropodactyl foot is the one studied by Miller and typified by members of the genus *Campephilus*, such as the imperial, ivory-billed and pale-billed woodpeckers. As in the other versions, when the bird climbs or clings to vertical surfaces the second and third toe are maintained in a splayed, upward-pointing arrangement. The greatly elongated fourth toe also points essentially upward. The hallux too is considerably lengthened and, in a curious development, it is shifted from its conventional position on the inside of the foot right around to the outer side, where it lies next to the fourth toe and points straight out to the side. Unlike the short hallux, this long digit is fully functional during climbing and clinging and has a long, strongly curved claw for effective gripping.

Besides having the most radical type of ectropodactyl foot, the *Campephilus* woodpeckers also have a unique way of positioning their legs when climbing and clinging. Most woodpeckers hold their legs more or less directly beneath their body, folded at the joints, so that the leg bones and the body are held away from the supporting surface. *Campephilus* woodpeckers unfold their legs and extend them sideways, as if hugging the tree. The tarsus (the part of the leg that attaches to the foot) is pressed against the tree trunk, but is protected from abrasion by a callus-like pad on the "heel." This wide-legged posture draws the body close to the tree and increases the contact of the ends of the tail feathers with the surface, helping to resist gravity.

The advantage of the *Campephilus* posture becomes evident if you think about a mountain climber on a narrow ledge. Her most secure stance is with arms outstretched to the sides and her body close against the cliff – essentially the imperial woodpecker pose. This reduces outward gravitational pull and increases the downward force, which she easily resists by keeping her feet firmly planted on the ledge. If she adopted a hairy woodpecker stance, folding her arms in front of her body as she faced the cliff, the outward gravitational component would increase. Experienced climbers also know that handholds reached with outstretched arms are more useful than those that are close to the chest. The arm muscles have a mechanical advantage in the extended position because they are at the beginning of their contraction cycle, instead of being already partly contracted, and because they are acting along the length of a long lever rather than working close to the fulcrum point.

Pale-billed woodpeckers and other *Campephilus* species may be ignorant of the laws of physics, but they have evolved a highly effective solution to the problem of large, heavy birds trying to climb vertical surfaces and excavate vigorously while clinging there. Small to medium-sized woodpeckers can manage these activities while gripping with the claws of three toes on each foot and bracing their stiff tail feathers against the trunk. The kings of the *carpinteros* operate by using all eight toes, the tarsi and the tail, and by hugging the tree with widespread limbs.

Woodpeckers in the genus *Campephilus* have an ectropodactyl foot with a long fourth toe that is pointed upward when climbing or clinging to trees. The hallux is also elongated and is extended out to the side during climbing or vertical perching.

e

d

c

b

a

Woodpeckers climb vertically using a technique known as hitching. The sequence of movements begins with the woodpecker pulling its body toward the tree trunk (b). Many woodpeckers, including the yellow-bellied sapsucker (shown here), keep their breast and abdomen close to the trunk as they stretch upward. (c) The woodpecker then momentarily releases its grip and swings both feet up to a higher position, while the tail acts like a spring, helping to propel the body upward (d–e).

When climbing on vertical surfaces a woodpecker can disengage its toes or tail for only a fraction of a second; it can never remove both supports at the same time or it will fall. These constraints have led to development of a climbing style called hitching. The movement begins with the woodpecker drawing its body toward the tree. It then lets go with both feet at once, swings the legs upward in unison, grasps the trunk again with the toes and pulls itself up to the new level, assisted by the spring-like action of the tail, which propels the body upwards. These actions are very quick, so don't be disappointed if you can't make out the details.

Some woodpeckers, such as the yellow-bellied sapsucker, hold the body close to the tree as they hop the feet up, and they keep the tail constantly in contact with the trunk throughout the climbing motion. Others, such as the black-backed woodpecker, hold the breast and abdomen well away from the trunk during the upward progression, which increases the outward gravitational pull while the feet are moving to their new purchase point. To compensate for this tendency to fall backwards, the woodpecker must flip its tail outward during the latter part of the movement.

The black-backed woodpecker's hitching movements are neither as graceful nor as efficient as the yellow-bellied sapsucker's. This is because the arrangement of muscles, bones and tendons that makes black-backed woodpeckers such strong and effective excavators is poorly designed for drawing the body inward and keeping it close to the trunk during upward movement. When excavating, black-backed woodpeckers maximize the impact of their blows by leaning back from the tree on straightened legs, with the breast and abdomen not touching the trunk, and striking with a forward rocking motion that uses the momentum of the whole body. Sapsuckers, on the other hand, keep the body close to the tree and use mainly neck action for delivering blows. In these and other woodpecker species there is a clear trade-off between the ability to deliver forceful blows and the smoothness and energetic efficiency of climbing.

The uneconomical hitching style of the black-backed and American three-toed woodpeckers influences their feeding movements. These anatomically very similar species are notably sedentary foragers. They tend to work intently on one area of a trunk for long periods and ascend slowly, often circling the tree in a tight spiral. In contrast, yellow-bellied sapsuckers are rapid climbers and may quickly travel long distances up tree trunks when gleaning insects.

Woodpeckers can and do hitch downward and sideways, but upward hitching is most common. This is partly because the most energetically efficient movement pattern for birds foraging in trees is to climb from a low point to a high point, then, assisted by gravity, coast down to a lower point on the next tree and begin hitching upward again.

Several other practical reasons cause woodpeckers to favor upward mobility when hitching. In a tail-first descent, a woodpecker cannot easily see where to place its feet after each hop and has to keep lifting its tail to avoid snagging

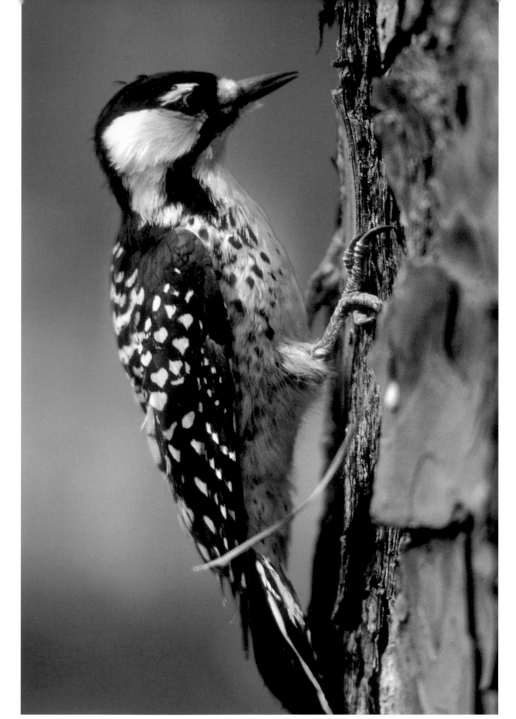

Tail and toes working together against gravity allow this red-cockaded woodpecker to move easily in a vertical plane.

it on the bark or other surface irregularities. One observer saw a pale-billed woodpecker that was hitching down a tree nearly fall when its tail slipped into an unnoticed cavity entrance. Besides awkwardness and potential risks, hitching downward is also likely to scare off any surface insects before the woodpecker can reach them with its bill.

Chapter 3

Communication

For many of us, the moment when winter gives way to spring is heralded by birdsong. The whistled refrains, the trills, the melodic pouring forth of pent-up passion – countless variations on the same optimistic message lift our spirits even though we humans are not the intended audience. Woodpeckers cannot sing and take no part in this vernal chorus, but they too have much to tell us about the turning of the seasons. The woodpecker year could be said to begin with the sound of drumming.

Drumming

Many North American woodpeckers drum at least occasionally throughout the year, but drumming is invariably more frequent and persistent just before and during the early weeks of the breeding season. Like birdsong, drumming plays an important role in establishment of territory, mate attraction and courtship during late winter and spring. At other times of the year it relates more to territorial defense and maintenance of pair bonds. Many species mix together drumming and vocalizations for more nuanced communication.

Generally both sexes drum, but not necessarily in the same way or for the same reasons. Females of many species drum more quietly, less often or for shorter periods of time than their male counterparts. Female Lewis's woodpeckers are thought to never drum, though the nearly identical appearance of males and females makes it difficult to determine the sex of the drummer unless the bird has been color-banded. Species that have no gender-related differences in drumming behavior include the downy, hairy, white-headed and Nuttall's woodpeckers.

A woodpecker drums by repeatedly striking a resonating object with the tip of its bill to produce a loud, rhythmic tattoo. It does so by using mainly the head and neck muscles rather than the whole-body action that some species use for excavation. Small indentations may be found at drumming sites, but no holes are chiseled during drumming. This activity is exclusively communicative, never a byproduct or extension of cavity excavation or foraging.

Nearly all species of true woodpeckers drum. So do most of their diminutive relatives the piculets. Within the bird world, drumming is a unique form of acoustical communication because it involves a separate instrument. The natural instrument of choice for woodpeckers is usually a tree, but not just any tree

His head a blur, a male downy woodpecker beats a rapid tattoo on a resonant snag.

will do. Dead trees have more resonance than live ones, most likely because of the lower water content of their wood cells. On the other hand, when fungi invade dead wood they destroy its elasticity and acoustical quality. Therefore the best options are a dead branch or dead tree that is still largely undecayed or the hollow trunk of a live tree.

In modern times human technology has provided a wealth of drumming-station alternatives, ranging from the obvious (telephone poles and fence posts) to the exotic (farm tractors, upturned metal boats, public-address system speakers). Anything goes, provided it reverberates to produce the loud, low-frequency sound that in most habitats is ideal for long-distance transmission. As many an exasperated homeowner knows from first-hand experience, woodpeckers often discover that stovepipes, rain gutters, aluminum roofs and wooden siding offer superlative sound quality.

Red-cockaded woodpeckers are at a disadvantage when it comes to drumming because they live in habitats where frequent fires remove most of the dead wood. Consequently their choice of instruments is usually limited to live pines, which are far less resonant than snags. Lacking suitable means for long-distance communication, red-cockaded woodpeckers drum less than many other woodpeckers and appear to do so primarily as a form of short-distance communication related to courtship. Other infrequent drummers include the gila, golden-fronted, red-bellied and Lewis's woodpeckers. At the opposite end of the spectrum, North America's most ardent drummers are the black-backed and American three-toed woodpeckers. Pileated woodpeckers are among the most impressive performers, hammering out tattoos that can be heard half a mile (800 m) away.

Woodpeckers of some species tend to favor particular drumming sites, most likely those that produce the best sound and provide the best vantage point for spotting predators or territorial intruders. Williamson's sapsuckers, which typically have two to four preferred drumming sites within their breeding territory, select them by systematically testing various possibilities, usually dead limbs. Less choosy woodpeckers apparently drum wherever it is convenient.

When woodpeckers hear drumming they react in a variety of ways. Typical responses, in order of intensity from low to high, include issuing alarm calls, approaching the drummer, drumming, flying over the drummer, performing certain displays, attacking or supplanting the drummer, and freezing in an anti-predation posture. When two woodpeckers drum back and forth, the participants may be of either the same or opposite sexes. Drumming duels usually occur between two males, but female Williamson's sapsuckers from neighboring territories interact this way early in the nesting season, and females of some other species may also do so. Male/female duets can be quite lengthy. Pale-billed woodpecker courtship duets, for example, have been known to go on for up to 20 minutes.

Lawrence Kilham, who devoted much of his life to studying woodpeckers, described two types of male/female duet performed by downy and hairy woodpeckers. One type, he wrote, reinforces the pair bond: "When things are going well, each bird drums, in unhurried fashion, in response to the drumming of the other." What he called the "tug-of-war type" of duet occurs when relations between a pair are troubled by lack of agreement on a nest site. Each member of the pair drums at its chosen location in an effort to persuade its mate to fly over and give the site due consideration. The duration of the duet and the rate of drumming indicate the intensity of the dispute. Kilham's observations of these species are likely relevant to some others as well.

Experienced listeners can identify certain woodpeckers by nothing more than the sound of their drumming, especially when they know which species are resident in the area. The *Campephilus* woodpeckers, for example, make loud double raps at widely spaced intervals. This signature pulse is no longer heard in the high-elevation pine and oak forests of the Sierra Madre Occidental, which were once the home of the imperial woodpecker, or in the cypress swamps and other former haunts of the ivory-billed woodpecker. The pileated woodpecker, the most likely candidate for confusion with the ivory-billed, beats a much different rhythm. Its loud, sonorous drum roll has a rapid introduction, settles into a slow, steady cadence and concludes with another rapid burst, becoming softer near the end, "similar to the rush of a receding car," in the words of one observer.

The slow and inconsistent drumming of the four sapsucker species is unlikely to be confused with that of other North American species. Each sequence includes a rapid introductory roll followed by a pause, then a varying number of loud, irregularly spaced single or coupled beats. Beyond this basic formula there is much variation in the length and composition of sequences. Even successive drum sequences by a single undisturbed bird may differ from one other.

Much more difficult to differentiate are the staccato drum rolls of the rest of the North American woodpeckers. Some of the subtle differences between them can be pinned down only with laboratory analysis, but others are discernable to the trained ear. The main defining characteristics of any species' typical drum sequence are the length of the roll, the total number of beats (individual strikes of the bill), the number of beats per second, the spacing between beats, and whether the tempo accelerates, decelerates or remains steady throughout.

This might seem like plenty of information to help woodpeckers tell each other apart, yet sometimes males of different species will enter into drumming duels against each other, or mismatched males and females will perform duets. Tape-recorded drumming often elicits incongruous counter-drumming as well. This has prompted suggestions that woodpeckers are unable to single out the drumming of their own species and that other signals, such as calls, are the key to species recognition.

Not so, according to a recent study by Danielle J. Dodenhoff, Robert D. Stark and Eric V. Johnson. After analyzing responses to both recorded and live drumming sessions and conducting playback trials involving eight species, these biologists concluded that a drum roll's cadence or tempo (the number of beats per second) encodes information about species identity, and that this information is understood by woodpeckers that hear it. They found that the intensity of a woodpecker's reaction to drumming by members of other species depends on the drum roll tempo. If the two species have a similar tempo, the listener responds the way it would to a member of its own species. If the tempos differ, it responds in a decidedly less demonstrative fashion.

This study showed that drumming tempo is an important species identifier for woodpeckers, yet Dodenhoff and her colleagues also noted that not every species has a unique tempo. How, then, do woodpeckers keep track of who's who? In some cases slight differences in the breeding schedule of two species with similar drum rolls may be sufficient to avoid mix-ups, but mostly the separation is spatial. Species that have similar rhythms usually have separate geographical ranges or local habitat preferences. If the ranges and habitats of two species overlap, they generally do not drum with an identical tempo. Under natural circumstances, ambiguity arises mainly during encounters between species that have a limited zone of range overlap or when a nonconformist drums noticeably faster or slower than others of its kind.

Tapping and Tongue Drumming

While woodpeckers are renowned for their drumming abilities, the rest of their percussive repertoire is less well known. At least half of all North American woodpecker species employ a form of short-distance communication known as tapping. Because tapping is relatively quiet and infrequent it is noticed only by astute observers, and it may be more widespread than we know. The main differences between drumming and tapping are tempo and context. In drumming, the strikes of the bill are usually too fast to be heard as separate beats. Taps, on the other hand, are generally delivered at a slow, countable rate. Woodpeckers tap in a variety of circumstances, apparently for different reasons in different situations.

Much of the tapping that has been observed has been associated with the process of choosing a nest site. When the paired birds are near each other, one may tap at a promising site, apparently to attract the mate's attention and express interest in the real estate. Red-bellied, red-headed and golden-fronted woodpeckers perform a highly ritualized version of this behaviour known as mutual tapping. It begins with the male tapping loudly but slowly to attract his mate to a potential nest site. She may respond by tapping simultaneously, sometimes with a synchronized rhythm. This apparently signals her approval of his choice and likely also plays an important role in reinforcing the newly established pair bond. During the course of excavation the pair will occasionally engage in additional mutual tapping sessions. If the cavity has been sufficiently excavated, the sessions take place with the male inside tapping on an inner wall and the female outside. When there is not enough room yet for the male inside, both birds will tap outside with his mate. If the female stops responding to her mate's invitations to join in mutual tapping, he will abandon the cavity under construction and start another. This suggests that the female uses this ceremony to communicate her continued acceptance of the site.

Another function of tapping in the course of nest site selection may be to test the thickness of the nest-cavity walls or general suitability of the nest tree. One pair of red-bellied woodpeckers was seen tapping extensively around their cavity after high winds broke off the top of the snag in which they were nesting.

The second most common tapping scenario is when one or both members of a woodpecker pair tap when they are about to trade places while excavating the nest, incubating or brooding. The returning partner may announce its arrival by calling or by drumming or tapping on either a nearby tree or the nest tree. The bird that is at the nest often replies by tapping on an inside wall of the cavity or on the lip of the entrance hole.

Sometimes woodpeckers tapping inside nest cavities may not be communicating. An incubating or brooding parent may tap briefly or for long stretches when its mate is not within earshot. These sounds may result simply from excavating efforts inside the cavity to enlarge the space or to produce fresh wood-chips for nest sanitation.

Tapping can also be a form of displacement behavior – a response to stress or uncertainty, such as when a woodpecker is thwarted in carrying out an intended activity or faces conflicting stimuli. Red-breasted, red-naped and yellow-bellied sapsuckers all perform displacement tapping in situations such as when an individual arrives at a feeding station and finds it occupied by other birds, when a parent returns to its nest with food for its young and is deterred by the presence of a human, or during the early part of the pair-formation process, when prospective mates are unsure whether the other's intentions are aggressive or amorous. Black-backed, lineated and pileated woodpeckers sometimes deliver loud single raps when they are disturbed or anxious, which may also be a type of displacement tapping.

Besides beating rhythms with the bill, at least two woodpecker species also use their tongues percussively. Red-cockaded and pileated woodpeckers tongue-drum by rapidly vibrating the tongue against a tree trunk or other surface, producing a soft, low *brr* that is similar to a rattlesnake's tail-rattling. Little is known about this rarely observed behavior. Its function seems to be related more to foraging than to communication.

Calls

Describing woodpecker calls, or those of any bird for that matter, is an uncertain business at the best of times. You and I probably hear things a bit differently even when we listen to the same call at the same time in the same location. Place us at different distances from the caller or vary the weather conditions or the habitat, and we are unlikely to come up with identical renderings of what we have heard. Complicating matters further are personal approaches to transliteration: I say *peek-it*, you say *pee-dink*; you say *churr*, I say *sk k-k-k-ah-er-r-r-r*. However, despite these complications, it is possible to learn to recognize many common woodpecker calls. An appreciation of their meanings can greatly enhance the experience of getting to know these birds.

There is much variation in the amount of calling done by different woodpecker species. Generally the least active drummers are the most active callers. The more sociable species are also notably vocal. Red-cockaded woodpeckers – cooperative breeders that live year-round in family groups and have few good drumming sites in their habitat – stand out as one of the most vociferous North American species. Acorn woodpeckers also call frequently during interactions with group members and neighbors. Other woodpeckers that are renowned for their noisy habits include the gila, red-bellied and red-headed. The golden-fronted woodpecker's conspicuously loud, harsh voice may be an adaptation to living in dry, open habitats where drumming sites are in short supply. At the other end of the scale, one of the most taciturn species is Lewis's woodpecker.

The vocal repertoire of many of the pied woodpeckers (members of the genus *Picoides*) includes half a dozen types of adult calls, classified according to context and presumed function – keeping in mind that we rarely know exactly what motivates a bird to behave in a particular way. For some species variations on these basic types produce a wide array of calls, while others get their message across more simply. The categorization of *Picoides* calls also has some application to woodpeckers in other genera.

For research purposes, ornithologists usually try to identify and label discrete vocal signals. This can be challenging because the calls of many species tend to grade into one another, with subtle shifts in the pitch, duration or spacing of notes, the volume of the call or other attributes. It is extremely difficult to determine whether each slight alteration changes the meaning of the call or whether its connotations are more broadly defined. Sometimes years of meticulous and patient fieldwork provide answers to such questions; mostly we have to settle for rough translations.

The most fundamental type of adult woodpecker vocalization, generally known as the call note, is associated with a range of emotional states, from relaxed to highly agitated. It commonly functions as a location call for communication between mates or members of family groups and for territorial pronouncements. When delivered with increased intensity it expresses alarm.

The call notes of many woodpeckers are single elements. A few species, such as the white-headed woodpecker, have a two- or three-syllable note. Call notes are often repeated in a loose series, especially when the caller is excited. Among the North American pied woodpeckers the call note is typically single and short, such as the black-backed woodpecker's *kyik* or the downy's *pik*. Other versions include the nasal *kint* of the pale-billed woodpecker and its *Campephilus* relatives, and the rolling *churrs* of the red-cockaded woodpecker and many members of the genus *Melanerpes*. The call note is an all-season vocalization for most species, but its rate of use invariably increases in late winter and spring.

Louder calls that carry over long distances are used by paired birds or family members to maintain contact with each other, and they often elicit an immediate reply. They are also used to assert territorial ownership. For all species these calls are most important during the breeding season. Species that maintain year-round social relationships or defend their territories through the winter are most likely to engage in long-distance communication outside of the breeding season. These calls have been assigned an assortment of labels: "rattle" or "trill" for many members of the genus *Picoides*; "whinny" for downy and hairy woodpeckers, because their renditions resemble a horse's neigh; "long call" for flickers and pileated and lineated woodpeckers.

Rattles, trills, whinnies and long calls typically consist of a series of similar notes delivered at a characteristic tempo. Sometimes this sequence is preceded by one or more discrete introductory notes, which often sound the same as the regular call note. The most complex rattle call heard in North America is the black-backed woodpecker's "scream-rattle-snarl" call, which may be delivered in its full three-part glory or with one or two elements omitted. During conflicts, black-backed woodpeckers often combine this formidable call with a display that incorporates a hunched posture, raised crest and swinging head. Perhaps the most famous long-distance woodpecker vocalization is the pileated

Perhaps the most famous woodpecker vocalization is the pileated woodpecker's cackling call, which echoes incongruously through steamy jungle scenes in old Hollywood movies.

woodpecker's cackling call, which echoes incongruously through the steamy jungle scenes of many old Hollywood movies.

The third type of vocalization is restricted to the breeding season and usually serves sexual or aggressive purposes, such as mate attraction or territorial announcement. Many species combine these calls with drumming, other types of calls or visual displays. For the *Picoides* woodpeckers, these are often referred to as kweek calls because they consist of squeaky *kweek*-like notes. In some species, such as the Arizona and Nuttall's woodpeckers, kweek calls are uttered more frequently by females than males. The opposite applies to the squeal call of the yellow-bellied, red-breasted and red-naped sapsuckers, which is used primarily by males. Sapsucker squeal calls are confined almost entirely to the early part of the nesting season. They are commonly intermixed with drumming and are often answered by a reply squeal call or drumming. As well, they frequently prompt the female to fly to the male, setting the stage for copulation.

The fourth type includes calls that relate to social situations, usually at medium to close range and with some degree of antagonism. Like the previous type, these calls are often associated with visual displays. They are used mostly during the breeding season, but they may be employed throughout the year, particularly by more gregarious species. The intensity, emphasis or form can change according to circumstances. Many members of the genus *Picoides*, as well as the northern and gilded flickers, have social/antagonistic calls that consist of a series of *wicka*s or similar sounds. Other examples of this type of call include the red-bellied woodpecker's *cha-aa-ah*, typically uttered during short-range aggressive or territorial encounters, and the repeated *urrk* calls often given by acorn woodpeckers just before they fly at a territorial intruder.

Intimate calls are muted vocalizations exchanged between members of a pair when they are near to one another, typically before or during copulation or when mates are trading places at the nest during excavation, incubation or brooding. These calls offer reassurance and reinforce pair bonds. The sounds of intimate calls vary widely, from the moans and low *keeus* of the pale-billed woodpecker to the white-headed woodpecker's soft *tyet* or *chuf* notes.

The sixth type of call is the scream, usually uttered by a woodpecker that has been captured by a predator or is being handled by a human. The adaptive value of screaming may be that these piercing calls occasionally attract other predators that try to steal the prize or otherwise distract the original attacker sufficiently that the victim can escape. Woodpeckers of some species occasionally scream when in dire straits during a battle with another member of the same species.

Vocal Development

Woodpecker vocalizations are primarily innate rather than learned, but that doesn't mean newly hatched chicks immediately start producing adult calls. Acquisition of vocal abilities takes time, and nestlings and fledglings have different communication needs than their parents.

The vocal development of white-headed woodpeckers is typical of that observed for many species. At hatching and for about the next seven days the chicks make soft *churr*s. By about the ninth day these sounds have become cricket-like and can be heard from outside the nest cavity. At the beginning of their second week the nestlings make the transition to louder *peep* notes. Around day 22, about four days before they leave the nest, they begin to try out both the two- and three-syllable forms of the adult call note, perching just inside the cavity entrance and alternating between nestling *peep*s and adult-like *pee-dink*s or *pee-de-dink*s. For a while after fledging their call notes remain noticeably weaker and less distinct than those of mature adults.

Although the nestlings of some woodpeckers may be silent for their first few days after hatching, at a very young age all species make some type of vocalization similar to the white-headed woodpecker's soft *churr*s. They produce these twittering, wheezy, raspy or droning calls almost incessantly during daylight hours. The nestling hum of some species, including the pileated woodpecker and northern flicker, sounds remarkably like the buzzing of bees in a hive, leading to speculation that it evolved to protect the young by sending a counterfeit warning to potential predators.

Even before their eyes open, woodpecker chicks can sense light through their translucent eyelids and they respond to changes in light intensity. They soon come to associate any sudden darkening of the cavity entrance with the arrival of a food-bearing parent, which they greet by breaking into a chorus of frantic begging calls. The hungry youngsters will respond with equal vigor if the light is blocked by a human hand, and even a cloud passing in front of the sun or the shadow of a branch may inspire a round of begging calls. Once the nestlings can see, they become more selective in their responses. By the end of the second week the sight or sound of a parent arriving at the nest brings forth the usual enthusiastic reception, but an unidentified object blocking the light is more likely to prompt the chicks to huddle silently at the bottom of the cavity.

The audibility of early woodpecker vocalizations varies between species. The quiet calls of very young red-breasted, red-naped and yellow-bellied sapsuckers can be detected only if you press one ear against the nest tree. In contrast, the begging calls of day-old downy woodpeckers may be heard from more than 30 feet (9 m) away. In all cases the volume increases as the days go by. Often during the latter part of the nesting period, active cavities can be easily located by listening for voluble nestlings.

The young of most species begin to produce rough renditions of adult calls as they prepare to leave the nest, but some nestling vocalizations are carried through into the fledgling period. Juvenile red-headed woodpeckers, for example, solicit food from their parents with noisy squeaks, chirps and purring sounds. Between the fledglings' raucous begging calls and the generally garrulous nature of this species, red-headed woodpecker families are hard to miss in summer. Red-cockaded woodpecker families also become more conspicuous at this time of year. For the first two to six weeks after leaving the nest, the fledglings' food-begging calls and squabbling to establish dominance hierarchies combine to make family groups even more audible than usual.

Visual Displays

In addition to acoustical communications, woodpeckers also employ a wide variety of ritualized visual displays to convey messages to members of their own and other species. What can be confusing to human observers is that courtship displays are frequently indistinguishable from antagonistic displays. This similarity arises from the social context in which woodpeckers operate.

For the most part, woodpeckers are aggressive territorial birds that spend much of their lives defending their nesting and roosting cavities and food sources, as well as the area around these scarce resources. Territorial aggression is mostly intrasexual – male against male, female against female – particularly in species with plumage differences that separate the sexes. The golden-fronted woodpecker is one of the few sexually differentiated woodpecker species in which territorial conflicts between members of the opposite sex are common.

The emphasis on same-sex aggression makes gender identification an important part of antagonistic displays. Sexual recognition is equally important in courtship displays, since each bird wants to establish whether the other is a potential mate. The result is that the same displays are used for both purposes at different times. Courtship displays also feature some of the same elements that signal dominance and submission during conflicts. Because males are normally dominant over females, establishing and maintaining pair bonds are essentially conciliatory activities that require both parties to overcome their instincts to attack or flee and to allow reproductive urges to take precedence instead.

The display repertoires of most woodpecker species are fairly similar. Postures and movements may be displayed in isolation or in combination and are often accompanied by specific vocalizations. One of the simplest and most common woodpecker displays is the raising of the crest, crown or nape feathers. For many species these are areas where sexual recognition characteristics, or sexual badges, are located. Erecting the head feathers identifies or emphasizes gender, as well as exaggerating the bird's size. Woodpeckers also draw attention to head markings by turning their heads or changing position relative to the antagonist.

Red-cockaded woodpeckers are unusual in having completely discretionary sexual badges. The male's "cockades" – the tiny streak of red feathers behind each eye – are normally concealed within the black crown feathers and exposed only during certain displays. Controlled expression of masculinity appears to be a key factor in this species' cooperative breeding system, because it reduces aggressive behavior within family groups.

An important display in the sapsucker repertoire is throat fluffing, in which the throat feathers are puffed out, often with the head angled upward and the bill raised. For yellow-bellied and red-naped sapsuckers this display plays an

A red-shafted northern flicker shows his colors as he drives away a rival.

important role in distinguishing between males, with their all-red throats, and females, with their white or partly white throats. The radically different plumage of male and female Williamson's sapsuckers leaves no room for error, but males still perform this display, which accentuates their gender by drawing attention to the red throat patch. Throat fluffing is of no use to red-breasted sapsuckers, since males and females have identical plumage.

A woodpecker's bill is its main weapon, so it is not surprising that this part of the body is highlighted in many displays. In the bill-pointing display, the bird holds a rigid pose with its head and neck extended and its bill aimed directly at its opponent. The body and tail are aligned with the head and bill. This aggressive display is transformed into an appeasement or submissive display when the head and bill are held at a higher or lower angle rather than pointing the bill straight at the other bird. Some species assume a hunched posture when the bill is lowered.

The bowing or bobbing display involves alternately raising the head, sometimes aiming the bill almost straight upward, then lowering the head and bringing the bill parallel to the ground. When sideways movements of the head and body are added, simple bowing is elaborated into the swinging display, in which the woodpecker traces circles or figure eights in the air with its bill as it raises and lowers its head and sways its body from side to side. Sometimes the head and bill are simply waved back and forth laterally, with little or no up-and-down movement.

Wing and tail actions often accompany other displays. Wing flicking and wing spreading are especially common in species that have stripes or other types of patterning on their wings. The degree to which the wings are spread depends on the intensity of the situation and the species. For example, during close territorial conflicts or when under attack, hairy woodpeckers will hold their wings at a high angle over the back in a posture known as the full-wing threat display. In tail spreading displays the tail feathers are fanned out and the tail may be angled to one side so that the undersurface is directed toward the opponent.

One of the most dynamic versions of the swinging display is carried out by northern and gilded flickers. Most commonly seen during the early part of the breeding season, it is used to defend breeding territories or mates. This display, which resembles a theatrical fencing duel, is performed by two male or two female flickers. Often they are watched or joined by a member of the opposite sex – generally the mate, if one of the birds is already paired. Without an audience the duel may proceed at a low intensity, but the arrival of an opposite-sex bird immediately results in a more vigorous performance by the original opponents.

In a typical flicker duel the rivals face off, usually on a branch, with their bills held slightly upward. They then begin to swing their heads, tracing aerial circles or figure eights with their bills, but rarely making contact with one another. This action is usually accompanied by wicka calls in rhythm with the swinging. Often the opponents will flick their wings or spread and angle their tails, flashing the brightly colored undersides at each other. Yellow-shafted flickers, which are the only North American flickers with a nape patch, usually erect these red feathers.

Sustained bursts of displaying and calling by the dueling flickers usually last five to ten seconds and are followed by a pause of about 30 seconds, then another brief burst of activity, continuing in this manner for several minutes at a time before the participants take a longer break. Then the contest resumes. Duels often go on for hours, sometimes extending through an entire day.

Like perched displays, ritualized aerial displays are employed by wood-peckers during both courtship and aggressive encounters. Sapsuckers often respond to territorial intruders with the bouncing flight display, in which the aggressor flies toward the intruder with a deeply undulating flight path and high-amplitude fluttering wing beats. Landing after a bouncing flight, the aggressor typically assumes the wings-up posture, with both wings out-stretched above the back and the throat-patch feathers fluffed.

Another sapsucker display, the moth flight, is characterized by a lowered head, hunched shoulders and rapid, shallow wing beats. It is performed in various aggressive and sexual contexts. Male Williamson's sapsuckers that have intruded into another male's territory often fly in this manner as they retreat.

Lewis's woodpeckers perform a flight display in which one member of a pair (often, or perhaps always, the male) circles the nest tree in a prolonged glide with the wings angled slightly upward. If a circle flight display ends with the flier landing next to its mate, the pair usually then copulate.

Fluttering aerial displays are common to many of the pied woodpeckers. The downy woodpecker's version – the butterfly flight display – is performed in early spring before nesting. It is named for the characteristic slow, weak, but-terfly-like wing flaps and the way the flier holds its wings high above its back at the top of the upstroke, especially as it glides into a landing. Typically the bird performing this display is a male pursuing a female. During the pursuit their path may include long, deep loops as well as stretches of level flying.

The fluttering flight displays of some pied woodpeckers are often accom-panied by muffled, irregular rustling sounds produced by the wing feathers. Sounds produced by aerially displaying sapsuckers include a snipe-like winnow and a ruffling noise. Yellow-bellied sapsuckers also occasionally punctuate ordi-nary flight with a loud clapping of the wings. It is likely that these sounds serve a communication function, but they are not yet well understood by biologists. Other woodpecker wing sounds include the almost musical *wurrp* with which flickers sometimes signal alarm as they fly, and the pale-billed woodpecker's occasionally heavy-sounding flight that contrasts with their normally silent wing beats. Observations suggest that pale-billed woodpeckers sometimes use these wing sounds to tell their nearby mate where they are going. Their heavy wing beats may also be heard during antagonistic encounters.

In this encounter between two yellow-shafted northern flickers, the female (at right) has claimed the dominant position.

Aggressive Encounters

In situations of conflict, visual displays and auditory communications usually serve to establish dominance and to signal intent, thereby avoiding the need for physical combat, which can be costly to both parties. Aggressive encounters frequently begin with supplanting behavior – one bird flies or hitches toward its adversary, which responds by retreating. They may then escalate to a chase, on foot or flying, and may finally reach a point where one bird launches a full-out attack.

Certain species seem more inclined than others to make bodily contact with adversaries. When fighting with others of their kind, it is not uncommon for pileated woodpeckers to strike at each other with their bills and wings. Golden-fronted woodpeckers also use their bills to stab at an opponent's head, and during airborne encounters antagonists may lock feet and tumble downward while exchanging jabs. Acorn woodpeckers occasionally also engage in aerial battles during power struggles and other territorial skirmishes, grappling with their feet and pecking at each other's heads as they fall. Now and then they fail to disengage in time to save themselves from hitting the ground, where they may remain for several seconds before they recover sufficiently to separate and fly away.

Aggressive encounters of all types are most frequent at the beginning of the breeding season. They typically peak during the egg-laying period and diminish considerably after hatching. For many species the size of the actively defended territory decreases during the breeding season, often being eventually limited to only the nest tree. Territorial boundaries may also shift between the breeding and non-breeding seasons. Red-bellied woodpecker territories, for example, dissolve at the end of summer, when the fledglings are dispersing, but are re-established before winter sets in. Until the next spring, males and females that were mated in summer may occupy completely separate or partially overlapping foraging territories, or they may share a territory; all other red-bellied woodpeckers are excluded.

Territories that woodpeckers actively defend through winter are nearly always associated with valuable localized resources. These may be food sources, such as the carpenter ant colonies that sustain pileated woodpeckers in this season of scarcity, or food storage sites such as acorn woodpecker granaries. Many species make little or no attempt to defend territorial boundaries outside the breeding season, since the energy required would be greater than what could be gained from having exclusive access to an area. But come the end of winter, when thoughts return to the elemental urge to reproduce, their territorial pronouncements will once again reverberate across the land.

Two male red-bellied woodpeckers spar outside a nest cavity while a female (top left) looks on.

Chapter 4

Nesting

Woodpeckers begin life in one of the most favorable environments that avian parents can provide for their offspring. Deep inside a cavity, eggs and nestlings are out of sight and out of reach of most predators and sheltered from the elements. As a result, woodpeckers have much greater nesting success than open-nesting birds such as warblers and thrushes. Open-nesting species suffer much higher rates of egg predation during the laying period than woodpeckers and continue to fare worse during incubation and after the eggs hatch, experiencing frequent losses from predation, exposure or starvation. An average of almost half of all open-nesting attempts are unsuccessful, without a single member of the brood surviving to the fledging stage. Woodpeckers may lose one or two nestlings, but rarely an entire brood. Depending on the species and local conditions, 75 to 100 percent of all woodpecker nesting attempts are successful – that is, they produce at least one fledgling.

Woodpeckers also have better nesting success compared to non-excavating cavity nesters such as house wrens. Birds that rely on prefabricated homes have limited choice and must often settle for old cavities in deteriorating trees, which no longer afford the superior insulation and security they provided for the original occupants. Previously occupied cavities are frequently infested with mites, lice or other nest parasites that have overwintered there and are ready to attack vulnerable nestlings the moment they hatch, weakening or killing them. Most woodpeckers avoid this problem by excavating a fresh cavity every year. Nesting in an old cavity requires less effort, but the end result is usually lower reproductive success. A study of yellow-bellied sapsuckers found that pairs that reused nest cavities fledged fewer young than pairs that nested in fresh cavities, despite the fact that the reusers laid larger clutches.

Cavity nesting is not without disadvantages, however. Suitable cavity sites are usually in short supply compared to sites that can accommodate open nests, cavity excavation is strenuous and time-consuming work, and woodpeckers often have to defend their cavities against other species that try to seize them for their own use. Nevertheless, the benefits outweigh the costs.

Demanding youngsters greet a red-shafted northern flicker upon her return to the nest.

Eggs

Woodpecker eggs, like those of other cavity nesters, are white. Hidden from view, there is no need for them to be camouflaged, and enhanced visibility in the dim light of the cavity may reduce the chance of accidental breakage by the parents. The surface texture is generally smooth and somewhat glossy. One early writer likened the ivory-billed woodpecker's eggs to "highly polished porcelain."

Compared to other birds, members of the Picidae family have relatively small eggs in relation to their body mass. Downy woodpecker eggs are about ¾ inch (1.9 cm) long and weigh less than one-tenth of an ounce (2–3 g). The ivory-billed woodpecker's eggs measured about 1.4 inches (3.6 cm) long, but no records were kept of their weight.

Once laying begins, female woodpeckers produce one egg a day, usually in the morning, continuing until the clutch is complete. Many, and perhaps all, woodpeckers are indeterminate layers. This means that the number of eggs females can lay exceeds the maximum clutch size. If some of their eggs are damaged or taken during the laying period, they will keep producing replacement eggs. In contrast, females of species that are determinate layers are physiologically incapable of producing extra eggs, even if their entire clutch is destroyed.

The woodpecker egg-laying record is held by a northern flicker that laid 71 eggs over a 73-day period in an attempt to compensate for an experimenter's relentless egg removal program. His efforts prevented the determined but luckless bird from ever achieving a clutch size of more than two. A similar deception induced a red-headed woodpecker to lay 32 eggs in one breeding season. After losing the first 28 eggs, she and her mate finally excavated a new cavity beyond the collector's reach, where she laid a new set and they successfully raised four young.

Under normal circumstances, the size of a northern flicker clutch ranges from three to thirteen – the highest upper limit for any North American woodpecker species. The maximum clutch size for red-headed woodpeckers is ten and for Lewis's woodpeckers, nine. With these and other woodpeckers, clutch size often varies widely between members of the same species. Factors that influence clutch size include habitat quality and the age of the pair – first-time breeders often produce smaller clutches than more experienced birds. For many North American woodpeckers, clutch size also corresponds to latitude: northern members of a species typically produce larger clutches than their southern relatives. Similarly, woodpeckers found mainly in the tropics tend to have smaller clutches than temperate-region species. Pale-billed and lineated woodpeckers, for example, usually produce clutches of only two or three eggs, about half the output of many more northerly woodpeckers.

Incubation

During the laying period woodpeckers sometimes leave their cavity unguarded for an hour or more at a time. Often, however, one member of the pair will perch outside the cavity or in the entrance hole to keep an eye on the nest. Woodpeckers may sit on their eggs for short periods before the clutch is complete, but sustained incubation usually does not begin until the last egg is laid. After that the cavity is nearly always occupied by an attentive parent.

Both parents participate in incubation, but the male always takes the nighttime shift throughout the nesting period. This is an unusual arrangement within the avian world. In other bird species that share incubation it is nearly always the female that stays on the nest overnight.

Each breeding season, mated birds of both sexes develop incubation patches, also known as brood patches, since they are used for brooding as well as incubating. They lose the feathers covering a specialized area of the abdomen and lower breast that is richly supplied with blood vessels, and the bare skin becomes soft and cushiony to allow the greatest contact between this heat delivery system and the eggs or, later, the nestlings. In acorn and red-cockaded woodpecker family groups, non-breeding helpers assist with incubation, though their brood patches are less well developed than those of the breeding birds and their participation is limited to a small part of the total effort.

For obvious reasons, one of the least-known aspects of woodpecker behavior is what they do inside their nest cavities. In the 1960s Jerome A. Jackson, one of North America's preeminent woodpecker experts, literally created a window into this mysterious realm by cutting out the backs of six nest cavities, half belonging to red-headed woodpeckers and the others to red-bellied woodpeckers. After removing the wood he fitted each cavity with a glass panel that he kept covered between observation sessions.

Watching from behind a blind several feet away, Jackson observed how the woodpeckers moved within the cavity. After entering, the arriving parent would walk headfirst, with its feet spread far apart, down the cavity wall below the opening. At the bottom it would turn around, keeping its tail raised out of the way, and settle on the eggs or nestlings with its incubation patch bared. Then it would fluff up its feathers, increasing their insulating value, and relax its wings, letting them rest on the cavity floor. Sometimes the incubating or brooding parent rested its bill against the cavity wall so its head was held upright. At other times it turned its head and tucked its bill under the scapular feathers on its back. Often the birds closed their eyes as if sleeping.

Observing a windowless woodpecker nest during incubation is nowhere near as fascinating as Jackson's experience, since the birds are at their least conspicuous during this time. Woodpeckers almost never leave their nests unattended during the incubation period, and if it is cold or rainy, the incubating bird will stay out of sight. In hot weather the parent on duty may sit in the entrance, sometimes panting to increase evaporative cooling, and occasionally neither parent may be present for a short interval. The length of time one bird spends incubating before trading places depends on the species, the time of day, the weather and possibly other factors. Daytime shifts may be as short as five to ten minutes or stretch to an hour or longer. Changeovers take place quickly, sometimes accompanied by intimate calls, tapping or both, but sometimes without any ceremony.

During incubation the parent's objective is to keep the eggs consistently at the optimum temperature for embryonic development, avoiding excessively

high or low temperatures. If the temperature inside the nest drops too low, the incubating bird must expend extra energy to keep the eggs warm. If the temperature rises too high, the bird will metabolize more water than usual in its efforts to cool the nest. In either case it must compensate by increasing its intake of food or water. Cavity nesters have an advantage over open-nesters because tree cavities provide a relatively stable, moderate microclimate. Compared to outside air temperatures, cavities are warmer in cold weather and cooler in hot weather. This is especially beneficial in environments with extreme weather conditions, such as deserts, mountains and boreal forests.

Most woodpeckers respond to disturbance at the nest in characteristic ways that can be useful for gauging the status of the nest, since these responses vary as the season progresses. If disturbed during the laying period – before incubation begins – the parents are generally quick to leave the nest and may stay away for a long time. During the first week after hatching, the brooding parent will also flush readily, but will usually remain nearby and quickly return to the nest if there is no further disturbance. Incubating woodpeckers, on the other hand, are notably reluctant to leave their nests.

The pronounced tendency of incubating woodpeckers to sit tight was well known to – and exploited by – 19th- and early 20th-century egg collectors. An incident reported in Arthur C. Bent's *Life Histories of North American Woodpeckers* was typical. One April morning in 1883, in California's San Bernardino Valley, oologist B.T. Gault saw a bird peek out of a nest hole and then retreat before he could identify it. After trying without success to scare the bird out of the cavity by banging on the trunk with the butt of his gun and shouting, he became impatient. "I finally resorted to my jackknife in order to enlarge the orifice," he wrote, "but, from its being such a tedious job, gave it up in disgust. The next morning I took a hatchet along with me, for I desired very much to know what that hole contained. It did not take me very long to cut a place large enough for me to get my hand in, and I was thoroughly surprised to learn that the bird was still on her nest." Gault removed the bird, a female Nuttall's woodpecker, and her six eggs, which he concluded were within a few days of hatching. His account makes no mention of the fate of the bird, but she was undoubtedly added to his collection along with the eggs.

<hr />

Members of the Picidae family have much shorter incubation periods than open-nesting birds of comparable size. This is an adaptation to the poorly ventilated environment at the bottom of a nest cavity. During embryonic development there is a constant exchange of gases through the eggshell: oxygen passes in and carbon dioxide passes out. The effectiveness of this exchange is reduced when there is a deficit of oxygen and an excess of carbon dioxide, exactly the kind of atmosphere that develops under an incubating parent in a tree cavity, especially at night, when the male does not leave the nest from dusk to dawn.

Although not yet three weeks old, these pileated woodpecker nestlings already bear rudimentary head crests, distinguishing the male (on top) from his female sibling.

Naked and sightless, a family of four-day-old northern flickers huddle in their nest. The pale knobs at the corners of their mouths are an aid to feeding. The white egg tooth at the tip of the beak, used to cut open the shell, will soon disappear.

As the chick grows inside the egg, its respiration rate increases and so does the potential for stress associated with shortage of oxygen.

The evolutionary solution to this problem has been a reduction in the period of development inside the egg, balanced by a corresponding increase in the period of development after hatching. Although a truncated incubation period means that woodpecker chicks hatch in a relatively immature state, the total developmental period for woodpeckers – the incubation phase plus the nestling phase – is about equal to that of other birds. Once hatched, the chicks are better able to cope with the low oxygen levels in the bottom of the cavity because direct lung breathing is more efficient than the exchange of gases through the eggshell. As well, the more frequent comings and goings of the parents once they have nestlings to feed increases the flow of fresh air from outside and encourages air circulation within the cavity.

Most North American woodpeckers incubate for about 10 to 14 days, and all of the eggs in the clutch hatch within a day or two of each other. The last-hatched chick sometimes quickly succumbs to starvation because it is smaller and weaker than its older siblings and therefore less able to compete for food.

Nestlings

Woodpecker chicks emerge from their shells with naked bodies, their pale pink skin so thin and translucent that organs and blood vessels are clearly visible. The hatchlings of some species show no sign of future plumage. On others, tiny dots mark the follicles from which feathers will soon push forth. With little capacity for regulating their body temperature, the young birds must be brooded almost constantly for the first few days of their lives. Not until at least halfway through the nestling period will they be physiologically able to warm or cool themselves as required. Even though cavities provide a considerable degree of protection against the elements, cold or wet weather during this vulnerable period is a common cause of nestling mortality. The amount of time spent actively brooding the young decreases as their thermoregulatory abilities improve, and some species discontinue brooding entirely during the last few days before the chicks leave the nest.

On the day that it hatches, a newborn woodpecker cannot support its own head for more than a second or two at a time. Nevertheless it will open its mouth wide and feebly crane its neck whenever one of its parents enters the nest. By the next day, hatchlings can extend their necks completely and hold their heads up for several seconds. The chick's eyes and ears are fused shut at first, but it can detect light through its eyelids and instinctively responds to the darkening of the entrance hole that indicates the arrival of a parent, usually bearing food. The eyes and ears open gradually. In downy woodpeckers, for example, the process starts around day four, and is not complete until day eight.

Within 24 to 48 hours of emerging, woodpecker chicks typically double their hatching weight. The rate at which different parts of the body develop is clearly related to priorities for survival. Mouth parts and lower limbs develop quickly, wings and plumage more slowly. Woodpecker hatchlings have a disproportionately wide gape, which makes an easy target for food deliveries, and large oral flanges. These pale, knoblike swellings on each side of the head at the base of the lower mandible help the parents locate the mouths of their hungry offspring in the dim light of the cavity. The oral flanges are also equipped with highly sensitive tactile nerve endings. If a nestling is not already gaping in anticipation of food, the parent need only touch one of the flanges and the bill will spring open. The width of the gape and length of the bill increase rapidly in the early days, allowing the nestlings to handle increasingly larger food items as their energy requirements accelerate. These developments are matched by large daily gains in balancing ability and leg strength.

The downy woodpecker is one of the few North American species whose nestling development has been studied closely. Other species develop at slightly different rates but follow the same general timeline. By four days of age, a downy woodpecker is able to raise itself to beg for food by extending its legs and stretching its body upward, but between feeding visits it rests. The chicks arrange themselves in the center of the nest, facing inward, and each drapes its long neck over the body of one of its siblings. When one of the parents arrives, the nestlings all raise their heads and reach up, uttering their plaintive begging calls, until each in turn is rewarded with a mouthful of food and lowers its head again. The last to be fed ends up with its neck and head on the top of the pyramid, conveniently claiming the best position to reach up first at the next mealtime. By about day 15, the young birds' legs are strong enough and their claws sharp enough that they can clamber up the nest-cavity walls, and they soon take to waiting at the entrance for their parents' arrival. They fledge when they are about 20 days old.

Northern flickers, being nearly twice the size of downies at maturity, take longer to develop. Nestlings of this species are only beginning to open their eyes by day 10 or 11, and they are not fully opened until the young birds are 12 to 15 days old. At first they huddle together at the bottom of the cavity between parental visits. Later, as their need to share body warmth decreases, they spread out. One observer noted that, starting around day 11 and continuing for the next week, the nestlings arranged themselves around the base of the cavity with their chins and throats pressed against the wall. This positioning may depend on the weather, since on hot days red-cockaded woodpecker nestlings of about the same age are similarly reported to sprawl along the sides of their nest cavities. By day 17 or 18 the nestling flickers begin climbing and, like other woodpeckers that are close to fledging, they often appear at the doorway during their last few days in the nest. They depart from the nest 24 to 27 days after hatching.

Woodpeckers are relatively slow to develop plumage, producing no down feathers and remaining naked for longer than most open-nesting birds. The first feathers, still enclosed in sheaths, start to emerge along the feather tracts about four days after hatching. Around the end of the first week the tips of the feather vanes begin to break from the sheaths; it takes a few more days for most areas of bare skin to be covered by growing plumage. By the time the nestlings begin popping their heads out to survey the world, they are almost fully feathered.

Feeding Nestlings

Midday is usually a time of rest for woodpeckers, but during the nestling period the fast-growing chicks must be constantly provisioned, and adults are often active from dusk to dawn. Although you will not be able to observe the nestlings directly until they are nearly ready to fly, the progress of their development can be deduced from the parents' activities.

For the first four to six days after hatching, the adults disappear completely into the cavity whenever they bring food and may not emerge for some time. After distributing the rations it has brought, the parent will either brood the nestlings or perch at the cavity entrance until its mate returns. The two then trade places, entering and exiting headfirst. By the end of the first week, however, the adults frequently leave the nest unattended in their haste to fill hungry mouths.

As the ability of the nestlings to reach up to receive food increases, the parents adjust their feeding methods. By day 10 to 13 they often do not enter far enough into the cavity to turn around. Instead they make their deliveries with the tip of the tail still visible through the doorway and then back out. From around the beginning of the third week, food transfer can be achieved with the parent thrusting only its head and neck into the cavity, and soon even that becomes unnecessary.

Nestlings that are mature enough to receive meals at the cavity entrance are often very assertive in their attempts to get fed, striking with their now well-developed bills at the food-bearing parent as well as at their siblings. If the adults fly directly to the entrance hole they risk an ill-considered jab from an overeager youngster. An indirect approach is usually favored at this stage, with the parent landing on the tree trunk below or to one side of the hole and hitching just close enough that the food can be delivered with an extended bill. While studying black-backed woodpeckers, Lester L. Short, one of world's leading Picidae experts, noted that the sword-waving nestlings "so besieged the adult that it often had to make several attempts before successfully 'running the gauntlet' into the nest."

Throughout the nestling period both parents contribute to the feeding efforts, assisted by non-breeding helpers in the case of acorn and red-cockaded woodpeckers. For the first week or so the parents rotate between feeding and brooding duty. Later, when the young do not require constant brooding, both parents can forage at the same time.

The nestlings' rapid growth is fueled by a protein-rich diet consisting primarily of insects, especially soft-bodied types such as caterpillars, beetle larvae, aphids and moths. Plant matter provides less protein than insects, but some woodpeckers, particularly in the genus *Melanerpes*, rely on plants to meet the escalating demand for food. Acorn woodpeckers break acorns into small pieces and feed them to their young from early on, substantially increasing the proportion of acorns in the diet as the nestlings mature. One study of gila woodpeckers in southern Arizona found that saguaro cactus fruit and pollen represented one-fifth of the food brought to the nest. A variety of fruits are prominent in the diet of red-bellied woodpeckers during the latter part of the nestling period.

Woodpeckers feed nestlings in one of two ways. A majority of species deliver food items whole or in pieces, one bill-full at a time. The alternative is regurgitation feeding, which is characteristic of species that specialize in preying on ants and their larvae. In North America the regurgitation feeders are the pileated, lineated and golden-olive woodpeckers and the northern and gilded flickers. The golden-olive woodpecker's close relative, the gray-crowned woodpecker, is probably part of this group, but this has not been confirmed by field observations. Ants dominate the nestling diet of Williamson's sapsuckers but, unlike other ant specialists, the parents carry all nestling provisions in their bill, mouth and throat, doling them out in an unregurgitated form.

Woodpeckers that feed by regurgitation store food for the nestlings in the crop, an expanded section of the esophagus that in northern flickers measures about 0.5 by 2.5 inches (1 by 6 cm). Parents forage until their crops are full, then return to the nest. During regurgitation feeding sessions the parent inserts its bill into the nestling's throat with their bills interlocked at right angles. It then disgorges the food from its crop with a series of vigorous pumping motions, sometimes accompanied by emphatic head shaking. The nestling may also jerk its head and suck at the parent's bill. The entire contents of the crop are not ejected in one go. During a single feeding visit the parent may feed each nestling more than once, withdrawing its bill from the nestling's mouth between deliveries. Once the chicks are old enough to be fed without the parent completely entering the nest cavity, convulsions of the adult's protruding tail and wing tips are a sure sign of a feeding session in progress.

Delivery of whole or pieced food is more straightforward. At first the parents simply deposit items in the hatchlings' wide gapes, but soon the young learn to coordinate their movements so that their bills connect effectively with the adult's bill and nothing is lost. For the first few days after hatching, prey brought to the nest by direct-feeding woodpeckers may be so small that they are hardly visible. As the nestlings grow, both their appetites and the size of the items they can handle increase, and parents will often arrive with their bills crammed full, insect wings and legs spilling out the sides. The adults sometimes prepare certain items to make them more manageable, removing the wings of moths or butterflies, crushing hard-shelled insects or compacting soft-bodied prey.

The frequency of feeding visits depends on many factors, including availability and nutritional value of the food, age and size of the brood, weather, time of day and method of food delivery. Feeding activity is usually most intense early in the morning and shortly before nightfall. The number of feeding visits per day usually increases rapidly during the first part of the nestling period and drops off a few days before fledging.

At times the feeding visits of direct feeders may be spaced only minutes apart. One researcher studying red-bellied woodpeckers saw the pace of feeding reach 40 to 45 visits per hour during the busiest periods – perhaps a record for North American woodpeckers. James T. Tanner, who studied some of the last known ivory-billed woodpecker nests in the 1930s, noted that the young were fed about 30 times a day early in the nesting period and about 15 times a day later on. Some of the prey brought to the nestlings were large enough for Tanner to identify from a distance as the larvae of a beetle commonly known as the hardwood stump borer.

Because regurgitation feeders can carry more food at one time, they bring meals less frequently than direct feeders. This may be advantageous because they are less likely to attract the attention of predators. The usual interval between feeding visits for pileated, lineated and golden-olive woodpeckers is from one to two hours. At one closely monitored northern flicker nest the

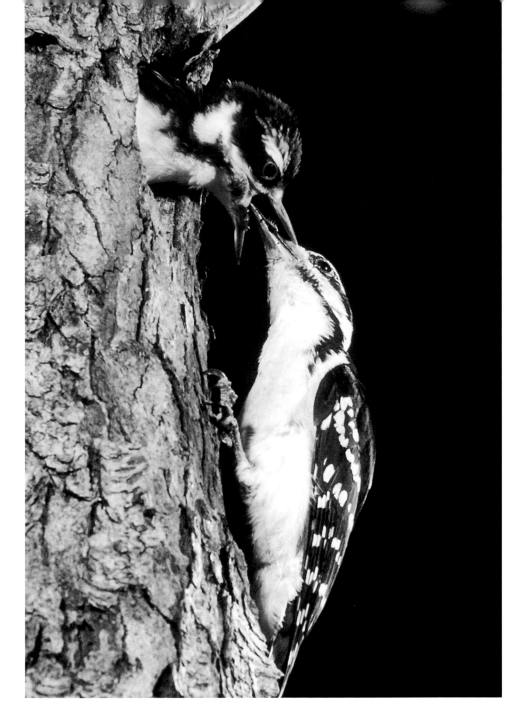

A hairy woodpecker delivers a meal to one of her offspring, identifiable as a male by the red spot on his forehead. In adult plumage his forehead will be black and he will be marked with red on the back of his head.

parents made 10 feeding visits on the day the chicks hatched and increased the feeding rate to 40 to 50 visits a day later in the nesting period.

Nest Hygiene

Like many birds, most woodpeckers remove eggshell fragments from the nest either immediately after hatching or within several days, though some species, such as the northern flicker and red-bellied woodpecker, leave the broken shells inside the cavity. But the enclosed environment of a cavity nest demands a level of hygiene that goes well beyond eggshell removal, and the most critical sanitation challenge is posed by the nestlings' bodily wastes. If these were left to accumulate throughout the entire nestling period, the cavity would soon become unlivable. The wastes are conveniently excreted inside tough, gelatinous fecal sacs, which a parent can easily pick up in its bill and remove from the nest. Any excess liquid is absorbed by the woodchips and fine wood shavings on the cavity floor; clumps of this material may also be carried away for disposal. Some woodpeckers regularly peck at the walls inside the cavity during the nestling period to add fresh layers of woodchips, either to cover debris or to help soak up feces.

The young usually defecate immediately after being fed, an action that the parent often stimulates by using the tip of its bill to gently prod the nestling's anal region. For the first few days after hatching, many woodpecker parents eat their offspring's fecal sacs. As repugnant as this may seem to humans, it is actually a very pragmatic practice. Not only does it keep the nest clean, it also allows the parents to recoup some nutritional value from food that was only partially digested as it passed through the hatchlings' inefficient digestive system.

Once the nestlings are a little older, the parents usually carry away the fecal sacs and dispose of them at some distance from the nest tree, where they will not draw attention to the nest. In many woodpecker species the males perform more of this nest sanitation duty than the females. Some species seem to drop the fecal sacs randomly, while others tend to deposit them regularly in one place. Sapsuckers are among the latter group and may use the same sanitation post from one breeding season to the next. After the sac has been dropped, sometimes with a few shakes of the head to free it, the woodpecker may wipe its bill on a branch.

Certain species and some individuals are more fastidious about nest sanitation than others. Most woodpeckers suspend their cleaning efforts a few days before fledging, probably because crowding inside the cavity makes it an impossible task. Red-bellied woodpeckers are perhaps the most negligent of North American woodpeckers. Beyond the first few days after hatching they no longer regularly remove fecal sacs or add fresh woodchips, and conditions inside the nest become increasingly unsanitary as eggshells, feces and dropped bits of food mount up and begin to decompose.

Nest sanitation also sometimes entails the removal of dead nestlings. Those that die at an early age, which is the most common time for nestling mortality, are carried away by one of the parents. Occasionally, however, an older nestling dies, and if its body is to heavy for an adult to lift, it must be left in the nest.

Learning Independence

As the end of the nestling period approaches, young woodpeckers instinctively prepare for life in the outside world. Regular ascents of the inside walls of the cavity toward the entrance strengthen their lower limbs and the muscles associated with the pygostyle and tail feathers. Although the fledglings' tails are noticeably shorter than those of adults, they serve the same bracing function.

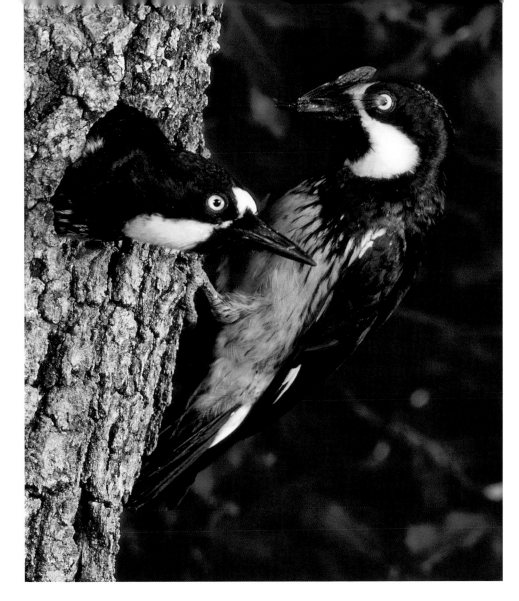

A male acorn woodpecker exits a nest hole while a female bearing food for the young waits to enter.

Older nestlings sometimes sleep clinging to one of the cavity's interior walls, as adults do.

There is no room inside the cavity for movements that would significantly strengthen flight muscles, but nestlings that are almost ready to fledge occasionally teeter on the rim of the nest hole and flex their wings. When they leave the nest the fledglings' wing flight feathers, like those of their tails, will not yet be fully grown. Their first flight will likely be inept and weak, and it will take from one to several days before they are capable of sustained flight.

During the final days before fledging, parents make fewer feeding visits and the nestlings usually lose weight, which may make easier the initial flight on untried wings. Hunger may also be a useful motivator for nest leaving. Nestlings sometimes launch themselves into the larger world spontaneously, but often they must be enticed out of their familiar surroundings. In some species the tried-and-true method of coaxing a reluctant youngster out of the nest is for a parent to hold food just out of reach. In its eagerness to eat, the nestling may lunge too far out of the entrance hole and find itself airborne, in which case it nearly always manages to flutter to a nearby perch. Pileated and white-headed woodpeckers generally take a different approach, encouraging their young to fly by calling and drumming near the nest tree. A disturbance at the nest, such as a threat from a predator, can also prompt flight-ready nestlings to launch.

In most species, once the young have left the nest they do not return, even if some of their siblings are still in residence. The nest may empty within a few hours of the first departure or it may take up to three days for all the nestlings to depart. Any members of the brood that linger in the cavity have an increasing incentive to leave, since the parents' primary focus becomes feeding the fledged young.

Acorn woodpeckers are an exception. The fledglings return to the nest at night to roost and during the day to cadge food being brought to the nestlings that have not yet fledged. If an acorn woodpecker family group nests a second time in the same breeding season, members of the first brood will sometimes help feed the second brood, but they may also enter the nest cavity and intercept provisions intended for the younger birds.

The first flight of many young woodpeckers is to the nearest tree, where they may perch for some time before making any further flying attempts. Lewis's woodpeckers usually do not go even that far; they typically spend two or three days exploring the nest tree after they leave the nest, but do not reenter the cavity.

Observations of recently fledged red-bellied woodpeckers show that the awkwardness of juvenile woodpeckers is not limited to flying. These young birds lack the tongue dexterity that is characteristic of this species, foraging with less coordination than adults. They also tend to get their tails wedged into bark furrows when hitching down tree trunks and may lose their grip or miss a foothold when trying to perch, sometimes falling several feet before recovering. Fledglings of other woodpecker species can be similarly ungainly.

Newly fledged woodpeckers are often inconspicuous as they quietly wait for their parents to bring them food. However, as their flying abilities improve and their confidence increases they usually start following the adults and begging loudly whenever they are hungry. Often the whole family stays together throughout the period of fledgling dependence, but in some species, such as the pileated and black-backed woodpeckers, it is common for the family to split in two, with each parent taking charge of part of the brood and operating independently.

The duration of the association between parents and offspring varies between species and largely depends on how quickly the fledglings can become proficient at foraging. Gleaning insects from tree surfaces is the most easily mastered feeding technique and requires the least physical development. Williamson's sapsuckers quickly figure out how to sustain themselves by gleaning and are usually self-supporting within two days of leaving the nest. Their parents leave them little choice in this matter, since they begin their post-breeding dispersal almost as soon as the young have fledged, or even sooner. Male Williamson's sapsuckers often abandon their broods one or two days before the nestlings are ready to fly.

Other sapsuckers allow their offspring a slightly longer grace period, feeding them insects for anywhere from a few days to two weeks after fledging. Yellow-bellied sapsuckers usually make their first attempts to drill sap wells within a few weeks of fledging, but often choose inappropriate sites, such as dead trees or tree species that produce little sap. By about six weeks of age they have learned to tap suitable trees.

Red-headed woodpeckers are strong fliers from early on and are able to catch insects on the wing soon after they leave the nest. However, for their first few weeks they generally stay very close to the parents, waiting to be fed, and do little independent foraging. By about the 25th day after fledging, the parents refuse to provide any more food, chasing away or even pecking at persistent beggars.

The feeding technique that requires the most physical development is subsurface foraging. It also involves a significant learning component before the woodpecker is able choose locations where prey are most likely to be found. As a result, species that forage primarily by excavating have some of the longest periods of juvenile dependency. Pileated woodpeckers stay with their parents for several months – until at least September – following them everywhere to receive both meals and foraging lessons.

Juvenile ivory-billed woodpeckers remained reliant on their parents for many months, possibly until or beyond the next nesting season. This exceptionally long period of dependency was likely related to how long it took for the bill to develop enough to be able to strip tight bark from trees and gain access to the large beetle larvae that sustained this species. The related pale-billed woodpecker also has a long period of juvenile dependency.

Once their offspring become independent, most woodpecker parents are finished with their reproductive efforts for the year, but they may exhibit a resurgence of courtship and nesting behavior. If conditions are favorable, members of some species will undertake a second or even a third nesting attempt in a single breeding season. Five of the North American species known to sometimes raise multiple broods are in the genus *Melanerpes*; these are the acorn, gila, golden-fronted, red-bellied and red-headed woodpeckers. Northern flickers and red-cockaded woodpeckers also produce an occasional second or third brood.

Pairs that make successive nesting attempts may or may not wait until the first brood is independent. Red-headed woodpeckers that lay second clutches often begin while they are still feeding fledglings from their first brood. Gila woodpeckers may also excavate a new nest cavity and incubate a second clutch while still feeding their first brood at the original nest. Observation of one pair of gilas showed that they accomplished this complex and taxing parenting feat by trading back and forth between incubation and food delivery – a departure from this species' usual division of labor, whereby males spend more time guarding the nest and females concentrate on feeding the young.

Chapter 5

Reproduction and Mortality

Woodpeckers, like all living beings, are profoundly shaped by the biological imperative to introduce as many copies of their genetic material as possible into the world before they die. Woodpeckers reach sexual maturity within their first year and will breed annually for the rest of their lives, provided they can acquire a breeding territory and a mate. If they can avoid predators, bad weather and food shortages, they may live for a decade or longer.

Mating Strategies

Monogamy is by far the most common mating system for birds in general. Likewise, within the Picidae family nearly all species approach breeding on the basis of one male, one female, one nest.

The duration of the pair bond varies among monogamous woodpecker species. In some species mates maintain loose bonds during the non-breeding season. In others they separate completely. Either way, pairings may last only a single season or for several years in a row. The pileated woodpecker is one of the few North American species known to mate for life, and the male and female usually stay close together throughout the seasons as they move about their permanent territory.

In many woodpecker species that do not have year-round territories, individuals commonly reclaim the same breeding territory – and often the same nest tree – each spring. If both members of a pair survive the winter, nest-site fidelity usually leads to renewal of the pair bond. Whether mates stay in contact through the winter or are reunited in spring, courtship is usually shorter and less intense for established pairs than for new pairs. This benefits established pairs by allowing them to start nesting earlier than first-time breeders and birds that are initiating new unions.

The second most common avian mating strategy is known as multiple-nest polygyny, in which one male mates with two or more females during a single breeding season and each female has her own nest. Multiple-nest polygyny is not a viable option for woodpeckers because the nest is always attended by the male at night, from the time incubation begins until the young depart. It is impossible for one father to fulfill this duty at two nests simultaneously. A few woodpecker species, none of them North American, are known to make rare attempts at this type of mating, but they usually fail to produce fledglings.

A pair of downy woodpeckers (male below) in autumn.

A third strategy is multiple-nest polyandry, in which one female mates with and lays eggs in the nests of two or more males. This situation is extremely uncommon among woodpeckers. It has been reported for only four species, with only a few documented cases.

The sole North American species known to practice multiple-nest polyandry is the northern flicker, normally a monogamous species. In 2001 biologist Karen L. Wiebe realized that a female flicker in her study area was simultaneously raising two broods with two males in separate nests about 500 yards (450 m) apart. The flicker began laying at the second nest while the clutch in her first nest was still being incubated. She divided her time between the two nests and assisted both males with incubation, brooding and feeding. Six young fledged from the first nest. Nine days later seven fledged from the second. With a reproductive output of 13 offspring that year, polyandry was clearly a profitable strategy for this female, but this was the only instance that Wiebe observed during four years of intensively studying northern flickers, and no other attempts have been reported elsewhere.

Multiple-nest polyandry probably remains rare among woodpeckers because nesting success usually requires the contributions of both parents, especially early in the nesting period, when almost constant incubation of the eggs and brooding of the young nestlings is needed. If one member of a pair dies or abandons its mate at this time, successful single parenthood is unlikely. Even once the nestlings are capable of keeping themselves warm, the effort of providing enough food for them may prove too exhausting for one adult. However, a few male woodpeckers have been known to successfully raise a brood on their own after losing their mates. Occasionally a bird that has lost its mate partway through the breeding season will attract a new partner that helps to care for the young despite having no genetic relationship to them. The payoff for the stepparent is that it establishes a pair bond, which increases its likelihood of breeding the following year.

Cooperative breeding differs significantly from the previous strategies, in that it is a group effort involving both breeders and non-breeding helpers that share the job of raising the young. Two North American woodpeckers, the red-cockaded and the acorn, are classified as cooperative breeders, though some breeding members of these species nest without benefit of helpers. Not surprisingly, nests tended by both breeders and helpers produce more fledglings than nests of unassisted breeders.

Red-cockaded woodpeckers are monogamous cooperative breeders. Each family group includes only one breeding pair. The other members of the group never fertilize or lay eggs as long as their status remains that of helper. Few male red-cockaded woodpeckers get an opportunity to breed until they are several years old, and some live out their lives as non-breeders. At first glance it seems that juvenile males would be better off striking out on their own, as most other woodpeckers do. However, it takes months or even years for a red-cockaded woodpecker to excavate a new nest cavity in a live pine, the only type of tree used by this species for nesting. This means that a young male without a territory is better off competing for a breeding vacancy in an established territory with existing cavities than trying to start from scratch in an unoccupied area.

Males have two ways of gaining breeding status. A juvenile can stay home as a helper and wait to inherit his natal territory when the breeding male dies, while also watching for vacancies to emerge in neighboring territories. Or he can disperse and search for a vacant territory, then try to attract a mate once he has acquired a home. Statistically his chances of success are about equal, regardless of which strategy he chooses. Males that remain as helpers tend to face a longer delay before breeding than those that depart, but departers have a higher mortality rate, as their wanderings take them into unfamiliar territory.

For young female red-cockaded woodpeckers the situation is different. Only males inherit territories, so the best strategy for their sisters is to disperse from the natal territory and search elsewhere for a breeding vacancy or the opportunity to depose a breeding female. Juvenile females almost never stay home and become helpers.

Acorn woodpeckers practice a very different sort of cooperative breeding. This species' unusual system of plural breeding is referred to as opportunistic polygynandry – a combination of both polygyny and polyandry that is adopted whenever the opportunity arises. Acorn woodpeckers live in groups of one to seven breeding males and one to three breeding females. If there is only one male and one female, they are necessarily monogamous, and in some populations of acorn woodpeckers this is the usual situation. When there is more than one member of either sex, the birds do not pair off. Instead all the breeding males compete with each other to mate with all of the breeding females, and the females lay their eggs in a single nest.

The non-breeding helpers are of both sexes and are usually the offspring of the breeders. Helpers may leave to become breeders in other groups that have breeding vacancies, but they can gain breeding status in their natal group only if all the breeders of the opposite sex disappear and are replaced by unrelated individuals. Co-breeding relationships between fathers and sons or mothers and daughters are relatively common, but incest almost never occurs, because breeding vacancies are always filled by outsiders; helper-daughters do not take their mother's place when she dies and helper-sons do not take their father's.

Opportunistic polygynandry influences the acorn woodpecker's breeding behavior in several ways. Acorn woodpeckers have briefer sexual engagements than other North American woodpeckers, with little or no pre-copulatory ritual. When there is more than one breeding male in a group, the females seem secretive about mating. If the other breeding males in the group observe sexual activity in progress they frequently try to interrupt it. Males also usually try to mount a female immediately after she finishes copulating with one of their co-breeders. As a result of this rivalry females often mate with more than one male during the egg-laying period. Since paternity is uncertain, all of the co-breeding males have a stake in raising the young.

Rivalry between joint-nesting female acorn woodpeckers also gives rise to a dramatic form of competition that biologists Walter Koenig and Ronald Mumme have dubbed the egg-demolition derby. In groups that have more than one breeding female there is a high rate of mutual egg destruction. When one female begins laying before her co-breeders, they frequently remove her eggs from the nest. The competing female carries the stolen egg to a tree and stores it in a crevice as if it were an acorn, which leads to its consumption by members of the group, often including the mother. The first-laying female often retaliates in kind. In one typical nest the first female laid four eggs, all of which were removed by her co-breeder. Two days later the second female started laying, and each of her three eggs was removed by the first female. Finally, after an 18-day break from laying, the two produced eggs at the same time and incubation proceeded without further destruction.

Although costly to the participants in terms of energy, egg-demolition derbies can go on for days or weeks. Their value is that they synchronize egg laying by joint-nesting females. If a female permits her co-breeder to get a head start and does not add her own eggs to the nest until some days later, she risks having her late-hatching young neglected in favor of the more advanced nestlings. The resolution of these contests is often reached when, for reasons that are not clear to biologists, one female finally allows her co-breeder's egg to remain in the nest and lays one of her own beside it. The females then complete the clutch over the next few days. Sometimes peace is established only when two females lay eggs simultaneously while inside the cavity together, since neither can distinguish her own contribution from her competitor's.

Although acorn and red-cockaded woodpeckers are the only true cooperative breeders among North American picids, there are occasional reports of nests of other species being attended by more than two adults. One threesome of red-breasted sapsuckers delivered food to a nest in Oregon, and a mixed group consisting of a male red-breasted sapsucker, a female red-naped and a female hybrid jointly tended a nest and reared five young together in northeastern California. In Ohio a researcher saw an extra female feeding nestlings at four of 13 downy woodpecker nests and was able to determine that none of the helpers was the daughter of the pair she was assisting. When there is no direct kinship to the nestlings, non-parental feeding is probably motivated by the possibility, however remote, of acquiring a mate. Unmated male Williamson's sapsuckers sometimes feed their neighbors' nestlings despite active discouragement from the parents. If a male of this species abandons its family before the young fledge, a bachelor will readily move in and take over his feeding duties.

Nest Site Selection

Once territorial boundaries have been defined and pair bonds cemented, the first order of business is to select a nest site. The ideal cavity tree is one that calls for minimal excavating effort and provides maximum shelter and security.

Species that are strong excavators generally choose live or recently dead trees with sound sapwood and decay-softened heartwood. Weaker excavators must settle for trees in more advanced stages of decay, and often begin their excavations in knotholes or cracks. Among the North American woodpeckers, relatively weak excavators include northern and gilded flickers and downy and red-headed woodpeckers, but even they have superior excavating skills compared to birds outside the Picidae family.

A gilded flicker surveys the world from the doorway of his saguaro cactus home.

Whether alive or dead, the ideal tree for cavity excavation has a hard outer shell and a yielding inner core. This condition is created by tree-decay fungi that attack the heartwood of live trees but not the sapwood. These fungi usually enter living trees through deep wounds caused by branch or top breakage, lightning strikes or frost cracks. Decades may pass before the tree dies. Meanwhile the central column of decayed wood becomes more extensive, offering increasing opportunity for cavity excavation. Some woodpeckers return year after year to the same tree – or even the same branch – and add another nest hole. If the decay column develops upward, each new excavation will be made higher than the previous year's nest. If the decay travels downward, the new nest will be lower. In Montana researchers found a larch tree that contained 40 red-naped sapsucker nests. The oldest were high up, close to where the trunk had snapped off and the decay fungi had entered, and subsequent ones were progressively lower.

In terms of protection from the elements, live wood is superior to dead wood, and the larger the diameter of the trunk or branch the better. Generally cavities in live trees heat and cool more slowly than those in dead trees, and cavities in large-diameter trees change temperature more slowly than those in smaller trees. As a result, cavities in large live trees are warmer at night and have more stable temperatures overall, while cavities in snags and in small-diameter trees are subject to greater temperature extremes, being hotter by day and colder by night. Position in the landscape is an additional consideration; exposed trees along the edges of stands cool more at night than trees deeper in the forest.

The internal temperature of a cavity is also affected by the orientation of its entrance to the sun and wind. In more northerly or high-elevation regions, which have cool summers and cold winters, woodpeckers often orient the cavity opening to take full advantage of solar heating. In hotter regions they may minimize heat in the nest by facing the cavity entrance away from direct sun; however, wintertime roosting cavities in these areas may have a different orientation to benefit from the sun's warm rays during the cooler months. In areas subject to the chilling effect of prevailing winds, cavity doorways are often on the sheltered side of the tree. Small to medium-sized woodpeckers often orient their cavities so that the doorway is on the underside of a branch or a leaning trunk, sometimes facing almost straight down, so it is sheltered from rain.

The cavity trees that are most impervious to the elements are also the best choice in terms of security. Large-diameter trees have room for cavities with thick walls and long entrance tunnels, which help deter marauders that try to tear open or reach into cavities. These trees are also likely to be tall, allowing the woodpeckers to reduce their exposure to snakes and other climbing predators by locating cavities high above the ground. Live trees are preferable to snags because they are less susceptible to wind damage and less vulnerable to certain predators.

As a rule, live wood provides a better defense than hard deadwood, which is better than soft, decayed wood. However, dead trees do offer certain security incentives. Predators, especially snakes, have more difficulty climbing smooth, branchless trunks than trees with limbs and rough or furrowed bark. Red-headed woodpeckers routinely select snags with the least amount of bark for their cavity trees, probably as a defense against tree-climbing snakes. Predator deterrence may also be why ivory-billed woodpeckers stripped away any bark directly below their cavity entrance holes. In addition, the lack of foliage on snags and on dead branches of live trees makes it easier for woodpeckers to fly directly to their entrance holes and harder for predators to lurk near cavities or to approach unseen.

Most woodpecker species prefer particular tree species as cavity trees; they are influenced partly by regional availability and partly by the qualities of the trees. Woodpeckers that excavate cavities in live wood usually select deciduous trees because most conifers respond to wounding by producing sticky resins, often in copious amounts. Conifer snags are favored by some woodpeckers because these trees are generally slow to decay after they die and can provide prime excavation potential for many decades.

In North America, trembling aspens, also known as quaking aspens, probably house more woodpecker cavities than any other tree species. The trembling aspen is the continent's most widely distributed tree species and it has numerous attributes that make it eminently suitable for woodpecker purposes. Aspens have relatively soft sapwood that is easy for woodpeckers to excavate into when the tree is alive; they produce little sap when wounded; they are susceptible to a type of decay fungus that produces an ideally soft core; they can remain standing for years after they die; and their bark retains its integrity even when wood decay is well advanced, a significant advantage for weak excavators. Aspens also offer relatively good security because they have very smooth bark and few branches on the main trunk.

Where suitable cavity trees are absent or scarce, some woodpeckers will use other types of plants. In desert habitats of the southwestern United States and northern Mexico, gilded flickers and gila woodpeckers strongly favor the lofty columns of saguaro cacti, while ladder-backed woodpeckers often nest in the easily excavated flower stalks of agaves.

The weaker excavators are by necessity relatively flexible in their choice of cavity sites, often excavating in wood that is well decayed or reusing old nest cavities. These species are also the most inclined to take advantage of human additions to the landscape. In the arid, largely treeless areas of the American Southwest, the proliferation of fence posts and telegraph poles during the late 1800s and early 1900s was instrumental in the range expansion of the golden-fronted and red-bellied woodpeckers. Farther north, settlement brought other novel opportunities. In the days when abandoned wagon parts still lay scattered across the open prairie, both northern flickers and red-headed woodpeckers occasionally nested in old wheel hubs. There were also reports of red-headed woodpeckers nesting between the shares of an upturned plow and in the box of a grain drill left standing in a field. Northern flickers have nested in barrels, a haystack and a crevice in an unused chimney. Unlike most woodpeckers, golden-fronted, red-headed and Lewis's woodpeckers and northern flickers sometimes raise their families in nest boxes.

Cavity Preparation

Cavity excavation appears to be fundamental to pair bonding. Woodpeckers that reuse existing cavities often spend some time renovating before they move in, cleaning out any accumulated debris or pecking at the inside walls and tossing chips out the entrance hole. Although this activity may have some practical benefits, its main function is most likely ceremonial.

During new home construction or renovations, woodpeckers like this red-breasted sapsucker, may be seen tossing out wood dust and shavings by the bill-full.

Males sometimes begin work on nest holes before they have acquired a partner. Unmated male Williamson's sapsuckers are particularly inclined toward excavating cavities and defending breeding territory in anticipation of winning a mate. Even if they are unsuccessful they often persevere long after their neighbors have begun nesting. One bachelor excavated four cavities in three trees before finally admitting defeat and abandoning his territory.

Normally both sexes participate in nest-cavity construction, but not equally. The division of labor depends largely on immediate circumstances and perhaps individual personality. Usually the male puts in more time on the job, but sometimes the reverse occurs. The females' limited contribution to excavation may be an adaptation to allow them to build their energy reserves for egg production. Females often increase their involvement near the end of the process, especially if the time for egg laying is fast approaching. They are more likely to play a dominant role in excavation if the nest is started late.

Nest cavities are usually excavated just before egg laying. Cactus-nesters such as the gila woodpecker and gilded flicker are an exception – they must complete their work several months before occupation to give the soft, moist inner pulp time to dry and harden. The year-round excavation work of red-cockaded woodpeckers is a unique response to unusual circumstances. The high sap production and hard sapwood of the live pines in which they nest and roost make the excavation process exceedingly slow. Whenever the resin flow becomes too heavy, the excavator must stop and wait until it stops and the sticky liquid crystallizes. Between these delays and the demanding task of tunneling through many inches of solid wood to get to the tree's decay-softened core, red-cockaded woodpecker cavities can take from several months to many years to complete.

The first step in any cavity excavation is to chisel a funnel-shaped hole, which is then steadily enlarged and deepened to form the entranceway. The woodpecker perches below the hole as it works. For the most part, any wood debris that accumulates in the opening is simply tossed to one side. As the work progresses, the excavator's head and shoulders start disappearing into the hole. Observers who are familiar with the sounds a particular woodpecker species makes when foraging will notice a difference in the sounds of cavity excavating. Downy woodpeckers, for example, pursue subsurface insects with a quiet, rapid rhythm that can be easily distinguished from the louder strikes and slower, more methodical pace of their cavity construction efforts.

Sooner or later the woodpecker starts digging down toward what will become the main part of the cavity. In live and recently dead trees, excavation of the vertical link to the nesting chamber does not usually begin until the tunnel has passed through the hard outer layer of sapwood and reached the softer heartwood. As downward excavation proceeds, the woodpecker perches on the lower rim of the entrance hole and leans ever farther inside, eventually leaving in view only its tail, joggling with each strike of the bill. At this point the only way the woodpecker can exit is to back up, a difficult exercise that often involves a certain amount of struggle and much mussing of feathers.

The situation improves once the woodpecker starts enlarging the main chamber. Soon there is enough room to turn around and exit headfirst. During the rest of the excavation process the woodpecker will often pop its head out the door and fling away a bill-full of woodchips or fine wood dust. Sometimes it may fly away and drop them elsewhere. When one member of the pair starts a new shift or the same bird returns after a break, the worker often begins with a session of flinging construction debris out the door. Fresh woodchips at the base of a tree are a sure sign of an excavation in progress or recently completed. New cavities may also be recognized by the contrasting color of the raw wood around the entrance hole.

The inner chamber of a finished nest cavity is more or less pear-shaped – if there is sufficient room for expansion at the bottom – or cylindrical if it is situated in a small-diameter trunk or branch. The final interior dimensions are governed by the size of the excavator. Ivory-billed woodpecker nest cavities were about 18 to 25 inches (45–64 cm) deep from roof to floor and about 9 to 11 inches (22–27 cm) in diameter at the widest point, near the bottom of the chamber. Downy woodpecker nest cavities range from about 6 to 12 inches (15–30 cm) deep, with an interior base diameter of about 2 to 3.5 inches (5–9 cm).

In most tree species the main chamber of a woodpecker cavity is usually contained within the heartwood. In ponderosa pines, however, the entire cavity is often in the outer wood. Unlike most other North American conifers, ponderosa pines have a very thick sapwood layer, which can comprise 50 to 75 percent of the tree's volume and typically decays quickly after the tree dies. Ponderosa pines also have very thick bark – up to four inches (10 cm) thick on mature trees. The bark remains intact for many years after the tree's death, providing a strong outer wall for cavities excavated in the sapwood.

To deter predators and minimize exposure to the elements, woodpeckers make their cavity entrance holes as small as possible. The primary architect of the nest cavity, usually the male, designs the entrance in relation to his body size. But a comfortable fit for him may be a tight squeeze for his mate, especially when she is ready to lay an egg. During the egg-laying period, biologist Lawrence Kilham watched one female downy woodpecker bow into her nest entrance 27 times as she attempted to enter it. After a pause she returned to the entrance and tried another 45 times before succeeding. Leaving the cavity was equally difficult; it involved a great deal of exertion and much head bobbing as she forced her body through the hole. Kilham also noted a female yellow-bellied sapsucker that, weeks after egg laying, still had to struggle to fit through the doorway of her nest when she was coming and going with food for her young.

Some woodpecker species, such as the downy, create cavity entrance holes that are remarkably perfect in their roundness. The rest are slightly to distinctly oval. Those of ivory-billed woodpeckers are about one inch (2.5 cm) higher than they were wide, possibly to provide head room for their exceptionally large crests. The egg-shaped nest-cavity entrance holes made by pileated woodpeckers may also be designed to accommodate head crests.

The length of time for nest-cavity excavation varies from species to species, taking three to six weeks for pileated woodpeckers, three to four weeks for white-headed woodpeckers and one to two weeks for the majority of other North American woodpeckers. The time required depends partly on external factors such as the condition of the tree, but often seems to be driven by the pair's sense of urgency. It is not advantageous to complete a cavity too far in advance, because this increases the length of time it will have to be defended against other birds that might try to commandeer it. On the other hand, not having the nest ready when conditions are best for egg laying is also undesirable. In an apparent effort to balance these concerns, woodpeckers often devote little time initially to excavation and then increase the length and frequency of their shifts as the work progresses.

Sometimes preparations for nesting are prolonged because the pair abandons their partially completed cavity and starts anew, presumably because the initial site was found to be unsuitable. This does not necessarily represent wasted effort – some incomplete nests are deep enough to be used as future roosting sites.

Nobody knows exactly how woodpeckers decide which tree is best for housing a cavity or whether they have ways of assessing the suitability of a site before they start work. Perhaps they recognize that fungal fruiting bodies, or conks, on the outside of a tree indicate the presence of internal decay. Or they may be guided by the presence of injuries such as broken tops or branch stubs, which mark entry points for decay fungi. However, heartrot can be present without any external signs, so they may need to make appraisals in other ways, such as by tapping with the beak to gauge the soundness of the inner wood. Whatever their methods, they are obviously not foolproof, since false starts are a regular occurrence for all species. White-headed woodpeckers (for reasons that are not yet understood) are especially prone to abandoning nest cavities in mid-excavation.

When mates change places during excavation they often engage in species-specific behavior that includes drumming, tapping, vocalizations or displays, alone or in combination. Nest-relief rituals may announce the partner's arrival and indicate its willingness to take over, or be used to summon the absent partner. They also help reinforce the pair bond. Some woodpeckers continue to perform these rituals during the incubating and brooding period, but not as frequently as during excavation.

Usually the bird that is outside the cavity will wait until its mate leaves before entering. Male lineated and pileated woodpeckers, however, seem prone to possessiveness. One male lineated woodpecker declined to leave the nest cavity on seven of 30 occasions when his mate came to relieve him. The female balked only twice, both times just before or during the egg-laying period; the male responded by climbing into the cavity on top of her and forcing her out. On two other occasions during the laying period the female reversed the situation and asserted her right of entry. One time when she entered the occupied cavity her mate departed after about 30 seconds, and the other time she left again almost immediately. Male pileated woodpeckers have been seen expelling their mates in the same manner during the egg-laying period.

Sexual Activity

Once the female begins laying, frequent mating is important to ensure that each day's egg is successfully fertilized. During this period woodpeckers often copulate several times a day, sometimes in quick succession. But an observation of a sexual encounter does not necessarily indicate that egg-laying is in progress. Woodpeckers usually begin copulating a week or so before the clutch is begun and incomplete mating attempts may occur even earlier. This advance sexual activity strengthens the pair bond. Often it occurs immediately after an intruder has been ejected from the pair's territory. Some woodpeckers continue with intermittent mating during the incubation period and after hatching; these copulations are not always fully completed.

Woodpeckers usually mate at or near the nest tree, generally on a horizontal branch or the broken top of a trunk. Pairs often favor a single site through-

These young northern flickers are almost ready to leave their nest. The first few weeks after fledging will be the most dangerous part of their lives.

out one breeding season. Either sex may initiate an encounter by drumming or calling, often from the designated copulation branch, or by tapping at the nest-cavity entrance. Intimate calls may be uttered by one or both birds before or during copulation.

When a female is ready to mate she perches lengthwise or crosswise on the branch. Females of many species assume a low crouched posture. Red-breasted, red-naped and yellow-bellied sapsuckers lift their tails and droop their wings slightly, holding them away from the body; sometimes they throw their heads up until the bill points almost backward. Female downy woodpeckers stand in a more upright position with the tail pointing straight out, head up and tilted backward, breast thrust out, and wings slightly dropped.

Once the female has assumed her invitation pose, the male hops or flutters onto her back. While she lifts her tail he slips gradually to one side, angling his tail underneath hers so that the cloacal (reproductive) openings of the two birds make contact. As he slides off her back he may maintain his balance by waving his wings or brace himself with one wing. The male ends up lying either alongside his mate or with his body more or less at a right angle to hers, some-times on his back. Males of some species, including sapsuckers and hairy, red-headed, red-bellied and golden-fronted woodpeckers, seem to be more likely than others to end up in a perpendicular final position.

Curiously, male woodpeckers nearly always fall to the left when copulating. One aberrant male pileated woodpecker consistently fell to the right, and he usually had to mount two or three times before the union was effectively com-pleted. During one mating session a lineated woodpecker was also observed falling uncharacteristically to the right.

Red-bellied, red-headed and golden-fronted woodpeckers also regularly per-form a sexual behavior known as reverse mounting, in which the female hops or flutters onto the male's back and remains there briefly. Reverse mounting is often followed by conventional copulation, in which the male mounts the female.

Successful copulation typically takes about 10 to 20 seconds, with the period of cloacal contact lasting from five to 15 seconds. Afterwards the male usually flies away immediately. The female may remain motionless on the branch for a while or may fly to another location. Both sexes commonly preen after copulating.

Mortality

Woodpeckers are much longer lived than many other birds because cavity dwelling significantly reduces vulnerability to predators and to inclement weather. Little is known about average life expectancy or maximum lifespan for most woodpecker species, but studies of marked individuals indicate that those who make it through their first year of life have a relatively high rate of year-to-year survival as adults and will probably live for several years or longer. Longevity records for North American species include a male acorn wood-pecker known to be at least 16 years old and a female hairy woodpecker of at least 15 years and 10 months. One male red-bellied woodpecker that was banded as a nestling was recaptured 12 years and one month later and judged to be in fine condition at that time.

Despite the advantages of cavity nesting, woodpecker eggs and nestlings are at risk from predators that can breach the defenses of the nest tree. Bears and raccoons sometimes succeed in tearing into cavities, especially if the walls are thin or the wood is rotten. The size of most entrance holes is no deterrent for small mammals. Chipmunks, squirrels, deer mice and weasels are among the most frequent raiders of woodpecker nests. A number of birds, including European starlings, English sparrows, house wrens, jays, crows and some species of woodpeckers, also prey on eggs and nestlings, sometimes in the course of trying to take over a nest cavity. In many southern regions of North America the most deadly cavity-nest predators are tree-climbing rat snakes and bull snakes.

Nocturnal invaders have the advantages of darkness and surprise, and male woodpeckers sleeping in the nest at night are sometimes killed along with their brood. In the daytime, however, parents are often able to fend off attacks. The woodpecker bill is a formidable weapon, and an adult striking from the protected vantage of the cavity entrance hole is usually able to repel an invader. Woodpeckers may also mount a fierce defense from outside the nest, flying at potential predators and trying to drive them off if they approach the nest too closely. One pair of red-bellied woodpeckers refused to tolerate a southern flying squirrel that was trying to roost in an abandoned cavity in their nest tree. They attacked repeatedly, and one of the birds grabbed the squirrel and tossed it to the ground at least twice.

The intensity with which woodpeckers defend their nests seems to be partly a species characteristic and partly a matter of individual temperament and other factors that may not be obvious to observers. Red-bellied woodpeckers are relatively aggressive and have proven themselves capable of forcing snakes climbing toward their nest to retreat by diving and striking at them, yet one timid pair kept their distance from a rat snake lurking visibly in a vacant cavity below their nest, eventually losing their brood to this predator. Acorn woodpeckers find strength in numbers, sometimes mobbing a snake as it climbs toward or enters a nest. They typically swoop at the marauder, pecking at its head or body, and have been known to pull a bull snake out of a cavity and force it to fall to the ground.

Once they leave the nest, woodpeckers face a different set of enemies, the most formidable being raptors, including northern goshawks, red-tailed hawks, Cooper's hawks, sharp-shinned hawks and American kestrels. Recently fledged birds are at significant risk because they are generally poor fliers and have not yet learned to recognize and avoid such dangers. One observer saw an American kestrel dispatch a couple of young Lewis's woodpeckers by swooping down from a perch and snatching each one as it emerged and began to climb up the nest tree for the first time. Adult Lewis's woodpeckers, on the other hand, have been known to battle with American kestrels and escape unharmed.

When experienced woodpeckers spot a bird of prey they usually move swiftly to the side of the trunk or limb opposite the predator's line of approach, then draw close to the tree and remain motionless and silent until the coast is clear. They may resort to evasive flight if necessary or duck into a cavity or dense foliage if either is nearby. Woodpeckers often make alarm calls when predators appear, and white rump patches or wing markings that flash when the bird takes flight may serve as visual warning signals for some species.

Although woodpeckers that regularly forage on or near the ground seem to suffer few losses to terrestrial predators, they must remain constantly alert to the danger. One of the few recorded observations of terrestrial predation describes a snake attack on an adult northern flicker in Tennessee. According to her account, Mrs. Sanford Duncan heard a commotion in her yard and found a group of flickers "dashing and darting at a bundle of something on the ground. Closer inspection with field glasses showed it was a snake, all tied up in a curious knot. He was too big for me to attack with the hoe I had, so I shot into the 'bundle' with a shotgun. As if by magic the snake flung himself into the air and fell, straightened out, over five feet long, and disclosed a full-grown Flicker that he had wrapped himself around many times. The Flicker was still alive, but died very shortly, probably from the gunshot that killed the bullsnake."

Most natural mortality of adult woodpeckers is due to predation, but starvation and inclement weather can take a toll, especially in winter. Some woodpeckers meet their demise in mishaps associated specifically with cavity use. The best cavity trees are usually the oldest in a stand and often their tops rise high above the rest of the forest canopy, where they may act like lightning rods. One observer found a female flicker burnt to death in her nest after the tree was struck by lightning. Because of interior decay, cavity trees are also susceptible to being blown down or snapped in two during storms. If woodpeckers are inside their roosting or nest cavities when these forces of nature strike, survival is simply a matter of luck. On the other hand, being outside during a storm can be equally risky. In a bizarre weather-related calamity, one red-bellied woodpecker died when it was blown into a tree trunk with such force that it was impaled on a branch.

Roosting

Other than when incubating eggs and brooding nestlings, woodpeckers almost never sleep inside cavities during the day. At night, however, adults of most species roost indoors. Juveniles generally have no choice but to sleep outside for the first several days or weeks after fledging – until they can find a vacant cavity or excavate a new one of their own.

Among North American woodpeckers the sapsuckers are the least inclined to use cavities for nocturnal roosting. Throughout the breeding season, adult females sleep in the open on a tree trunk, often sheltered by foliage. As with other species, male sapsuckers begin occupying the nest cavity at night during the later stages of excavation and continue to sleep there until their offspring fledge, or a few days before. After the young leave the nest, male sapsuckers return to sleeping outdoors. During the non-breeding season yellow-bellied sapsuckers never use cavities, while Williamson's sapsuckers roost in old nest holes or natural cavities. Little is known about the roosting habits of red-breasted and red-naped sapsuckers during migration and through the winter.

When woodpeckers sleep outside they typically do so in a vertical position, hanging onto a tree trunk or other perpendicular surface, with the head turned and the bill tucked under the scapular feathers on the back to minimize heat loss. Often they will seek the shelter of an overhanging limb or some other protected niche. Northern flickers sometimes spend nights under the eaves of buildings or beneath bridges.

When roosting in cavities, woodpeckers often sleep clinging to an inner wall. A biologist studying white-headed woodpeckers in Oregon observed that they sometimes slept on the floor of the cavity with their tail propped up against a wall and their head tucked to one side. This sleeping position may also be

White-headed wood-peckers usually excavate a new nest cavity each spring. Come winter, the vacated quarters may be among the night-time roosts used by this male.

used by other species. Cavities offer woodpeckers two significant advantages over open roosting: security and comfort. Like many birds, woodpeckers have poor nocturnal vision and are extremely vulnerable in the dark. Once they are settled into a cavity for the night – having first checked to see that no enemy lies in wait – they are hidden from view and out of reach of most predators.

Adults of many woodpecker species maintain one or more alternative roost sites. This ensures that accommodation is available even if a cavity is taken over by a trespasser, a cavity tree is felled by the wind or a prowler forces a sudden evacuation at night. Pileated woodpeckers, among others, will quickly leave their roost and relocate if they hear a mammal climbing the tree (or a human

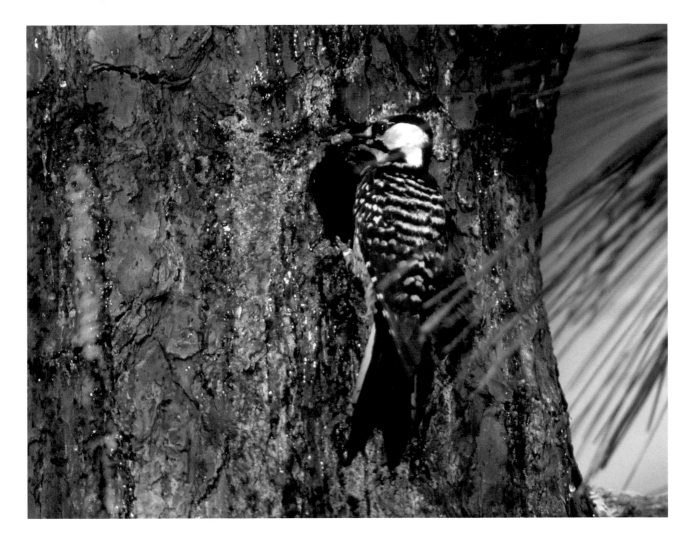

scratching the trunk). Having access to multiple roosts may also serve other functions. Woodpeckers probably reduce their risk of predation if they periodically vary where they spend the night. For species with large home ranges, using roosts in different areas reduces the commuting distance to various foraging sites, thus conserving energy.

Two species whose roosting habits have been closely studied are the pileated and white-headed woodpeckers. Pileated woodpeckers tracked in the Pacific Northwest during the non-breeding season used from four to 11 roost trees apiece. White-headed woodpeckers in central Oregon used as many as 13 different roost trees over a five-month period, changing sites weekly to biweekly. In summer and early fall the white-headed woodpeckers usually roosted in cavities, but sometimes tucked in under sloughing bark or in cracks and crevices in tree trunks. After the first snowfall in November they always slept in cavities, and each bird used the same roost hole for most of the rest of the winter.

It is not surprising that white-headed woodpeckers choose to pass winter nights in enclosed roosts. In Canada and throughout much of the United

Red-cockaded woodpeckers deter climbing snakes by surrounding cavity entrances with shallow holes that ooze sticky sap. Fresh clear resin on the trunk indicates an active nest or roost cavity where daily pecking at the tree wounds maintains the flow.

States, night is a critical time for overwintering birds. Temperatures plummet after sunset and there is no chance to refuel during the long hours of darkness. On a cold, blustery winter night there is no better place for a woodpecker than inside a tree cavity. Thermal inertia ensures that the interior of the cavity cools more slowly than the outside air, while the solid walls cut the wind, reducing convective heat loss. In addition, the woodpecker's own body heat raises the cavity temperature. A researcher who measured the temperature inside roost cavities of hairy woodpeckers in midwinter in Minnesota found that they averaged 37 to 43 degrees Fahrenheit (3°–6°C) warmer than the exterior of the tree. During the most extreme weather in winter, energy conserved by cavity roosting may tip the scales between survival and death. Even in areas with relatively mild winters, cavity roosting helps offset the energy stress that can arise when cool temperatures combine with limited food supplies and reduced foraging time.

Acorn woodpeckers are the only North American picids that routinely roost communally. On most nights throughout the year, two or more acorn woodpeckers from the same family group share a single cavity. The average number of co-roosting birds is three, but groups of up to 14 have been counted. Some communally roosting bird species reduce individual heat loss by crowding together, but acorn woodpeckers are not huddlers. Nevertheless, they realize significant energy savings simply by sharing their quarters. A study of acorn woodpeckers conducted at the Hastings Natural History Reservation in California found that when the outside air temperature was 32° Fahrenheit (0°C), the temperature inside an unoccupied cavity averaged 40° Fahrenheit (4.4°C), but in a cavity occupied by four woodpeckers it averaged 50.5° Fahrenheit (10.3°C). At the same outside temperature, a woodpecker roosting alone raised the cavity temperature to only 42° Fahrenheit (5.5°C).

Even though the thermal benefits of communal roosting increase with the number of birds, whole family groups of acorn woodpeckers seldom roost together in one cavity. The reason they split up at night may be to reduce the risk of their entire genetic investment being wiped out by a single calamity. Besides the obvious hazards of predator attack or cavity branch breakage, there is also the possibility of accidental entrapment, a fate that befell one group at the Hastings Reservation. Two males that had been roosting together apparently tried to leave simultaneously and ended up with their shoulders wedged so tightly into the opening that they could go neither forward nor back. Their dehydrated remains were found stuck in the doorway and the body of a female was found inside, where she had expired because of her forced confinement. Other members of the group survived this fatal incident, but the loss left them unable to defend their territory from usurpers and they were subsequently driven off.

The only other North American species that has been observed to break the pattern of solitary roosting is the pileated woodpecker. Researchers infrequently come across a pair spending the night under the same roof. There is also one record of an adult male sharing a roost cavity with a juvenile.

Cavities created specifically for roosting are usually excavated after the breeding season, before winter sets in, and they are often completed more quickly than nest cavities. Downy woodpeckers, which may work on nest cavities for up to 20 days, have been known to complete roosting cavities in as little as three to four days. If the woodpecker is lacking nighttime shelter, this speediness can be a product of necessity. As well, roosting cavities are often not as deep as nest cavities.

Because sleeping quarters need not meet such exacting specifications as the cavities that house vulnerable eggs and nestlings, some woodpecker species rarely or never excavate specifically for roosting. Instead they make use of old nest cavities (not necessarily of their own making), holes abandoned after false starts, natural openings or niches in trees. Several species of woodpeckers occasionally roost in nest boxes.

A large investment of time and energy is required to produce cavities big enough for pileated and lineated woodpeckers, so members of these species often roost in hollowed-out sections of trunk in large-diameter trees infected with heartwood decay. Many hollow-trunk roosts have multiple natural doorways created by knotholes, cracks and open tops. Pileated and lineated woodpeckers sometimes also excavate secondary openings. Although a roost with a single opening is more protected from the elements, extra doorways provide emergency exits in case of predation.

In his study of pileated woodpeckers in west-central Alberta, Richard L. Bonar found that they seldom excavated cavities outside the breeding season. Each pair produced only one new cavity annually, plus a few excavations that stopped at the shelf or shallow cavity stage. These unfinished excavations were sometimes completed and used for nesting the following year. Although they never excavated cavities specifically for roosting, these woodpeckers had a plentiful supply because they added new cavities to their territories at a faster rate than the old ones were eliminated by storms and natural attrition. They also conducted regular maintenance on roosting cavities throughout their territories, regularly removing debris deposited by other occupants and chiseling off any ingrowing wood around the entrances of cavities in live trees.

Chapter 6

Feeding Habits

Feeding habits are one of the most extensively studied aspects of woodpecker biology. Because the search for food occupies a large part of all woodpeckers' lives and is easily observed, early naturalists took many notes on diet and foraging behavior. This research became more formalized in the 1880s with the emergence of the field of "economic ornithology," the study of the interrelationship between birds and agriculture, focusing on avian consumption of farm crops and insect pests. In 1885 the U.S. Department of Agriculture established a new division devoted entirely to economic ornithology, and a wealth of data was gathered over the next half century, when interest in this field was strongest. As ecological studies gained favor in the latter half of 1900s, the emphasis shifted, but interest in food habits remained keen and new information continues to emerge.

Diet

All members of the Picidae family are at least partially insectivorous, and some are almost entirely so. Insect eggs, larvae, pupae and adults are all featured on the menu, along with other invertebrates, particularly spiders. The two groups of insects that are most widely eaten by woodpeckers are ants – in all their life stages – and larval and adult beetles.

Ants dominate the diet of woodpeckers in several genera, including *Colaptes* (represented in North America by the northern and gilded flickers), *Dryocopus* (pileated and lineated woodpeckers) and *Piculus* (golden-olive and grey-crowned woodpeckers). Ants are also the primary prey of adult red-cockaded woodpeckers and the main nestling food for Williamson's sapsuckers. Some of these species are specialists, concentrating on one or two species of ants that are particularly abundant in their usual habitats. Arboreal ants are favored by all except the flickers.

As part of a comprehensive survey of woodpecker feeding habits published in 1911, U.S. Department of Agriculture biologist Foster E.L. Beal examined the stomach contents of 684 northern flickers. He found ants in 524 of the stomachs, 98 of which contained no other food. One of the stomachs was stuffed with more than 5,000 ants, and two others contained more than 3,000 each. Beal also counted 2,600 ants in the stomach contents of a pileated woodpecker.

A large dragonfly proves a mouthful for this recently fledged northern flicker.

The word *Campephilus* is Greek for "caterpillar-loving." The name of this genus refers to the ivory-billed woodpecker's preferred prey, although "beetle-larvae-loving" would have been a more accurate moniker. *Campephilus* woodpeckers, including the ivory-billed, imperial and pale-billed, specialize in preying on very large, tree-dwelling beetle larvae, particularly those of long-horned beetles.

Several other woodpecker species are equally dependent on specific types of arboreal beetle larvae and often eat little else. Black-backed woodpeckers favor the larvae of wood-boring, engraver and mountain pine beetles. American three-toed woodpeckers zero in on bark beetle larvae. Many other woodpecker species include beetle larvae in their diets on a more opportunistic basis. They consume them when they are readily available but, unlike the specialists, do not normally focus their search efforts on this food source.

Woodpeckers in the genus *Melanerpes* are renowned for their fondness for fruits and nuts, but all North American woodpeckers consume some plant foods, whether seasonally or year-round, in large quantities or small. Besides berries, fruits, nuts and seeds, various species also consume sap, flower nectar, cambium (the single layer of cells between the woody part of a tree and the bark), catkins and flower buds. When settlers from other parts of the world brought new domestic crops to the continent, some woodpecker species quickly gained an appreciation for these foreign foods, often incurring the wrath of farmers, orchardists and gardeners as a result.

A number of species rely on particular plant foods to sustain them through the parts of the year when insects are in short supply. The white-headed woodpecker's fall and winter dependence on pine seeds ties this species to western forests dominated by large-coned pines. Seasonal dependence on nuts is characteristic of the aptly named acorn woodpecker, as well as the red-headed and Lewis's woodpeckers; the winter movements of these species are strongly influenced by mast crops.

A handful of woodpecker species around the world have developed the habit of drilling shallow holes in live trees or shrubs and feeding on the collected sap, but none so famously as the four members of the genus *Sphyrapicus* – the true sapsuckers – whose tongues are specially modified for this form of feeding. Sapsuckers consume sap year-round and at times exist on almost nothing else. Most other North American woodpeckers limit their sap feeding to occasionally pilfering from other species' sap wells or enjoying sap exuded by natural tree wounds. The exceptions are the American three-toed and acorn woodpeckers.

Sap wells made by acorn woodpeckers are defended and shared by all members of a family group and are often kept active for several years. In New Mexico, sap is almost exclusively a springtime food for acorn woodpeckers. In California they exploit this resource in early spring (February and early March) and midsummer (July and August), especially if they have depleted their acorn stores. Acorn woodpecker sap wells are scattered in a nonlinear arrangement,

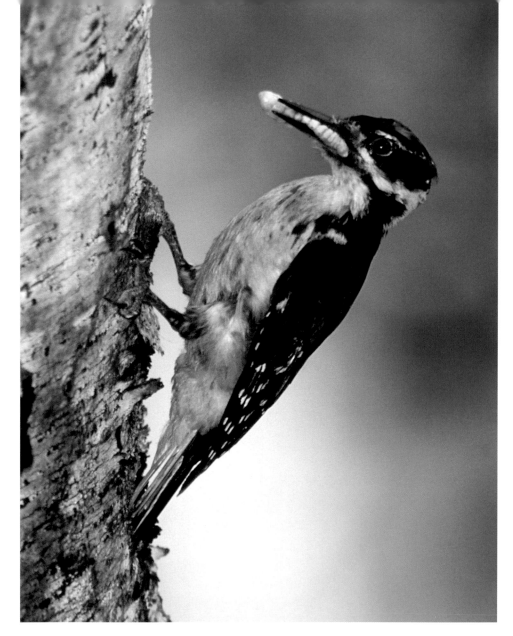

Wood-boring beetle larvae are typical fare for hairy woodpeckers. This resident of the Sierra Nevada is distinguished from relatives on the eastern side of the continent by his drab underparts and reduced white markings on his wings.

like the holes they make for storing acorns, but are smaller in diameter and shallower than the storage holes. In comparison, sapsucker wells are drilled in neat lines.

Eurasian three-toed woodpeckers regularly create sap wells and drink from them, but sap feeding by the closely related American three-toed woodpecker was until recently thought to be uncommon. While working in the boreal forests of Quebec in the late 1990s, biologists Louis Imbeau and André Desrochers found that American three-toed woodpeckers had ringed many black spruce trees with rows of sap wells that extended from the base of the trunk to the crown. Whether this little-studied species feeds as extensively on sap in other parts of North America remains unknown.

Along with their usual diet of insects and plant matter, some woodpeckers also dine intermittently on vertebrate fare. Many North American woodpeckers now and then eat bird eggs or nestlings, which are sometimes killed in the course of nest-cavity takeover attempts. Predation on small mammals, amphibians and reptiles is less common. The most frequent hunters of such quarry are red-headed and red-bellied woodpeckers, which typically pounce on their victims as they cross open ground, grabbing them with their bills. These small animals are dealt with in the same way that woodpeckers deal with large invertebrates. They are either battered against a tree or pecked to death, then torn into pieces if too large to be swallowed whole.

Woodpeckers are not typical scavengers, but over the years a number of observers have seen downy and hairy woodpeckers picking fat from large mammal carcasses. Like the suet we offer in backyard feeders, fat is a high-energy food source that is especially valuable during times of food scarcity. Pileated woodpeckers also scavenge, a fact that has only recently been documented. In April 2000, biologists working at the Tyson Research Center in Missouri were surprised to see a female pileated land on a large fresh beef bone they had put out for the wolves they were studying. The woodpecker perched on the bone and used powerful blows of her bill to remove pieces of cartilage and muscle, which she consumed on the spot. She fed this way for about three minutes, until the wolves approached and frightened her off.

In the early 1900s naturalist M. French Gilman indulged the gila wood-peckers that came to his feeding table in Arizona by providing them with both raw and cooked meat as well as suet. All the offerings were readily consumed, but the woodpeckers had discriminating tastes. "Their favorite cut of beef was the T-bone steak and we always left some meat on the bone for them," wrote Gilman. "They picked it clean, and if a new supply was slow in coming the softer parts of the bone were devoured."

Although woodpeckers can't catch aquatic prey, both red-bellied and red-headed woodpeckers have been seen dining on fish on at least one occasion. They presumably found this food washed up along a shore.

The essential minerals required by woodpeckers are mostly obtained from their normal diet. During the egg-laying period, however, females require large amounts of calcium for the proper formation of eggshells. A calcium deficiency can result in thin eggshells, reduced clutch size or reduced hatching success. Females of some species of birds supplement their diets during the egg-laying period by eating calcium-rich substances such as snail shells, calcareous grit or bone. How woodpeckers deal with this problem is mostly unknown, but observations of red-cockaded woodpeckers have provided some interesting insights.

The calcium supplement of choice for this species appears to be bone fragments that are regurgitated in pellet form, along with other undigested prey remains, by owls or hawks. During an intensive two-year study Richard R. Repasky, Roberta J. Blue and Phillip D. Doerr observed two instances of female red-cockaded woodpeckers eating bone from raptor pellets. The two females consumed small pieces of bone on the ground and carried larger pieces to nearby trees, where they pecked at them and wedged them into the bark for later use. The biologists also noticed activity that seemed to be associated with a search for calcium sources. Although red-cockaded woodpeckers rarely descend to ground level, Blue saw one female repeatedly fly down to the ground to investigate scraps of white paper, and on several other occasions Repasky watched a female hitch down to the base of a tree and hop between trees while scanning the ground. These behaviors were seen only around the time of laying.

While observations of feeding are common, woodpeckers are rarely seen drinking. This is partly because many species can satisfy most of their water needs directly through the food they eat. During the times when sapsuckers and other sap-feeders are enjoying their liquid diet they seldom need to drink free water. Other woodpeckers benefit from the high moisture content of fruits, berries and the juicier kinds of insects when these foods are in season.

Seeds and nuts, on the other hand, are very dry, and species that consume them in large quantities may be thirstier than others. Acorn woodpeckers drink often from water-filled holes in trees during the rainy season and from springs and other groundwater sources during the dry season, when they may visit one watering place as many as three times in a day. White-headed woodpeckers, whose diet is dominated by pine seeds, drink frequently from pools, creeks, rain puddles and melted snow, and sometimes from hollows in trees.

Many woodpeckers are reluctant to leave the safety of trees, but they can usually find all the water they need in depressions on horizontal limbs or in cavities and knotholes. Some may also drink from leaves or needles laden with dew or raindrops. Species that do some of their foraging on the ground are more inclined to drink from puddles, ponds and streams.

In areas where winter temperatures drop below freezing, the usual sources of water for thirsty woodpeckers are melted snow and dripping icicles. One determined – or desperate – red-headed woodpecker was seen chipping a hole in a frozen pond. As well as drinking from the water it exposed, it also ate some of the ice.

Foraging Techniques

Woodpeckers use a wide range of techniques to obtain their food. Specialists mostly employ one or two techniques for which they are particularly well adapted anatomically and use others secondarily as the need arises, if at all. Generalist feeders use any or all of the techniques in the woodpecker repertoire, but may lack the proficiency of the specialists.

The signature woodpecker foraging technique is subsurface excavation to reach prey hidden in the wood of a tree. When excavating, woodpeckers generally strike at a slight angle, alternating from side to side with each blow or delivering several strikes from one side followed by several from the opposite side. Depending on the woodpecker species and the targeted prey, the resulting holes may be shallow or deep, small or extensive.

Woodpeckers may chop through any bark present on the tree or use other techniques for dealing with this obstacle. Members of the genus *Campephilus* specialize in stripping large sections of bark from live or recently dead trees by

delivering oblique blows and then prying with their powerful, chisel-like bills. Species such as the American three-toed woodpecker are experts at bark scaling: loosening and detaching pieces of bark with lateral blows and quick upward or sideways flicks of the bill, as well as sometimes pulling bark loose with the bill. On conifers with bark made up of layers of plate-like pieces, some woodpeckers remove the bark by scratching with their feet, a form of bark scaling sometimes referred to as flaking. Arizona woodpeckers regularly remove bark by scratching, usually using both feet at once. White-headed woodpeckers occasionally use this technique.

Scaling and flaking are the red-cockaded woodpecker's most important foraging techniques and are most efficient and effective on old pines, which have larger and looser bark plates than younger trees. Red-cockaded woodpeckers mostly dislodge the bark by flicking and pulling with their bills, but sometimes they scrabble with their feet. When members of this species are foraging in a pine stand their presence is often revealed by a shower of bark flakes falling steadily from on high. In territories where red-cockaded woodpecker groups are active, some pines will be so thoroughly worked over that their trunks become smooth and conspicuously red-toned.

Bark removal and subsurface excavation account for 70 to 80 percent of the black-backed and American three-toed woodpeckers' foraging activities and are key to these species' ability to live year-round at northern latitudes. While many other insectivorous birds must fly south for the winter to avoid starvation, these woodpeckers can remain on or near their breeding territories throughout the non-breeding season, avoiding the dangers and costs of migration. Even for less specialized woodpeckers these feeding techniques offer a form of insurance in temperate regions – they guarantee a source of food in winter when surface insects are scarce.

Before removing bark or excavating, woodpeckers sometimes tap on the foraging substrate. Red-headed woodpeckers, for example, have been observed to deliver a few sharp raps here and there on a tree, turn their head as if listening and then drill directly into the wood and extract a beetle larva. Biologists have speculated that tapping may provide clues to finding food in a particular spot or may induce subsurface prey to betray their location by making audible movements.

Another common woodpecker foraging technique is probing with the bill and tongue to investigate cracks, crevices or holes and to extract prey. Probing may follow excavation or be employed separately. Some species, such as Nuttall's woodpecker, favor the poke-and-peer approach, frequently turning the head from side to side for visual inspection between explorations with the bill. Depending on the species, woodpeckers probe anywhere that food might be found, including into wood, bark, earth, ant or termite mounds, fruits, flowers, epiphytic plants and tangles formed by vines.

Woodpeckers that specialize in deep probing have extremely long tongues, often enhanced with sticky saliva and a modified tip. The red-bellied wood-

Unlike most woodpeckers, downies are light enough to forage on weed stems. Using his pick-like bill to pierce a goldenrod gall, this male is after the insect larva concealed within.

With characteristic agility, a male ladder-backed woodpecker hunts for insects in a flowering shrub.

pecker's barbed and pointed tongue can be extended at least 1.4 inches (3.5 cm) beyond the tip of the bill and is highly maneuverable, making this species one of the most adept at extracting food from crevices. With a maximum tongue reach of 1.6 inches (4 cm), northern and gilded flickers can easily lap up ants running about on the ground or infiltrate subterranean ant nests. Their long, pointed bills are also well designed for their terrestrial feeding habits and appetite for ants.

Strong excavators generally have intermediate-length tongues, since probing is not their primary foraging technique. White-headed and red-headed woodpeckers do little or no probing and have relatively short tongues. The red-headed woodpecker's limited reliance on probing is also reflected in the hair-like, rather than barbed, bristles at the tip of its tongue. The shortest-tongued North American woodpeckers are the sapsuckers.

Woodpeckers that use a variety of foraging techniques are best able to deal with changing circumstances, as a researcher who observed a female golden-fronted woodpecker with a broken tongue found out. Throughout the 10-month period when the woodpecker was present in his study area, the tip of her tongue was discolored and stuck out to one side from the base of her bill for about 0.8 inches (2 cm). Although golden-fronted woodpeckers are mainly gleaners, they do about 20 percent of their foraging by probing. The injured bird foraged only by gleaning, but was able to survive and even managed to supplant another female and pair up with that bird's mate. However, the disability may have been an impediment to a normal lifestyle, since she and her mate showed no sign of nesting. Observations ended after she abruptly departed from her territory one day and never returned.

All woodpeckers, specialists and generalists alike, obtain at least some of their food by gleaning, or picking surface prey from bark, exposed wood, foliage or the ground. Even when woodpeckers are more intent on excavating or bark scaling, they are bound to notice insects and spiders on the surface as they work their way up trees, and it would be inefficient for them to ignore this food and pass it by. Focused gleaning activity is often characterized by rapid movement up tree trunks and along branches or twigs.

In addition to these arboreal and terrestrial foraging techniques, some woodpecker species also pursue insects aerially. This technique goes by a variety of names, including hawking, sallying and flycatching. Sallying flights are usually made from a perch that provides a good view over open habitat, such as a snag, a leafless branch that extends high above the tree canopy, a telephone pole or a fence post. Red-headed, acorn and Lewis's woodpeckers are among the species that are most proficient and spend the most time capturing prey on the wing.

When foraging aerially, red-headed woodpeckers sometimes fly straight up in the air and back to their perch. On other occasions they follow a more elliptical path – straight out horizontally or swooping high or low – traveling up to 55 yards (50 m) from the starting point. The acorn woodpecker's flights are often nearly vertical. The woodpecker usually targets a specific insect and takes about five seconds to seize it and return to its perch, though longer chases may last up to 43 seconds. During flycatching sessions acorn woodpeckers usually sally out at one- or two-minute intervals, but they have been observed making as many as six flights per minute.

Lewis's woodpeckers are probably the most versatile flycatchers in the woodpecker family. They engage in both short-distance and long-distance hawking to capture prey they spot while scanning from a perch. These sorties generally begin with continuous flapping. After the targeted insect has been captured, short flights end with a direct return to the perch, while long flights continue with extended gliding and sporadic flapping. During non-targeted foraging flights the woodpeckers stay airborne for prolonged periods – from several minutes to at least half an hour – alternating between flapping, lengthy glides and complex maneuvers as they search for and pursue insects. Non-specific foraging flights can last up to eight minutes. One study of Lewis's woodpeckers conducted in Montana during the breeding season found that they spent 25 percent of their 14-hour day in the air and averaged 440 flights per day.

Feeding Strategies

Although particular foods and foraging modes are characteristic of different woodpecker species, there is considerable variability. Differences in regional insect and plant communities mean that members of widespread species are unlikely to eat exactly the same foods throughout their range. Conspicuous seasonal differences in diet and feeding strategies are also common, since foods that are abundant in some months are often in short supply during others. Even the time of day may influence feeding habits. During the sizzling months of summer gila woodpeckers usually limit their feeding on saguaro flowers and fruits to the cooler hours; when the sun is high they forage in the shady interiors of leafy trees.

Many woodpecker species exhibit sexual differences in feeding techniques, diet and foraging sites, either seasonally or year-round. In some cases these are correlated with anatomical differences between the sexes. Male Arizona woodpeckers, for example, have longer bills than females and obtain more of their insect prey by excavating, while females more often forage by scratching bark from tree trunks with their feet. Male downy woodpeckers typically concentrate their foraging on thinner branches and weed stems, leaving the large branches and trunks to the females. A female will usually shift to smaller-diameter branches when there is no male present to keep her in her place, suggesting that this pattern is based on male dominance. Partitioning of food resources between the sexes, whether by anatomical or behavioral means, is important for many woodpecker species because it allows mated pairs to make the most efficient use of the territory they share during the breeding season or throughout the year.

Storing Food

The strong bills and well-developed pecking abilities of woodpeckers are useful not only for obtaining food, but also for processing anything that cannot be consumed whole. This includes foods that are too hard, too bulky or both, such as nuts, large seeds, hard-bodied insects, snails and eggs. Woodpeckers usually carry such items to a crack or crevice, bark furrow or forked branch that can serve as an anvil. Once the item is wedged in place, the bird hammers with its bill to break the food into manageable pieces or split the outer covering so the edible contents can be picked out. The North American woodpeckers that most frequently use anvils are those that eat the most nuts and seeds – the acorn, Lewis's, red-headed and white-headed – but many other species occasionally process food this way.

Woodpeckers sometimes leave bits of food in their anvils and may return later to eat them. More sophisticated and deliberate forms of food storage likely evolved from this primitive form of food caching. Regular food storage is uncommon in the woodpecker family but is characteristic of several species in the genus *Melanerpes*, the most famous being the acorn woodpecker.

The acorn woodpeckers with the most highly developed food storing habits live in California. The granary or storage trees of these populations are an impressive testimony to their industriousness. Each family group has one primary storage tree and from one to half a dozen secondary trees. These granaries are pocked with individually drilled holes, each the perfect size to hold a single acorn, and every autumn the group fills as many holes as possible

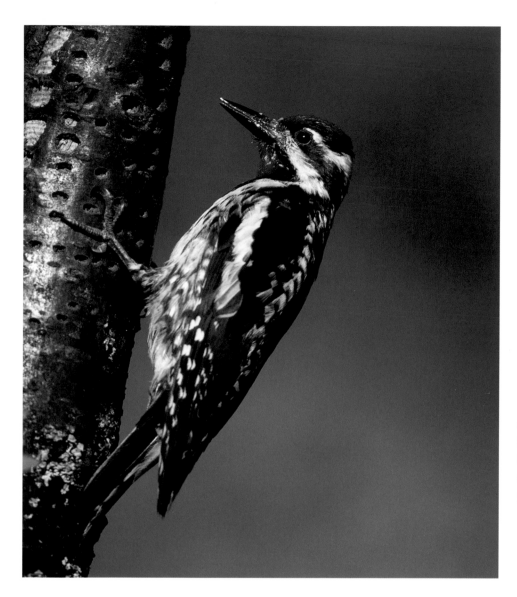

A yellow-bellied sap-sucker works on his sap wells, the source of much of his daily nutrition.

with provisions for the lean times to come. They add new holes to their gran-aries throughout the winter, taking about an hour to drill each one, though the work is not done in a single session. Given the other demands on their time and energy, a family group of five could be expected to create about 480 holes a year. Even if they lost none of their old holes to weathering and decay, it would take them more than eight years to produce a modest granary of 4,000 holes. Little wonder that these sites are fiercely defended.

Acorn woodpeckers also make use of unconventional storage sites offered by their human neighbors. Besides drilling holes into utility poles, fence posts and wooden buildings, they have been known to tuck acorns under roof tiles and into automobile radiators. This kind of innovation does not pay off when the acorn goes right through an opening and falls into an empty space, but some wood-peckers refuse to be deterred by the disappearance of their loot. In a vacant house in California more than 62,000 acorns were found stashed irretrievably in door and window casings. And in Arizona acorn woodpeckers deposited 485 pounds (220 kg) of acorns in the depths of a wooden water tank, apparently in a single year.

Red-bellied, red-headed and Lewis's woodpeckers also typically stockpile food, mostly in the autumn for winter and early spring consumption. Unlike the acorn woodpecker, none of them create their own storage nooks, nor do they usually store nuts whole. Red-bellied woodpeckers store a wide variety of foods, including nuts, corn kernels, grapes, seeds, berries and insects. In captivity, members of this species also cache inedible objects such as nails, toothpicks, slivers of wood, paper clips and wads of paper. Typical storage sites for this long-tongued species are deep cracks and crevices in trees or posts and tangles of vine roots attached to trunks. Red-bellied woodpeckers are scatter-hoarders; their widely distributed sites may be anywhere from right beside where the food was gathered to more than 100 yards (90 m) away. They do not defend their storage sites, but their preference for openings that are two to three inches (5–7 cm) deep deters most would-be thieves.

Like acorn woodpeckers, Lewis's woodpeckers are larder-hoarders. Their food storage sites – usually natural cracks and crevices in trees or posts – are concentrated in one defendable area. Mated pairs sometimes develop and guard larders jointly, but storage is more often a solo effort. The most commonly stored foods are acorns and other nuts, broken into pieces, and whole corn kernels. These provisions form the mainstay of their diet through the winter, and the amount of food amassed by a single individual can be substantial. One Lewis's woodpecker accumulated more than 10,000 kernels of corn, which it tucked into cracks in the dried wood of four telephone poles.

Lewis's woodpeckers are at their most aggressive when defending their larders in fall and winter, driving away all interlopers, whether they are members of the same species or another. In the winter much of their time is also spent turning stored food items and repositioning them in the same or different sites. This careful tending may limit the amount of decay due to fungal growth.

Red-headed woodpeckers uniquely combine scatter-hoarding and larder-hoarding behaviors. An individual will first store acorns or other nuts in one area, then later re-store the same items in separate sites widely scattered around its territory. Any nuts that were originally stored intact are broken before re-storing. The initial use of larder storage allows red-headed woodpeckers to harvest food with maximum efficiency during the gathering period, when competition may be stiff. The re-storing may be done to make the stored food less vulnerable to raiders and to minimize fungal decay. These woodpeckers typically store their provisions in fractures, fissures, knotholes, tree cavities and spaces under sections of loose bark. Cracks in railroad ties and gaps under roof shingles sometimes substitute for natural sites. They frequently hammer items so firmly in place that other birds such as blue jays are incapable of removing them.

Red-headed woodpeckers are the only North American woodpeckers known to sometimes cover or seal in stored food. They do this most often in

November and December, particularly after heavy rains, and typically use pieces of wet bark or wood. Sometimes the woodpecker excavates an opening in a hollow section of a dead trunk or branch, inserts the food, then plugs the opening with splinters of wet wood, which harden as they dry. This effectively hides the cache from view and makes it accessible only by chiseling out the plug.

When insects, particularly grasshoppers, are abundant, they too may be cached by red-headed woodpeckers. Sometimes the woodpeckers kill their prey first, but often they store them alive and kicking, wedged in so tightly that escape is impossible. When naturalist A.V. Goodpasture encountered this practice for the first time, he was horrified. In an account published in *Bird-Lore* in 1909, Goodpasture describes finding a live June bug that had been consigned to a crack in the top of a stump by a red-headed woodpecker. "And what a prison he was in!" he exclaims. "It was a thousand times worse than the Black Hole of Calcutta. They had turned him on his back and pounded him into a cavity that so exactly fitted him that he could move nothing but his legs, which were plying like weaver's shuttles in the empty air."

Applied Ingenuity

In obtaining and handling food many animals reveal problem-solving abilities that go beyond instinctive actions. This type of higher learning was demonstrated by a few resourceful red-headed woodpeckers in South Carolina that contrived an alternative method for shelling nuts and extracting pine seeds from cones. They placed the nuts and pinecones on a road at Huntington Beach State Park and waited for cars to drive over them, then retrieved the edible portions.

In another striking example of applied ingenuity, a gila woodpecker figured out a way to enhance the diet of his offspring by bringing them honey from a saucer. To do this he gouged pea-sized pieces of bark from a stump on which the saucer was sitting and immersed the pellets in the syrupy liquid before carrying them to the nest. He employed this procedure repeatedly over many days and expanded it to include grains and sunflower seeds as dippers. Sapsuckers sometimes dip insects in sap before feeding them to nestlings, but this gila's inventiveness went one step further and was out of character for his species.

When probing in tree crevices, extracting prey from excavations or manipulating food at anvils or storage sites, woodpeckers sometimes drop items or strike them so hard that they ricochet away. But they usually manage to make a quick recovery before any morsel is lost. Most commonly they do this by pressing their breast or belly against the tree to trap the falling item. The woodpecker then reaches down with its bill and retrieves the rescued piece of food.

Some species of woodpeckers also have a knack for catching food with their wings by quickly hunching forward while partially extending the wing on the side where the item is falling and pressing the breast against the tree trunk. If the save is successful, the food will be caught in the pocket formed by the wing and breast against the trunk and can be easily recovered from there. Most

A quiet pool offers this golden-fronted woodpecker an opportunity to quench his thirst. Most woodpeckers are rarely seen drinking or bathing.

North American woodpeckers, except flickers, regularly catch food with their breasts, but so far only downy, hairy, pileated, red-bellied, acorn and red-cockaded woodpeckers have been observed performing the wing-catching trick.

Preening, Bathing and Anting

Although preening appears to be a leisure activity, it is vital for keeping plumage in prime condition and removing dirt and external parasites from feathers and skin. When preening, a woodpecker sweeps its bill through its feathers to work in the oily secretions produced by the uropygial gland, which is located on the rump, and may draw the flight feathers of the wings and tail through the bill. Periodically it may scratch its head and neck with its toes, shake and fluff its body plumage or rub its face against a tree trunk or branch. Other birds commonly accompany preening with leg and wing stretches, but such moves are awkward and infrequent for woodpeckers because they often preen while clinging vertically to a tree. Woodpeckers preen regularly during all seasons, but more frequently during the breeding season and when molting.

Breeding season preening is often associated with drumming or territorial calling, and on these occasions it may be mainly a displacement activity used to relieve nervous tension during or after conflicts. Nest excavation may also call for extra grooming activity to remove bits of construction debris or to deal with plumage that is in disarray because of backward exits from incomplete cavities.

Most adult woodpeckers begin their annual molt after their young have fledged and they complete the process before winter. However, migration alters the schedule for some species. Migratory red-headed woodpeckers interrupt the wing molt immediately after it starts and complete it after arriving at their wintering destination. Lewis's woodpeckers may also temporarily suspend their molt or draw it out to as late as February, replacing the wing and tail feathers early and the body feathers later. Williamson's sapsuckers complete the molt of their flight feathers before fall migration, but continue to replace body feathers as they move south.

Preening sessions are often accompanied by sunbathing. In a typical sunning posture the woodpecker perches or stretches out on a branch or the flat top of a broken tree trunk with its back to the sun, wings extended, wing and tail feathers fanned and crown feathers raised. If the sunning perch is relatively narrow, the bird's wings may droop down on either side. Woodpeckers are usually very lethargic when sunning and often seem to enter a stupor or fall asleep. Red-cockaded woodpeckers may remain immobile for five to ten minutes before resuming preening. Other woodpeckers indulge in shorter sunning bouts lasting only a few minutes.

Water bathing is a less common woodpecker pastime than sunbathing, but members of many species will occasionally dip and splash in puddles on the ground, in water pooled in depressions on horizontal branches or at the edges of ponds, springs or creeks. Hairy and downy woodpeckers occasionally bathe in snow, using the same dipping motions they use when cleansing themselves in water. Downy and red-bellied woodpeckers sometimes opt for a dust bath.

A few woodpecker species are among the more than 200 bird species known to perform an intriguing behavior known as anting, which may have a grooming function. "Passive" anting involves flattening the body against the ground among live ants and allowing them to crawl through the feathers before picking them out in a ritualized manner. In "active" anting the bird picks up a live ant, inserts it among its feathers with a stroking or jabbing motion, then discards it, repeating the action numerous times with other ants. Sometimes insects or objects other than ants are used, but biologists still refer to the activity as anting. Many explanations for this behavior have been proposed, including repelling external parasites, inhibiting the growth of fungi and bacteria or relieving itching. Confirmation of its purpose awaits further research.

Northern and gilded flickers regularly ant, both actively and passively. The only other North American woodpeckers for which anting has been reported are the golden-fronted, red-headed and red-bellied woodpeckers and Williamson's sapsucker. The single documented instance of anting by a golden-fronted woodpecker comes from southern Mexico; the activity was carried out using small paper wasps.

Chapter 7

Relationships with Other Species

No man is an island, nor is any woodpecker. Like all living beings, woodpeckers are members of ecological communities. Their existence is interwoven with those of trees, tree-decaying fungi, insects, other prey, food-producing plants, secondary cavity users, competitors, predators and parasites. The more we learn about these relationships, the better we can understand woodpeckers and how their lives intersect with our own.

Ecosystem Architects

One exceptionally important community role of woodpeckers is that of keystone habitat modifiers or ecosystem architects. A keystone species is an organism that exerts an influence on the structure and function of its community that is disproportionately large relative to its own abundance. Woodpeckers do this by excavating cavities that are subsequently used by non-excavating species and by weak excavators.

The species that benefit from woodpecker construction are mostly birds and mammals. Among the dozens of North American secondary cavity users are various species of perching birds (including swallows, bluebirds, chickadees, wrens, flycatchers, titmice, starlings and house sparrows), ducks, birds of prey (owls and kestrels), and small to medium-sized mammals such as bats, flying squirrels, other tree squirrels, chipmunks, mice, woodrats, weasels, martens, fishers and raccoons. Tree-climbing snakes and tree frogs round out the list. Many woodpeckers, especially the relatively weak excavators, at times also take advantage of secondhand cavities.

Most cavity-nesting birds are dependent on suitable cavities for raising their young. So are a few mammals. For other species, access to a warm, dry cavity during periods of extreme weather can make the difference between life and death. Tree cavities created by weathering and decomposition – often referred to as natural cavities – are generally in short supply compared to woodpecker-excavated cavities, which have the added attraction of being designed to provide maximum security and shelter.

Biologists often represent the manifold connections between primary cavity excavators – woodpeckers – and secondary cavity users as a "nest web" or "cavity web." Interest in nest webs is relatively new and there have been few long-term investigations of these relationships. One of the most comprehensive

A hairy woodpecker stands her ground during a chance encounter with a forest neighbor.

to date is an eight-year study carried out in an area of mixed coniferous and deciduous forest in central British Columbia by Kathy Martin, Kathryn E.H. Aitken and Karen L. Wiebe. Over the eight years they found 1,692 occupied tree cavities. The occupants included seven woodpecker species, 13 other bird species (including black-capped chickadees and red-breasted nuthatches, both weak excavators that sometimes create their own cavities) and six small mammal species. Woodpecker-excavated cavities were about 10 times as numerous as natural cavities.

A particularly interesting finding from this study is that the leading cavity supplier was not the community's largest woodpecker species (the pileated) nor one of its strongest excavators (the black-backed and American three-toed woodpeckers). Northern flickers are relatively weak excavators, but because they are the most abundant woodpeckers in this community and the second largest, they claimed the distinction of being the architects of more than half of the occupied cavities.

Studies in other areas have also shown that one or sometimes two woodpecker species are the foremost real estate developers in those ecosystems, creating a majority of the cavities that support the community's nest web. The principal cavity provider in the western hemlock and Douglas fir forests of Washington's Olympic Peninsula is the hairy woodpecker, and in the pine forests of the southern United States it is the red-cockaded woodpecker. In burned ponderosa pine and Douglas fir forests in Idaho, the main supporting species are the hairy woodpecker and the northern flicker. The saguaro-dominated ecosystems of the Sonoran Desert also acquire most of their cavities from two excavators, the gila woodpecker and the gilded flicker. Their contribution is particularly important because cavities do not form naturally in saguaro cacti.

⸺⸻◆⸻⸺

Although many, and perhaps all, nest webs are centered on one or two key woodpeckers, it is important to remember that severing any strand in a web compromises the integrity of the whole. Because large woodpeckers generally have extensive territories and low population densities, they produce fewer cavities per unit area than most other woodpeckers and are unlikely to be one of the principal cavity providers in a community. However, their unique contribution cannot be matched by any of the smaller species. We can only speculate about the community impacts felt as the imperial and ivory-billed woodpeckers disappeared, but we can gain some retrospective insight by considering the importance of North America's next largest woodpecker, the pileated.

Pileated woodpeckers provide nesting, roosting and denning habitats for other species through three different processes: excavation of nest cavities, including those left uncompleted; excavation of openings into hollow trees for use as roosts; and foraging excavation. For certain North American species such as martens, goldeneyes and boreal owls, pileated woodpecker nest cavities are the only woodpecker-excavated cavities that have sufficiently large doorways and inner dimensions. Many other secondary users, including small cavity-nesting ducks and owls, can use smaller woodpecker cavities but prefer the roomy abodes of pileated woodpeckers. Shallow incomplete cavities are often deep enough to accommodate squirrels, bats or small birds.

Like most other woodpeckers, pileated woodpecker pairs create a new nest cavity each year. These strong excavators generally select very sound trees, which are not easily toppled or broken by wind and may stand for many years or even decades after their initial occupancy. In active territories a surplus of cavities tends to accumulate over time. During a five-year study of pileated woodpeckers in west-central Alberta, biologist Richard L. Bonar tracked cavity production and loss in the territories of 14 pairs. He counted four to 48 cavity trees per territory, with one to 11 entrances per tree; one territory had 90 cavities. In contrast, in the entire study area he found only 15 natural cavities that were comparable in volume and entrance size to the pileated woodpecker cavities. Mated pileated pairs exclude all other members of their species from their territory on a year-round basis, sharing only with their offspring before they disperse and occasionally tolerating the presence of unmated, non-territorial individuals. Over the course of a year the territorial owners use many different roosts, including old nest holes, but on any given night plenty of cavities are available for other users.

Although pileated woodpeckers seldom excavate cavities expressly for roosting, they do create entrances into trees that have been partially hollowed out by heartwood decay. If the tree has no natural openings or is open only at the base, the woodpecker's work provides or improves access for secondary cavity users. These chimney-like trees are particularly favored by Vaux's swifts and some species of bats.

The deep foraging excavations of a pileated woodpeckers create alcoves that are sheltered enough to be used occasionally for overnight roosting by other birds, including brown creepers and hairy woodpeckers. In rare instances they may even provide admittance to a compartment within a tree trunk. Researchers studying big brown bats in British Columbia found a maternity colony in the hollow center of a ponderosa pine; the bats came and went through a hole that had been opened up by a pileated woodpecker digging for insects.

Across the pileated woodpecker's range, at least 38 vertebrate species use its nesting and roosting cavities. In any one area the number is usually about 18 to 20. No other North American woodpecker is known to support so many secondary cavity users. The red-cockaded woodpecker has the second longest list of associates, but many of the 24 vertebrate species that use its cavities do so only after the holes have been enlarged by pileated woodpeckers. Northern Mexico's two largest surviving primary cavity excavators, the lineated and pale-billed woodpeckers, probably also provide cavities for an extensive community of secondary users, but these relationships remain largely unstudied.

—————⋙◆⋘—————

Desirable woodpecker cavities can lead to fierce struggles for possession by prospective secondary tenants, including members of woodpecker species that sometimes reuse old cavities for nesting. The ability of the rightful owners to resist takeover attempts depends on the relative size and aggressiveness of the opposing parties. Red-bellied woodpeckers, for example, often lose their nest cavities to European starlings, and less frequently to northern flickers and red-headed woodpeckers. However, they usually prevail in competitions with golden-fronted woodpeckers and will forcibly evict downy and red-cockaded woodpeckers from their nest cavities. These home invasions can be violent. Red-bellied woodpeckers trying to oust red-cockaded woodpeckers will strike and grab with their bills and try to drag them from the cavity, sometimes injuring or killing the defender in the process. When other woodpeckers are the aggressors, their tactics are similar.

One of the most aggressive secondary cavity nesters in North America is the European starling, a Eurasian species that was brought to the New World by highbrow colonists who aspired to import all the birds mentioned in Shakespeare's writings. After a number of fruitless introduction attempts, success was finally achieved with the release of about a hundred starlings in New York's Central Park in 1890 and 1891. The birds did not move far beyond the city at first, but after the turn of the century their descendents began spreading rapidly across the continent, reaching the Pacific coast by 1950. Although present in northern Mexico since the 1940s and in northern Alaska since the 1960s, this species may still be slowly expanding its range southward and northward.

Within decades of the establishment of breeding populations of starlings in North America, concerns were being raised about this species' impact on native cavity-nesting birds. Since then their aggressiveness in appropriating nest cavities has been well documented. The largest woodpeckers can probably hold their own against most starling attacks, and species that live in dense forests rarely cross paths with these nest pirates, but most other woodpeckers are potential victims. Small woodpeckers should be exempt from harassment because of the size of their cavities and entrance holes, which starlings cannot squeeze through, but this is not always the case. Starlings have been known to stick their heads into downy woodpecker cavities and peck at the nestlings, injuring them and sometimes causing the parents to abandon the nest.

These pugnacious birds do not hesitate to take on woodpeckers that are considerably larger than themselves. In one instance a starling landed on the back of a northern flicker that was on the ground and pecked at it repeatedly. The flicker appeared unable to escape, but was saved when its assailant noticed the human observer and flew away. Although sometimes able to fight back successfully, northern flickers regularly lose nest cavities to starlings and may be forced to delay breeding until the starlings have chosen their nest sites and started incubating.

Yet size isn't everything. In contests with other woodpeckers that are as big as or bigger than starlings, the outcomes vary. Lewis's woodpeckers dominate in nearly all interactions with European starlings, even when a single woodpecker is up against more than one adversary, and they rarely lose nests to starlings. In Arizona's Sonoran Desert, where starlings commonly nest in saguaro cactus cavities, they seem to have little impact on gilded flickers but significantly decrease the number of nesting gila woodpeckers. In a single nesting season a pair of gila woodpeckers often loses two or three successive cavities to starlings.

One of the best defenses woodpeckers have against starlings is simply not to be in the wrong place at the wrong time. Species that normally initiate nesting during the same period as starlings fare worse than those that nest later. In Ohio, biologist Danny J. Ingold studied red-bellied woodpeckers, which nest at the same time as starlings, and red-headed woodpeckers, which lag about two weeks behind, and found that the red-bellied woodpeckers bore the brunt of starling competition for newly excavated cavities. They were forced to surrender nearly 40 percent of their cavities, while a few weeks later the red-headed woodpeckers lost only 15 percent to late-nesting starlings. Although the red-headed woodpecker's combative nature makes this species more resistant to bullying, the difference in losses was primarily due to timing.

A number of species, including red-bellied, acorn and hairy woodpeckers and northern flickers, typically respond to starling interference by delaying nesting, but this solution is not without drawbacks. Each species' breeding season is timed to coincide with one or more factors that will affect clutch size and survival of nestlings and fledglings: good weather, an abundance of food, little competition with other native species and enough time for the young to mature before winter. Late nesters may lay fewer eggs and raise fewer or less robust young or forego the opportunity to produce a second brood. Based on his studies, Ingold concluded that northern flickers and red-bellied woodpeckers whose nesting was postponed by starlings had significantly lower seasonal reproductive output than those that suffered no setbacks.

Even woodpeckers that can successfully defend their nests against starlings may pay a price if conflicts reduce foraging time or elevate stress levels. Yet Walter D. Koenig, one of the leading experts on acorn woodpeckers, believes there is reason for optimism. After analyzing data from nearly a century of Christmas bird counts and 40 years of breeding bird surveys, both up to 1996, he believes that North American woodpeckers are holding their own against the starling invasion. However, Koenig cautions that although it has been decades since starlings invaded most of the sites he considered, it is possible that their effects on some species are only now beginning to appear. He also notes that populations of woodpeckers and other native cavity nesters may yet suffer significant declines if densities of starlings continue to increase. Only continued monitoring at both the local and continental levels and additional in-depth studies will tell us whether starlings are a long-term threat.

Although nest cavities are often the focus of fierce struggles for control, woodpeckers sometimes nest in the same tree as European starlings and other potential competitors. Once each pair has claimed its space there is usually little or no aggression between the different species, though skirmishes occasionally occur. Surprisingly, when there are no better options available, woodpeckers will sometimes share their nest trees with potential predators such as American kestrels or red squirrels. One pair of brave (or foolhardy) Lewis's woodpeckers nested in a cavity on the underside of a large branch that supported a red-tailed hawk's nest – almost directly above the entrance to their cavity.

For one pair of Williamson's sapsuckers, nest-tree sharing went far beyond the normal level of intimacy. The sapsuckers had excavated a cavity just below an older hole that was subsequently claimed by a pair of mountain chickadees. After the sapsuckers' eggs hatched, but before the chickadees had begun laying, the weak partition between the bottom of the upper apartment and the entrance tunnel to the sapsuckers' cavity collapsed. This sudden introduction to the neighbors' nestlings seems to have confused the chickadees' parental instincts. Instead of finding a new home and producing a brood of their own, they stayed and helped to feed the young sapsuckers.

Roosting cavities are usually not defended with the same vigor as nest cavities, especially by woodpeckers that have alternative roosts available. Even North America's largest woodpeckers seldom try to evict squatters. If a pileated woodpecker finds its intended roost taken when it arrives at dusk, it usually flies directly to a different one. However, the spaciousness of their roosts allows them to occasionally share these quarters. One researcher reported two instances of pileated woodpeckers spending the night in the same hollow tree as another woodpecker, in one case with a hairy woodpecker that had already claimed the space, and in the second case with a northern flicker that entered after the pileated woodpecker had already settled in. Another biologist observed a pileated woodpecker roosting in a cavity occupied by nesting Vaux's swifts.

Keystone Feeding Relationships

The community influence of woodpeckers is not limited to providing prime real estate for secondary cavity users. Some species also establish unique feeding opportunities for other wildlife. Sapsuckers in particular play a keystone role by catering to a wide range of sap lovers. Sap-well drilling and maintenance require a large investment of time and energy, so sapsuckers vigorously defend their well systems against raids by members of their own and other species, except for their mates and their young of the year. But despite their vigilance, uninvited guests frequently appear.

Hummingbirds have an especially close relationship with sapsuckers. This is not surprising, since tree sap is remarkably similar in both sucrose content and liquidness to the nectar of flowers favored by hummingbirds. In eastern North America ruby-throated hummingbirds often build their nests near yellow-bellied sapsucker wells and tag along after the sapsuckers during the day. In the West, rufous, broad-tailed and calliope hummingbirds associate in the same way with red-breasted and red-naped sapsuckers. During migration, sap wells may be critical refueling stations for these hummingbird species and perhaps others.

Ruby-throated and rufous hummingbirds have the longest migration routes and the most northerly breeding distribution of all hummingbirds, and biologists suspect that sapsuckers may have a lot to do with this. There is strong evidence that the timing of these hummingbirds' arrival in spring – often before flowers are in bloom – and the northern limits of their breeding range are determined by the sapsuckers' migratory schedule and distribution. From July to early September in some parts of western North America, sapsucker drillings provide such an important energy source for rufous hummingbirds traveling south that they will pause in their journey for up to a week and defend a feeding territory around a group of wells. When one hummingbird moves on, the territory is claimed by another migrant within a couple of hours.

Numerous other birds also partake in the sweet delights of the sap well, at least occasionally. These include six warbler species (Nashville, orange-crowned, Wilson's, Cape May, black-throated blue and yellow-rumped) and four woodpecker species (downy, hairy, red-bellied and white-headed), as well as white-breasted nuthatches, ruby-crowned kinglets, white-crowned sparrows, pine siskins, common goldfinches, mountain chickadees and house wrens. For the warblers especially, sap wells may provide a vital dietary supplement in late summer, when the availability of insects and flower nectar begins to decline.

Several small mammals that show a fondness for sap use diverse strategies for obtaining it. Chipmunks make furtive raids and are often quickly chased away by sapsuckers, while red squirrels approach boldly to lick at the sap for 20 minutes or longer, paying little heed to the sapsuckers' scolding. Jumping mice may limit their forays to nighttime. Wasps, bees and a variety of other insects also feed at sapsucker wells.

Much less is known about interlopers' use of Williamson's sapsucker and American three-toed woodpecker sap wells, but these resources are undoubtedly exploited by many of the species that use other sapsucker wells. In central California, acorn woodpecker sap trees are commonly visited by white-breasted nuthatches, Anna's hummingbirds, Nuttall's woodpeckers, oak titmice and chipmunks, all of which are chased away by the sap-well owners if caught in the act.

Woodpeckers whose foraging specialties are excavating and bark removal provide a different type of feeding opportunity for other members of their communities. Their activities expose prey or open up deep dining possibilities for birds that are less proficient at getting beneath the surface. Boreal chickadees, for example, will feed at the base of trees where foraging American three-toed woodpeckers have left piles of bark chips, which usually contain some beetle larvae and pupae that the woodpeckers have missed.

The extensive feeding excavations of pileated woodpeckers attract a variety of followers, including downy, hairy and red-bellied woodpeckers, Williamson's sapsuckers, northern flickers and house wrens. Depending on their own abilities, these birds may excavate and probe within the pileated woodpecker's foraging pits or simply hunt for prey overlooked by their inadvertent host. For these associates the sound of a pileated woodpecker's loud foraging blows may be the equivalent of a dinner bell.

Mixed-Species Feeding Flocks

In many avian communities a common type of feeding relationship is the mixed-species feeding flock – a loosely organized band of birds that travel and forage together for prolonged periods, moving more or less as a group while maintaining a comfortable distance between individuals. Certain species typically act as flock leaders and are followed by a variety of attendant species. The composition of a flock shifts and changes throughout the day as different birds join or leave.

Most woodpeckers that participate in feeding flocks do so as followers, but red-cockaded woodpeckers play a dual role. Compared to other insectivorous birds of the southern pine forests, red-cockaded woodpeckers are late risers. While these woodpeckers are still in their roost holes, a diverse group of feeding companions typically convenes in the vicinity of their cavity-tree cluster. The red-cockaded woodpeckers emerge shortly after dawn. Once they begin foraging, the assembled company moves off through the forest. These flocks usually stay relatively coherent until late morning, when the woodpeckers reduce their feeding activity.

The frequent use of cavity-tree clusters as assembly points for southern pine forest feeding flocks suggests that red-cockaded woodpeckers are important members, but the group dynamics are not yet fully understood. For the most part the woodpeckers seem to pay little attention to their flock-mates except for generally coordinating their movements with the rest of the group and reacting to alarm calls that signal a predator's approach. Sometimes the woodpeckers lag behind; but at other times flock movements appear to be influenced by their foraging agenda.

The two species most intimately linked with red-cockaded woodpeckers in these flocks are the brown-headed nuthatch and the eastern bluebird. These birds often follow red-cockaded woodpeckers closely for prolonged periods in one-on-one pairings, with the follower consistently remaining within three feet (1 m) of the woodpecker as it progresses. This behavior is apparently motivated by the opportunity to apprehend prey disturbed by the woodpecker's bark scaling and pecking. Attendant species are often seen darting out to capture insects that take flight from sites where red-cockaded woodpeckers are working.

The main benefit of feeding-flock relationships for red-cockaded and other woodpeckers is that they provide additional eyes and ears to monitor for approaching hawks or other predators. Research on downy woodpeckers has shown that they spend less time cocking their heads and scanning their surroundings for signs of danger when they are with feeding flocks than when alone. With more time freed up for foraging, downies in feeding flocks capture prey at a faster rate than do solitary individuals.

Meanwhile there is no disadvantage to keeping company with non-woodpeckers because they are not rivals for foraging sites or food. However, competitive pressure between closer kin usually dictates that the number of woodpeckers in a feeding flock is low, except for family groups of red-cockaded woodpeckers. Participation is often circumscribed by territoriality. An individual may join a flock as it enters its home range, then drop out when the group moves beyond its familiar margins.

In the southern pine forest haunts of the red-cockaded woodpecker, feeding flocks are active throughout the year, except during the nesting period, and may have as many as 50 members. In Louisiana and eastern Texas the most common year-round species in these assemblages are brown-headed nuthatches, pine warblers and Carolina chickadees, which are often joined by red-cockaded, red-bellied and downy woodpeckers, tufted titmice and a variety of other birds. In North Carolina as many as seven woodpecker species have been seen in a single flock. During winter the ranks are swelled by various migrants such as warblers, kinglets, brown creepers and bluebirds.

This composition is characteristic of feeding flocks of arboreal insect-eating birds throughout much of North America. The species mix varies regionally, but certain families of birds are routinely represented. In temperate areas feed-

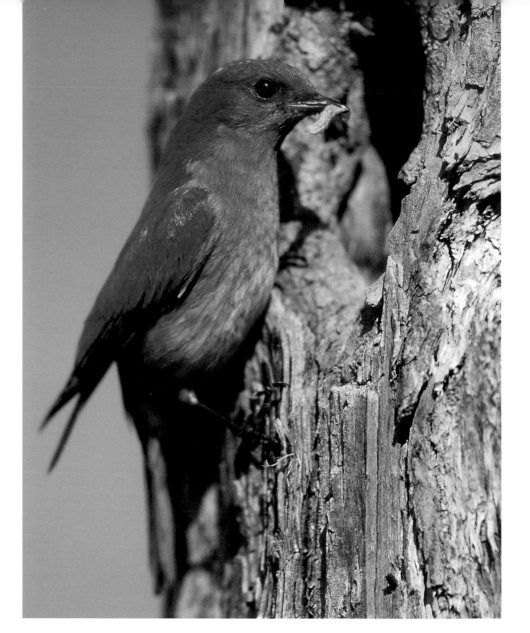

An eastern bluebird bearing a tasty morsel for his brood alights outside the nest hole he has inherited from a woodpecker neighbour.

ing flocks almost always coalesce around chickadees, titmice or both, which serve as flock leaders and sentinels. These birds are prominent as core species probably because they are quick to sound the alarm when predators come into view. Typical attendants besides woodpeckers include nuthatches, kinglets, bushtits, warblers, verdins and brown creepers. These flocks generally number up to about two dozen birds.

Feeding flocks are most important for woodpeckers during the non-breeding season, when territorial instincts are muted and high energy demands coincide with food scarcity. Downy woodpeckers team up with others more readily when food is in short supply, and the incidence of hairy woodpeckers joining feeding flocks increases with decreasing temperature. Hairy woodpeckers are only occasional participants in feeding flocks and tend to remain near the periphery of these groups.

In the evergreen oak woodlands of Arizona, woodpeckers seen in mixed-species feeding flocks include ladder-backed and Arizona woodpeckers, red-naped sapsuckers and northern flickers. The core species are usually either common bushtits or bridled titmice. Northern flickers also forage with Mexican jays in the oak savannas of Arizona, though the two species eat different foods. In these flocks the flickers follow the jays and heed their warnings about approaching hawks or northern harriers. Northern flickers spend more time foraging when they are in the company of Mexican jays than in flicker-only flocks. In tropical and subtropical forests, antwrens are the most common core species in feeding flocks. Golden-olive woodpeckers are regularly seen with such groups and lineated woodpeckers are occasional joiners.

Predator/Prey Relationships

Several species of woodpeckers are highly dependent on certain types of insects, and their fortunes rise and fall with the availability of their principal prey. Conversely, the woodpeckers significantly influence the population dynamics of these insects. The best-studied of these relationships are the ones between woodpeckers that specialize in subsurface feeding through excavation and bark removal and several families of wood-boring and bark beetles, which include some of the most injurious insects native to North America's coniferous forests.

Bark beetles are small, often cylindrical beetles in the Scolytidae family. In summer, female bark beetles bore through the bark of mature live trees to lay their eggs in the underlying phloem, which is made up of live nutrient-transporting cells. After the eggs hatch the larvae live in the inner bark, eating phloem tissue and creating a network of galleries until they are ready to pupate. When metamorphosis is complete, a new generation then chews its way out of the tree and flies off to breed and find fresh egg-laying sites, leaving behind a dying tree. The entire life cycle usually lasts about 12 months but in some cases may take more than a year.

The wood-boring beetles are represented by two families: the Buprestidae, commonly known as metallic or jewel beetles because of the adults' shiny green, blue or copper-colored bodies; and the Cerambycidae, or long-horned beetles, named for their long antennae. Female wood-borers lay their eggs underneath bark or in bark crevices. Some target live trees, while others seek out recently dead ones. Certain species use infrared sensors to detect forest fires and home in on the fire-killed trees they prefer as egg-laying sites. Upon hatching, wood-borer larvae may stay close to the surface or may tunnel deeper. The larvae of some species spend their first summer in the inner bark and subsequently move into the sapwood. Eventually, after pupating, the new adults emerge.

Bark beetles and wood-borers are always present in North America's coniferous forests, but their numbers fluctuate with changing weather and forest conditions. Populations may be small and localized or they may rapidly increase to epidemic levels. Like fire, beetles that attack live trees play a role in rejuvenating older forests and creating a mosaic of variably aged stands across the landscape. Insects that follow in the wake of forest fires or tree-killing beetles hasten the processes of decomposition and nutrient recycling. Unrestrained insect population growth would be detrimental in the long run, but healthy ecosystems have natural checks and balances, including the presence of woodpeckers.

When it comes to mediating outbreaks of bark and wood-boring beetles, two characteristics of woodpeckers set them apart from other vertebrates. One is their unparalleled ability to expose and extract prey from underneath bark or deep inside trees. The other is that, unlike many other insect-eating birds, most woodpeckers are nonmigratory, so the impact of their predation is not limited to the breeding season. In many parts of Canada and the United States resident woodpeckers are the primary avian insectivores throughout the winter, when eradication of tree-dwelling beetle larvae and pupae can significantly reduce the likelihood of major population increases during the following year.

In addition to their effectiveness as predators, some woodpecker species are also very quick to respond to increases in beetle populations, in a variety of ways. One basic response is concentration of foraging effort on the more readily available prey, which can result in remarkable consumption rates of the target species. During one spruce bark beetle epidemic, the stomachs of a sample of American three-toed woodpeckers contained an average of 915 larvae, and researchers estimated that each bird would fill its stomach several times in a day. Based on the caloric content of the larvae and the daily energy expenditure of American three-toed woodpeckers, an individual needs to eat about 3,300 of these small grubs a day to fuel itself adequately and survive in zero-degree (−18°C) winter weather.

Another common response to insect outbreaks is a sudden increase in the number of woodpeckers on the scene as newcomers flock in from other areas to enjoy the abundance of prey. During southern pine beetle irruptions in the southeastern United States, pileated, downy, hairy, red-bellied and red-cockaded woodpeckers may all converge on affected stands, leading to woodpecker densities that are from three to 58 times greater than in unaffected areas. In boreal forests outbreaks of spruce bark beetles attract downy, hairy and American three-toed woodpeckers, especially the latter. Threefold to sevenfold increases in woodpecker density are typical of aggregations during the breeding season. In winter the densities may increase to 30 times the densities in uninfested stands. At such times it is not uncommon to see up to a dozen woodpeckers feeding on the same tree.

Besides providing a sudden wealth of feeding opportunities, outbreaks of tree-killing insects such as bark beetles produce a surge in the availability of suitable cavity trees. When this occurs, local woodpecker populations may be augmented through increased reproduction over several years, as well as by immigration. Red-cockaded woodpeckers, which nest exclusively in live pines, are the only woodpeckers that do not benefit from large-scale tree die-off.

Besides consuming prey in large numbers, woodpeckers also indirectly affect populations of bark and wood-boring beetles in the course of foraging.

After woodpeckers have punctured, thinned or removed a tree's bark, any remaining beetle eggs, larvae or pupae are more exposed to other vertebrate and invertebrate predators and to parasites. The beetle broods also lose some of their protection from extreme temperatures and desiccation. These secondary effects of woodpecker feeding activity are responsible for at least as much mortality as direct consumption, and possibly more.

Although woodpeckers cannot prevent insect epidemics from occurring, they are important control agents that help keep insect populations at endemic or moderate levels. By delaying population explosions and hastening the decline of outbreaks after they peak, woodpeckers are instrumental in increasing the length of time between outbreaks and maintaining natural balance in forest ecosystems.

Fungal Colonization

Over the years some biologists have speculated about whether subsurface foraging by woodpeckers plays a role in inoculating trees with the wood-decaying fungi that make cavity excavation possible. The first detailed study to tackle this question head-on was recently conducted by Kerry L. Farris, Martin J. Huss and Steve Zack in the Cascade Mountains of Oregon and California. It focused on newly dead ponderosa pines that had been killed by bark and wood-boring beetles and on four beetle predators: white-headed, American three-toed, black-backed and hairy woodpeckers.

In one part of the study the researchers measured the wood density of pines that had been subject to varying levels of woodpecker feeding activity and determined that heavily used foraging trees had softer, more decayed sapwood than trees that had received little woodpecker attention. In the other part they looked at what types of microscopic life woodpeckers might be transporting from tree to tree. They did this by capturing a number of birds – both woodpeckers and non-cavity-nesters – and swabbing their beaks. As it turned out, the non-cavity-nesters mostly had fungus-free beaks, but more than half of the woodpeckers had fungal material on theirs.

The trio's findings suggest that woodpeckers probably promote fungal colonization of dead trees by puncturing bark and fragmenting the underlying wood as they forage, and that they are important carriers of fungi that contribute to the decomposition of trees – at least in ponderosa pine forests. With typical scientific prudence the authors of the study caution that there is still much to be learned about the connection between woodpeckers and tree-decay fungi. Nevertheless, their work underscores the intricate nature of the relationships between woodpeckers and other members of their ecological communities.

Fist-sized, squared-off foraging holes are a sure sign that a pileated woodpecker lives nearby.

Chapter 8

Woodpeckers and Humans

The human bond with woodpeckers is an ancient one. There is evidence that a woodpecker cult existed in Neolithic times in Europe, when much of that continent was covered with oak forests, and throughout history in almost every part of the world woodpeckers appear in legend and folklore, often cast as supernatural beings. In North America they figure in the stories of many indigenous societies and are frequently linked with the sun or fire, perhaps because of their bright red or yellow head markings.

The belief that woodpeckers possessed prophetic powers was intriguingly widespread. Traditional cultures in places as widely separated as Britain, Guyana and Borneo credited these birds with the ability to forecast rain or to predict other events, such as the sex of an unborn baby. In ancient Rome an agricultural deity named Picus, one of Saturn's sons, was famed for his talents as an augur and soothsayer. According to the Roman myth, Picus was hunting in the forest one day and met the sorceress Circe out gathering herbs. Although it was love at first sight on her part, he rejected her advances. Furious, Circe transformed the unfortunate youth into a woodpecker, robbing him of his manly prowess, but even in his feathered form he retained his gift for divination. Picus's story was recalled by the classically educated biologists who first assigned scientific names to the woodpeckers. The Eurasian genus *Picus* commemorates this god, as does the woodpecker family name, Picidae.

Outside the mythological realm, for thousands of years the primary relationship between humans and woodpeckers was that of hunter and quarry. Now we hold in our hands the fate of entire species, not just individual birds. In North America the greatest threat to woodpeckers over the past 150 years has been habitat loss caused by settlement, agriculture and forestry. In some places the habitat of certain species has been entirely eliminated. Elsewhere habitat quality has degraded to the point where woodpecker populations in those areas have declined significantly.

Habitat loss can also take the form of fragmentation: formerly extensive ecosystems are reduced to scattered patches too small to support viable populations and too isolated from other remnants of intact habitat for individuals to move between them. Habitat destruction, degradation and fragmentation continue at an alarming rate, but attitudes toward the natural world are shifting. With our growing awareness of the ecological importance of woodpeckers and

A generally adaptable species, the red-bellied woodpecker has fared better than most North American woodpeckers over the past century.

appreciation of these birds for their intrinsic value, the conservation initiatives that gained momentum toward the end of the 20th century may ultimately define a new human relationship with woodpeckers.

Traditional Uses

The vivid head plumage of a number of woodpecker species and the colorful flight feathers of flickers were widely used by North America's first peoples to beautify special-occasion garments. Other woodpecker body parts, particularly the powerful bills of the larger woodpeckers, were used to embellish sacred objects, to treat diseases and other ailments, as talismans, and for decorative purposes.

During the course of their epic journey across North America at the beginning of the 19th century, explorers Meriwether Lewis and William Clark collected a number of cultural artifacts from the people they met along the way. One of these, which came from either the eastern Plains or the western Great Lakes region and now resides in the Peabody Museum of Archaeology and Ethnology at Harvard University, was a ceremonial pipe adorned with beading, feathers and an ivory-billed woodpecker head. Ivory-billed woodpeckers were esteemed far beyond the lands where they lived and were transported great distances via the continental trade networks that thrived before European contact. Besides being used to enhance ceremonial objects, these woodpeckers' scarlet-crested scalps and large, pale bills were also worn by warriors and carried in medicine bundles by people in many parts of North America.

Pileated woodpecker body parts and plumage were also desirable trade items for indigenous people living outside this species' range. Some were carried as far from their source as Colorado, where archaeologists digging in the 1930s found two woodpecker bills, one from a pileated and the other from an ivory-billed, buried with the skeletons of a man and woman from an unidentified tribe. California's Pomo tribe hunted pileated woodpeckers within their own territory and used their red head feathers as a form of currency. In California and southern Oregon, and probably in other parts of the acorn woodpecker's range, this species was prized for its striking plumage and the ease with which large numbers of these communally roosting birds could be caught. Some California tribes built special devices to trap acorn woodpeckers as they emerged from their cavities in the morning.

The renowned artisans of the Pomo tribe traditionally decorated their exquisite coiled baskets with bird scalps or individual feathers, including those of acorn woodpeckers and northern flickers. Acorn woodpecker heads or crown patches also served to embellish garments and headdresses worn by shamans and dancers of a number of California and southern Oregon tribes. One elaborate full-length cape was completely covered with the red crown feathers of several thousand birds. On the Great Plains, the Cherokee and some other tribes regarded the red-headed woodpecker – North America's most pugnacious picid – as a symbol of war, and they sported its head as a battle ornament.

Hunting Woodpeckers for Food and Profit

The acorn woodpecker may be the only woodpecker species that was regularly eaten by North American native peoples. Likewise, settlers from Europe and other parts of the world generally rejected these birds as food, except when motivated by hunger and a lack of alternatives.

Nineteenth-century naturalist John James Audubon wrote of the pileated woodpecker, "Its flesh is tough, of a bluish tint, and smells so strongly of the worms and insects on which it generally feeds, as to be extremely unpalatable." He said much the same about red-headed woodpeckers, minus the mention of flesh color, and reported that the red-bellied woodpecker "feeds on all sorts of insects and larvae . . . and at certain periods its flesh is strongly impregnated with the odour of its food."

It was not that Audubon had an oversensitive nose. Most members of the woodpecker family have a conspicuous scent, whether dead or alive. Biologists do not know its exact source, but as Audubon suggested it may be at least partially attributable to diet. There is also some evidence that preening oils produced by the uropygial gland play a role. The intensity and character of the odor are variable, from unpleasantly pungent to merely musty. One experienced woodpecker biologist compared the smell to dirty clothes that have sat too long in the laundry hamper. Red-cockaded woodpeckers have a resinous fragrance, which may be related to their close association with live pines.

The northern flicker is one of the few species that was deemed palatable by European immigrants and their descendents. Arthur C. Bent, an eminent chronicler of bird lore, recalled that during his boyhood in the late 1800s flickers were considered legitimate game. Bunches of these birds, known locally as partridge woodpeckers, were often seen hanging in game dealers' stalls in the eastern United States. They were, he added, "very good to eat."

A popular tactic used until early in the 20th century to procure flickers was described by New Jersey ornithologist Witmer Stone in his 1937 book, *Bird Studies at Old Cape May*. Each year hunters prepared for the fall migration by fastening poles or fence rails to the tops of low pines and cedars at Cape May Point. These perches, which extended high above the tree canopy, were irresistible to the tired southbound birds. As soon as half a dozen or so flickers had lined up on a pole to rest, the gunner who had been hiding below would step out and rapidly pick them off. Stone reported that a pair of men could fill six fruit baskets with flickers in a single morning and that knee-high piles of corpses were a frequent sight.

Flicker hunters were not the only North Americans profiting from killing woodpeckers at this time. From the mid-1800s to the early 1900s, enthusiasm for collecting birds and their eggs was rampant among both amateur naturalists and professional ornithologists. Although many of these specimens were ultimately used to further scientific knowledge about woodpeckers, there was also much waste and senseless slaughter. In 1908 *The Condor* published a dispatch decrying the ignorance and greed that were often associated with the collecting

Stored acorns add an unplanned decorating touch to this cabin wall, where an acorn woodpecker searches for an empty hole in her family's unconventional granary.

craze. The correspondent, Austin Paul Smith, relayed a story told to him by a prospector who had been working with a partner in the mountains of Chihuahua, Mexico, where imperial woodpeckers were still common, though they were already becoming rare elsewhere. The partner had heard that there was money to be made from collecting these birds, but wrongly assumed that it was the large, pale beaks that were in demand, not prepared skins. "Working on this idea," wrote Smith, "he shot some seventeen of the magnificent creatures in the course of a few months, and cut off the bills, figuring them at $25.00 each, until, on reaching civilization again, he was chagrined to find his material utterly worthless."

The Nuisance Factor

In the past, wanton killing of woodpeckers was often carried out to prevent them from consuming or damaging agricultural crops, even though their defenders pointed out their beneficial predation on injurious insects. Early European settlers considered the red-headed woodpecker to be a serious agricultural pest, little realizing that the changes they had wrought upon the landscape were exacerbating the situation. Losses were greatest during the period when small farm holdings existed amid a patchwork of woodland habitat, offering convenient nesting sites close to an abundance of food from cornfields, orchards and gardens. In an effort to combat the problem, colonial authorities in one area paid a bounty of twopence for every red-headed woodpecker killed.

In the West, Lewis's woodpeckers infuriated commercial orchardists because of their habit of sampling one piece of fruit after another, spoiling far more than they ate. A study of the economic status of woodpeckers in Oregon in the 1920s found that Lewis's woodpeckers were destroying train-carloads of apples and pears annually in some orchards, particularly those near wooded habitat. One grower said he had been able to halve his losses with daily hunting patrols, but grumbled that "one man can not keep them out of a seven acre orchard entirely, as they will work one end while you are scaring them out of the other."

All four species of sapsuckers have also at times fallen afoul of human interests because of their sap-well drilling habits. Early lumbermen complained that their attacks on growing trees caused scars and blemishes in the wood. In 1911 a U.S. Department of Agriculture report on the impact of woodpeckers on trees and wood products estimated that sapsuckers were responsible for nationwide losses of more than 1.25 million dollars annually. No attempts were made to keep the forests free of woodpeckers, but many fruit growers were quick to shoot at sapsuckers seen working in their orchards, despite evidence that the trees did not usually suffer permanent damage.

Woodpeckers who showed too much interest in wooden buildings, fence posts or utility poles were also labeled pests and considered expendable until well into the 1900s. The shooting of 22 red-headed woodpeckers over a year in the mid-1800s to protect a church steeple in Texas from their excavating efforts was an all too common scenario. In Texas, golden-fronted woodpeckers wreaked such havoc on telephone and telegraph poles in the late 19th and early 20th centuries that the affected company owners lobbied for the species' protected status to be revoked. Once they achieved this goal they organized an extermination campaign that took a noticeable toll. Elsewhere the woodpecker most frequently responsible for pole damage was the red-headed. In 1897 the Kansas City Electric Car Company went so far as to hire an official red-headed woodpecker exterminator to protect the wooden poles that supported the tramline's feed cables. On one of his first days on the job he shot 19 of the offending birds.

Structural damage to utility poles by foraging and cavity-excavating woodpeckers continues to plague utility companies throughout North America, costing them thousands of dollars for every pole that must be replaced. Shooting the perpetrators is no longer socially or legally acceptable, but most other deterrents that have been tried over the years have proved to be impractical, uneconomical or both. The most cost-effective and successful solution currently used is to replace solid wood poles with poles made from steel, concrete, fiberglass or laminated wood, none of which hold any attraction for woodpeckers.

Doing away with conventional utility poles has the added benefit of eliminating a woodpecker health hazard. Most wooden poles are impregnated with creosote before they are installed, and despite its strong odor this oily preservative does not discourage woodpeckers from excavating nest cavities in the poles. Unfortunately, creosote in high concentrations kills the developing embryos in most eggs and quickly finishes off any chicks that do hatch. Although weathering eventually reduces the concentration of toxic chemicals in the wood, these deadly effects are evident for at least four years after freshly creosoted poles are erected.

———❖———

As in centuries past, North Americans today sometimes experience problems with woodpeckers drumming on or excavating holes in their houses. Nowadays, however, this crime rarely nets the troublemaker a death sentence. Even the most aggravated homeowner must consider the fact that it is illegal to kill woodpeckers, except under a permit issued by the appropriate government authorities, who must first be convinced that all nonlethal options have been exhausted.

Prevention is naturally the best solution. If you are beginning new construction in woodpecker territory, avoid eliminating existing woodpecker habitat on your property and choose your materials carefully. Woodpeckers generally prefer untreated or stained wood over painted wood, and cedar or redwood over other types of wood siding. They avoid very smooth wood surfaces because these do not provide adequate footholds.

When a woodpecker turns its attention to an existing building, the first step in resolving the problem is to determine the nature of its activity. Foraging, cavity excavation and drumming are motivated by different stimuli and have different effects, so the methods of dealing with these are not identical. It is uncommon for woodpeckers to forage on buildings, because they rarely find any food. If they do locate a food source in the walls of your house, they are probably doing you a favor by warning you about a larger problem that needs to be addressed. The best way to avoid this kind of woodpecker damage is to prevent insects from invading in the first place, by sealing cracks and protecting the wood against moisture. Foraging excavations can generally be recognized as small, shallow, irregularly shaped holes that may be scattered over a wide area.

Excavation of nesting or roosting cavities in buildings often indicates a local shortage of suitable trees. In some cases woodpeckers will agree to use artificial cavities instead, but merely erecting a few nest boxes will not likely solve the problem. One of the most effective and long-lasting remedies against excavating woodpeckers is to exclude them from the problem area by creating a physical barrier – with netting. Experts recommend using a 3/4-inch (2 cm) mesh. At least three inches (7.5 cm) of space should be left behind the netting and the edges should be secured so that birds cannot get underneath. Alternatively, the damaged site may be covered with hardware cloth or metal or plastic sheathing.

Stationary models of owls, snakes or other predators are seldom effective as visual deterrents. Mobile silhouettes of birds of prey or shiny plastic or metallic strips suspended from the eaves or near the problem area are more often successful in dissuading aspiring drummers or excavators. Loud noises may also scare woodpeckers and discourage them from returning, especially if this scare tactic is employed at the first sign of activity and used consistently until the woodpecker moves on for good.

If a cavity has already been excavated by the time it is noticed, be sure to determine whether it contains eggs or nestlings before you take any action. If there is a family in residence, avoid doing anything that will upset or drive off the parents until after the young have fledged.

When woodpeckers drum on buildings this is sometimes a comment on the scarcity of natural sites, but often it seems they are simply attracted to the superior acoustics offered by wooden siding and metal structures. Some people are willing to tolerate the disturbance, knowing that drumming causes little or no physical damage and is largely a seasonal activity, but others find the noise unbearable in the early morning hours or when it continues incessantly for weeks on end.

One way to discourage drumming is to dampen the resonance of the site by filling in hollow spaces or by covering the surface with fabric or foam. Another solution is to use netting or hardware cloth to eliminate access to the drumming site. Other remedies that cure excavating problems may deter drummers, but woodpeckers with territorial aspirations can be extremely persistent. Once barriers, repellants or deterrents are in place, providing an alternative drumming site may help convince the woodpecker to leave your house alone. A drumming post can be made by taking two boards and nailing them together at one end so they reverberate when struck, then attaching them to a tree trunk or other vertical surface.

People who have struggled to prevent woodpeckers from treating their houses like trees might take comfort in knowing that not even leading scientists are immune from such problems. In June 1995, shortly before the scheduled launch of the space shuttle *Discovery*, NASA technicians at the Kennedy Space Center in Florida discovered that the brown foam insulation covering the shuttle's external fuel tank had been riddled with more than a hundred holes, some of them up to four inches (10 cm) in diameter, while the spacecraft sat on the launch pad. The date of liftoff was postponed and an investigation was initiated. Not until a video surveillance camera caught them in the act did it occur to anyone that woodpeckers might be to blame.

The culprits were northern flickers. They had been drawn to the area by foraging opportunities in the surrounding fields, but had found that suitable nest sites were in short supply and competition from European starlings was stiff. In their search for other nesting options the flickers tried excavating into the insulation on the fuel tanks, only to hit hard metal a few inches in every time. Once the problem was identified, flicker deterrents were deployed, the damage was repaired and – more than a million dollars later – the shuttle proceeded on its journey.

From Forests to Tree Farms

The colonization of North America led to the felling of an almost unimaginable number of trees. Before the arrival of the first European explorers, the dominant vegetation type on the continent was forest. Only the most arid and most northerly regions lacked trees. In what is now Canada approximately 1,097 million acres (444 million ha) of the country's total land mass of 2,278 million acres (922 million ha) was forested. In the contiguous United States, forests covered an estimated 820 to 850 million acres (332 to 344 million ha) of the total 1,903 million acres (770 million ha). By 1920 the lower 48 states retained only 138 million acres (56 million ha) of original forest, much of it in the West. The devastation north of the border was less severe, but only because there were fewer inhabitants. In heavily settled parts of eastern Canada the degree of loss was as great as in the eastern United States.

Much of the preliminary forest clearing was done to make way for farms and homes, but demands for wood soon outstripped this initial timber supply. The settlers used wood to build houses and barns, fence their land, heat their homes and cook their meals. Furniture, tools, wagons, boats and countless other items, from cradles to coffins, were made of this ubiquitous material. Dependence on wood in daily life would not noticeably diminish until alternatives became readily available in the 20th century. Meanwhile, with industrialization of the continent in the 19th century came rapid population growth and an associated demand for building lumber and firewood, as well as massive use of wood by industry and to build the immense railway network needed to move people and goods across the continent. Every mile (1.6 km) of track laid required approximately 3,200 wooden ties, and the ties were replaced every three or four years.

Large-scale commercial exploitation of North America's forests began in the mid-1800s and proceeded as a full-frontal assault until well into the 1900s. By the turn of the century the forests of the Great Lakes states and some parts of eastern Canada had been essentially liquidated. A couple of decades later the southern pine forests were largely gone and the lumber barons' invasion of the forests west of the Great Plains was rapidly picking up steam. Decimation of the western forests may have been averted only because of intervention by political leaders in both countries who realized that this style of forestry made very poor economic sense. Some politicians were swayed by conservationists who decried the ecological costs of systematically laying waste to these forested lands, but the driving force behind the change was the need to guarantee a long-term timber supply.

The idea of managing forests with a view to meeting future as well as present needs was introduced to North America in the 1890s. As new policies and practices became established over the next several decades, forestry became less like mining and more like farming. In a few areas the end of the era of unrestrained logging was good news for woodpeckers, but generally habitat losses continued to mount under the new system of intensive forest management for sustained yield.

To achieve their goal of sustainability the new generation of professionally trained foresters set about replacing naturally diverse and dynamic forest ecosystems – which they saw as infested with insects and disease and cluttered with worthless deadwood – with same-age, single-species stands of trees. The tree species were selected for their commercial value and tended with an emphasis on maximizing the yield of wood fiber while minimizing the costs of production and harvesting. From the woodpeckers' perspective the most damaging practices associated with the intensive forest-management model have been elimination of standing dead trees and large logs, implementation of short-rotation harvesting regimes, suppression of fires whenever possible and systematic salvage logging of stands killed by fire or insects.

During the early days of forestry in North America, loggers concentrated on felling the most valuable timber. They generally bypassed snags and live trees with decay indicators such as broken tops, and left rotting logs lying in place. Eventually these old-growth remnants were incorporated into the new forest that grew up around them. But foresters trained in the ways of intensive management called for using every possible scrap of wood and removing all

Radiant in the early morning light, a golden-fronted woodpecker pauses on his journey.

logs and other large woody debris in preparation for replanting. Concerns about the inherent instability of dead and deteriorating trees also led to the introduction of safety standards that made felling these trees mandatory wherever forestry workers might be at risk.

This campaign to "clean up" the forest coincided with the introduction of the idea that trees should be harvested like any other crop, on a planned cycle, or rotation. The forest industry's commercial goals dictate that logging rotations are much shorter than the natural lifespan of a tree. Depending on the tree species being grown and the regional conditions, stands in many intensively managed forests are cut every 60 to 100 years. In the southern United States, loblolly and slash pine plantations may be managed under rotations as short as 35 years for trees grown for sawtimber, and 20 years for those grown for pulp production. Foreshortening the natural cycle of tree growth, decay and death depletes and ultimately eliminates the supply of old large-diameter, heart rot–infected live trees and snags on which most woodpecker species depend for nesting and roosting. The loss of this biological legacy and of healthy old large-diameter trees also deprives a number of species of essential foraging habitat.

White-headed woodpeckers are seasonally dependent on pine seeds, and many populations are sustained by ponderosa pines. Dense stands of young trees cannot meet their needs since ponderosa pines do not begin to produce significant cone crops until they are 60 to 100 years old. As well, the best seed supply comes from large, dominant trees growing in open, uncrowded situations. Red-cockaded woodpeckers show a marked preference for foraging on the largest and oldest pines available, especially those that are more than 60 years old. Biologists believe they prefer large trees because these offer a greater surface area for foraging. Old trees may be favored because of bark characteristics that affect foraging success, such as large, loose bark plates that are easily flaked off. The type or abundance of invertebrates living on and in these trees may also contribute to their desirability. For pileated woodpeckers, high-quality foraging habitat includes rotting logs more than 15 inches (38 cm) in diameter, as well as large dead trees, which are the preferred home of this species' primary prey, the carpenter ant.

In addition to becoming more intensive during the 20th century, forestry has also become more extensive. An ever-increasing demand for wood products has accelerated the rate of cutting in previously untouched forests, even those that were once considered not valuable enough to warrant the effort of logging them. At the same time, technological innovations have hastened the speed at which trees can be felled and hauled away, and opened up areas that were formerly too remote or inaccessible to be of interest. Woodpeckers with large territorial requirements and low population densities are often the hardest hit by the magnitude of modern forestry because viable populations of these species cannot be supported within small fragments of intact habitat.

Pileated woodpecker territories cover from hundreds to thousands of acres, depending on local forest characteristics and the quality of the habitat. In the

Rocky Mountain foothills of west-central Alberta, near the northern limits of this species' range, one pair's year-round territory can encompass as much as 8,150 acres (3,300 ha). In regions with less severe winters their territories are typically much smaller, but even the most compact pileated woodpecker territories are far bigger than the 5 to 30 acres (2–12 ha) required by downy woodpeckers, which are at the other end of the territorial needs scale.

Fire Suppression and Salvage Logging

In the early 1900s a group of influential North American foresters began campaigning to reduce the amount of timber lost to fire, and by the 1940s their doctrine of prevention and suppression had achieved primacy. Large sums of money were dedicated to deploying firefighting technology and manpower, and Smokey Bear was recruited to spread the message that fire was an enemy of wildlife, loggers and wilderness-loving citizens. Throughout this period a few renegades tried to defend the place of fire in natural ecosystems, but made little headway against the dominant view. Today the ecological benefits of fire are more widely recognized, yet the forest industry is still loath to let future profits go up in flames and many members of the public are harshly critical when they encounter burned-over landscapes.

In some regions the natural fire regime is one of frequent low-intensity fires, which burn only the groundcover and understory vegetation, leaving mature trees largely unharmed. In other areas the normal interval between fires is much longer, and the accumulated combustible material eventually fuels ferocious conflagrations that charge through the forest canopy, killing almost every tree in their path. Associated with each type of regime are plant and animal species that are expressly adapted to survive the flames or to take advantage of post-fire conditions. For these species fire is an boon, not a disaster.

Among North American woodpeckers the black-backed is the most dependent on severe, stand-replacing fires. This species has an extensive distribution but is largely restricted to areas of recently burned coniferous forests. After a tree-killing fire, wood-boring beetles converge to lay their eggs in the wood of the dead trees, and black-backed woodpeckers follow to seek out their primary prey, larval wood-boring beetles. Within two to three years the larvae complete their metamorphosis and emerge as adults and the feast is over. At that point the woodpeckers move on to another area of forest that has been stocked with prey, usually by fire, but sometimes by high winds, flooding, insect damage or some other large-scale disturbance.

Black-backed woodpeckers are found in low numbers in some areas of unburned and undisturbed forest, but these appear to be "sink" habitats, so named because the number of young fledged each year is less than the total adult mortality. The persistence of black-backed woodpecker populations in these low-quality habitats probably depends on birds dispersing from older burned forests and traveling in search of the next beetle bonanza. If fires are suppressed, "source" habitats disappear and the population fades into oblivion. Prescribed burning, in which fires are deliberately lit and allowed to burn over a designated area, has now become a standard forest-management tool. Usually these are planned as moderate, manageable understory fires, which means they do not meet the needs of species like the black-backed woodpecker. For some other woodpeckers, such as the red-cockaded and Lewis's, prescribed burning more closely resembles the natural fire regime to which they are adapted.

The acute decline in red-cockaded woodpecker populations over the past 150 years is largely due to logging of the longleaf pine forests that once covered more than 62 million acres (25 million ha) of the southeastern United States, but fire suppression practices that rendered large portions of the remaining habitat unusable also bear some of the blame. Historically, low-intensity understory fires swept through this region several times a decade, usually during the growing season, between late spring and early fall. The longleaf pine is superbly adapted to this fire cycle and red-cockaded woodpeckers are uniquely specialized for living in the resulting savanna-like landscape of widely spaced pines growing above a low understory of grasses and herbaceous plants. Without regular burning, shrubs and deciduous trees gain ground, crowding the mature pines, preventing pine regeneration and making the habitat unsuitable for red-cockaded woodpeckers.

On the opposite side of the continent, Lewis's woodpeckers are closely associated with another fire-adapted tree species, the ponderosa pine. Recently burned ponderosa pine forest provides the best breeding habitat for these woodpeckers. The abundance of suitable cavity trees in such areas is an obvious attraction, but the ideal foraging environment may be just as important – there are plenty of well-positioned sites for perching between foraging flights, the wide spacing of the trees offers good visibility and lots of space for aerial maneuvers in pursuit of prey, and the shrubby understory hosts a profusion of insects.

While frequent low-intensity fires clearly play a critical role in maintaining the kind of ponderosa pine forest that Lewis's woodpeckers favor, recent research suggests that occasional stand-replacing crown fires may be equally important. One apparent benefit is reduced predation pressure. In separate studies of black-backed and Lewis's woodpeckers biologists have found that nest predators such as squirrels, snakes and raccoons are initially rare or absent from forests after severe, large-scale fires and take years to return, giving the woodpeckers several breeding seasons of respite.

———⊰◈⊱———

Despite the determined efforts of forest managers to quell all fires and preclude insect outbreaks, these natural disturbances continue to make their mark on North America's forests. Woodpeckers don't necessarily get to enjoy the resulting habitat, however, because the fire- or insect-killed trees are often quickly removed to claim the wood for commercial purposes and clear the land for replanting. Salvage logging has long been common in North America, but it became much more prevalent in the 1990s, when many jurisdictions adopted regulations that promoted this practice or made it mandatory.

Salvage logging is not an environmentally benign activity. It impedes nutrient recycling, hinders natural regeneration of trees and understory plants and eliminates post-fire habitat that is essential to a number of species, including American three-toed, black-backed and Lewis's woodpeckers. The large-diameter trees that the salvagers covet are the same trees that are most valuable to the woodpeckers as foraging, nesting and roosting sites.

Ecosystem-based Management

Although intensive management practices still dominate the North American forest industry and the continent's last uncut forests are fast disappearing, the situation is not entirely hopeless. Over the past few decades a new approach to forest management that goes by a variety of names, including holistic forestry, ecoforestry and ecosystem-based forest management, has been emerging. Once dismissed as the ramblings of naïve tree-huggers, the principles of ecoforestry are now starting to be accepted and put into practice by both government and industry, though not yet to the degree needed to reverse the biodiversity losses of the past.

The most important principles of ecosystem-based forest management are ecological responsibility and balanced use. In practical terms ecological responsibility means protecting and maintaining all the parts and processes that contribute to fully functioning ecosystems: parts such as dead trees, woodpeckers and bark beetles; processes such as fungal decay and fire. Balanced use implies taking into consideration the needs of all users, human and nonhuman. The old industrial model was predicated on growing selected tree species as a cash crop. The new ecological model recognizes forests as complex, self-renewing systems from which a limited amount of wood can be judiciously harvested. Although ecosystem-based management has been proven viable in demonstration forests in various regions, large-scale implementation appears to be still many years away – too many for a species on the edge such as the red-cockaded woodpecker. Its fate in the meantime depends on the effectiveness of intensive single-species management tools and procedures.

When the red-cockaded woodpecker gained federal protection as an endangered species in 1973, it was a species in crisis, so much so that all the monitored populations except one continued to lose ground through the rest of that decade and into the next. Recovery efforts finally began to show some results in the 1990s, with many populations stabilized and some beginning to increase, yet others continued to decline and most remained precariously small. In 2003, when the second revision of the official species recovery plan was released, the total population stood at 14,068 individuals living in 5,627 social groups in 11 states – less than 3 percent of the species' estimated abundance at the time of European settlement.

In their book *The Red-cockaded Woodpecker: Surviving in a Fire-maintained Ecosystem*, senior red-cockaded woodpecker biologists Richard C. Conner, D. Craig Rudolph and Jeffrey R. Walters discuss short- and long-term strategies for the recovery of this species. The short-term plan focuses on protection of existing cavity trees from logging, installation of cavity restrictors to prevent pileated woodpeckers from enlarging the entrance holes of existing cavities, provision of artificial cavities to prevent territory abandonment and encourage population expansion, translocation of individuals or pairs to augment populations that are in immediate danger of dying out and to reintroduce the species to suitable but unoccupied habitat, controlled burning during the growing season to prevent deciduous trees and shrubs from growing up around the pines in occupied territories, and removal of deciduous trees and shrubs that have encroached upon the longleaf pines. They describe this as an emergency strategy, a necessity for now and probably for the next 20 to 30 years, to deal with the unnatural conditions that have put this species on the road to extinction.

But this approach would not be appropriate forever. Conner, Rudolph and Walters say that the emphasis must eventually shift to ecosystem management based on regular controlled burning during the growing season and silvicultural practices that promote the development of mixed-age forests with large numbers of well-spaced old trees, which will provide an abundance of high-quality nesting and foraging habitat capable of supporting high densities of red-cockaded woodpeckers. "In short," they conclude, "the long-term strategy is to maintain forests that resemble those that existed when Europeans first arrived in North America, and to allow the woodpeckers to fend for themselves within the ecosystem to which they are so well adapted." This forestry prescription could be equally well applied to any of the continent's woodpecker species that have declined over the past 150 years because of our voracious appetite for wood products.

Agriculture

Agricultural societies were already well established in some parts of North America when the first Europeans arrived, but the amount of land under cultivation was insignificant compared to the total land mass. From the 1600s on, European-style agriculture became a major contributor to woodpecker habitat loss as the settlers spread out across the continent, clearing land to plant crops wherever they went. Woodpecker species that require large expanses of old-growth forest were the most immediately affected. Those that favor relatively open habitats and younger forest adapted more easily. Some initially benefited from the new food sources provided by farmers, but they lost this advantage in many areas as the patchwork of mixed-crop fields, pastures and woodlots was replaced with sprawling monocultures devoid of suitable nesting habitat and, in the case of crops such as cotton and tobacco, offering no sustenance.

Direct habitat destruction is the most obvious impact of agriculture on woodpeckers, but it is not the only one. In the Sonoran Desert, irrigated crop fields are progressively replacing saguaro cactus ecosystems and depriving gila woodpeckers of essential nesting and foraging habitat. Even where the desert habitat remains intact, the woodpeckers are not secure. Agricultural development has increased the pressure from European starlings, which compete aggressively for nest cavities, reducing the gila woodpeckers' nesting success and sometimes causing them to abandon otherwise suitable breeding habitat. Starlings that nest in saguaro cactus ecosystems obtain nearly all of their food from nearby agricultural areas and cannot survive in this arid environment without the insect prey that the irrigated fields support.

So far, saguaro-nesting gilded flickers seem to be little affected by the starling invasion of the Sonoran Desert, perhaps because they are larger than gila woodpeckers and better able to defend their cavities. However, if the number of gila woodpeckers declines significantly – and with them the abundance of gila woodpecker cavities – or starling populations increase, the starlings may become more forceful in their attempts to commandeer gilded flicker cavities. A scarcity of gila woodpecker cavities could also have a profound effect on a number of secondary cavity users, including elf owls, western screech-owls, brown-crested and ash-throated flycatchers, purple martins and American kestrels.

For several woodpecker species, the most serious agricultural threat comes from livestock. Grazing and trampling by cattle or sheep alter habitats by hampering the regeneration of trees. In arid regions, riparian (streamside) habitats are particularly vulnerable. In the southwestern United States and parts of Mexico, grazing damage to oak and pine/oak woodlands inhabited by acorn woodpeckers is thought to be contributing significantly to population declines. In these same areas, heavy grazing in riparian habitats is reducing the abundance of sycamores, which are among the most important nest trees for Arizona woodpeckers. Excessive demand on groundwater sources also threatens sycamores, because both seedlings and mature trees require a permanently high water table to survive.

Settlement

As the human population of North America has increased, natural ecosystems have been progressively replaced by homesteads, villages, towns, cities, suburbs, hobby farms and vacation properties. In many cases the woodpeckers that historically inhabited these areas have been evicted to make way for the new residents, but some species have persisted.

Most North American woodpeckers are not particularly shy of humans. Whether they remain in settled areas depends mainly on the availability of suitable habitat, especially potential cavity sites. Even in large cities woodpeckers of many species can find suitable abodes and sufficient food in established residential neighborhoods, parks, golf courses, cemeteries and other green spaces. But urban development leaves no room for woodpeckers that require large areas of mature forest or have other specialized needs.

A dripping tap becomes a drinking station for this resourceful male red-bellied woodpecker.

In arid regions, where trees are naturally scarce, the shelterbelts, shade trees and ornamentals that have been planted over the years have increased the amount of habitat for some woodpeckers and allowed a few, such as the golden-fronted, to expand their ranges. However, the human inclination to "green up" the landscape is not advantageous for woodpeckers that are adapted to desert living. A study conducted around Tucson, Arizona, showed that gila woodpeckers can coexist with low-density residential development – two houses per 2.5 acres (1 hectare) – but only if the native vegetation is maintained. It is important that large saguaro cacti are preserved and replacement generations of saguaros allowed to grow. As well, homeowners must accept that nature can be messy. When a gila woodpecker or gilded flicker starts excavating a cavity in a saguaro, the cactus will try to seal the wound by exuding a tar-like substance that is notorious for staining sidewalks and the clothing of passersby. Provided you avoid getting water in the hole, which will harm the plant, you can simply rinse off the black ooze when the woodpecker is absent.

More problematic for some people is the fact that the damage inflicted by the excavator may eventually kill the cactus, depending on the placement of the cavity. This is unavoidable, but perhaps a small price to pay for a front-row seat for watching woodpeckers and the secondary cavity nesters that will follow after they vacate the premises.

Desert dwellers are not the only ones who need to develop a tolerance for nature's untidiness and cycles of life and death if they wish to save a place for woodpeckers in their midst. Throughout North America the modern predilection for cutting down dead and aging trees and pruning away dead branches has been a significant factor in the recent declines of many woodpecker species that were once relatively abundant in cities and towns. This purging of dead-wood is often justified as a safety measure without proof that the limb or tree actually presents a threat. A professional arborist can assess the situation and may be able to suggest a solution that eliminates the hazard while retaining part of the tree for future woodpecker use. Branches and trees that are not positioned where they might fall on someone or cause property damage can be left alone, yet they are often removed for aesthetic reasons. Conservation of woodpecker habitat in settled areas calls for a new way of seeing. When we behold dead and dying trees through the eyes of woodpeckers, it is easy to see their beauty and their usefulness.

Feeding stations and surrogate cavities can never take the place of natural foraging and nesting sites, but they can compensate in a small way for habitat lost to settlement while giving interested humans an opportunity to become better acquainted with woodpeckers. The easiest way to entice woodpeckers into your yard is by offering food. Peanut butter, sunflower seeds, nuts, fruit and dried corn on the cob are popular with many species. A few of the more omnivorous woodpeckers appreciate meat scraps. And, above all, woodpeckers love suet.

Because of its high calorie content, suet is especially welcome to birds in winter, when energy demands are high and other foods may be scarce. They will also consume it eagerly at other times of year, but it is best to discontinue this treat from late spring to early fall, because suet melts in warm weather. When woodpeckers feed on heat-softened suet their facial plumage becomes saturated with the fat, which inflames the feather follicles and causes the feathers to fall out. Fortunately the damage is not permanent and the bare-faced birds will regrow their feathers once the cause of the problem is removed.

The downy woodpecker is among the five most common feeder-visiting birds in North America. Other species that regularly patronize feeding stations include the gila, golden-fronted, hairy, ladder-backed, pileated, red-bellied, red-headed and white-headed woodpeckers and the northern flicker. Downy and gila woodpeckers occasionally imbibe sugar-water from hummingbird or oriole feeders. These two species and hairy woodpeckers will also drink from bird-baths or other containers. Golden-fronted and red-headed woodpeckers are more likely to quench their thirst with water dripping from a tap or running in a drinking fountain. Any of these species may also take the occasional dip in a birdbath or fountain.

While it is relatively easy to attract woodpeckers by catering to their appetite, convincing them to take up residence in backyard birdhouses is another matter. Unlike secondary cavity nesters, most woodpeckers generally ignore nest boxes because cavity excavation is such an important breeding season ritual. However, woodpecker species that commonly reuse cavities from year to year sometimes show an interest in alternative sites, including nest boxes intended for ducks, owls, American kestrels or other secondary cavity nesters.

The most likely woodpecker candidates for nesting in boxes are northern flickers and members of the genus *Melanerpes*, especially red-bellied, red-headed, golden-fronted and Lewis's woodpeckers. These species also some-times roost in nest boxes during the non-breeding season. There are a few reports of hairy and downy woodpeckers nesting in boxes, but downies are more inclined to use them as winter roosts. Nuttall's woodpeckers have occa-sionally been known to roost in bluebird boxes.

Custom-built woodpecker nest boxes should be made with rough wood on both the interior and exterior walls to provide good footholds for vertical perching. Because many woodpeckers have a strong urge to at least go through the motions of excavation, the box can be made more attractive by covering the bottom with a one- or two-inch (2.5–5 cm) layer of wood shavings, which the woodpeckers may toss out the door in preparation for nesting. Any wood shavings left inside will help the parents keep the nest clean during the nestling period. Some people find that northern flickers prefer boxes that have been packed completely full of sawdust before they are put in place. Experimentation is the best way to learn what appeals to your own local woodpeckers.

The dimensions of the box should be guided by what woodpeckers nor-mally build for themselves. A box that measures 12 to 15 inches (30–38 cm) in height with a six-by-six-inch (15 cm by 15 cm) floor will suit most medium-sized woodpeckers. Flickers require more spacious quarters: a box height of 16 to 18 inches (41–46 cm) and a seven-by-seven-inch (18 cm by 18 cm) floor. Downy woodpeckers can make themselves comfortable in a box that is 8 to 12 inches (20–30 cm) high with a three-by-three-inch (7.5 cm by 7.5 cm) floor and will face less competition for ownership of this kind of compact apartment than they would for a larger box. Entrance hole sizes for each species are listed in Chapter 9. The hole should be positioned about two to three inches (5–7.5 cm) below the top of the box.

Alternatively, artificial cavities can be made from tree trunk sections or large branches. Log-section cavities are generally better insulated than boxes and may provide greater protection against predators. One technique for construct-ing this type of home is to saw a log in half lengthwise and use a chainsaw or chisel to partially hollow out each half, then reattach them. Another method is to carve out the chamber with a chainsaw by working from the top. In either case a doorway is drilled in the front and the finished abode is roofed with a slab of wood. At the Hastings Reservation in California, acorn woodpeckers occasionally roost in log-section cavities made with the first technique.

A unique type of housing designed specifically for red-cockaded wood-peckers has played an important role in the recovery of this species since the early 1990s. Recognizing that the energy and time demands of cavity excavation in live pines are a significant constraint on red-cockaded woodpecker population expansion, biologists have developed two techniques for creating prefabricated housing. One involves drilling two holes in a tree and excavating a chamber, then sealing one of the holes, leaving the other as the entrance. The other entails cutting away a section of a tree trunk and inserting a wooden box with an entrance hole in the outer wall.

The first major test of the effectiveness of cavity inserts and drilled cavities came in September 1989, after Hurricane Hugo struck Francis Marion National Forest, home of what was at the time the second-largest red-cockaded woodpecker population in existence. The hurricane destroyed 87 percent of the active cavity trees, rendering most territories uninhabitable and reducing the number of breeding groups from 470 to 249. Over the next four years hundreds of artificial cavities were installed, and by 1994 the number of groups had climbed back up to 353 – a level of recovery that would have taken more than 15 years if the woodpeckers had been left to excavate their own replacement cavities.

Watching Woodpeckers

Whether you limit your observations to your backyard or venture farther afield, the visibility and fascinating behaviors of woodpeckers make them among the most rewarding birds to watch. Most North American species can be easily identified, often without binoculars, and some have recognizable calls or drumming patterns. Birders whose interest extends beyond checklists may be inspired by the example of Lawrence Kilham, the author of *Life History Studies of Woodpeckers of Eastern North America*. A virologist by profession and a passionate amateur ornithologist, Kilham spent more than 25 years studying woodpeckers in his off-hours, primarily in the eastern United States, with side trips to Panama, Costa Rica and Guatemala.

Kilham's sustained interest in woodpeckers was fueled by a desire to learn as much as possible about the species common to his region, "how they scratched, preened, foraged, bred, interacted with other species, and communicated by means of displays, drumming, and vocalizations." Being a meticulous observer with an inquiring mind, he made note of details such as the black-and-white markings visible on the underside of a downy woodpecker's tail when it leans into the nest cavity to feed its young – and realized that these patterns varied enough from bird to bird that he could use them to recognize individuals.

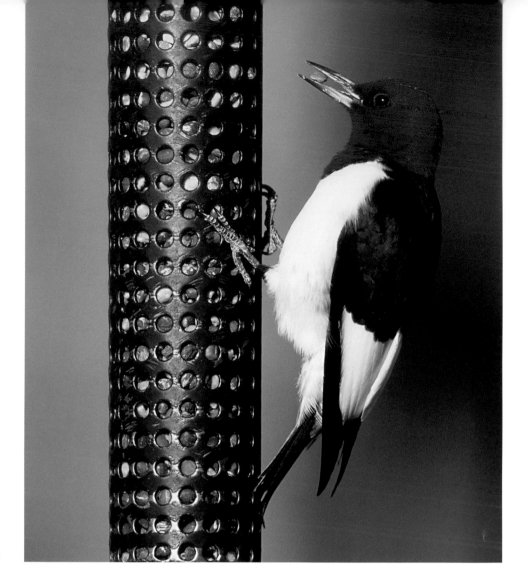

Red-headed woodpeckers will readily take peanuts from a feeder, eating some on site and carrying others away to cache for later consumption.

This proved to be useful for keeping track of the number of feeding trips made by each parent at times when they were coming and going so quickly that he missed seeing the head well enough to determine the bird's sex. Kilham also observed that downy and hairy woodpeckers have distinct individual markings on the back of their heads, which he used to identify known birds.

Kilham's favorite time of day for observing woodpeckers was first thing in the morning, because their cavity roosting habits made it easy to predict where they could be found. "Just wait until an hour after sunrise," he wrote, "and the chances of locating a Hairy or Downy in a reasonable time can be slim. These birds move over large areas in winter and one can easily come back empty-handed in places like New Hampshire. But, in taking the trouble to be by a roost hole at dawn, I have had some of the best birdwatching. It is in the first half hour of day that woodpeckers can be most active in foraging, courtship, play, and other aspects of their behavior."

If you are not an early riser and you miss the woodpeckers' morning debut, you may be able to trick them into appearing later. If you have a knack for mimicry you may be able to lure downy woodpeckers into view by duplicating the tapping sounds these birds make as they forage. In pileated woodpecker country try clapping your hands with slightly cupped palms or knocking slowly against a tree with a stick to imitate the loud blows these woodpeckers deliver when excavating in search of prey. There is a good chance that any territorial pileated woodpecker within hearing distance will come to investigate. Other birds that like to forage alongside pileated woodpeckers may also be attracted.

Whether you watch woodpeckers purely for pleasure or engage in more serious study, do not underestimate the value of your observations. There is still much to be learned about woodpeckers, especially species and populations that live in regions less frequented by humans. We can all contribute to filling the many information gaps. Williamson's sapsucker is a perfect example of a woodpecker that offers great scope for research by biologists and sharp-eyed birdwatchers alike. This species has received little scientific attention in the United States and almost none in Mexico. Nearly everything that is known about its breeding biology comes from studies conducted at two sites, one in Colorado and the other in Arizona; the details of its wintertime existence are sketchy and its migration ecology is largely a mystery. Although populations appear to be on a downhill slide, there is not enough population data to know for sure. We've come a long way from the time when male and female Williamson's sapsuckers were thought to belong to entirely different species, but our ignorance still outweighs our knowledge.

Conservation of Williamson's sapsuckers, and of other woodpeckers, will ultimately depend on our deepening our understanding of every aspect of their lives and making wise use of what we learn. Our ancestors looked to woodpeckers to predict the future. Now we must take responsibility for determining what becomes of the descendents of Picus.

Chapter 9

Species Profiles
Introduction

North American Species Profiles

While there are many similarities between woodpecker species, no two are exactly alike. The profiles in this chapter describe unique attributes of North America's 28 woodpecker species and summarize significant facts about their lives: what they look and sound like; where they live; how they behave; and what threats or advantages they face in the modern world. A good field guide can be a useful complement to the profiles, providing illustrations that highlight identifying characteristics, and, in some cases, sonograms that visually depict vocalizations. Each profile includes a range map and the following nine sections.

Identification
The identification section gives body size and describes the main characteristics of the adult plumage, including markings that distinguish males from females. Woodpeckers seen in action may appear slightly smaller than the listed lengths, since length is usually determined from museum specimens laid on their backs and measured from the tip of the bill to the tip of the tail.

Distribution
This section provides a broad outline of the species' range. For migratory species, the breeding and winter ranges are described separately. For all others, "range" refers to their year-round place of residence. Among these resident species some individuals may move short distances after the

breeding season, dispersing juveniles may wander and populations may periodically irrupt and spread out beyond the main range. These types of movements are described in the migration section.

Habitat
This section describes general habitat requirements as well as essential habitat characteristics or components. Seasonal changes in habitat use are noted.

Voice
The voice section describes the main adult vocalizations and summarizes their presumed functions. Information about function is omitted for the call note, which seems to serve the same purposes for all North American woodpeckers. It is generally used as a location signal for maintaining contact between members of a pair or social group. When delivered with greater intensity, frequency or both, it appears to express excitement or alarm.

Drumming and Tapping
Key characteristics of drumming and tapping are given in this section, with some additional information about activities associated with these forms of communication. The timing of drumming and gender differences are mentioned only when they diverge from standard practice. Most species increase the frequency and intensity of drumming sessions from late winter through spring but may occasionally drum at other times of the year. During the breeding season, drumming

is normally most frequent in the early morning and just before sunset. In most species both sexes drum, but males typically do so more than females.

Feeding
This section summarizes dietary preferences and typical foraging behavior, including seasonal variations, and notes unusual food-handling techniques and food-storing habits.

Breeding
Breeding information includes mating strategies, nest site preferences, clutch size, annual number of broods and size of cavity entrance hole. Unless otherwise noted, all species are monogamous and raise only a single brood each year.

Migration
Most North American woodpeckers are not migratory, but many make short-distance seasonal movements after the breeding season. Juvenile dispersal typically also occurs in fall and winter. Both types of movements are sometimes referred to as wandering. A few species are irruptive, meaning that populations periodically experience dramatic, short-term increases in response to temporary environmental changes, such as insect outbreaks. During population irruptions woodpeckers often travel far beyond the boundaries of their regular range. This section covers migratory movements, wandering and population irruptions.

Conservation
The conservation section describes the current status of the species and lists the main factors responsible for declining or increasing populations.

Species List

Genus *Picoides*
American three-toed woodpecker (*Picoides dorsalis*)
Arizona woodpecker (*Picoides arizonae*)
Black-backed woodpecker (*Picoides arcticus*)
Downy woodpecker (*Picoides pubescens*)
Hairy woodpecker (*Picoides villosus*)
Ladder-backed woodpecker (*Picoides scalaris*)
Nuttall's woodpecker (*Picoides nuttallii*)
Red-cockaded woodpecker (*Picoides borealis*)
White-headed woodpecker (*Picoides albolarvatus*)

Genus *Melanerpes*
Acorn woodpecker (*Melanerpes formicivorus*)
Gila woodpecker (*Melanerpes uropygialis*)
Golden-fronted woodpecker (*Melanerpes aurifrons*)
Lewis's woodpecker (*Melanerpes lewis*)
Red-bellied woodpecker (*Melanerpes carolinus*)
Red-headed woodpecker (*Melanerpes erythrocephalus*)

Genus *Sphyrapicus*
Red-breasted sapsucker (*Sphyrapicus ruber*)
Red-naped sapsucker (*Sphyrapicus nuchalis*)
Williamson's sapsucker (*Sphyrapicus thyroideus*)
Yellow-bellied sapsucker (*Sphyrapicus varius*)

Genus *Colaptes*
Gilded flicker (*Colaptes chrysoides*)
Northern flicker (*Colaptes auratus*)

Genus *Piculus*
Golden-olive woodpecker (*Piculus rubiginosus*)
Gray-crowned woodpecker (*Piculus auricularis*)

Genus *Dryocopus*
Lineated woodpecker (*Dryocopus lineatus*)
Pileated woodpecker (*Dryocopus pileatus*)

Genus *Campephilus*
Imperial woodpecker (*Campephilus imperialis*)
Ivory-billed woodpecker (*Campephilus principalis*)
Pale-billed woodpecker (*Campephilus guatemalensis*)

AMERICAN THREE-TOED WOODPECKER
Picoides dorsalis

Most woodpeckers have four toes on each foot. In some species, however, evolution has led to the loss of the first toe, or hallux. This trait gave rise to the common name "three-toed woodpecker," which is now shared by two species that were formerly considered as one. The Old World representative is now known as the Eurasian three-toed woodpecker and retains the original scientific name, while its New World relative is officially identified as the American three-toed woodpecker.

Within the Americas the only other three-toed picid is the black-backed woodpecker. Asia has five such species: the Himalayan and common flamebacks and the olive-backed, pale-headed and bamboo woodpeckers. In the case of the Himalayan flameback only about 20 percent of the population are truly three-toed; the rest have a small vestigial hallux.

The effectiveness of the three-toed grip is attested to by a 1909 account by avian collector Major Allan Brooks, who wrote, "When shot, even if instantly killed, three-toed woodpeckers . . . have a marvelous faculty of remaining clinging to the tree in death. Where the trunks are draped with moss, it is impossible to bring one down, except when winged – then they attempt to fly, and fall to earth; but when killed outright they remain securely fastened by their strong claws. The only chance is to leave the bird and visit the foot of the tree when the relaxing muscles have at length permitted the body to drop – usually within two days."

American three-toed woodpeckers exhibit a notable lack of wariness around humans, an attribute that made them easy targets for Brooks and other marksmen with scientific or less lofty objectives. In modern times this fearlessness has facilitated less deadly forms of study as researchers have been able to observe these woodpeckers close up and at length. Unfortunately many gaps remain in our scientific knowledge of this species, which is difficult to find because of its extremely quiet demeanor, especially in fall and winter, and naturally low population densities.

Identification
This medium-sized woodpecker (length: 8 inches, or 20 cm) and the black-backed woodpecker are the only North American woodpeckers with three toes on each foot. Its white underparts are heavily barred with black on the sides and flanks. The back is brownish black along the sides, with varying amounts of black-and-white barring down the center, depending on geographical location: mostly white in the Rocky Mountains; heavily barred with black in the East; intermediate from Alaska to Oregon. The wings are black with some white barring. The rump and central tail feathers are black, with an increasing amount of white on the outer tail feathers. The head is mostly black with two variable white facial stripes. In the eastern subspecies these stripes are least prominent and the white stripe over the eye is sometimes absent. The male's large yellow crown patch is usually bordered with white streaks. The female's crown is black, streaked with white.

Distribution
The American three-toed woodpecker's range includes nearly all of Canada and Alaska south of the treeline, except most of coastal Alaska and British Columbia, the unforested southern parts of the prairie provinces and the southeastern corner of the Atlantic provinces. The range extends a short distance south of the international border into New England and northeastern New York,

and runs south to Arizona and New Mexico following the western mountains.

Habitat

American three-toed woodpeckers inhabit dense boreal and montane coniferous forests at elevations of 4,300 to 9,000 feet (1,300–2,750 m) in the West and 1,200 to 4,100 feet (365–1,250 m) in the East. They favor mature or old-growth forests with plenty of standing dead or dying trees, and areas where fire, insects, disease, flooding or wind breakage have increased prey abundance. They avoid young forests and clearcuts. Moist or swampy areas may be preferred, especially in eastern North America. During population irruptions some individuals move into urban areas.

Voice

American three-toed woodpeckers are much less vocal than many other woodpeckers. The year-round call note is a high-pitched *pik*, given singly or in a loose series. All other calls are believed to be restricted to the breeding season. The rattle call, often given in flight, is usually associated with threat or territorial displays; it consists of six to 26 notes repeated at a steady rate of about 11 notes per second. Aggressive encounters with members of the same or other species may be accompanied by a long series of loud, squeaky *kweek* notes. Repeated *wicka*s are given during interactions with other species. Low-pitched intimate calls are exchanged by mates.

Drumming and Tapping

This species and the black-backed woodpecker drum more than most other woodpeckers. American three-toed woodpeckers vary the tempo of their drum sequences, apparently to convey different messages. Fast drumming is usually a response to drumming by other members of the same species or by black-backed woodpeckers, and most likely serves a territorial function. Slow drumming is less frequent and mostly used as a breeding communication or location signal between mates. Drum rolls in both categories last slightly longer than one second and the tempo increases toward the end. The average fast drum roll consists of 16 strikes (about 14 beats per second). Slow drum rolls average nine strikes (about 11 beats per second).

Feeding

American three-toed woodpeckers primarily eat bark beetle larvae, which live in the cambium just beneath tree bark. They also prey on wood-boring beetle larvae during their initial cambium-dwelling stage, before they move deep into the sapwood. They forage by delivering glancing blows with the bill to remove the bark and expose larval galleries and by excavating, usually no deeper than the cambium layer. American three-toed woodpeckers forage exclusively on conifers, favoring dead or dying trees and concentrating on the trunk. They typically spend a long time working each section, with frequent quiet pauses, and often completely strip the trunk of bark before moving to another tree. They also consume small quantities of sap and cambium from the sap wells they drill in live conifers.

Breeding

American three-toed woodpeckers breed farther north than any other North American woodpecker. Pair bonds do not seem to be maintained through winter and the proportion of pairs that remate is not known. Usually a new nest cavity is excavated annually. Nest trees may be coniferous or deciduous and are usually dead; live nest trees commonly have heart rot. The clutch size ranges from three to seven, but is usually four. Cavity entrance hole diameters range from 1.5 to 1.8 inches (3.8–4.5 cm).

Migration

Western populations are nonmigratory. Possible southward migration in central and eastern North America is difficult to document because of this species' generally low abundance. Localized population irruptions occur sporadically south of the breeding range, mainly in the East, but also into the southern Prairie provinces. These are usually associated with a forest fire, insect outbreak or arboreal disease such as Dutch elm disease.

Conservation

Population densities are highly variable, but generally low, making it difficult to assess overall trends. Apparent declines are likely related to modern forestry practices. These woodpeckers' large home ranges make them sensitive to forest fragmentation. Short cutting rotations, fire suppression and salvage logging of burned and insect-infested trees reduce the availability of their prey.

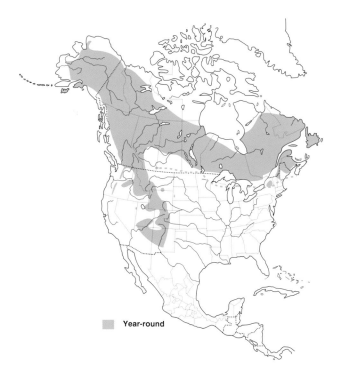

Year-round

ARIZONA WOODPECKER
Picoides arizonae

Despite its relatively loud drum rolls and wide array of calls, the Arizona woodpecker has a reputation for being quiet and secretive, especially during the early part of the nesting season. In April and May, pairs forming or renewing bonds and establishing territories are as noisy and conspicuous as many other woodpeckers. Since mated birds generally do not stay close together, long-distance vocalizations and drumming play an important role in maintaining contact. However, during egg laying and incubation their voices largely disappear from their woodland abode.

Throughout the incubation period and for several days after the eggs hatch, one parent – either the male or the female – is nearly always in the nest cavity. Whenever the off-shift parent returns to the nest to incubate the clutch or to bring food to the nestlings and brood them while its mate forages, it signals its arrival with a soft *tuk-tuk-tuk*. This nest-relief call prompts the attending parent to emerge and switch places. Later the parents will use the same call to summon their newly fledged young when they have food for them.

Although the covert behavior of nesting Arizona woodpeckers frustrated egg collectors, many observers have found this species to be much more approachable than other woodpeckers. Juveniles are particularly unwary. In 1904 ornithologist Harry Swarth wrote about an episode in which an acquaintance was watering his horse. As the thirsty animal drank, a young Arizona woodpecker flew down from a nearby oak, landed on the horse's hind leg and gave it a couple of vigorous raps. The startled response of both horse and human caused the bird to momentarily retreat, but a minute later it was back to its investigations, this time hammering on one of the horse's front legs. Some spirited bucking convinced the assailant to give up its deluded effort, but did not scare it away. The woodpecker was still sitting on the edge of the well when the horse and rider left.

Identification

The Arizona woodpecker is the only North American member of the genus *Picoides* that is patterned in brown and white instead of black and white. The body plumage of this medium-sized (length: 7–8 inches, or 18–20 cm) woodpecker is mostly brown above and white with brown spots and streaks below. The dark brown nape, crown, forehead, ear patches and mustache stripes contrast with the other portions of the head, which are largely white. Males have a narrow red band across the back of the head that females lack. In fresh fall plumage the wings, back and rump are the same dark brown as the head parts, but their color fades during the year because of wear. The brown spotting on the white breast and belly becomes increasingly pronounced in spring and summer as the white feather tips get worn away.

Distribution

In the United States, the Arizona woodpecker is found only in the mountains of extreme southwestern New Mexico and southeastern Arizona. South of the Mexico–U.S. border the range follows the Sierra Madre Occidental to Jalisco, then runs east along the south rim of the Mexican plateau to Michoacán. Until recently the Arizona woodpecker was considered a subspecies of Strickland's woodpecker. When the two were split, the older name was kept for the species residing in the high mountains of central Mexico.

Habitat

In the northern part of their range Arizona woodpeckers typically inhabit montane oak or pine/oak woodlands and associated sycamore/walnut riparian areas, mostly between 3,900 and 6,900 feet (1,200–2,100 m). Their elevational distribution may be influenced by competition with hairy woodpeckers, which nest at higher altitudes, and ladder-backed woodpeckers, which occupy lower areas. In the southern part of the range Arizona woodpeckers are more often found in pine woodlands and at elevations up to 7,900 feet (2,400 m).

Voice

This species' year-round call note is a long *peep*. The loud, harsh rattle call is a rapid sequence of seven to 30 notes; it is a common response to disturbance. A female will usually reply to her mate's rattle call or drumming with single or repeated *kweek*s. A twitter consisting of kweek-like notes (four to 12 per second) often alternates with wicka calls, in which the *wicka*s are repeated about five times a second. The Arizona woodpecker's large vocal repertoire also includes intimate calls and several other calls exchanged between mates during the breeding season.

Drumming and Tapping

Drumming typically consists of a sustained series of loud rolls, each about 12 beats long. The number of rolls per minute averages 3.5, but the rate can increase to 11 per minute. Males drum more frequently than females and in longer sequences. During nesting season Arizona woodpeckers usually drum in the morning. Individuals may also drum after emerging from the nest following an incubation shift.

Tapping is uncommon and done only by males. After performing a courtship display flight a male may tap loudly, usually five to 11 times, at his partially excavated cavity to attract his mate.

Feeding

Arizona woodpeckers prey mainly on larval and adult insects, particularly beetle larvae. These very active foragers spiral rapidly up the tree trunk and out onto the smaller branches, then fly to the next tree and start again close to the ground. Individuals have been recorded as working 47 to 69 trees in an hour. Their main foraging techniques are prying and probing into crevices with their bills and scratching away loose bark using both feet. They sometimes excavate larvae from trees or the dead flowering stalks of agave. They also eat fruits and acorns.

Breeding

It is not clear whether Arizona woodpeckers maintain pair bonds through winter. Nest cavities are usually excavated in deadwood and are not reused. Tree species typically used for nesting are oaks, sycamores, maples, cottonwoods and walnuts. The few clutches that have been counted contained two to four eggs. Cavity entrance hole diameters range from 2 to 2.2 inches (5–5.7 cm).

Migration

This species is nonmigratory. Some individuals move to lower elevations during some winters, perhaps prompted by food scarcity.

Conservation

Population trends are unknown because of lack of information about historical abundance. Habitat in northwestern Mexico is being fragmented rapidly and destroyed by rural development and logging. Habitat in the United States is less vulnerable because of its low commercial value. In both countries lowering of the water table and heavy grazing in riparian areas threaten the survival of sycamores, which are important nest trees.

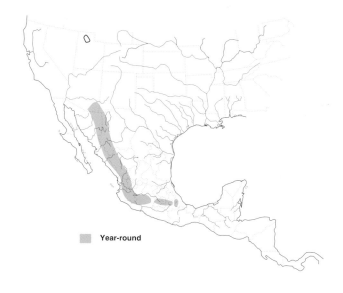

■ Year-round

BLACK-BACKED WOODPECKER
Picoides arcticus

Fire is a natural part of the vast boreal and montane forests that are home to the black-backed woodpecker. It is also an essential element in the survival of this widespread but generally rare species. At first glance a forest of charred trunks rising above scorched ground may look devastated, but there is life as well as death in the aftermath of a severe burn. Once the last embers have cooled, wood-boring beetles converge on the fire site to take advantage of the ideal egg-laying conditions they find there. And in their wake come hungry black-backed woodpeckers, some traveling hundreds of miles to enjoy the two- to four-year feast of beetle larvae.

In the early 1900s U.S. Department of Agriculture biologist Foster E.L. Beal carried out a comprehensive survey of woodpecker feeding habits to determine the economic impact of these birds. He estimated that a single black-backed woodpecker would typically eat 13,675 larval long-horned beetles (wood-boring beetles of the Cerambycidae family) each year. The stomachs of many of the woodpeckers he examined contained 15 to 20 long-horned beetle larvae, and one held 34. Assuming that the birds would fill their stomachs several times a day, Beal thought it likely that they would eat 50 larvae daily during the half of the year when their nutritional needs were greatest and 25 a day during the other six months of the year.

Biologists refer to the black-backed woodpecker as an irruptive species, meaning that local populations irregularly experience abrupt and substantial, though temporary, increases in response to favorable environmental change. Population irruptions of black-backed woodpeckers are associated with insect outbreaks, which are usually triggered by fire. Throughout North America black-backed woodpecker breeding densities are much higher in recently burned forests than in areas that have remained untouched by flames for many years. Unfortunately a century of fire suppression and post-fire salvage logging has greatly reduced the availability of the habitat this species needs to thrive.

When searching for black-backed woodpeckers, be prepared to use your ears as much as your eyes. Charcoal-colored dorsal plumage makes these birds hard to spot against the trunks of burned trees, but the sounds of their vigorous excavating, as well as their contact calls and drumming, should alert you to their presence.

Identification

This species gets its name from its entirely black back, which contrasts with its white underparts and black-and-white barred sides. The wings and tail are also black except for white barring on the primaries and white outer tail feathers. The head is mostly black, with a long white stripe below each eye. A prominent yellow cap distinguishes males from females. This medium-sized woodpecker (length: 9–10 inches, or 23–25 cm) is one of only two North American woodpeckers that have three toes on each foot instead of the usual four.

Distribution

The black-backed woodpecker's range stretches across Canada south of the treeline and east of the Pacific Coast Mountains, with absences in southern areas of the prairie provinces and parts of southern Ontario and Quebec. The range extends north into the interior of Alaska and south into mainly mountainous regions of Montana, Wyoming, Idaho, Washington, Oregon and California, as well as the Black Hills (South Dakota and Wyoming) and the extreme northeastern U.S. from Minnesota to Maine. During population irruptions black-backed woodpeckers sometimes move well south of the border states in winter.

Habitat

The breeding range extends across the boreal and montane coniferous forests of Alaska, Canada and the northern United States. Within this wide territory black-backed woodpeckers are habitat specialists, favoring fire-killed stands or other areas affected by outbreaks of wood-boring beetles. However, during winter population irruptions they often move into urban areas.

Voice

The black-backed woodpecker's year-round call note is a fast double-click that sounds like *kyik* or *chet*. The complex rattle call consists of three elements in various combinations, including the full three-part scream-rattle-snarl. It is often given in flight and is associated with establishing territory and antagonistic encounters with members of the same or other species. Other breeding season vocalizations include the wicka call and the intimate call.

Drumming and Tapping

This species and the American three-toed woodpecker drum to a greater degree than most other woodpeckers. A typical black-backed woodpecker drum roll lasts about 1.5 to two seconds, with an increase in tempo toward the end. Females drum slightly faster than males – about 20 beats per second, compared to the males' 18. Repeated drum rolls are usually spaced 30 to 40 seconds apart. Black-backed woodpeckers sometimes deliver single raps when disturbed or just before roosting.

Feeding

The larvae of wood-boring beetles, engraver beetles and mountain pine beetles – obtained by excavating – are this species' most important prey. Black-backed woodpeckers congregate in areas where populations of these insects have increased rapidly after a fire or, less frequently, after some other large-scale natural disturbance such as flooding or wind throw. Other invertebrate prey, obtained mostly by gleaning, and plant foods such as wild fruits, nuts and cambium make up a small part of their diet.

Breeding

Black-backed woodpeckers nest in live or dead trees, using a wide variety of deciduous and coniferous species. They appear to maintain pair bonds year-round. Pairs nearly always excavate a new cavity each year. Clutch size is usually three to four, but ranges from two to six. Nests may be initiated later than normal if fire provides new breeding opportunities in previously unsuitable habitat; egg laying may start within days after burning ends. Cavity entrance holes are approximately 1.7 inches (4.4 cm) in diameter.

Migration

Regular migration does not occur, but some individuals in eastern areas wander a short distance south of the breeding range during winter. Irruptive movements in response to insect outbreaks are often over very long distances.

Conservation

Natural fluctuations in black-backed woodpecker populations make it difficult to determine a trend in overall numbers. It is clear, however, that fire suppression and salvage logging after forest fires are reducing the availability of essential habitat and may lead to local or regional extirpation. Prescribed burning programs will not solve this problem, since these controlled, low-intensity fires are intended to avoid the hotter, stand-replacing fires that produce the conditions black-backed woodpeckers require.

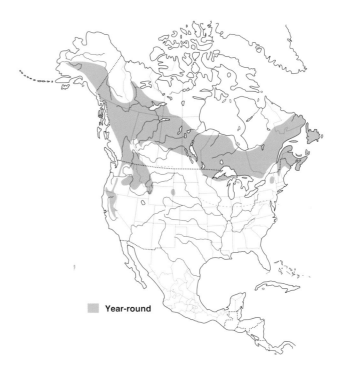

Year-round

DOWNY WOODPECKER
Picoides pubescens

The downy is the smallest woodpecker living in Canada and the United States, but it is much better known than most of its larger relatives. It is found widely across the continent and it is the most common woodpecker in eastern North America. The downy woodpecker has adapted readily to life in settled areas throughout its range and is a familiar visitor to backyard feeding stations in winter.

Downy woodpeckers are very active foragers, moving incessantly as they glean insect eggs from leaves and bark, probe into cracks and excavate for prey living just below the surface of tree trunks and branches. The muted but persistent tapping that accompanies their excavating activities sometimes attracts other downy woodpeckers. Humans with a talent for mimicking this tapping are often able to entice these engaging little birds closer for a better view.

Although downy and hairy woodpeckers have very similar plumage patterns, they can be distinguished by relative bill size. The downy's bill is shorter than the length of its head from front to back, while the hairy woodpecker's bill is as long as or longer than its head. The names of the two species refer to the appearance of the feathers that form the white stripe down the back: soft and downy in one case; fine and filamentous, or hair-like, in the other.

The downy's pristine, snowy white to off-white underparts are a useful distinguishing feature but can sometimes be a source of puzzlement because of their susceptibility to staining. No need to call the birdwatchers' hot line if you see a purple-breasted downy look-alike. You haven't discovered a new species – just spotted an individual that has been feeding on pokeberries or mulberries. Similarly, black walnuts can leave a yellow tint. In regions with red soil downy woodpeckers sometimes end up with red-tinged bellies, while black-fronted individuals are not uncommon in areas where trees are charred by frequent prescribed burning. One crimson-bellied downy was discovered to be visiting a hummingbird feeder regularly and slopping red-dyed sugar-water onto itself. The bluish hue on another individual was attributed to its habit of foraging on stained wood siding.

Identification

A distinctive white stripe runs down the center of the downy woodpecker's black back, and its unmarked underparts are white in most parts of its range. In the Pacific Northwest the dorsal stripe and underparts are pale gray-brown, and in parts of the south-central and southeastern United States the underparts are drab gray. The central tail feathers are black and the white outer tail feathers are marked with a few black bars. The wings are black with white spots. The head is marked with contrasting areas of black and white. Males have a narrow red patch on the nape, which is black in females. At only 6 to 6.7 inches (15–17 cm) in length, this woodpecker is smaller than all the others within its range.

Distribution

This species' range covers much of Canada and the United States. Downy woodpeckers are thinly distributed in the northern halves of all Canadian provinces and absent from northern Alaska and most parts of Canada's northern territories. They are also absent from southern regions of the U.S. from California to Texas.

Habitat

Downy woodpeckers are strongly associated with deciduous trees and are often found in open

deciduous woodlands or riparian forests. In regions dominated by conifers they favor mixed forests and those with a well-developed deciduous understory. They are also common in orchards and treed urban areas.

Voice

Most of the downy woodpecker's calls are given throughout the year. The flat *pik* that is the regular call note changes to a higher-pitched *peek* or *kweek*, repeated at a rate of three to four notes per second, as the caller's level of excitement increases. The whinny – used in forming pair bonds, signaling location and asserting dominance – is a rapid series of 11 to 25 notes, descending in pitch and shortening through the call. The raspy multipart sputter call may express dominance. Various low intimate calls, both soft and harsh-sounding, are given by mates in close proximity.

Drumming and Tapping

Drum rolls usually last 1.5 seconds or less, with a tempo of about 16 to 18 beats per second, decelerating slightly toward the end. They are broadcast at a rate of about nine to 15 repetitions per minute.

Downy woodpeckers of both sexes tap to attract their nearby mate to a potential nest site. They typically tap nine or 10 times in a row at a rate of about three or four taps per second.

Feeding

The diet is dominated by insects but also includes fruits and seeds. Downy woodpeckers are very active foragers, mostly using gleaning, probing and shallow excavating to obtain prey. In late winter and early spring they occasionally lick sap from sapsucker wells or tree wounds. Differential use of foraging sites has been well studied for this species – males tend to concentrate on small-diameter tree limbs and trunks and the stems of tall weeds; females focus on larger branches and tree trunks.

Breeding

Pairs with a plentiful food supply seem more likely to stay together year-round. Some pairs that separate through winter may reunite in spring. Nests are nearly always excavated in wood with advanced heart rot, either in snags or dead limbs of live trees, most often deciduous species. Cavities are used for only one nesting season. Clutch size ranges from three to eight. Cavity entrance hole diameters range from 1.1 to 1.5 inches (2.8–3.8 cm).

Migration

There is ongoing debate as to whether downy woodpeckers in some areas undertake seasonal migration or whether records of long-distance movements represent one-way dispersal.

Conservation

Populations have declined in some regions and increased in others, probably in response to habitat alteration by agriculture, forestry and urbanization. Overall this species is not threatened.

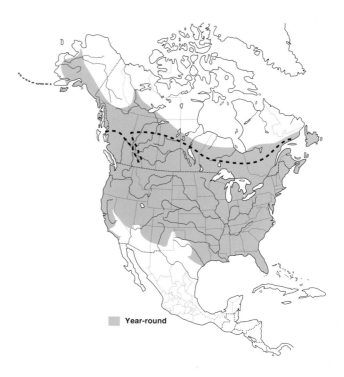

■ Year-round

HAIRY WOODPECKER
Picoides villosus

The hairy woodpecker has one of the most extensive ranges of any North American woodpecker and is one of the continent's most geographically variable birds. A northern birdwatcher seeing a Central American hairy woodpecker for the first time would probably recognize the species, but might be confused by unfamiliar elements of its appearance.

A student of biology, however, might remember that the hairy woodpecker is a textbook example of Bergmann's Rule, an ecogeographical principle that addresses size differences within widely distributed bird and mammal species. The rule states that members of populations living in colder regions generally have larger bodies than their warm-region relatives. Why? Because larger mass results in a lower surface-to-volume ratio, which reduces relative heat loss – an advantage in chilly climates and a disadvantage in hot ones.

As predicted by Bergmann's Rule, the body mass of hairy woodpeckers decreases gradually but significantly from north to south throughout the species' range, as well as from higher (cooler) to lower (warmer) elevations at any given latitude. Males from Alaska weigh about 3.3 ounces (95 g), while those from Chiapas, Mexico, weigh only about 1.5 ounces (44 g). The same trend is also seen in other widespread species. Alaskan downy woodpeckers, for example, are about 12 percent larger than members of the same species living in Florida.

In addition to size differences, hairy woodpeckers also exhibit a daunting array of regional variations in plumage coloring and patterns. In general, those living east of the Rocky Mountains and in the boreal forests of Alaska and Canada's northern territories have light-colored underparts ranging from pure white to buff-tinged white. Most populations from the Rockies west to the Pacific and south to Central America have darker underparts in shades that include whitish drab, grayish brown, sooty brown and, in Costa Rica and Panama, smoky cinnamon.

Within some western and southern populations the "white" areas on the head, back and wings take on the darker color of the underparts. In many of these populations the prominence of the mid-dorsal stripe or the amount of spotting on the wings is reduced compared to most eastern populations. Hairy woodpeckers living in very humid regions also tend to have less white spotting on their backs. And isolated populations, including those on islands such as Newfoundland and the Bahamas, tend to have more black streaking on their flanks, black barring on their backs and black markings on their outer tail feathers.

Another notable plumage discrepancy is the size of the red head markings that identify adult males. Throughout much of the species' range this sexual badge is a band across the back of the head. In eastern North America, however, it is often reduced to a red spot on either side of the head, separated by black. Fortunately the average person does not need to keep track of all these permutations of plumage and size. Ornithologists who have devoted years to this woodpecker still can't agree as to whether there are 17 subspecies, 14 or 21.

Identification

Like the very similarly patterned downy woodpecker, the hairy woodpecker is distinguished by the white or off-white stripe down the center of its black back and its plain white or off-white underparts. The black wings are variably marked with white spots and the tail is black except for white outer tail feathers. The head is marked with contrasting areas of black and white. On males the white stripe above the eye meets the narrow band of red across the nape. In eastern North America this nape patch is often reduced to two lateral spots. Females have no red head markings. This small to medium-sized species varies in length from 6.5 to 10.2 inches (17–26 cm), depending on geographic location.

Distribution

The northern limit of this species' range runs close to the treeline and stretches across the continent from central Alaska to Newfoundland. The range extends throughout most of Canada and the U.S., except some non-forested parts of southern Alberta and Saskatchewan and the western and southern states. Farther south the range becomes discontinuous, but includes northern Baja California and many highland areas from eastern Sonora to western Panama. Hairy woodpeckers are also resident in the Bahamas.

Habitat

Hairy woodpeckers inhabit a diversity of mature forest habitats, favoring deciduous or mixed woodlands in many regions. In parts of the southern United States, open pine forest is preferred. Urban areas with mature trees sometimes attract this species, especially in winter.

Voice

The hairy woodpecker's year-round call note is a loud, sharp *peek* that becomes a strident *cheerk* in its most intense form. The whinny, used for long-distance communication, often begins with one or two abbreviated *peek*s followed by a rapid series of lower-pitched notes. A harsher, extended version of the whinny signals alarm. A series of notes that sound like *kweek*, *woick* or *joick*, depending on the intensity of the call, may be uttered as a greeting between mates or during interactions with woodpeckers of other species. Repeated *wicka* notes may accompany conflicts with other hairy woodpeckers, especially between two males. Intimate calls include soft *teuk* notes, often given by a female when approaching her mate.

Drumming and Tapping

The hairy woodpecker's rapid drum rolls are about one second in length, with a steady tempo of about 26 beats per second. The usual delivery rate is four to five drum rolls per minute, but repetitions of 26 rolls per minute have been recorded. Males usually drum more than females.

During nest-site selection either the male or the female may tap to attract its nearby mate to a potential nest site. The beat is slow, typically two or three taps per second.

Feeding

The diet is dominated by insects, both adults and larvae, gathered primarily by gleaning or excavating and occasionally by flycatching. Hairy woodpeckers also consume some fruits, seeds and other plant materials, including sap from sapsucker wells or tree wounds, and they sometimes visit feeders in winter.

Breeding

The pair bonds of hairy woodpeckers are maintained year-round in at least some cases and may be lifelong. Nest-tree selection varies geographically. In some areas live trees with heart rot are preferred. In others nest cavities are typically excavated in snags or dead branches of live trees. Affinities for either deciduous or coniferous trees are also regional. Clutch size ranges from three to seven. The hairy woodpecker's cavity entrance holes are slightly oval and vary in size geographically in relation to varying body size. In the northeastern United States the average diameter is approximately 2 inches (5 cm).

Migration

In Mexico and Central America this species is nonmigratory. More northerly populations are usually described as permanent resid ents, but some birds undertake seasonal movements that have been interpreted as limited migration.

Conservation

Populations appear to be gradually declining in some areas, most likely because of habitat fragmentation, loss of mature forest and competition with European starlings.

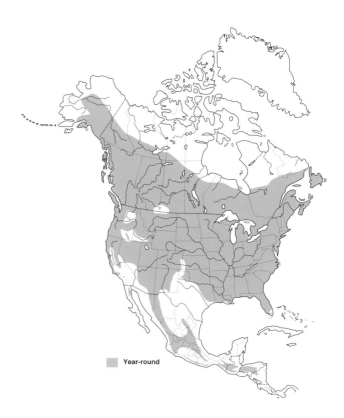

Year-round

LADDER-BACKED WOODPECKER
Picoides scalaris

In most regions where it lives, the ladder-backed woodpecker is easily distinguished from its relatives. In extreme southern California and northwestern Baja California, however, the ranges of this species and Nuttall's woodpecker overlap slightly. The two are very close in size and similar in appearance, creating an identification challenge for birdwatchers.

Ladder-backed and Nuttall's woodpeckers both respond to vocalizations and drumming of the other species, although there are discernable differences in these. Expert human listeners – and presumably the woodpeckers – know that the single *peek* call note of the ladder-backed is louder and often higher pitched and longer than Nuttall's *pit* note. More obvious is the difference in how each species strings these call notes together. The ladder-backed woodpecker's rattle call, which is much like the downy's whinny, descends in pitch at the end and trails off without a decisive conclusion. Nuttall's woodpeckers have a crisp rattle that ascends slightly at the end and concludes with a distinct "t" sound.

Where these two species meet, their ranges fit together almost like pieces of a puzzle. The abrupt border between them is defined largely by habitat preferences. One place where this has been well documented is in San Diego County, California. Here Nuttall's woodpeckers are a common resident of the riparian, oak and mixed conifer woodlands along the county's coastal slope, while ladder-backed woodpeckers are restricted mainly to the thorn scrub and agave habitats of the drier east slope. The only significant area of shared terrain is a narrow zone, perhaps no more than five miles (8 km) wide, along the east slope, where wooded canyons reach like fingers down toward the desert. In this zone the distance between the territories of the two species can be negligible, with Nuttall's woodpeckers nesting in the relative lushness of the canyons and ladder-backed woodpeckers on the arid open hillsides nearby.

Where habitat and landscape promote a greater degree of contact, territorial behavior plays a more significant role in keeping these woodpeckers apart. They both defend their territories against intruders of their own and the other species. However, despite their usual segregation, hybridization is frequent in Baja California between Ensenada and San Quintin. Mixed matings are also regularly reported from a few parts of California, including Kern and San Bernardino counties.

Identification

Horizontal black-and-white barring on its back and wings gives this small woodpecker (length: 6.3–7 inches, or 16–18 cm) its name. The three outermost pairs of tail feathers are also broadly barred in black and white, while the rest of the tail is black. The dull off-white underparts are tinged gray, buff or brown and marked with dark streaks and spots on the sides. The black eye-line and mustache stripe on either side of the head join near the nape and are offset by white to buffy brownish white markings. The dusky nasal tufts blend into the black forehead. The male has a vermilion crown flecked with white and black on top, becoming solid red at the back. Females have no red head markings, but sometimes have some white spots on their black forehead and crown.

Distribution

The ladder-backed woodpecker's range includes much of the southwestern U.S., from California to Texas, and nearly all of Mexico. Scattered populations are found as far south as Nicaragua.

Habitat

In the United States this species occupies primarily desert habitats, including desert scrub, thorn forests and mesquite grasslands, but some populations are found in riparian, desert-edge and piñon juniper woodlands. Habitats in Mexico are similar, with the addition of relatively open deciduous and pine/oak woodlands.

Voice

The call note is a short, high-pitched *peek*. This is also the basic component of the rattle call, a series of 12 to 25 notes delivered rapidly (about 10 notes per second) with a marked drop in pitch at the end. Both calls are given year-round. During the breeding season, rattle calls are often associated with drumming and kweek calls, which consist of one or a series of *kweek* notes typically given during conflicts or encounters with ladder-backed woodpeckers or members of other species.

Drumming and Tapping

Ladder-backed woodpeckers drum very rapidly, averaging 28 to 30 beats per second in drum rolls that last slightly less than one second. The tempo decreases slightly toward the end of the roll. Drumming is limited to the months of February to April.

Feeding

Ladder-backed woodpeckers feed largely on adult and larval insects, found mostly by probing, tapping and gleaning. Their foraging involves much twisting, turning, fluttering and sideways movement. Typical foraging sites include Joshua trees (often in old seed clusters or new flowers), cholla and prickly pear cacti, mesquite and agave, as well as deciduous trees such as cottonwoods, willows and oaks, where these occur in their range.

Breeding

The duration of pair bonds is not known. Nest cavities are excavated in Joshua trees and other yuccas, agave stalks, saguaro cacti and various deciduous trees. Fence posts and utility poles are also used. No research has been done on reuse of nest cavities from year to year. Clutch size ranges from two to seven, but is usually four or five. Ladder-backed woodpeckers occasionally hybridize with Nuttall's or hairy woodpeckers. Cavity entrance holes are approximately 1.6 inches (4 cm) in diameter.

Migration

Ladder-backed woodpeckers are nonmigratory.

Conservation

Populations trends are not well documented, but the limited data suggest declines in some areas.

Year-round

NUTTALL'S WOODPECKER
Picoides nuttallii

Florence Merriam Bailey, an ardent Victorian-era advocate of using opera glasses instead of shotguns to study birds, was one of the first ornithologists to closely observe Nuttall's woodpeckers. After watching them forage she noted that this species "has a nuthatch-like way of flying up to light on the underside of a limb, and when hanging upside down turns itself around with as much ease as a fly on a ceiling."

Decades later a comprehensive analysis of the feeding behavior of Nuttall's woodpeckers was carried out by Alden H. Miller and Carl E. Bock, who found these birds were more versatile and acrobatic than woodpeckers such as the hairy and downy, and switched frequently and erratically from one foraging method to another. Miller and Bock reported that their subjects frequently hopped from one part of a tree to another, "often almost crept ... along a foraging surface, assuming a rather humped position, with the bill thrust ahead or somewhat tangentially," perched crosswise on small branches "with the tail thrust ventrally but not in contact, as a balancer," climbed about in foliage clusters while fluttering and balancing with the wings, hung upside down from slender twigs, foraged mostly by bark scaling, probing and gleaning, and "pursued insects in the air, tumbling out from or down through the foliage in the process." Many other North American woodpeckers include some of these behaviors in their repertoire, but only the ladder-backed matches this species' nimble and eclectic style.

Identification

This small (length: 6.3–7 inches, or 16–18 cm) woodpecker's back and wings are marked with broad black and narrow white horizontal bars. The white underparts are streaked or spotted with black along the sides. The central tail feathers are black and the outer ones white, sparsely spotted with black near the tips. The head is marked with contrasting areas of black and white. The male's black forehead and crown are streaked with white, while the back of his head and upper nape are bright poppy red to scarlet vermilion. Females have no red head markings, but sometimes have streaks of white in the black forehead and crown.

Distribution

Nuttall's woodpecker has a very limited range. It runs the length of California, mostly west of the deserts and Sierra divide, and extends a short distance into northwestern Baja California.

Habitat

In the northern part of its range this species is strongly associated with oak woodlands. Farther south, oaks decrease in abundance and Nuttall's woodpeckers have an increasing affinity for riparian woodlands.

Voice

Throughout the year Nuttall's woodpeckers use both single (*pit*) and double (*pitit*) call notes. In winter and spring the double, which consists of paired, nearly identical components, is more common than the single. The somewhat metallic-sounding rattle call consists of 14 to 45 call notes delivered at about 19 notes per second, ascending slightly in pitch toward the end. From fall through spring rattle calls are used for establishing territories and as a long-distance contact call. They are often associated with drumming. The kweek call, a series of *kweek* notes, is given mainly by females in late winter and spring, often as a long-distance signal for interaction with a male.

Drumming and Tapping

The average tempo of Nuttall's woodpecker drum rolls is about 21 beats per second, increasing toward the end. Drum rolls are approximately one second in length and are delivered 20 times an hour during peak drumming periods. Males drum more often than females.

Feeding

Nuttall's woodpeckers primarily eat insects, supplemented with small amounts of plant matter such as berries, flower buds and sap. Depending on local habitat, they forage in oaks, other deciduous trees and gray pines, locating their prey by probing, limited excavating to widen crevices, gleaning and bark scaling.

Breeding

Mated pairs remain within their shared territory year-round. Time spent together ranges from 80 percent in February to none after their young disperse in August. Pairs often exchange calls when foraging during fall and winter. Nest cavities are usually excavated in deadwood of deciduous trees; new cavities are excavated every spring. Clutch size ranges from three to six. Nuttall's woodpeckers occasionally hybridize with ladder-backed and downy woodpeckers. Cavity entrance holes are approximately 2 inches (5 cm) in diameter.

Migration

Although nonmigratory, some Nuttall's woodpeckers move upslope in autumn, out of the foothills and canyons where they breed, to higher mountain ranges.

Conservation

Population declines are occurring in central and southern California. Habitat destruction due to residential and agricultural development is undoubtedly to blame. At the same time Nuttall's woodpeckers have moved into some urban areas where they were previously absent, such as central San Diego, probably because maturing trees are providing newly suitable habitat in what was originally sage scrub.

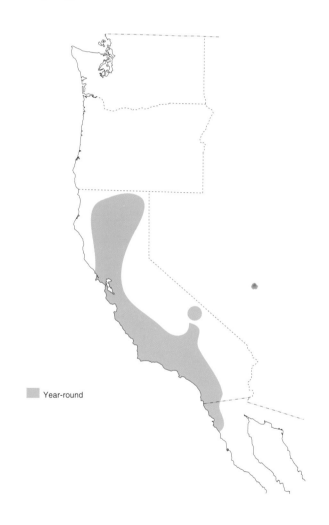

■ Year-round

RED-COCKADED WOODPECKER
Picoides borealis

Many woodpeckers prefer to nest in dead, decay-softened wood, which is easily excavated. Those that nest in live trees generally avoid conifers because of the gummy resins they produce when wounded. But in the fire-prone pine forests of the southeastern U.S. trees are in short supply. Red-cockaded woodpeckers have adapted to this environment by becoming the only North American woodpeckers that nest exclusively in live pines.

To reach the heartwood of a pine that is large enough to accommodate a cavity, a red-cockaded woodpecker must tunnel through three to six inches (8–15 cm) of sapwood. As soon as the assault begins the tree responds by exuding copious amounts of resin, which threatens to make a sticky mess of the woodpecker's feathers. This is no mere inconvenience. Faulty tunnel construction can be fatal, as evidenced by the occasional red-cockaded woodpecker that is found dead in a cavity entrance, trapped in a pool of resin.

When the resin flow becomes excessive the woodpecker must stop excavating and wait until the flow stops and the liquid crystallizes. Then work can resume, but only for a short time. Depending on the thickness of the sapwood and the tree's resin-generating capacity, it can take from several months to a few years to reach the non-resin-producing heartwood. If there are long interruptions a dozen or more years may pass between initiation and completion of a cavity. The bird that begins construction may not be the one who finishes the job.

The difficulty of excavating into live pines is balanced by the fact that these cavities are much more secure and long-lasting than those made in snags or deciduous trees. Red-cockaded woodpecker nest cavities often remain in use for two decades or longer. This species' cooperative breeding social system – which holds the promise of cavity inheritance for males that remain on their natal territory as non-breeding helpers – is directly tied to both the constraints and the rewards of being specialized live-pine excavators.

Not only have red-cockaded woodpeckers evolved the ability to use live pines as cavity trees, they have also managed to turn the trees' resin production to their advantage. Shortly before a new cavity is ready for occupation, its creator drills small, shallow holes into the tree trunk all around the entrance. The resin that oozes from these holes and runs down the trunk will soon form a highly effective deterrent against tree-climbing rat snakes, the most deadly enemy of cavity-nesting birds in the American southeast.

The woodpeckers ensure a continuous flow of resin by pecking at existing wells every day, often just before entering to roost for the night. They also regularly add new wells. Eventually the system of wells may extend six to 10 feet (2–3 m) above and below the entrance. On cavity trees that have been used for many years, the buildup of white crystallized resin coating the trunk resembles melted candle wax. A tree that is in current use is distinguished by the presence of fresh, clear resin and the reddish appearance of the wells that are being actively worked. Cavity trees can also be recognized by their relatively smooth trunks. By flaking away loose bark, red-cockaded woodpeckers improve their defenses in two ways: snakes have more difficulty climbing without bark furrows to wedge their scales into, and the resin flows more evenly.

Identification

This medium-sized (length: 8–9 inches, or 20–23 cm) woodpecker is named for the male's distinguishing feature, a tiny red streak on the side of the head behind each eye. However, the 12 to 16 red feathers that form each cockade are usually hidden by the black crown feathers, and males cannot be reliably differentiated from females except in the hand or when they are displaying. Both sexes have a black-and-white barred back and wings and white or pale gray underparts spotted and streaked with black along the sides of the breast and belly. The central tail feathers are black, while the outer ones are white with several black spots. The forehead, crown and nape are somewhat glossy black. The large white cheek patches contrast with black mustache stripes that extend down to the sides of the breast.

Distribution

Red-cockaded woodpeckers were once resident throughout much of the southeastern U.S. from central Texas and Oklahoma to the Atlantic coast, with the northern boundary of their range running roughly from Missouri to New Jersey. Today the remaining populations are highly fragmented and generally concentrated in southern parts of the historical range.

Habitat

The best habitat is provided by pure stands of widely spaced mature longleaf pines with a low understory of herbaceous plants and grasses. Frequent growing-season fires are required to maintain this savanna-like forest type and prevent the incursion of hardwood trees and shrubs, which make the habitat unsuitable. Loblolly and shortleaf pine forests also support populations in some areas. Other pines are less frequently used.

Voice

Red-cockaded woodpeckers are much more vocal than many other species, communicating year-round with a large and variable array of calls. They are noisiest after leaving their roosts in the morning and when returning to the cavity-tree cluster in the evening, but family members maintain an almost constant chatter throughout the day. If they come close to each other while foraging they exchange soft chortles, and they appear to call whenever they move from tree to tree. The call note given by undisturbed individuals is a long *churt*. In the presence of humans or when otherwise disturbed, it changes to a more emphatic *sklit*. The rattle call, a series of notes that descends toward the end, is often given when flying into the cavity-tree cluster or toward the nest. Calls given when defending the nest or territory, as well as in several social contexts between family members, include repeated *she-u* or *whe-u* notes and *wic-a* notes. Shrill *kweek*s are delivered singly or in a short series after feeding the young and at other times during the year.

Drumming and Tapping

Red-cockaded woodpeckers drum mostly on live pines, which lack the resonance of deadwood, so their drumming is relatively quiet. It is also infrequent. Solitary males are the most active drummers. Most drumming is done within or near the drummer's cavity-tree cluster.

Feeding

The diet is dominated by invertebrate prey (adults, larvae and eggs), including ants, beetles, cockroaches, centipedes and spiders. Red-cockaded woodpecker foraging is concentrated on large old live pines. The most frequently used foraging techniques are bark scaling and flaking. Some insect prey are also obtained by excavating in dead branches, gleaning and probing. Group members forage together, often within a few inches of each other. Males concentrate on the branches and upper trunk and females on the lower trunk, often below the lowest branches. Pine seeds and berries are eaten in season and groups living near cornfields may feed intensively for several weeks on corn earworms excavated from standing plants.

Breeding

Red-cockaded woodpeckers are cooperative breeders and typically live in small social groups consisting of a monogamous breeding pair and one or more non-breeding helpers. Most helpers are male

offspring that stay with their parents instead of dispersing. Groups may have up to five helpers, but most have one or none. Breeding pairs often mate for life. When the breeding male dies, one of the helpers inherits the territory; if the breeding female is his mother she leaves to find a new mate. Not all groups nest every year. Those that do nest generally raise one brood, rarely two. Clutch size ranges from two to five. Nest cavities are excavated in large live pines, often with heartwood decay, and are used for many years. The average diameter of cavity entrance holes ranges from 2.2 to 2.8 inches (5.6–7.1 cm).

Migration
Red-cockaded woodpeckers are nonmigratory.

Conservation
This once relatively common species has disappeared from much of its original range because of habitat loss and fragmentation. The U.S. government officially listed the red-cockaded woodpecker as an endangered species in 1970. Development and implementation of effective habitat management policies have been slow. Some populations are now stable or increasing as a result of intensive habitat management, but many are still declining, isolated or both.

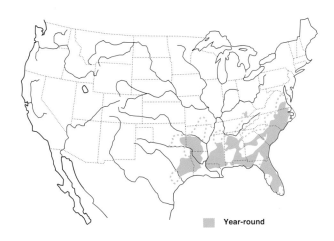

Year-round

WHITE-HEADED WOODPECKER

Picoides albolarvatus

White-headed woodpeckers live exclusively in western North American forests dominated by large-coned pines. Ponderosa pine is the principal tree species throughout much of their range, yet extensive areas of the West have plenty of ponderosa pines and no white-headed woodpeckers. The reason for their absence from these apparently favorable habitats is one of the many unanswered questions about this little-studied species.

These pine-seed specialists are most numerous in habitats with more than one pine species, probably because tree diversity ensures a more reliable food supply. In the Pacific Northwest, for example, ponderosa pines produce heavy cone crops only every fourth or fifth year. Besides ponderosa pine, other preferred species are sugar, Jeffrey and Coulter pine. White-headed woodpeckers avoid forests dominated by species with small or closed cones, such as singleleaf piñon and lodgepole pine. They occasionally eat the seeds of knobcone pine and white fir.

Pine seeds are an essential part of the diet in all seasons, but most important in fall and winter, when insect prey may be scarce. Sugar pines provide food only from August to October, since they shed their seeds in early fall. Pine species that hold their seeds longer can provide year-round sustenance, but peak use is generally from late summer through winter.

With most pine species white-headed woodpeckers obtain seeds by probing into open cones or drilling into closed cones. Large seeds extracted whole or nearly whole are taken to a makeshift anvil, usually located on the same tree or another one nearby. The woodpecker wedges the seed into a bark crevice and breaks it apart by hammering with its bill, then eats the pieces.

When foraging on unopened sugar pine cones white-headed woodpeckers use their bills to carve a series of furrows down the length of each cone, from which they extricate the seeds. They can be highly efficient in their harvest. At one study site in northern California white-headed woodpeckers destroyed one-third of the healthy cones in a sugar pine stand during late August and September, including 85 percent of the 358 cones on one hard-hit tree.

To avoid contact with the sap that often drips from pine cones, foraging white-headed woodpeckers cling acrobatically to the sides or bottom of the cone and hold their bodies well away from it as they work. In southern California the large, spiky cones of the Coulter pine present a formidable foraging challenge that may account for the long bills of the most southerly white-headed woodpecker subspecies, which resides from San Diego County to the San Gabriel Mountains. On average their bills are about 11 percent longer than those of their northern relatives.

Identification

This medium-sized woodpecker (length: 8.3–9 inches, or 21–23 cm) is easily identified by its unique plumage. Its entirely white face, throat and crown " The black back and breast have a slightly bluish gloss. The only white below the head is the white patch on each wing, which is visible when the bird is perched as well as in flight. The male has a narrow band of scarlet across the nape that the female lacks.

Distribution

The white-headed woodpecker's range runs discontinuously from the extreme southern interior of British Columbia south through Washington, Oregon, Idaho, California and the Lake Tahoe area of western Nevada.

Habitat

White-headed woodpeckers are restricted to montane coniferous forests dominated by one or more large-coned pine species. They require an abundance of mature pine trees because larger and older trees produce the most seed. They also need snags or other suitable nesting sites. The best habitats have widely spaced large-diameter trees and sparse understory vegetation.

Voice

The white-headed woodpecker's year-round call notes have either two syllables (*pee-dink* or *peek-it*) or three (*pee-de-dink*). The rattle call consists of rapidly repeated sharp *peek* notes. In its short form it starts with the *pee-dink* note, followed by four to 11 *peeks*. Rattle calls are given throughout the year, but most commonly during territorial disputes and other interactions with members of the same species just before and through the breeding season. During the early part of the breeding season, communication between pair members often involves long, slow sequences of loud, squeaky *kweek* notes. The intimate calls exchanged between mates include low repeated *tyet* or *chuf* notes.

Drumming and Tapping

White-headed woodpeckers drum with an even tempo of about 20 beats per second. The average length of drum rolls is one second.

Males drum more frequently than females. Males tap during the nest-site selection process. During incubation, both males and females often tap from inside the nest cavity while incubating and at the entrance before exchanging places with their mate.

Feeding

The white-headed woodpecker's diet consists mainly of insects, both adult and larval, and pine seeds. The relative importance of these foods varies seasonally, with seed consumption generally concentrated in fall and winter. The most common insect prey are ants, beetles and scale insects obtained from tree trunks, branches and needle clusters, primarily by shallow excavating, bark scaling with the bill or feet, gleaning and shallow probing. Occasional foods include sap from sapsucker wells, mullein seeds and insects caught in flight.

Breeding

This species appears to maintain pair bonds year-round. Clutch size ranges from four to seven. Pairs do not seem to lay replacement clutches if the first clutch or brood is lost. They normally excavate new nest cavities each spring, often making numerous false starts that produce incomplete, unused

cavities. White-headed woodpeckers nest lower than most other woodpeckers, often within 10 feet (3 m) of the ground, regardless of the tree's height. Typical sites are conifer snags, stumps and leaning or fallen trees. Live trembling aspens, dead tops of conifers and fence posts are sometimes used. Cavity entrance holes are slightly oval, with a diameter of about 1.9 inches (4.8 cm).

Migration

Although generally a resident species, between August and April individuals sometimes move to lowland habitats up to 90 miles (145 km) away from known breeding areas.

Conservation

Suitable habitat for white-headed woodpeckers is considerably fragmented by topography, and therefore so are populations. Habitat fragmentation and loss are currently increasing because of fire suppression, short cutting rotations, same-age forest management and snag removal by forestry companies and firewood cutters. Population trends are unclear because of lack of survey data and natural rarity north of California, but there is evidence of declines in British Columbia, Washington, Oregon and Idaho.

■ **Year-round**

ACORN WOODPECKER

Melanerpes formicivorus

Acorn woodpeckers are renowned for their unique method of stockpiling food. In autumn they gather acorns and hammer them into nut-sized concavities in storage trees, often referred to as granaries. The holes are predrilled, usually in winter, and the storage capacity of granaries increases year by year as new holes are added. While some granaries have only a few holes, successive generations of woodpeckers can increase the number to thousands if the tree remains standing. One prodigious granary tree reported in 1923 had 50,000 holes, representing more than a century of effort. The thick bark of the living trees used as granaries protects them from harm, since the shallow holes do not penetrate to the sapwood. Groups that have filled their existing granary facilities may also store acorns in old nesting and roosting cavities.

This signature food-hoarding behavior is almost universal among acorn woodpeckers in California, where there is significant seasonal variability in the abundance of insects and other foods. Elsewhere within the species' range, however, not all populations rely on granaries. Members of one intensively studied population in southeastern Arizona cache only small quantities of acorns in natural tree cavities and crevices, and migrate south once these stores have been depleted. In the tropics acorn woodpeckers are less inclined to hoard. When they do store food, it is typically in bromeliads, under loose bark or in other natural nooks and crannies.

This species' other claim to fame is its cooperative breeding habits, though the particulars of its social life vary from population to population and within populations. Acorn woodpeckers in many populations live year-round in plural breeding groups consisting of up to seven mate-sharing males and up to three joint-nesting females. Within other populations most breeding is by monogamous pairs. In all cases family groups may also include one to 10 offspring from previous years that help with incubation, care of nestlings and territorial defense. These non-breeding helpers may be up to five years old.

When death leaves a group with no more breeders of one sex, dramatic power struggles ensue. Non-breeding helpers from other groups compete – either as individuals or in same-sex sibling gangs – for the right to fill the vacancy. These intense contests are marked by days or weeks of continuous chasing, fighting (occasionally with full-body contact), vocalizing and drumming. The largest team usually wins. This sibling coalition then shares breeding status in the new group, while the losers return home and wait for another opening to appear. Helpers regularly make systematic forays in search of reproductive opportunities, traveling distances of up to nine miles (15 km) during their searches.

Because breeding vacancies are filled from outside the family group, there is little chance of incest. Co-breeders of the same sex are nearly always closely related to each other – either as siblings or as parents and offspring – but breeders of the opposite sex are nearly always unrelated.

Identification

The acorn woodpecker's unusual black-and-white facial markings and white eyes give it a clownish appearance. The male's crown is entirely red. On females a wide black band separates the red on the back of the crown from the white forehead. The back, tail, wings and breast band are mostly glossy black. Small white wing patches and a white rump patch are visible in flight. This is a medium-sized woodpecker, with an average length of about 9 inches (23 cm).

Distribution

The acorn woodpecker's range runs discontinuously from northwestern Oregon to southwestern California, with isolated populations at either end of the Baja peninsula. From Arizona, New Mexico and Texas the range crosses the international border and runs south along the Pacific and Atlantic slopes to central Mexico and down through Central America to northern Columbia.

Habitat

Acorn woodpeckers only live in or near habitats with plenty of oak trees. These include oak or mixed pine/oak woodlands, riparian corridors, Douglas fir, redwood or tropical hardwood forests and treed urban areas. The critical components are mature oaks in sufficient number to produce large crops of acorns, and suitable nesting, roosting and storage trees.

Voice

The most common vocalization throughout the year is a series of *waka*s, usually repeated several times in rapid succession. This call is given as a salutation when a group member lands near other members, flies past or departs, and during boundary disputes and other intergroup interactions. Another year-round call, *karrit-cut* or sometimes simply *karrit*, is associated with territorial defense and detection of predators such as hawks or owls. *Urrk* and *garrick* calls are also given during boundary disputes and power struggles.

Drumming and Tapping

The average length of an acorn woodpecker's drum roll is little more than half a second. These concise rolls consist of two to 20 strikes delivered at a slightly accelerating tempo that averages about 17 beats per second. Drumming is often associated with territorial encounters with members of other groups, particularly power struggles. Lone individuals rarely drum. There is some preference for established drumming sites.

Feeding

Insects, captured on the wing or gleaned from trees, are the species' favored food and are sometimes stored in tree cracks or crevices. Acorns are supplemental, but can comprise more than half of the adult diet. Before being eaten, acorns are broken into pieces at anvil sites on the upper surfaces of horizontal branches. Other nuts, including almonds, walnuts, hazelnuts and pecans, and piñon seeds are also eaten and may be stored like acorns. Seasonal foods include oak catkins and fruit. Acorn woodpeckers also drill sap wells, which are shared and defended by all group members. Sap feeding is mostly limited to spring and, in California, midsummer. In temperate regions group members generally forage independently; in tropical areas they often forage together.

Breeding

Acorn woodpeckers are plural breeders. Family groups of up to 13 breeders and helpers have been observed, but the most common group size is two to three. Nest cavities are excavated in large dead or live trees, often on the undersides of limbs, and may be reused for many years. Co-breeding females lay their eggs in a shared nest. The usual clutch size is four if there is a single breeding female and five for joint nests. Groups often raise a second brood in one season, and occasionally a third. In the United States nest-tree species include oak, cottonwood and ponderosa pine. Cavity entrance holes are approximately 2 inches (5 cm) in diameter.

Migration

Although the acorn woodpecker is mostly a sedentary species, acorn crop failure sometimes prompts winter wandering. One population usually migrates between breeding grounds in southeastern Arizona and wintering areas in Mexico's Sierra Madre, but occasionally it remains on the breeding grounds through winter when food supplies are sufficient.

Conservation

Numbers are probably declining. A major contributing factor in many areas is habitat loss caused by overgrazing, which prevents regeneration of oaks, or by urban development. As well, granaries and cavity trees are often felled for firewood or due to safety concerns. European starlings are aggressive, increasingly numerous competitors for nest holes. Occasionally acorn woodpeckers are shot, legally or otherwise, to protect nut and fruit crops.

Year-round

GILA WOODPECKER
Melanerpes uropygialis

Sexual dimorphism – differences between males and females in overall size and in the proportions of some body parts – is a characteristic of many woodpecker species, especially in the genus *Melanerpes*. Because these physical differences are generally associated with differences in foraging behavior and diet, they reduce competition for food between mates. Size differences may also be used to advantage if members of a pair divide parental duties, each bird specializing in those tasks for which its size makes it more efficient. This seems to be the case with gila woodpeckers.

Among gila woodpeckers, males are about 14 percent heavier than females and their bills are about 14 percent longer than those of their mates. A study of this species at Saguaro National Monument in Arizona showed that this pronounced size difference influenced behavior in a number of ways. When the gila woodpeckers foraged on desert shrubs such as foothill paloverde or desert ironwood, the males concentrated most of their effort on the trunks and large limbs, while the females divided their time almost equally between small branches, large branches and trunks. Their preferred foraging techniques differed as well, with males doing more excavating for subsurface larvae and females doing more gleaning for surface insects. These patterns are consistent with observations from other areas.

During the nesting period the males generally spent more time guarding the nest than the females did. They were also more aggressive than their mates, attacking and driving off other birds, especially other gila woodpeckers, at roughly twice the rate of the females. At one intensively studied nest the male averaged 8.7 attacks per hour, while the female's hourly average was 4.6 attacks.

If a female was guarding a nest or offspring when a serious attack occurred, she would give alarm calls until her mate arrived to relieve her.

It would appear that the males take the lead in defending the nest and young, and perhaps also the female, because of their larger body size. The maternal role, on the other hand, emphasizes food deliveries to the nestlings. Between 7 a.m. and noon the females made an average of 12 feeding trips per hour, while the males maintained an average rate of eight trips an hour.

An interesting aspect of this division of labor is that it is not inflexible. Short-term role switching was observed on a number of occasions, such as when a disturbance at one nest made the female unwilling to go away and forage. For two days her mate took over nestling feeding duties and concentrated on foraging instead of defense, while she remained vigilant near the nest. Sexual dimorphism clearly disposes male and female gila woodpeckers to perform different parental functions, but an individual's behavior at any given time depends largely on what its mate is doing.

Identification

When perched, the gila woodpecker has a zebra-striped appearance created by the horizontal black-and-white barring on back, wings and tail. In flight its white wing patches are conspicuous. The head and underparts are grayish tan to pale brown, tending to yellow on the belly and whitish on the forehead. Males are distinguished by a small bright vermilion cap, but females occasionally have a few red crown feathers. The body length of this medium-sized woodpecker is about 8.5 to 9.5 inches (22–24 cm), with males being about 14 percent heavier and longer-billed than females.

Distribution

The gila woodpecker's range in the U.S. is centered in southern Arizona, extending slightly into southeastern California, southern Nevada and southwestern New Mexico. Its range stretches south of the international border through Baja California, except the northwest corner, and from Sonora and Chihuahua south to Jalisco.

Habitat

This species inhabits arid regions and is closely associated with saguaro cactus deserts. It is also found in open to semi-open forests, riparian woodlands, plantations and residential areas, provided suitable nest trees are available. It lives mostly at elevations between sea level and 3,280 feet (1,000 m).

Voice

These vociferous woodpeckers have two main calls. One consists of single vibrato *churr* note or repeated *churr*s separated by intervals of less than one second. This rolling call is used by pairs to maintain contact when moving independently around their territory and for advertising territorial boundaries. It is given much more frequently by males than females. The second call apparently signals alarm, often in response to human presence or vocalizations by other species. This call, a series of harsh *pip*s, is given by females more than males. Variability in the delivery of these calls suggests that they may be used for individual identification.

Drumming and Tapping

Gila woodpeckers are infrequent drummers and there is little documented information about their drumming. The beat is described as loud and steady.

Feeding

A variety of insects gathered by probing, gleaning and excavating in trees, shrubs and cacti make up the largest part of the diet throughout most of the

year. The flowers and fruit of saguaro and other cacti are important seasonal foods, as are mistletoe berries in some areas. Gila woodpeckers sometimes also eat small lizards, earthworms, the eggs and nestlings of various songbirds, corn, cultivated fruits and pecans.

Breeding

Gila woodpeckers prefer to nest in large saguaro cacti, where available. Cavities in cacti are excavated months in advance of nesting so the inner pulp can dry and harden. They also nest in other columnar cacti and various deciduous and palm trees. The average diameter of cavity entrances is about 2 inches (5 cm), but the oval holes are often up to ½ inch (1.3 cm) taller than wide. Up to three broods may be raised in one season and nests are generally used for several consecutive years. This species is probably monogamous, but little is known about courtship or pair formation. Clutch size ranges from two to seven, with three to four eggs being most common. In Mexico gila woodpeckers occasionally hybridize with golden-fronted woodpeckers.

Migration

This is primarily a nonmigratory species. Some individuals make short movements northward or to higher elevations in winter.

Conservation

Numbers have recently declined in southeastern California after apparently increasing in the 1930s and 1940s in response to tree planting. Trends elsewhere are less clear. The primary threats are loss of saguaro cacti due to residential development in the Sonoran Desert and nest-hole competition from European starlings.

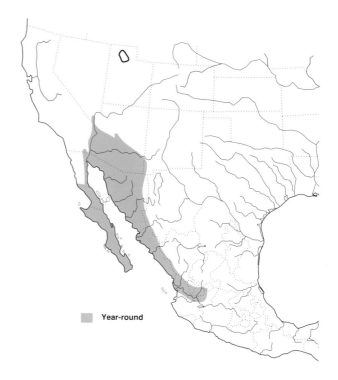

■ Year-round

GOLDEN-FRONTED WOODPECKER
Melanerpes aurifrons

During the late 1800s and early 1900s the golden-fronted woodpecker was one of the least popular birds in Texas. By 1866 Western Union Telegraph had strung 75,000 miles (120,000 km) of wire across the United States and the miracle of nearly instantaneous long-distance communication was transforming the country. The advent of the telegraph line had also transformed the landscape for several woodpecker species, perhaps none more so than the golden-fronted, but woodpeckers and humans were at odds about the best use of telegraph poles.

One witness described how a telegraph line running from San Antonio, Texas, to a ranch nine miles (14 km) away was practically destroyed by golden-fronted woodpeckers: "they came from all sides, from far and near, and made fresh holes every year, sometimes as many as five or six in a single pole."

"In this species," wrote another contemporary observer, "we have a woodpecker which for centuries had been pecking into hard mesquite trees. Along came the soft pine poles and these same birds immediately literally ate them up. I have seen 16 holes, three of which were deep enough for nesting sites, in one small pole, not over 10 inches [25 cm] in diameter." In response, legislation was passed permitting the extermination of golden-fronted woodpeckers. Railway section crews were given shotguns to dispatch any offending birds and independent hunters were encouraged to assist in the control efforts. By the 1930s this species, though still fairly abundant, was much less common than in previous decades.

Despite this period of intense persecution, the golden-fronted woodpecker gained ground later in the 20th century. In 1900 the species' U.S. breeding range was restricted to west-central and southern Texas. Over the next hundred years its range expanded in all directions: 109 miles (175 km) east, 186 miles (300 km) west, 249 miles (400 km) northwest and 174 miles (280 km) north. After crossing the state line into southwestern Oklahoma, golden-fronted woodpeckers began nesting there in the late 1950s.

New nesting and foraging sites provided by utility poles and fence posts played an important role in this range expansion, but other influences were also at work. The overall density of mesquite trees increased throughout the southwestern United States during the 1900s, allowing golden-fronted woodpeckers to move into areas that had once been inhospitable grasslands. Meanwhile, additional habitat was created in and near towns as the shade trees planted by settlers matured and small oases flourished around artificial water reservoirs. Golden-fronted woodpeckers were well positioned to take advantage of these environmental changes. Their tendency to wander far from breeding areas during late summer and winter offered plenty of opportunities for finding newly suitable habitat. The only competitors for the new habitat were ladder-backed woodpeckers, which are much smaller and appear to occupy a different ecological niche. Competition with red-bellied woodpeckers, on the other hand, may be limiting the golden-fronted woodpecker's eastward expansion.

Identification

This medium-sized (length: 8.5–10.2 inches, or 22–26 cm) woodpecker's scientific name, *aurifrons*, is a misnomer; it translates as "golden forehead" – when in fact only the nasal tufts and nape are golden – and is probably the origin of its equally misleading English name. Black-and-white barring on the back and wings give this bird a zebra-striped appearance. The white rump contrasts female lacks a crown patch and has a buff-yellow nape and nasal tufts. In summer members of this species sometimes have purple-stained faces from eating prickly pear cactus fruit.

Distribution

Within the U.S., golden-fronted woodpeckers are resident from southwestern Oklahoma through central Texas to the Mexican border. In northern Mexico their range extends from the Gulf coast west to Coahuila, Durango, Zacatecas, Jalisco, Colima and Michoacán. It continues from southern Mexico through Central America to northern Nicaragua.

Habitat

Golden-fronted woodpeckers live in open to semi-open habitats from sea level to about 8,200 feet (2,500 m). In the United States and northern Mexico they are most closely associated with mesquite brushlands and riparian corridors, but also frequent oak/juniper savannas, second-growth woodlands and suitable urban environments. Although arid areas are favored throughout much of this species' range, some populations in Oaxaca, Mexico, inhabit tropical evergreen forests.

Voice

This species is extremely vocal throughout the year and its loud, harsh voice is conspicuous. A call consisting of rapidly repeated *chuh* notes (also written as *chah-aa-ah*) is heard year-round, but more so in winter, and appears to serve as a location announcement and territorial call. During the breeding season, widely spaced *churr*s or *krr-r-r-r*s are used to advertise territorial boundaries and attract or communicate with mates. The warning call directed at intruders of the same or different species, including humans, consists of a series of raspy *kek* notes. Repeated *tsuka* notes may be exchanged during territorial disputes or close contact between birds that are not mates. The intimate call is a low *grr*.

with the mainly black tail. White patches are visible in flight. There is pronounced geographic variation in the rest of the plumage. The subspecies found in the United States and northern Mexico has smoky to drab gray underparts, with a yellow patch on the abdomen. The head is the same shade of gray, with markings that distinguish the sexes. The male has orange-yellow nasal tufts. His nape is the same color, mixed with crimson and scarlet, and his crown patch is crimson. The

Drumming and Tapping

Golden-fronted woodpeckers drum less frequently than many other woodpeckers. Drumming sequences last approximately one second and are often repeated a number of times in a drumming bout. Sequences consist of a rapid roll with a fairly constant tempo, either delivered alone or preceded or followed by one to five slow beats. Females very rarely drum.

During courtship paired birds sometimes tap in rough synchrony at a potential nest site. Golden-fronted woodpeckers also engage in displacement tapping.

Feeding

Golden-fronted woodpeckers mostly forage arboreally or on the ground in open areas with little brush. Ground foraging is rare in summer and common in winter. On trees they find a wide variety of insect prey, mainly by surface gleaning, but also by probing into holes and crevices and pecking away bark. Some insects are also captured on the wing. Cactus fruits, berries, nuts, corn and other plant foods constitute as large a part of the diet as insects. A few observations have been made of apparent predation on vertebrates, including a lizard, a mouse and bird eggs.

Breeding

Golden-fronted woodpeckers raise one or two broods each year, usually laying clutches of four or five eggs, up to a maximum of seven. Some, but not all, pairs stay together through winter. Nest cavities are excavated in live or dead deciduous trees, as well as utility poles and fence posts, and are often reused in subsequent years. Nest boxes are occasionally used. This species occasionally hybridizes with red-bellied woodpeckers in south-western Oklahoma and gila woodpeckers in Mexico. Cavity entrance holes are slightly oval, with an average diameter of approximately 2 inches (5 cm).

Migration

Golden-fronted woodpeckers are nonmigratory.

Conservation

Within the United States populations are generally stable or slightly declining, except for increases associated with the 20th-century range expansion. Numbers are thought to have fallen in the early 1900s because of shooting intended to reduce woodpecker damage to utility poles and fence posts. Information about population trends elsewhere is lacking.

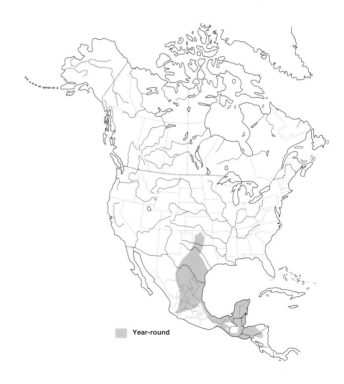

■ Year-round

LEWIS'S WOODPECKER
Melanerpes lewis

Members of this species are easily distinguished from even their closest relatives by plumage and flying style. When Lewis's woodpeckers travel between foraging locations or perches their flight is usually direct and characterized by continuous flapping, instead of the intermittent flap-bounding that produces the typical undulating flight path of other woodpeckers. Their foraging flights are also distinctive.

During spring and summer Lewis's woodpeckers feed mainly by catching insects in the air. One type of aerial foraging, known as hawking, is done from a perch such as a snag, pole or fence post that affords an unobstructed view of the surrounding area. Some hawking flights are short sallies directly to an insect and then back to the perch after the quarry has been captured and eaten. In these flights flapping is continuous between take-off and landing, and there is no gliding. Other sorties are longer and include changes in altitude, periods of continuous flapping alternating with prolonged glides, sharp banking and complex maneuvering achieved by asymmetrical wing and tail movements. Between either long or short flights Lewis's woodpeckers scan continuously for flying prey. If an insect comes within range they may snap it out of the air without even launching.

Lewis's woodpeckers engage in extended, nonspecific foraging flights, sometimes in the company of flocks of swallows or swifts feeding over open water or fields. During all types of aerial foraging, Lewis' woodpeckers capture their prey with their beaks. Having a relatively wide gape compared to other woodpeckers, they are well suited for snatching insects from the air.

Despite being slow fliers, migrating Lewis's woodpeckers may move 60 to 600 miles (100–1,000 km) between breeding and wintering grounds. Migratory routes and distances are not well known and may vary from year to year, depending on food supplies along the way.

Migrating Lewis's woodpeckers travel by day, flying from 10 to more than 500 feet (3 to 150 m) above the ground and generally following a direct course, sometimes circling and occasionally perching in trees. Compared to their behavior in summer and winter, they are much more gregarious during migration and during the nomadic interlude that often precedes fall migration. In California, during one September week in 1940, more than 5,000 birds were counted passing over a 3.2-mile-wide (5 km) area. About a fifth of this number were seen during a half-hour period one morning. The rest passed by in smaller groups at intervals of 30 minutes or more.

Observers at various locations have recorded migratory groups ranging in size from two to 150 individuals. Migrants leave their breeding grounds in late August or early September and arrive at wintering areas between mid-September and mid-October. They travel more quickly in spring, departing from their winter homes in mid- to late April and reaching their destinations by early May.

Identification

Lewis's woodpeckers are easily identified by their medium-large size (length: 10.2–11.5 inches, or 26–29 cm) and unique plumage. Males and females are essentially identical. The crown, nape, back, wings and tail are glossy greenish black and the rest of the face is mostly deep red. A silvery gray collar encircles the neck and merges with the gray upper breast, which shades into pinkish red on the lower breast, flanks and belly. The plumage of the throat, neck and underparts appears coarse and hair-like.

Distribution

The boundaries of this species' breeding range are irregular, approximately corresponding to the distribution of ponderosa pine. It extends from southern British Columbia to southern New Mexico and from western California to eastern Colorado. The winter range overlaps the southern half of the breeding range, with scattered occurrences south of the breeding range to northwestern Baja California and extreme northern Sonora and Chihuahua.

Habitat

Lewis's woodpeckers are burned-pine-forest specialists. They breed in open habitats, favoring ponderosa pine forests that are subject to frequent low-intensity fires and cottonwood-dominated riparian woodlands. The most important features are widely scattered trees, including large snags, and a brushy understory that harbors plenty of insects. Prime winter habitats are those that offer abundant seasonal foods and sufficient storage sites, such as oak woodlands and nut orchards.

Voice

Lewis's woodpeckers are less vociferous than many other woodpeckers and, calling mainly during the breeding season. One male-only call, used to attract mates and defend nesting territory, consists of three to eight loud, harsh half-second-long *churr* notes repeated in quick succession. The chatter call – a series of short squeaks of varying character – is given mostly by males and may signal aggression. Although most common during courtship, it is a year-round vocalization. Alarm calls may be given any time by either sex in response to potential predators or disturbance by humans or livestock. Alarm notes are uttered singly or in bursts. The male's note (*yick*) is distinct from the female's (*yick-ick*).

Drumming and Tapping

The typical drum sequence is a low-intensity roll, sometimes followed by several beats spaced up to about half a second apart. Drumming is limited almost entirely to the courtship period and even then it is relatively sporadic. Lewis's woodpeckers never drum in winter. During the breeding season unmated males drum about 2.5 times an hour and mated males drum about once every five hours. Drumming is thought to be done by males only.

Feeding

During the breeding season Lewis's woodpeckers feed largely on insects, mostly caught in midair, but also gleaned from trees and bushes or the ground. Their principal prey are ants, bees, wasps, beetles and grasshoppers. In fall and winter they concentrate on acorns, cultivated nuts, corn, fruits and berries. Before eating or storing nuts (and some other foods, such as large insects), they break them into manageable pieces using the top of a pole or broken snag as an anvil. Nut fragments and corn kernels are stored in natural cracks and crevices in trees. Winter storage sites are aggressively defended and tended diligently. Adults with nestlings sometimes store insects when supplies are abundant.

Breeding

Limited research shows that at least some Lewis's woodpeckers keep the same mate from year to year. Although they are territorial, nests may be clustered within a small area, sometimes even in the same tree. New nests are excavated in coniferous or deciduous trees that have wood softened by advanced decay. Lewis's woodpeckers frequently reuse old cavities, either their own or those of hairy woodpeckers or northern flickers. Natural cavities and nest boxes are also used. Clutch size ranges from five to nine, and is usually six or seven. Cavity entrance hole diameters range from 2.4 to 3 inches (6.1–7.6 cm).

Migration

Birds that breed in the northern half of the range mostly winter in more southerly or coastal areas.

Other populations stay put or migrate short distances, some switching strategies from year to year depending on food availability. In late summer large nomadic flocks often move locally to higher elevations or orchards before migrating.

Conservation

This species has experienced significant declines throughout its breeding range in the past half-century, but its naturally sporadic distribution complicates assessment of trends. Its range expansion in southeastern Colorado is probably due to increases in mature cottonwoods and cornfields. It has disappeared from parts of its historic range, including southwestern British Columbia and northwestern Washington and Oregon, as fire suppression, commercial forestry, cattle grazing and urban development have changed the landscape. Lewis's woodpeckers often abandon their nests if humans approach closely.

Breeding

Year-round

Wintering

RED-BELLIED WOODPECKER
Melanerpes carolinus

For those who think of woodpeckers as insectivores that drill holes in trees to find their prey, the red-bellied woodpecker's eclectic diet and diverse foraging techniques may come as a surprise. Would you expect to see a woodpecker clinging to a grapefruit, feasting on its juicy pulp? How about hunting lizards? These are but two of the many ways this opportunistic generalist feeder fuels itself.

Among the plant foods eaten by red-bellied woodpeckers are corn, wild and cultivated nuts (acorns, hickory nuts, pecans, beechnuts, hazelnuts), wild berries, cultivated fruits (grapes, citrus fruits, mangoes, persimmons) and sunflower seeds. These woodpeckers also occasionally drink sap from sapsucker wells, nectar from blossoms or sugar-water from hummingbird feeders. The types and amount of food consumed vary regionally, but plants tend to dominate the diet, particularly in fall and winter.

When foraging for nuts and fruits, red-bellied woodpeckers demonstrate considerable versatility, perching upright or hanging upside down – on a branch, a berry cluster or a large fruit – or hovering momentarily. One bird may return to feed for several days on a single large fruit such as an orange. Hard-shelled seeds and nuts are wedged into a fissure in a tree trunk or pole and hammered with the bill until broken into edible portions.

Red-bellied woodpeckers also eat a multitude of invertebrates, including beetles, weevils, ants, grasshoppers, cockroaches, caterpillars, stinkbugs, spiders, millipedes and snails. They locate and capture most of these prey by moving about the trunks and branches of snags and live trees, gleaning from surfaces, probing into crevices and revealing hidden quarry by pecking, scaling away bark and excavating into sapwood. They also capture flying insects on the wing.

This species' appetite for vertebrates and bird eggs may be the most unexpected facet of its feeding ecology, although it is not the only North American woodpecker with this propensity. Red-bellied woodpeckers have been known to eat small lizards (both green and brown anoles), tree frogs, small mammals, small fish (most likely scavenged along a lakeshore) and nestling birds (red-cockaded and hairy woodpeckers, American redstarts, Carolina chickadees and house wrens, among others). Their victims are dispatched by thrashing them against a tree or pecking them to death, and they are then torn into pieces and devoured. This approach is also used to contend with large caterpillars and other invertebrates that are too big to swallow whole. Vertebrate prey form only a very small part of the red-bellied woodpecker's diet, but almost anything it can subdue is probably fair game.

The red-bellied woodpecker's flexible feeding habits have almost certainly played a role in its northward and westward range expansion during the past half-century and in its numerous sporadic appearances, often during winter, beyond the edges of its established range. By following forested river valleys into the Great Plains, red-bellied woodpeckers have found new habitat in the maturing trees planted by settlers in areas that were once open prairie. Perhaps equally important, on the prairies and elsewhere they have found increasing numbers of backyard bird feeders. And being opportunists, they have not hesitated to dig right in.

Identification

This medium-sized woodpecker (length: 9.5 inches, or 24 cm) has a zebra-striped appearance when perched that is created by the horizontal black-and-white barring on the back and wings. When the wings are extended the black outer part shows black with a white patch. The central and outermost tail feathers are broadly marked with black and white, while the others are solid black. The rump is largely white. The male's bright red cap covers the forehead, crown and nape, sometimes varying to pinkish or reddish orange on the lower forehead. The sides of his head and neck are gray, flushed orange or pinkish around the bill, cheeks and chin. Females have red only on the nape (with occasionally a few red feathers in the center of the gray crown) and less extensive pinkish areas on the face. Despite its name this woodpecker's belly coloring is indistinct. The underparts are primarily grayish white, with a pale red or occasionally orange patch between the legs. The female's belly patch is smaller and less vivid than the male's.

Distribution

The red-bellied woodpecker's current range covers much of the eastern half of the United States (mostly east of the Great Plains) from the Gulf coast to the Great Lakes and extends north into extreme southern Ontario. This represents a northward and westward expansion from the historical range. There have been numerous scattered sightings from places outside the main range – north to central Ontario and southern parts of Saskatchewan, Manitoba, Quebec, New Brunswick and Nova Scotia, and west to eastern parts of Idaho, Montana, Wyoming, Colorado and New Mexico.

Habitat

Red-bellied woodpeckers inhabit a wide range of forest types, typically with fairly high tree density and well-developed mid- and understory vegetation. Breeding records also exist from open country in Texas, where utility poles and fence posts substituted for nest trees. They will nest in urban areas if there are sufficient mature trees and snags. This species usually resides at elevations below 2,000 feet (600 m), except in the Appalachians, where it is found up to 3,000 feet (900 m).

Voice

This species is extremely vocal throughout the

year and particularly in late winter and spring. The year-round call note is the rolling *kwirr* or *churr*. *Cha* notes are used for long-distance communication or expression of alarm and are most frequent during the period after pair bonds are established and before nesting. Short-range *cha-aa-ah*s are typically given in territorial or antagonistic situations. The *che-wuck* call is made frequently prior to pairing, as well as year-round during conflicts. The intimate call exchanged by mates is a low *grr*.

Drumming and Tapping

Red-bellied woodpeckers do not drum as much as many other woodpeckers, and females drum much less frequently than males. Drum rolls are about one second long with a tempo of about 16 to 18 beats per second, accelerating slightly toward the end. They are sometimes preceded by a few well-spaced beats.

Males use tapping, along with drumming and *kwirr* notes, to attract females. Once he has attracted a mate, the male taps loudly but slowly (about three taps per second) to signal interest in a potential nest site. If the female accepts his choice she responds with synchronized or simultaneous tapping. These mutual tapping sessions continue throughout the excavation period, with both birds outside the cavity or, if excavation is sufficiently advanced, with the male inside and the female outside.

Feeding

Foods consumed by red-bellied woodpeckers include nuts, fruits, seeds, insects and other invertebrates, bird nestlings and other small vertebrates, bird eggs, sap and flower nectar. They employ a full range of foraging techniques. Sometimes, especially in fall, they store food in scattered undefended sites such as deep cracks or crevices in trees or posts.

Breeding

Pair bonds dissolve after the young disperse and are re-formed between early winter and late spring. The annual number of broods ranges from one to three, with multiple broods more common in the south. The average clutch size is four. Nest cavities are excavated in snags or dead portions of live trees, either deciduous or coniferous. Pairs usually excavate a new nest cavity each year, often directly below the previous year's nest. If available, they often usurp red-cockaded woodpecker cavities for nesting. In southwestern Oklahoma red-bellied woodpeckers occasionally hybridize with golden-fronted woodpeckers. Cavity entrance holes are slightly oval, with a diameter of about 2.3 inches (5.8 cm).

Migration

Although the red-bellied woodpecker is not generally considered a migratory species, northern populations may shift south during severe winters. In the South some movement to areas with better winter food supplies apparently occurs.

Conservation

Populations have been increasing significantly for many years and the species' breeding range has expanded since the mid-1900s. In much of the southeastern United States this is the most abundant woodpecker. Because of its broad habitat adaptability, the red-bellied woodpecker has a much lower risk of becoming endangered than most other North American woodpeckers.

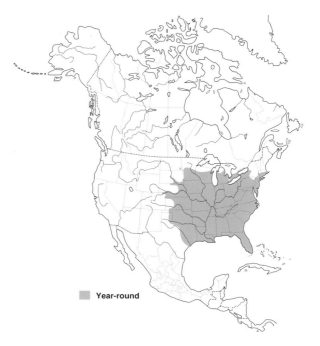

■ Year-round

RED-HEADED WOODPECKER

Melanerpes erythrocephalus

Many early European settlers in North America were closely acquainted with the red-headed woodpecker. Patchwork clearing of forests created ideal nesting habitat and these adaptable birds quickly developed an appetite for domestic crops including berries, orchard fruits, peas and corn. Variously known as shirt-tail birds, white-shirts, half-a-shirts, flag birds, jellycoats and flying checkerboards, these woodpeckers were a familiar, though often unwelcome, denizen of colonial villages and farms. "I would not recommend to anyone to trust their fruit to the Red-heads," wrote John James Audubon in 1840, "for they not only feed on all kinds as they ripen, but destroy an immense quantity besides."

In the 1870s red-headed woodpecker populations swelled in response to an irruption of Rocky Mountain grasshoppers, which swarmed by the billions from Canada to Mexico and from Iowa to California. The relationship between the woodpeckers and their periodically plentiful prey was a longstanding one, but this was its final enactment. The last sighting of a live Rocky Mountain grasshopper was in 1902. These misnamed insects (actually North America's only locusts) were driven inadvertently to extinction by habitat destruction in the limited breeding areas occupied during the low phase of their population cycle.

The subsequent decline of the red-headed woodpecker in the early 1900s was temporarily reversed after two foreign fungal diseases arrived in North America: chestnut blight in 1904 and Dutch elm disease in 1930. As these relentless tree-killers produced a short-term superabundance of nesting sites, red-headed woodpecker numbers increased dramatically, peaking around the mid-1900s.

Superimposed on this history of large-scale population fluctuations is a regional pattern of widely varying winter numbers in the northern part of the range. Some winters, red-headed woodpeckers are most numerous in the West; in others, in the East. It depends on the supply of hard mast, their primary winter food. Fall migrants will travel only as far as required to find sufficiently large crops of acorns, beechnuts, pecans or other nuts.

It is difficult to determine long-term population trends for a species that is so erratic, both naturally and in response to human activities. Nevertheless, the evidence points to significant declines in many parts of the species' range.

Identification

This medium-sized woodpecker (length: 7.5–9.5 inches, or 19–24 cm) is easily identified by its unique plumage, which is identical for both sexes. The head, neck, throat and upper breast are entirely crimson. The rest of the underparts are white, rarely tinged with dull yellow, orange or red. A narrow black line neatly separates the red hood from the white breast. The upper back and outer parts of the wings are glossy black with a slight green or blue sheen, contrasting boldly with the white lower back and rump and large white wing patches. These white areas are prominent in flight. The tail is mostly black, with white margins on the outer feathers and narrow white tips on all but the central feathers.

Distribution

The breeding range covers much of eastern North America, from southern Saskatchewan to southern New Brunswick in the north and from southeastern Texas to central Florida in the south. The western edge runs from eastern Montana to eastern Texas. Breeding is rare in the Atlantic provinces and New England states. The breeding and winter ranges overlap except in the northwestern and northern parts, where red-headed woodpeckers are usually absent in winter, and in central Texas and along the Gulf Coast, where they sometimes winter but do not breed.

Habitat

Red-headed woodpeckers breed in a variety of open deciduous and coniferous forests, generally nesting near the edges. They also nest in fields with scattered trees and in urban parks. Areas with numerous snags, such as beaver ponds or flooded bottomlands, may attract large breeding concentrations. In winter critical habitat components are food trees, usually oaks, and snags for roosting. Along the western edge of the winter range, red-headed woodpeckers often visit pecan orchards. Migration habitats include oak woodlands and fruit orchards.

Voice

These boisterous woodpeckers communicate with a wide variety of chirps, cackles and harsh calls. The year-round call note is a loud *tchur*, becoming shriller when given during chases and other high-intensity situations. During the breeding season, males attract mates and may defend territory with rapidly repeated *queer*s or *qee-ark*s. The winter territorial call sounds like *quirr* or *kikarik*. Repeated chattering *rrr* or *cuh* notes are often given by parents of young nestlings when exchanging places.

Drumming and Tapping

Drum rolls of about one second in length, with a tempo of 19 to 25 beats per second, are typically repeated in sets of two or three. Individuals often have a favorite drumming site. Males drum more frequently than females.

During nest site selection the male may tap at a prospective site to attract his mate; she will signal approval by joining him in synchronized or simultaneous tapping. Mutual tapping sessions also occur during excavation, either with both birds outside the cavity or with the male inside and female outside.

Feeding

This is one of the most omnivorous woodpeckers in North America. During the breeding season as much as 40 percent of foraging effort may be devoted to capturing airborne insects with swift, agile sallies from a perch. Red-headed woodpeckers also frequently drop from perches to seize terrestrial prey such as grasshoppers, worms, lizards and mice, and to forage directly on the ground. Bark gleaning and excavation for are less common foraging modes. Bird eggs and nestlings are sometimes eaten. The summer diet is about two-thirds plant matter, including nuts, seeds, corn and wild or cultivated fruits. In winter they mainly eat acorns or other nuts, but will catch aerial insects on warm days. Seasonally abundant foods such as nuts and insects (particularly grasshoppers) are cached in holes and cracks in trees and posts, behind loose bark or under roof shingles. Large items are broken at an anvil site before being stored or eaten.

Breeding

Although red-headed woodpeckers do not appear to maintain pair bonds through the winter, they may breed with the same mate for several years. Pairs often return to the same tree or limb for several years and sometimes reuse their old cavities. Some pairs raise second, and possibly third, broods during a single breeding season. Clutch size ranges from three to 10, usually four to seven. Nest cavities are typically excavated in dead deciduous or coniferous trees (preferably without bark), dead portions of live trees or utility poles. Red-headed woodpeckers regularly take over other species' active or abandoned nest holes and occasionally use natural cavities or nest boxes. Cavity entrance holes average about 2.3 inches (5.8 cm) in diameter.

Migration

All populations seem to wander in search of food after the breeding season. Some from the south may move north in winter. Northern and western populations are the most migratory, but timing and distances moved vary widely from year to year. Spring migration is probably mainly nocturnal. In the fall migrants travel by day, perhaps so they can assess mast crops. Flying 50 to 650 feet (15–200 m) above the ground, they move silently, alone or in small groups, and often in the company of blue jays.

Conservation

Red-headed woodpecker numbers have fluctuated greatly over the past 200 years. High death rates from motor vehicles are a suspected cause of declines in the mid-20th century, before members of this species learned about the danger of foraging on or beside roads. Reasons for the current decreasing trend may include reduced availability of suitable cavity trees due to modern agricultural and forestry practices, and snag removal in urban areas. In Florida the red-headed woodpecker is the fastest-declining cavity-nesting bird.

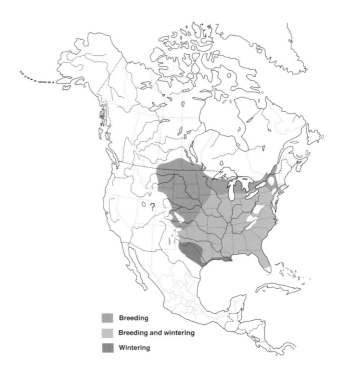

■ Breeding
■ Breeding and wintering
■ Wintering

RED-BREASTED SAPSUCKER
Sphyrapicus ruber

Because of their behavioral and ecological similarities, the red-naped, red-breasted and yellow-bellied sapsuckers were at one time classified as a single species. The varying amount of red on their heads was not considered sufficient to separate them. During the 1980s and 1990s the American Ornithological Union revised this classification, drawing on the latest genetic studies and other new information to make their decisions. First the red-breasted sapsucker gained full species status alongside the yellow-bellied. Then several years later the red-naped was split off from the red-breasted. Interestingly, this is the same order of divergence that paleontologists believe was followed by the ancestors of these birds as they evolved.

Because these three species are so closely related, they occasionally hybridize where their breeding ranges overlap. Biologists are not certain what prevents interbreeding from happening more often or, conversely, why it sometimes does occur. One proposed isolating mechanism is related to the fact that males of each species have more red coloring than females of the same species. Therefore it is thought that when a male encounters a female of a redder species (for example, a yellow-bellied male and a red-breasted female), he normally treats her as an intruding male and drives her away. This theory is supported by the observation that in most mixed pairs the male belongs to the redder of the two species, so the female's coloring would not have elicited aggression.

The timing of courtship may also play a role in preventing interbreeding in regions where the species overlap. The theory in this case is that by the time the yellow-bellied and red-naped sapsuckers return to their breeding grounds, the less migratory red-breasted sapsuckers will have already paired off.

The breeding range of yellow-bellied sapsuckers overlaps with other sapsuckers in two areas: in northeastern British Columbia with the red-breasted, and in southwestern Alberta with the red-naped. Hybridization has been recorded in both areas. There is a greater convergence between the breeding ranges of the red-breasted and red-naped sapsuckers. The two species are known to nest side by side and sometimes interbreed in a number of areas, including central British Columbia; Vancouver Island; along the crest of the Cascade Mountains in Washington; Modoc County, California; and Eureka County, Nevada. They also share breeding habitat in other parts of California and Nevada, but there have been no reports of hybridization from these sites.

Identification

The red-breasted sapsucker is a medium-sized woodpecker (length: 8–8.5 inches, or 20–22 cm), with no difference between the plumage of males and females. The head, neck and breast are almost entirely vermilion, except for a black spot in front of each eye and a whitish stripe extending from the nasal tufts to below each eye. Below the breast the underparts are yellow or yellowish white, marked on the flanks with dark Vs or streaks. The back, tail and wings are largely black, except for a varying amount of white or yellow spotting on the back, a white rump, white barring on the central tail feathers and elongated white wing patches. Compared to its northern counterpart the southern subspecies has slightly paler red parts, a longer white facial stripe and less distinct separation between red and yellow on the underparts.

Distribution

The red-breasted sapsucker's breeding range follows the Pacific coast south from southeastern

Alaska and northwestern British Columbia to northwestern California. It widens and reaches its eastern limits in central British Columbia, continuing south through western Washington and Oregon and into northern and east-central California, and touching into western Nevada near Lake Tahoe. There are isolated breeding populations in mountainous areas of southern California. The winter range extends from coastal and southwestern British Columbia south through the breeding range, as well as outside the breeding range throughout the rest of California and into northwestern Baja California.

Habitat

Red-breasted sapsuckers breed in a variety of habitats, most commonly coniferous forests or deciduous and riparian woodlands. Second-growth forests, old burns and orchards may be used if snags are present. They winter in dense to open coniferous or deciduous forests, and during migration probably use habitats that are similar to those used in summer and winter. This species is found from sea level to about 9,900 feet (3,000 m).

Voice

Throughout the year red-breasted sapsuckers use the *waa* call to signal low-intensity alertness or, in the harsher form of this call, high-intensity alarm. The squeal call, consisting of up to 16 repeated *kwee-urk* notes, is given mainly by males early in the breeding season and is related to mate attraction and sexual activity. Rapidly repeated raspy notes known as dry chatter are given during territorial disputes or by pair members during courtship. This call is given only in flight and is most common during the early part of the nesting period. A variety of intergrading vocalizations collectively known as the interaction-call complex include loud sequences given in flight by territorial birds chasing intruders, other loud calls that are a regular part of aggressive interactions between unrelated individuals, and soft calls commonly exchanged between mates and family members whenever they meet or approach one another.

Drumming and Tapping

The drumming of all sapsucker species is slow and irregular, with considerable variation in duration and rhythm. Red-breasted sapsucker drum sequences usually begin with an introductory roll of several rapidly repeated beats delivered at a tempo of about 22 beats per second, followed by a pause, then a number of slow beats that may be heard as singles or as couplets (or occasionally triplets) with a very brief interval separating the two (or three) beats. The average length of one complete sequence is 1.5 seconds. Males drum more frequently than females.

Mated red-breasted sapsuckers tap during various types of encounters with each other, including changeovers during nest excavation and incubation. Upon the arrival of the absent mate the bird at the nest taps with a stilted rhythm on the lower rim of the entrance hole or on the inside of the cavity. During incubation and brooding the arriving bird often taps once or several times at one or more places on the nest tree before going to the cavity entrance. Red-breasted sapsuckers tap as a displacement behavior in a variety of circumstances.

Feeding

Red-breasted sapsuckers select mostly conifers for sap feeding and may be attracted to trees that already have sap wells or are seeping sap because of an injury. Their diet also includes insects, spiders, fruit, cambium, phloem and seeds. Invertebrate prey are usually obtained by gleaning or fly-catching.

Breeding

Red-breasted sapsucker pair bonds are usually renewed from year to year if both partners survive. Clutch size ranges from four to seven. Nest cavities are excavated in snags or dead or decaying parts of live trees; a variety of deciduous and coniferous species are used. Nest trees are often reused, but a new cavity is excavated for each breeding season. Red-breasted sapsuckers sometimes hybridize with red-naped or yellow-bellied sapsuckers. Cavity entrance holes average about 1.8 inches (4.6 cm) in diameter.

Migration

The northern subspecies (*S. r. ruber*), found from Alaska to Oregon, is nonmigratory along the coast, but inland-breeding populations tend to move to coastal areas in winter. The southern subspecies (*S. r. daggetti*), which breeds in California and Nevada, tends to winter at lower elevations in California and Baja California.

Conservation

The number of red-breasted sapsuckers fluctuates widely in British Columbia, perhaps because of periodic extreme winter conditions that cause tree sap to freeze. Populations are increasing in Oregon, decreasing in California and apparently stable elsewhere. Historically sapsuckers risked being shot because of the damage they did to orchard trees. Today the primary threat is habitat loss.

- Breeding
- Breeding and winter
- Winter

RED-NAPED SAPSUCKER
Sphyrapicus nuchalis

The red-naped sapsuckers and the other three members of the genus *Sphyrapicus* are named for their practice of drilling evenly spaced rows of shallow holes in live trees or shrubs and feeding on the sap that collects within them. This is a partial misnomer, since they actually lick up the sap with their brush-tipped tongues.

Sap wells are drilled just deep enough to penetrate the outer bark and reach either the underlying phloem, which transports sugars and other synthesized foods through the plant, or the xylem, the water-conducting tissue in the woody part of the plant. Once the bark has been pierced, sap quickly begins to fill each hollow. Left alone, however, the flow will soon cease, so sapsuckers spend much of their time tending their well systems.

Sap is a year-round part of the sapsucker's diet and at times may be the only food consumed. In addition to providing sap the wells also sometimes provide supplementary prey in the form of ants, small flies and other invertebrates that get trapped in the sticky fluid. Parents of nestlings sometimes take insect prey to sap wells and dip them in the sap before delivering them to their offspring, perhaps to enhance the nutritional value of the food.

Red-naped sapsuckers vary their sap-feeding activities through the year. In early spring, when they first return to breeding areas, they tap the xylem of conifers such as Rocky Mountain juniper, Douglas fir, lodgepole pine and white spruce. Then, as buds begin to form on trembling aspens and black cottonwoods, the sapsuckers turn their attention to these trees. On both coniferous and deciduous species, xylem wells are recognizable as parallel rows of round holes that usually encircle the trunk.

As deciduous trees and shrubs leaf out, attention shifts to these species and to drilling shallower, laterally rectangular wells that reach only to the phloem. Like xylem wells, the phloem wells are drilled in parallel rows and typically extend all the way around the trunk or stem. Holes in offset rows are likely exploratory wells. Persistent efforts to keep the sap flowing can eventually extend individual phloem wells until they merge with those above or below. Small stemmed shrubs such as willow are often killed by a season of sapsucker feeding, but other species survive and are used in successive years.

Identification

The red-naped sapsucker's strongly patterned head is striped black and white, with a black line separating the poppy-red forehead and crown from the red nape patch. The male's entire throat and chin are red. Most females have a white upper throat and chin, with red only on the lower throat, but some have more extensive red. Below the red throat both sexes have a black bib. The rest of the underparts are pale buff or yellow, fading to dull white on the sides, which are marked with black V-shaped bars. The black back is heavily spotted with white or brownish white. The rump is white and the tail is mostly black, except for some black-and-white barring in the center. The black wings are spotted with white near the tips and have elongated white patches. This medium-small woodpecker is 7.5 to 8.3 inches (19–21 cm) in length.

Distribution

Red-naped sapsuckers breed in the Rocky Mountain region from central British Columbia and Alberta south to Arizona and New Mexico. The breeding range also extends south through the mountains of central and eastern Washington and Oregon. There are isolated breeding populations to the west in eastern California and western Nevada

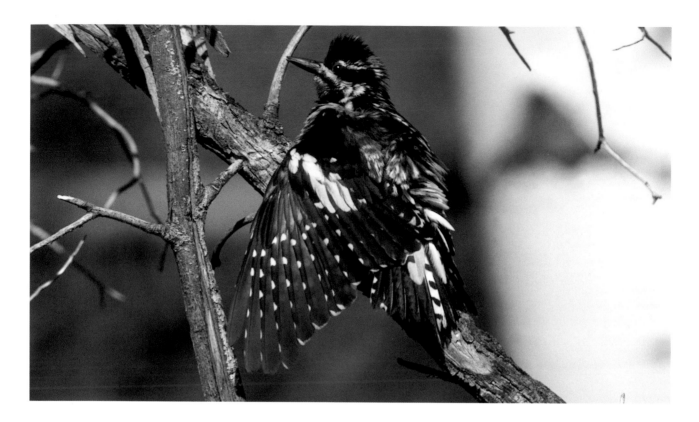

and to the east in the Cypress Hills (Alberta and Saskatchewan) and around the Black Hills (South Dakota, Wyoming and Montana). In the U.S. this species winters from southern California, Nevada and Utah through most of Arizona and New Mexico to southwestern Texas. In Mexico they winter in Baja California and throughout the northwest, south to Jalisco and east to Tamaulipas. The winter and breeding ranges overlap in New Mexico and Arizona and extreme southern Utah.

Habitat

The most common breeding habitats are deciduous or mixed woodlands, or deciduous groves within coniferous forests, logged areas or open rangeland from 1,000 to 9,900 feet (300–3,000 m) in elevation. Occasionally red-naped sapsuckers nest in residential gardens. They do not breed in oak or oak/pine woodlands, but they do use these habitats, as well as other woodland habitats and orchards, during migration and in winter. On their wintering grounds in Mexico they are found from sea level to 8,200 feet (2,500 m).

Voice

Throughout the year red-naped sapsuckers use the *waa* call to signal low-intensity alertness or, in the harsher form of this call, high-intensity alarm. The squeal call, consisting of up to 16 repeated *kwee-urk* notes, is given mainly by males early in the breeding season and is related to mate attraction and sexual activity. Rapidly repeated raspy notes known as dry chatter are given during territorial disputes or by pair members during courtship. This call is given only in flight and is most common during the early part of the nesting period. A variety of intergrading vocalizations collectively known as the interaction-call complex include loud sequences given in flight by territorial birds chasing intruders, other loud calls that are a regular part of aggressive interactions between unrelated individuals, and soft calls commonly exchanged between mates and family members whenever they meet or approach one another.

Drumming and Tapping

As with other sapsuckers, the drumming of this species is slow and irregular, with considerable variation in duration and rhythm. Red-naped sapsucker drum sequences usually begin with an introductory roll of several rapid beats delivered at a tempo of about 24 beats per second, followed by a pause, then a number of slow beats that may be heard as singles or as couplets (or occasionally triplets) with a very brief interval separating the two (or three) beats. The average length of one complete sequence is 1.7 seconds. Repeated sequences by lone drummers that are not responding to other woodpeckers are spaced on average about half a minute apart. Males drum more frequently than females.

Red-naped sapsuckers tap during various types of encounters with their mates, including changeovers during nest excavation and incubation. Upon the arrival of the absent mate the bird at the nest may tap with a stilted rhythm on the lower rim of the entrance hole or on the inside of the cavity. During incubation and brooding the arriving bird often taps once or several times at one or more places on the nest tree before going to the cavity entrance. Tapping as a displacement behavior occurs in a variety of circumstances.

Feeding

In addition to sap, this species' diet includes insects and spiders – mostly obtained by gleaning or fly-catching – and plant matter such as fruit, cambium, phloem, seeds and aspen buds.

Breeding

If both partners survive, red-naped sapsucker pair bonds are usually reestablished in spring. Live trembling aspens with heart rot are the most frequently selected nest trees. Various other deciduous trees (live or dead) and conifers (usually dead) are also used. Nest cavities from previous years are sometimes reused. New cavities are often excavated in trees with old nest cavities. Clutch size ranges from three to seven. Hybridization may occur with any of the other three sapsucker species. The red-naped sapsucker's slightly oval cavity entrance holes are about 1.7 inches (4.3 cm) high and 1.5 inches (3.8 cm) wide.

Migration

Most red-naped sapsuckers spend the winter south of the breeding range in New Mexico, Arizona, southern California or Mexico. Breeding and wintering ranges overlap in Arizona and New Mexico. In southern parts of the wintering grounds females are more common than males; the reverse is true in northern areas. Migrants leave breeding areas from late August to October, generally returning in April or May.

Conservation

Populations appear to be generally stable, but habitat loss and degradation may affect local numbers. Extreme drought has intermittently led to an absence of red-naped sapsuckers in breeding areas in Utah and southern Idaho. Historically sapsuckers were considered destructive orchard pests and were often shot.

Breeding
Breeding and winter
Winter

WILLIAMSON'S SAPSUCKER
Sphyrapicus thyroideus

During his tenure as curator of ornithology at the Academy of Natural Sciences in Philadelphia, John Cassin was the first person to formally report on the species we now know as Williamson's sapsucker. In an 1852 publication Cassin described an adult female specimen from the academy's collection, misidentifying it as a male and coining the name "black-breasted woodpecker" for this bird.

The first true male of this species to receive scientific notice was collected by John Strong Newberry in 1855 as he traveled with a surveying party sent west to ascertain the best railway route from the Mississippi to the Pacific. Although Newberry's official position was that of acting assistant surgeon and geologist, he also had a keen interest in the flora and fauna he encountered along the way. Newberry's 1857 account of his journey cataloged his various discoveries, including the "Williamson's woodpecker," which he had named in honor of the expedition's leader, Lieutenant Robert Stockton Williamson.

These cases of mistaken identity went unchallenged for the next 15 years and were reinforced by repeated publication. Then in 1873 Henry Henshaw, ornithologist for the George Wheeler Geographic Survey West of the 100th Meridian, came upon a nest in Colorado being tended by one bird that met the description of the black-breasted woodpecker and another that looked like a Williamson's woodpecker. Based on his field observations, Henshaw had already become suspicious that the two species were actually one, but had surmised that their plumage differences were related to maturity, not gender. Not until he had secured both members of the ill-fated pair, taking them as they left the nest after delivering food to their young, was he certain they were an adult male and female of the same species.

After more specimens were killed and examined it became clear that the birds previously described as adult female Williamson's woodpeckers were actually juvenile males, and those thought to be adult female black-breasted woodpeckers were juvenile females. The early ornithologists' confusion is understandable. No other woodpecker species has such dissimilarity in the appearance of the two sexes. Their classification efforts were further confounded by the fact that juveniles quite closely resemble adults of the same sex. Henshaw's 1875 report on the birds he had collected during the expedition finally set the record straight.

Identification

Williamson's sapsucker is a medium-sized woodpecker (length: 8.3–9.5 inches, or 21–24 cm) with strongly differentiated sexes. The male has an iridescent black head with white mustache stripes, a white stripe above each eye and a scarlet chin and throat. The breast, sides, back and tail are also iridescent black. In contrast, the belly is bright yellow, the rump is white and the lower flanks are barred black and white. The wings are mostly black with a few white spots near the outer edges and large white patches.

The female's back, sides, tail and wings are mostly black with heavy horizontal barring in sepia or off-white. The rump is white. The entire breast may be barred, becoming darker at the center, or barred on the sides and solid black in the center. The belly is pale yellow. The dark brown to tawny or buffy head is streaked with black in the mustache area, on the sides and back of the crown and on the nape. Some females have a few reddish orange or black feathers on the chin and throat.

Distribution

Williamson's sapsuckers breed from southern British Columbia through the western states and into northern Baja California, with many range discontinuities and isolated populations because breeding is restricted to middle and high-elevations. Breeding areas in British Columbia, the Pacific states and Baja are in the interior mountain ranges. The easternmost states where breeding occurs are Montana, Wyoming, Colorado and New Mexico. The winter and breeding ranges overlap in extreme southern Oregon, California, Nevada, Arizona, New Mexico and Baja California. Williamson's sapsuckers also winter outside the breeding range in southern California and northern Baja, and from Arizona and New Mexico (and rarely Texas) south through western interior Mexico from Sonora and Chihuahua to Michoacán, and less commonly east to Coahuila and Nuevo León.

Habitat

Williamson's sapsuckers breed at mid to high elevations in open montane forests, either coniferous (including spruce/fir, Douglas fir, lodgepole pine, ponderosa pine) or conifer-dominated with some trembling aspens. They use a wide variety of habitats during migration. Individuals wintering in western Mexico favor high-elevation pine/oak forests. In the southwestern United States the typical winter habitats are low- to mid-elevation oak/juniper and pine/oak forests. In southern Arizona the females tend to winter at lower elevations than the males.

Voice

Males use single or repeated *cheeur* notes, often in association with drumming, for territorial announcement, mate attraction and as an alarm signal. Females occasionally give a higher-pitched version of this call. A hoarse *ca-haw* (its second syllable lower pitched, longer and less emphatic than the first) is often given at the beginning of a territorial or courtship encounter, while a rapid guttural trill frequently marks the end. Close-range calls exchanged between mates vary from slow sequences of *ch* notes to rapid bursts of many soft chatter notes. When intruders approach a nest or sap tree, Williamson's sapsuckers commonly respond with a short guttural roll that drops rapidly in pitch.

Drumming and Tapping

Williamson's sapsucker drum sequences begin with one or two rapid, steady rolls, followed by several – often three or four – irregularly spaced loud strikes. One complete sequence can be three seconds long. Males drum most commonly in early morning during the courtship period, but only in late afternoon once pair bonds are formed. Females drum less often and more quietly than males. Female drumming may be limited to the early part of the nesting season and to same-sex encounters. Most pairs have two to four preferred drumming sites within their territory.

Feeding

Early in the breeding season Williamson's sapsuckers consume only conifer sap and phloem. During the nestling period they switch to an insectivorous diet of mainly ants, augmented by some beetles, aphids and other insects. They take prey mostly by gleaning from tree surfaces, less often by shallow excavating or probing. Occasionally they forage for ants on the ground or catch insects on the wing. Outside of the breeding season sap and phloem are the principal foods, but berries are also eaten.

Breeding

Williamson's sapsucker pairs separate after their young fledge and little is known about year-to-year mate fidelity. Clutch size is three to seven, usually four to six. Where available, live trembling aspens with heart rot are usually preferred for nesting; dead conifers and aspens are also used.

Most pairs excavate a new nest cavity each spring, often in a tree with old cavities. Williamson's and red-naped sapsuckers occasionally hybridize. Cavity entrance holes average about 1.7 inches (4.3 cm) in diameter.

Migration

Some populations are migratory, while others are resident. The western subspecies is largely resident, with some birds traveling as far south as Baja California. Some members of the eastern subspecies reach central Mexico. Migrants head south from September to October, depending on the region. They return in early spring, mostly in March or April, with males leading by one or two weeks. Females probably migrate farther south than males. During migration Williamson's sapsuckers form small flocks. There is also a general pattern of downslope movement after the breeding season.

Conservation

In recent decades populations have declined significantly throughout this species' range, especially in the Pacific Northwest. Loss of breeding habitat, particularly nest trees, due to intensive forest management may be a factor. Williamson's sapsuckers are relatively tolerant of human activity near their nests.

Breeding
Year-round
Wintering

YELLOW-BELLIED SAPSUCKER
Sphyrapicus varius

Like red-naped sapsuckers, yellow-bellied sapsuckers vary their sap-feeding activities according to the seasons. When they reach their breeding grounds in early spring they start by drilling xylem wells, which tap into the tissue that conducts fluids up the stem. When deciduous species leaf out they switch to drilling only as deep as the phloem, which lies just inside the bark and transports foods synthesized in the leaves to the rest of the plant. The phloem sap of summer is a rich food source, with a sucrose content of up to 25 percent, depending on the tree species. Phloem sap produced by the same plants in winter contains only 1 to 5 percent sucrose, and xylem sap's sucrose content is usually 2 to 3 percent. In winter, when sap provides a more dilute energy source, sapsuckers may spend much of their day drilling wells and feeding at them.

Xylem wells are round about 0.1 inch (2.5 mm) in diameter and usually arranged in short rows of three to 15 holes. Sapsuckers feed from xylem wells by inserting the bill straight in and probing with the tip of the tongue. Phloem wells begin as horizontal slits and are gradually enlarged to form rectangles that extend vertically up the tree. Sap seeps from the exposed wood and collects at the base of the rectangle. Besides licking up the sweet liquid, sapsuckers also eat cambium and phloem removed while creating and maintaining the wells.

Yellow-bellied sapsuckers typically drill two to 20 new phloem wells a day. The average well reaches a length of about half an inch (13 mm), but can be longer. The birds usually feed at and enlarge a well for several consecutive days. Once the flow of sap stops, a new well is begun just above the old one. Sap oozing from the active well at the top often runs down the trunk into the lower holes and onto the bark. A sapsucker arriving to feed at an active well system sometimes seems to lick along a line starting low on its column of old holes and moving up the trunk to the top one. This feeding technique may take advantage of the higher concentration of sugar in sap that has run down the trunk and evaporated.

Identification

This medium-small woodpecker (length: 7.5–8.3 inches, or 19–21 cm) is poorly named, since all sapsuckers have some yellow on the belly. In this species the lower breast and belly are pale yellow, offset by a black bib on the upper breast and brownish or dull white sides with black V-shaped bars. The black back is heavily spotted with white or brownish white. The rump is white and the tail is mostly black, with white bars on the central feathers and white outer margins. The black wings are marked with white spots and elongated white patches. The head is striped black and white with variable poppy-red or crimson markings. Males have two areas of red: the crown and forehead, and the chin and throat. Most females have the same red forehead and crown as males, but on some females these areas are entirely black, mixed black and red, or black with buffy markings. The female's chin and throat are white, occasionally with some red mottling.

Distribution

The northern boundary of the breeding range runs from eastern Alaska across northern Canada to central Quebec, southwestern Labrador and southern Newfoundland. The range includes northeastern British Columbia, most parts of the other provinces, parts of the northern states from North Dakota to New England and scattered locations south through the Appalachians to Tennessee and North

Carolina. There is no overlap between the breeding and winter ranges. This species winters in the southeastern U.S., throughout Mexico except the northwest, south to Panama and in many parts of the West Indies.

Habitat

During the breeding season yellow-bellied sapsuckers are found at elevations of up to 6,600 feet (2,000 m) and favor young forests dominated by deciduous species. They also nest in riparian woodlands and scattered stands of deciduous trees left after conifers have been logged. Their diverse migration habitats include woodlands, orchards, coastal palm groves and scrublands. In winter they frequent forest edges or other semi-open habitats, including those modified by human activities. Their wintering areas range in elevation from sea level to 9,800 feet (3,000 m).

Voice

The yellow-bellied sapsucker's year-round *waa* call (also described as *chee-aa*) signals low-intensity alertness or, in its harsher form, high-intensity alarm. The squeal call – six to 10 *kwee-urk* notes repeated at a rate of 1.5 to two notes per second – is mainly given by males early in the breeding season and is related to mate attraction and sexual activity. The rapidly repeated raspy notes of the dry chatter call are given only in flight, typically during territorial disputes or by pair members during courtship. A variety of intergrading vocalizations collectively known as the interaction-call complex range from loud sequences, such as the *weetick*s given in flight by birds chasing territorial intruders and the *juks* that are invariably part of aggressive interactions between unrelated individuals, to soft *week*, *wurp* or *quirk* notes commonly exchanged between mates and family members whenever they meet or approach one another.

Drumming and Tapping

Yellow-bellied sapsuckers drum in a slow, irregular manner, with widely varying duration and tempo.

The rapid introductory roll is followed by a pause, then a number of slow strikes that may be heard as single beats or as couplets with a very brief interval separating the paired beats. Most males show a strong preference for one or two established drumming sites. Females drum less often, more quietly and more briefly than males. Yellow-bellied sapsuckers rarely, if ever, drum in winter.

Mated yellow-bellied sapsuckers tap during various interactions with each other, including changeovers during nest excavation and incubation. When the absent mate arrives the bird at the nest taps on the lower rim of the entrance hole or inside the cavity. A bird arriving to relieve its mate during incubation and brooding often taps once or several times at one or more places on the nest tree before going to the cavity entrance. Displacement tapping also occurs under other circumstances.

Feeding
Sap comprises about 20 percent of the annual diet, and during certain periods it may be the only food consumed. Yellow-bellied sapsuckers also eat insects and spiders (obtained by gleaning, bark scaling and fly-catching), fruit, cambium, phloem, seeds and aspen buds.

Breeding
Yellow-bellied sapsuckers usually mate with the same partner each year if both birds survive. They often return to the previous year's nest tree and sometimes re-nest in the same cavity. Clutch size is two to seven. Most of nests are excavated in live trembling aspens with heart rot. Other deciduous trees in the same condition are also used, but rarely conifers. This species sometimes hybridizes with red-naped or red-breasted sapsuckers. Cavity entrance holes are about 1.3 to 1.6 inches (3.3–4 cm) in diameter.

Migration
Yellow-bellied sapsuckers are the most migratory North American woodpeckers. They return to breeding areas in April or May, depending on location and weather. Previous breeders arrive before first-time breeders. In September or October juvenile and adult females depart first, followed by juvenile males, then adult males. Females outnumber males wintering in Mexico, Central America and the West Indies. Males are more numerous in the northern part of the wintering range. Yellow-bellied sapsuckers are quiet during migration and often rest motionless against a tree trunk during the day. Migratory flights are nocturnal, sometimes resulting in fatal collisions with telecommunications towers and tall buildings. Loose aggregations are sometimes seen during migration.

Conservation
In the past half-century populations have decreased in New Brunswick and the southern Blue Ridge Mountains, increased in some eastern states and remained stable elsewhere. Yellow-bellied sapsuckers may be more numerous now than before European settlement because they prefer the young forests that have replaced much old growth. In the past sapsuckers were often shot because they were considered an orchard pest.

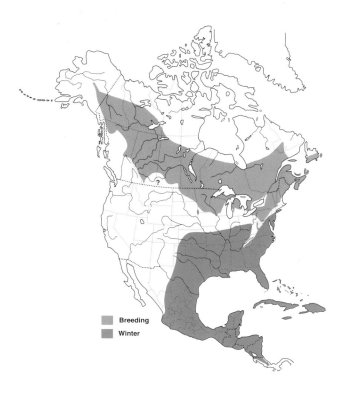

Breeding
Winter

GILDED FLICKER
Colaptes chrysoides

Travelers in the Sonoran Desert sometimes come across strange slipper-like objects, apparently made of wood, lying on the ground. These mysterious items are found only in the part of the desert where saguaro cacti grow – extreme southeastern California, southern Arizona and northwestern Sonora state in Mexico. The saguaro, with its tall, fluted columnar stem and upward-curving branches, is probably the most widely recognized plant of the Sonoran Desert. But few first-time visitors would guess that the "wooden slippers" are a product of these magnificent cacti and are fashioned by woodpeckers, most likely either the gilded flicker or the gila woodpecker.

The stem and branches of a saguaro cactus contain two kinds of soft tissue for storing water: outer cortex and central pith. A vertical skeleton of parallel woody rods surrounds the pith, providing support, and is the primary conduit for water transport. Woodpecker excavation into the succulent outer cortex causes little harm to the cactus aside from loss of a minimal amount of water-storing capacity. The plant simply seals off the wound with a hard, impermeable layer of cork, forming the durable "slipper" that will remain intact long after the cactus has fallen and its soft tissues have decayed.

However, skeletal rods that are damaged by excavating woodpeckers seldom regenerate fully, and complete or partial severing of the rods is usually detrimental – or even fatal – to a saguaro. The loss of structural support makes the plant susceptible to decapitation by strong winds. Injury to the rods also reduces capacity for water transport, resulting in a water deficit that can kill tissue directly and increases the risk of tissue death due to freezing.

Woodpecker cavities in saguaros are of two main types: smaller cavities excavated entirely within the outer cortex, causing no harm to the skeleton, and larger ones made by chiseling through a number of skeletal rods to accommodate a nest chamber carved out of both cortex and pith tissue. Skeleton-damaging cavities are almost invariably located within 10 feet (3 m) of the top of a cactus stem. Here the rods are thinnest and least resistant to the woodpecker's efforts, but they are also closest together. The nearer to the apex a woodpecker excavates, the greater the likelihood that it will sever all the skeletal rods. And the more rods it cuts, the shorter the life expectancy of the cactus.

Saguaro slippers have characteristic shapes and bear distinctive scars that provide clues about the original position of a woodpecker cavity. Outer-cortex slippers typically have a somewhat flattened nest chamber that is wider from side to side than from front to back. They are also usually scarred with vertical lines where the back wall made contact with the woody skeleton.

The remains of pith-penetrating cavities can be recognized by the pattern of scars left by the severed rods at the top of the nest chamber. If the entire ring of rods was cut, the small, round scars form a complete circle. A semicircle or crescent indicates that the excavation damaged only part of the skeleton. The smaller the diameter of the circle or semicircle, the closer to the apex the cavity was located.

Some researchers believe that smaller saguaro cavities – those contained within the outer cortex – are excavated by gila woodpeckers and that the larger, apex cavities created by cutting through skeletal rods are mostly the work of gilded flickers. What is certain is that both species require saguaros that are at least 16 feet (5 m) tall for nesting and roosting, because shorter plants lack the girth to accommodate even a small cavity. With an average growth rate of approximately one foot (30 cm) every five years, saguaros are not usually suitable as nest sites until at least 80 years old.

Identification

The gilded flicker is named for the yellow undersides of its wings and tail and the matching wing and tail feather shafts. This medium-large (10.2–12 inches, or 26–30 cm) woodpecker's buffy brown back and wings are marked with dark brown bars. The tail is dark brown and the white rump is conspicuous in flight. The underparts are off-white with black spots, and a large black crescent forms a bib across the upper breast. Both sexes have a rufous yellow crown and gray throat and ear patches. Males have red mustache stripes.

Distribution

The gilded flicker's range extends from southwestern Arizona south along Mexico's Pacific slope from Sonora to northern Sinaloa and through all of Baja California except the extreme northwest.

Habitat

This species is strongly associated with saguaro deserts, but it also inhabits riparian woodlands in arid areas. It is found mostly at elevations below 3,000 feet (900 m).

Voice

Since the gilded flicker's recent promotion from its status as a subspecies of the northern flicker, no comprehensive study of its calls has been undertaken. However, differences between the two are likely negligible. The call note is a single, explosive *peah* (sometimes written as *klee-yer*). The long call consists of loud *wik* or *kick* notes repeated at about seven notes per second for up to 20 seconds. Both are heard most commonly during pair formation and territory establishment. The distinctiveness of long calls and *peah*s given by different flickers suggests these may be used for individual identification. Long calls are given more by males than by females, often alternating with drumming. The gilded flicker's most complex and variable vocalization is the wicka call given in a territorial or courtship context during close interactions between two, three or four adults. This quiet call is a series of regularly spaced seesaw notes, variously transcribed as *wik-a*, *wik-up* or *ta-week*, repeated for up to four seconds.

Drumming and Tapping

This species' nonvocal communication is believed to be similar to that of northern flickers, which drum from established sites with a rapid, even tempo of about 22 beats per second, each drum roll lasting slightly more than one second. Males drum more than females. They increase their drumming and decrease their use of long calls when a female is nearby and calling.

Northern, and presumably gilded, flickers engage in ritualized tapping when one member of a pair has been working on nest excavation and the other returns from elsewhere. Positioned either inside or outside the cavity, the bird at the nest delivers from two to 20 or more slow taps on the rim of the hole while its mate watches. The arriving bird then takes over excavating and the other usually departs. The taps are delivered at a rate of two to three per second, with a slight pause between each sequence.

Feeding

Gilded flickers are primarily ground-feeding insect eaters. They use their bills to probe and dig in the soil and their long tongues to glean surface prey from the ground. Details of their diet are not well known, but ants are almost certainly a major component. They also feed on cactus fruits in season and on stored corn.

Breeding

Limited research suggests that gilded flickers are monogamous and raise one brood annually. The average clutch size is about four. In the desert they mostly nest in saguaro cacti and occasionally in Joshua trees. In riparian habitats they nest in cottonwoods and willows, in either snags or dead

portions of live trees. Gilded flickers hybridize with red-shafted northern flickers in central and southern Arizona, primarily in riparian areas along streams flowing from the mountains into the Sonoran Desert. The gilded flicker's oval cavity-entrance holes are on average about 3.3 inches (8.4 cm) high and 2.8 inches (7 cm) wide.

Migration

Gilded flickers are nonmigratory.

Conservation

Gilded flickers were once fairly common in southeastern California along the Colorado River Valley, but are apparently now extirpated from this area, probably because of habitat destruction. Populations in south-central Arizona are stable or possibly increasing. In Mexico they may be declining because of ongoing conversion of Sonoran Desert habitats into irrigated farmland. European starlings appear to have little effect on the reproductive success of gilded flickers nesting in saguaros, despite their negative impact on gila woodpeckers using the same habitat.

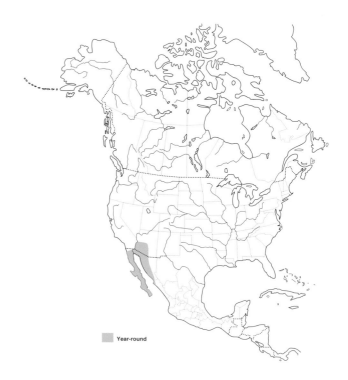

■ Year-round

NORTHERN FLICKER
Colaptes auratus

The two North American subspecies of the northern flicker – the red-shafted and the yellow-shafted – have an intriguing relationship. Descended from a common ancestor, they were divided into separate, isolated populations by the vast ice sheets of the Pleistocene epoch and lived apart for thousands of years. By the time the glaciers had retreated and the populations were reunited, each had evolved unique plumage characteristics, though they remained fundamentally alike in their behavior and ecology.

The line that now divides the yellow-shafted flicker from its red-shafted relative runs diagonally from the northwestern corner of North America down toward the Gulf of Mexico. But instead of each subspecies faithfully keeping to its own side, the two mingle in a broad hybrid zone that extends from southern Alaska to the Texas panhandle, following the eastern slope of the Rocky Mountains for much of its distance and reaching its greatest width in the northern Great Plains states and a short distance north of the Canadian border. This zone of flicker interbreeding corresponds with the transition zone between the wetter ecosystems of eastern North America and the relatively drier ecosystems of the West.

Sporting plumage with every imaginable combination of ancestral traits and intermediate characteristics, crosses between yellow- and red-shafted flickers seem designed to baffle unsuspecting birdwatchers, especially when they show up as migrants outside the hybrid zone. A typically confusing hybrid might have a gray throat and brown crown (like a red-shafted flicker), a black mustache and tan ear-patches (like a yellow-shafted), and feather shafts and wing and tail linings in a golden orange shade midway between yellow and red. Despite the abundance of mixed-up northern flickers

along the length of the hybrid zone, the parent subspecies are not in any danger of disappearing. Geneticists have calculated that the hybrid zone has existed for at least 4,000 to 7,500 years and that its position and width have remained stable since the late 1800s, or perhaps even longer.

The yellows and reds of the northern flicker's feathers are produced by carotenoid pigments. Flickers can synthesize some pigments, such as the melanins that produce various browns and blacks, but an experiment conducted by zoologist Frederick H. Test showed that they depend on food sources to obtain carotenoids. When Test fed captive flickers on food that contained almost no carotenoids, the new flight feathers they grew were progressively more pallid, eventually becoming very pale yellow. Once carotenoids were restored to their diet by adding grated raw carrot, the flickers went back to producing normal-colored feathers. Since carotenoids occur widely in plants and in many herbivorous insects, the natural diet of flickers contains numerous potential sources of these pigments.

In Test's experiment the loss of standard coloring happened gradually, over a period of two to four months, because the birds drew on pigment stored in body fat and in the liver and other organs until this supply was depleted. Their ability to use carotenoids once they were reintroduced was almost instantaneous. Based on feather growth rates and the narrowness of the zone of transition from washed-out to full-strength color, it took only a few hours for pigment concentrations in the developing feathers to build to the maximum level.

This experiment also demonstrated that whether a flicker has red- or yellow-tinted feathers is genetically encoded. Diet, stress and other environmental factors can cause variations, but the

basic color depends on how the bird metabolizes the carotenoids it ingests. All of the captive flickers had the same nutritional regime. On the carotenoid-deficient diet, they all regenerated progressively paler flight feathers. But when they ate the carrot-enriched food, each bird resumed growing plumage of its original color.

Identification

The northern flicker is the second-largest surviving woodpecker in Canada and the United States (length: 12–14 inches, or 30–35 cm). There are four distinct subspecies, two of which live in North America and are similar in most aspects of their plumage: buffy brown back and wings with dark brown bars; a black crescent across the upper breast; black-spotted off-white breast and belly; dark brown tail feathers; and white rump, which is conspicuous in flight.

The yellow-shafted subspecies is differentiated by the yellow coloring of the wing and tail feather shafts and the undersides of the wings and tail. The breast and belly are also tinted yellow. Other distinguishing characteristics are the tan throat and ear patches, gray crown and red nape patch. Males have black mustache stripes, which females lack.

The red-shafted flicker has salmon-red wing and tail feather shafts and linings, and sometimes a pinkish hue on the breast and belly. This subspecies has a gray throat and ear patches, a brown crown and no nape patch. Males have red mustache stripes.

Distribution

Northern flickers breed throughout most of Canada and the United States south of the treeline, except southeastern California, southwestern Arizona, southeastern New Mexico and central and southwestern Texas. The separation of the red- and yellow-shafted subspecies is described on the previous page. Red-shafted flickers also breed in Mexico's western and eastern Sierra Madres and south through the interior to Oaxaca.

In winter some members of both subspecies move south, sometimes into the other subspecies' breeding range, and some remain resident. The winter range extends along the Pacific coast from southern Alaska south, across most of southern Canada, throughout the U.S. (including southern non-breeding areas), throughout the Mexican breeding range and into non-breeding areas in northeastern Mexico from Coahuila to Tamaulipas.

Two other subspecies of northern flicker reside outside of North America: the Cuban flicker, in Cuba and on Grand Cayman Island, and the Guatemalan flicker, from extreme southern Mexico to northern Nicaragua.

Habitat

During the breeding season northern flickers inhabit a wide variety of open woodland or forest-edge habitats, including pastures, logged or burned forests and urban areas, provided they have potential nest trees and areas of short grass or bare ground for foraging. Habitat preferences during migration and winter are not well known. Unavailability of ants in winter may encourage movement to habitats where foods such as berries are available.

Voice

The call note is a single, explosive *peah* (sometimes written as *klee-yer*). The long call consists of loud *wik* or *kick* notes repeated at about seven notes per second for up to 20 seconds. Both are heard most commonly during pair formation and territory establishment. The distinctiveness of long calls and *peah*s given by different flickers suggests these may be used for individual identification. Long calls are given more by males than by females, often alternating with drumming. This species' most complex and variable vocalization is the wicka call given in a territorial or courtship context during close interactions between two, three or four adults. This quiet call is a series of regularly spaced seesaw notes, variously transcribed as *wik-a*, *wik-up* or *ta-week*, repeated for up to four seconds.

Drumming and Tapping

Northern flickers drum with a rapid, even tempo of about 22 beats per second, each drum roll lasting slightly more than one second. The interval between repeated rolls ranges from 10 seconds to more than 40 seconds. Males drum more than females. They increase their drumming and decrease their use of long calls when a female is nearby and calling. Both sexes use established drumming sites around the breeding territory.

Ritualized tapping occurs during nest excavation when the absent mate returns from elsewhere. Positioned either inside or outside the cavity, the bird at the nest delivers from two to 20 or more slow taps on the rim of the hole while its mate watches. The arriving bird then takes over excavating and the other usually departs. The taps are delivered at a rate of two to three per second, with a slight pause between each sequence.

Feeding

Northern flickers forage primarily on the ground, using their bills to probe and excavate in the soil for insect prey, especially ants, and gleaning ants from the ground. During fall and winter both North American subspecies increase their consumption of berries and seeds, but the yellow-shafted more so than the red-shafted. Northern flickers also occasionally visit feeders in winter.

Breeding

Northern flickers are mostly monogamous, but several instances of polyandry have been documented. Nest cavities are typically in snags or dead portions of live trees, either deciduous or coniferous, and sometimes in utility poles, fence posts or wooden buildings. The oval entrance holes are about 3.2 inches (8 cm) high and about 2.9 inches (7.4 cm) wide. This species reuses old nest cavities more than most other woodpeckers and will use nest boxes. The average clutch size is about six, but varies from three to 13. Pairs occasionally raise a second or third brood in one year. Red-shafted flickers hybridize with gilded flickers where their ranges overlap.

Migration

Northern breeding populations of both the red- and yellow-shafted subspecies winter in more southerly locations. Yellow-shafted flickers that breed south of latitude 37° north are largely non-migratory. Some red-shafted flickers undertake altitudinal rather than latitudinal migrations. These include Rocky Mountains breeders that winter on the Great Plains. Migrants travel in loose flocks ranging in size from a few to more than a hundred birds.

Conservation

The familiarity and abundance of the northern flicker masks a steady decrease in numbers throughout North America. The total decline from 1966 to 1991 was 52 percent for yellow-shafted flickers and 19 percent for red-shafted flickers. Factors contributing to this decline probably vary regionally, but likely include loss of suitable nest trees and degradation of terrestrial foraging habitat. Nest competition from European starlings seems to be a contributing factor in at least some areas.

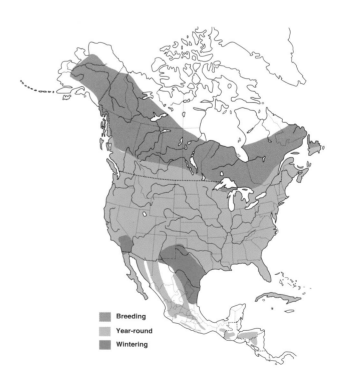

Breeding

Year-round

Wintering

GOLDEN-OLIVE WOODPECKER

Piculus rubiginosus

The golden-olive woodpecker is a polytypic species, meaning that within the group of birds that bear this name are a number of well-differentiated subspecies. At one time or another polytypic species are invariably the subject of taxonomic debates between "lumpers" (who endorse the amalgamation of all the subspecies under one species name) and "splitters" (who contend that certain subspecies are sufficiently distinct to be recognized as species in their own right). The golden-olive woodpecker is no exception. The only points that all taxonomists agree on are that this species is highly variable in its appearance and that there are a multitude of subspecies – between 19 and 25, depending on who's counting.

One subspecies of golden-olive woodpecker that some ornithologists would like to see promoted to species status is officially known as *Piculus rubiginosus aeruginosus*. Its English name is the bronze-winged woodpecker. Living only in eastern Mexico, from Nuevo León and Tamaulipas states to central Veracruz, this is the most northerly subspecies and the only one that can be considered North American. The amount of range overlap, if any, between this subspecies and its neighbor to the south is not clear.

Those who champion the bronze-winged woodpecker's recognition as a separate species cite plumage differences and distinctive vocalizations. Their opponents argue that the subspecies *aeruginosus* is no more idiosyncratic than some others, such as *tucumanus*, the southernmost subspecies, found from southern Bolivia to northwestern Argentina. They also note the high degree of individual variation in plumage pattern and color within many of the subspecies.

Although debates between lumpers and splitters may seem like nothing more than academic squabbles that have no bearing on "real" life, they can have significant implications. Governments and the general public tend to be far more willing to take measures to protect species rather than subspecies, especially if a species occurs nowhere else. For example, if the bronze-winged woodpecker were endangered it would have a much higher profile as a uniquely Mexican species than in its current manifestation as one of at least 19 subspecies living in more than a dozen different countries. Fortunately, all subspecies of the golden-olive woodpecker, including *aeruginosus*, remain fairly common at this time and their well-being is not tied to the results of this name game.

Identification

The plumage and size of the golden-olive woodpecker vary throughout its range. At 9 to 9.5 inches (23–24 cm) in length, the subspecies found in northern Mexico – known as the bronze-winged woodpecker – is larger and longer-tailed than those to the south. This subspecies has a green back and bronzed green wings. The tail is brownish olive, becoming darker near the feather tips. The pale lemon to cream underparts are coarsely scalloped with dark olive markings, rather than barred as in other subspecies. The face, throat and chin are largely pale and the crown is gray. Females have a small band of red on the nape below the crown. The male's red nape band is more extensive, running along the edges of the crown to a point just behind the eye. Males are also distinguished by their red mustache stripes.

Distribution

The bronze-winged subspecies' range extends along Mexico's Atlantic slope from central Nuevo

León and Tamaulipas to central Veracruz. It is apparently separate from the rest of the golden-olive woodpecker's range, which continues, with several more breaks, south through southern Mexico and Central America to Peru and northern Argentina.

Habitat

The golden-olive woodpecker occupies a wide variety of habitats throughout its range. The bronze-winged subspecies favors humid to semi-arid areas in the lowlands and foothills of the Atlantic slope, from near sea level to about 6,900 feet (2,100 m). Common vegetation within these habitats includes cottonwoods, mesquite and cacti. These woodpeckers may be found along the edges of or deeper within forests, as well as in plantations and clearings with scattered trees.

Voice

Like other members of the genus *Piculus*, golden-olive woodpeckers are more often heard than seen, because they are fairly secretive in their habits. The vocal repertoire of the bronze-winged subspecies is distinct from that of the more southerly subspecies. The call note is a single or repeated sharp, nasal *kyow'n* or *chey-eh*. Another frequent call, probably used for long-distance communication, is a rattle-like series of sharp *weeyk* or *wheeir* notes given at a steady rate of about two per second. Guttural chattering notes may be heard at close range.

Drumming and Tapping

The characteristics of this species' drumming have not been documented.

Feeding

Golden-olive woodpeckers eat ants, termites and the adults and larvae of wood-boring beetles. Fruits and berries are a rare addition to their diet. When foraging on trunks they ascend slowly as they probe, pry and excavate into soft bark or the soft green wood of live trees. They often probe into vines, dense foliage, clusters of epiphytes and moss on branches, and also tear apart bromeliads and cocoa pods to get at insects living inside.

Breeding

Golden-olive woodpeckers are apparently monogamous, the duration of pair bonds is unknown. Nest cavities are excavated in dead or live trees. The few clutches that have been counted contained two to four eggs.

Migration

These woodpeckers are nonmigratory.

Conservation

Golden-olive woodpeckers are generally common, but population trend data are not available. Because they are relatively versatile they are less vulnerable to habitat loss than many other woodpecker species.

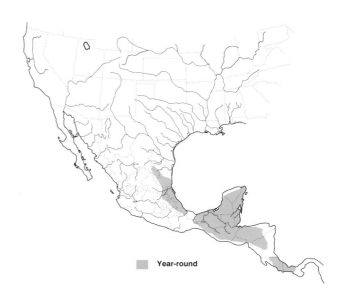

Year-round

GRAY-CROWNED WOODPECKER
Piculus auricularis

Most people who are familiar with the birds of Canada and the United States do not expect to find woodpeckers arrayed in shades of green, yet this color is prominent in the plumage of many woodpecker species from other parts of the world. The genus *Piculus* is primarily tropical in its distribution, as are many of the other green picids. The gray-crowned and golden-olive woodpeckers are the only two representatives of this genus whose ranges extend into the subtropics of northern Mexico.

True green pigmentation is rare in birds, and the *Piculus* woodpeckers are among the many that owe their coloring to other pigments. Close examination of the gray-crowned and golden-olive woodpeckers' plumage reveals that they are tinted by two different pigments that are distributed through separate components of the individual feathers. The view through a 10-power microscope shows that within each dorsal feather the rachis (the central shaft) and the barbs (the row of filaments on either side of the shaft that form the vane) are yellow, while the barbules (the tiny filaments that run along the sides of each barb) are black. Without magnification, the combined effect makes the feathers appear olive-green.

The first scientific description of the gray-crowned woodpecker was published in 1889. More than a century later these birds remain largely unstudied. This neglect is due partly to their lack of visibility. Like its other *Piculus* relatives the gray-crowned woodpecker often goes unnoticed by human observers because of its cryptic green plumage, small size and relatively quiet and sedentary habits. This species' limited range within an economically poor country has also contributed to the meagerness of our scientific knowledge.

Mexico is a country of remarkable biological diversity. Its western side, from Sonora and Chihuahua south to Oaxaca, is particularly significant as a center of biological uniqueness. Forty-six bird species, including the gray-crowned woodpecker, are endemic to western Mexico – that is, they are found nowhere else. In recent years biologists A. Townsend Peterson and Adolfo G. Navarro-Sigüenza, of the United States and Mexico respectively, have been working to draw attention to the outstanding concentration of endemic birds in western Mexico. This situation, they note, presents both a challenge and an opportunity for conservation efforts. A challenge because of the paucity of large-scale, effective reserves in western Mexico. An opportunity because the convergence of endemic species in discrete parts of the region, including the Sierra Madre Occidental in the north, is conducive to developing cost-effective conservation strategies by focusing on priority areas.

Identification
This little-studied species is variously reported to be either small (length: 6.3–6.5 inches, or 16–17 cm) or medium-sized (length: 7.5–8.3 inches, or 19–21 cm). The dominant body color is olive-green, with the wings more bronzy and the underparts marked with pale lemon to cream bars. The tail is brown, paler underneath and darker near the tip. The face is grayish buff and a gray cap extends from the nape to the bill. Males often have flecks of red along the sides of the cap and are distinguished by red mustache stripes, which females lack.

Distribution
This species' range runs in a narrow strip along Mexico's Pacific slope from southern Sonora and Chihuahua to southern Oaxaca.

Habitat

Gray-crowned woodpeckers inhabit a variety of humid to semi-humid forests, primarily pine/oak and pure oak woodlands in the northern part of its range. Farther south, habitats include tropical evergreen and deciduous forests. They are found from the lowlands to the foothills of Mexico's Pacific slope, from 3,000 to 7,900 feet (900 to 2,400 m).

Voice

The gray-crowned woodpecker's call note is a sharp, slightly explosive *kee-ah*. A shrill rattle consisting of rapidly repeated *churr*s is likely used for long-distance communication. Other vocalizations include a *growh* call that is described as both gruff and mewing. Members of this species are usually heard before they are seen.

Drumming and Tapping

The characteristics of this species' drumming have not been documented.

Feeding

The diet includes insects and berries. Details of foods eaten and foraging techniques are unavailable.

Breeding

This species' breeding habits are unknown. They are likely similar to the golden-olive woodpecker's.

Migration

Gray-crowned woodpeckers are nonmigratory.

Conservation

Gray-crowned woodpeckers are fairly common to common throughout their range and do not face any known threats. However, the lack of population data and field research on this species creates uncertainty about its status.

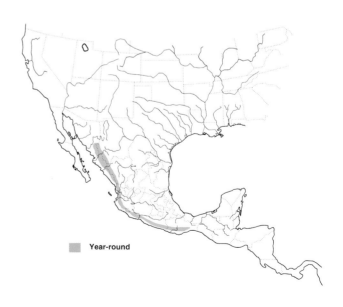

■ Year-round

LINEATED WOODPECKER
Dryocopus lineatus

At least 60 percent of the world's woodpeckers feed on ants, and some eat little else, especially at certain times of the year. The widely distributed genus *Dryocopus* includes a number of ant-loving species, including Eurasia's black woodpecker, the white-bellied woodpecker of southern and eastern Asia, the North American pileated woodpecker and the lineated woodpecker, a largely Central and South American species whose range extends to northern Mexico. *Dryocopus* is Greek for "tree cleaver," and members of this genus typically live up to their name.

Among the lineated woodpecker's preferred prey are the aggressive stinging ants of the genus *Azteca*, which live in large, hollow chambers in the bamboo-like trunks and branches of *Cecropia* trees, commonly known as trumpet trees. These specialized insects gain some of their nutrition from tiny oil- and protein-rich food packages produced by these trees. In exchange for food and lodgings, the ants help safeguard their host plants against leaf-eating herbivores by attacking invaders. If a major disturbance occurs, the ants swarm out of the tree to protect their nests and broods. But this proves a poor strategy when the assailant is a lineated woodpecker, since these birds seem not to be bothered by the defenders' sharp bites and caustic chemical secretions.

In his 1969 publication *Life Histories of Central American Birds*, ornithologist Alexander F. Skutch described the lineated woodpecker's adept approach to ant eating. "I have often watched these woodpeckers perforating the soft wood that surrounds the wide central cavity of the thinner trunks and branches – no difficult undertaking for bills as strong and sharp as theirs. Then they busily extract from the interior objects which are doubtless either the *Azteca* ants or their larvae and pupae.

From time to time, they interrupt this activity to collect the little ants which run confusedly over the bark. Or they may merely hammer on the branch, without perforating it, until the ants come pouring out through the doorways . . . . Then the woodpecker eagerly picks the ants off and devours them."

In pursuit of other types of insects, foraging techniques used by lineated woodpeckers include prying or pulling loose bark from dead trunks or branches with their bills, excavating deeply into either live or decaying wood and probing with their long, flexible tongues. Occasionally they feed on the ground, tossing aside fallen leaves in search of prey.

Lineated woodpeckers typically feed in one place for 10 to 15 minutes, then fly to another, distant tree. Since their territories are large, it is easy for them to fly out of an observer's sight. Attempts to follow or find them are helped by this species' active and noisy habits. Pairs usually stay close to each other, exchanging frequent contact calls. The fledglings are strong fliers from the start, and family groups of four to six birds may be seen foraging together after the young leave the nest.

Identification

This large woodpecker (length: 12.2–13.5 inches, or 31–34 cm) has a black back, tail, wings and neck, except for a white stripe on each side that begins at the bill and runs below the eye and black ear patch, then down the side of the neck, ending partway down each side of the back. The facial portion of this white stripe may be indistinct or absent on the subspecies found in western Mexico. The breast is black and the rest of the underparts are whitish with black barring. The female has a black forehead and large, tufted red crest. The male's red crest extends from forehead to nape. Males also have red mustache stripes, which females lack.

Distribution

In western Mexico the lineated woodpecker's range reaches north to southern Sonora and follows the Pacific slope southward. In eastern Mexico it extends as far north as Nuevo León and follows the Atlantic slope southward. These separate arms meet in the narrowest part of the country. The range continues south through Mexico and Central America and encompasses much of northern South America through to southern Brazil.

Habitat

Lineated woodpeckers live in humid, transitional and moderately dry habitats, from wet forests to dry woodlands or scrub. Although sometimes found in relatively dense forest, they prefer open areas such as forest patches and edges or clearings and pastures with scattered trees and plantations. In Mexico they are found from sea level to 5,200 feet (1,600 m).

Voice

The lineated woodpecker's long-distance call, used for communication between mates and territorial announcement, is a series of eight to 30 rapidly repeated *wik* notes. At higher intensity the notes become loud *wuks* that diminish toward the end of the call. During nest excavation a loud *pik* or *chik* may be given singly or repeated for several minutes. This sharp note is also combined with a rolling element to form the two-part *pik-urrr-r-r* or *chik-urrrrr* call, given during nest excavation and as a response to disturbance. Low intimate calls are exchanged by mates.

Drumming and Tapping

The lineated woodpecker's loud drum sequence starts with five to eight slow beats, which are followed by a long, accelerating roll. Sequences last two to three seconds and may be repeated one to three times a minute.

During nest excavation either the bird at the nest or the one arriving may tap rapidly on the rim of the entrance hole or from within the cavity before trading places. Parents may respond to an intruder near the nest or a similar disturbance by delivering single loud raps.

Feeding

Insects commonly eaten by lineated woodpeckers include all the life stages of ants, adult and larval wood-boring beetles, caterpillars and the egg cases of grasshoppers and related insects. They forage mostly on trees, both live and dead, and sometimes on sugar cane and cacao pods. They also eat some fruits and seeds.

Breeding

Lineated woodpeckers maintain pair bonds throughout the year, are apparently monogamous and probably raise one brood a year. Mates call frequently to each other and often forage close together. Nest cavities are excavated in snags or dead portions of live trees. Nest trees are often along forest edges or in isolated stands within open habitats. The usual clutch size is two or three. Nest-cavity entrance holes are approximately 3.2 to 3.5 inches (8–9 cm) in diameter.

Migration

These birds are nonmigratory.

Conservation

Lineated woodpeckers are fairly common to common throughout most of their range, including Mexico. This species does not face any known threats and can survive in many human-altered habitats, provided enough nesting and foraging trees remain. However, there is little comprehensive data on population trends.

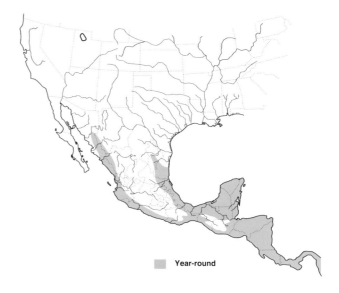

■ Year-round

PILEATED WOODPECKER

Dryocopus pileatus

With the demise of the imperial woodpecker and the near extinction of the ivory-billed, the pileated woodpecker gained the distinction of being the largest living member of the Picidae family in North America. This crow-sized woodpecker plays a vital ecological role in the forests where it lives, creating nesting, roosting and denning quarters for a wide variety of cavity adopters. The next largest picid in Canada and the United States – the northern flicker – is about half the size of the pileated woodpecker and is a much weaker excavator, so its cavities are smaller and of poorer quality than those of the pileated. At least 38 species of vertebrates (plus an uncounted number of invertebrate species) make use of vacant pileated woodpecker cavities.

The pileated woodpecker's distinctive nest holes and foraging excavations are highly visible signs of their presence in an area. Nest-cavity entrance holes are egg-shaped, measuring about 4.5 inches (11.5 cm) vertically and about 3.5 inches (9 cm) across. Roost portals look much the same unless the woodpecker has used a natural gap or opening instead of excavating its own entrance.

During the winter pileated woodpeckers concentrate their foraging activities on live or recently dead trees that house colonies of carpenter ants. These trees have hard, undecayed sapwood, which protects the ants and their eggs and larvae from all but one predator. Only the pileated woodpecker is suitably equipped to expose the honeycombed heartwood where the ants dwell in winter. Pileated woodpeckers may defend their territories year-round to ensure exclusive access to these known and dependable food sources.

These woodpeckers were dubbed logcocks by early North American settlers because much of their summertime foraging is on fallen trees, along with standing dead trees that are in more advanced states of decay. In summer they also do some searching for new carpenter ant colonies in live or undecayed trees and glean ants from the surface at previously excavated sites. Once a pileated woodpecker has located a carpenter ant colony it will return to feed there repeatedly for several years.

Pileated woodpecker foraging excavations are typically rectangular, often several inches deep and more than 12 inches (30 cm) in length. On standing trees they are usually located near the base of the trunk, with the long axis running vertically. Excavations can be so extensive that they topple the tree. Large woodchips often litter the ground around trees or logs where pileated woodpeckers have been foraging.

Identification

The pileated woodpecker, with a length of 16–19.3 inches (40–49 cm), stands out as North America's largest surviving woodpecker. Males are 10 to 15 percent heavier than females. "Pileated" means "crested," and one of this species' most recognizable features is its bright red crested cap. On males the red extends from the bill to the nape. The female's cap is smaller, extending back from the top of the crown. Males are also distinguished by red mustache stripes, which females lack. Overall the plumage is mostly a very dark brown, but it appears black. Contrasting white facial markings include a white stripe that runs from the bill across the cheek and down the neck to the sides of the breast. When the wings are folded they appear almost entirely black. In flight a large expanse of white shows on the undersides of the wings when seen from below, but only a small amount of white is visible on the upper sides of the extended wings.

Distribution

The pileated woodpecker's range stretches from southern Florida to northern Alberta. It covers most of the eastern U.S. west of the Great Plains from eastern North Dakota to eastern Texas, and extends north into southern Canada from the Atlantic to Manitoba. It continues across the prairies (excluding the unforested southern parts) to British Columbia, extending back into the U.S. through western Montana, northern Idaho and eastern Washington and Oregon and down the Pacific coast from southern British Columbia to central-eastern California.

Habitat

Pileated woodpeckers inhabit a variety of forest types, both deciduous and coniferous, and forest edges. They breed in young forests only if these have retained enough old large dead or decaying trees and logs to meet nesting, roosting and foraging needs.

Voice

The loud, high-pitched, nasal call note, given singly or in series, is usually represented as either *wuk* or *cuk*. The functions of this year-round call include territorial proclamation and communication between mates. Alarm is expressed with a loose, irregular series of these notes. During long flights individuals often utter sporadic *wuk*s. As with all of the pileated woodpecker's vocalizations, female calls are higher pitched than those of males. A loud, shrill *g-waick* or *woick* call is given during encounters with territorial intruders. Mated birds call frequently in the vicinity of the nest during courtship. A common courtship call consists of five or six repeated mewing or whining notes. Pair members often greet each other, especially at the nest, with repeated *wichew* notes.

Drumming and Tapping

The pileated woodpecker's forceful drumming is loud and resonant. The one- to three-second drum roll starts fast, slows to an even rhythm of about

15 beats per second, then speeds up while becoming quieter near the end. Rolls are commonly repeated four to seven times in a row. Continuous drumming has been documented for up to three hours, with 40- to 60-second intervals between drum rolls. Females drum less frequently than males.

Tapping by pileated woodpeckers takes several forms. One is rapid bursts of about one second in length, given at a potential nest site. Double taps may also be associated with nest selection or with copulation. Another form is a series of slow taps delivered by the bird in the nest when its mate arrives to take over excavation work or incubation or brooding duties. When disturbed, pileated woodpeckers sometimes deliver one or several loud raps.

Feeding

Ants, especially carpenter ants, are the pileated woodpecker's most important food, followed by wood-boring beetle larvae. Additional foods include other insects and seasonally abundant berries and fruits. During winter the primary foraging method is deep excavation. Through the rest of the year, prey are also captured by gleaning, shallow excavating and bark scaling, and plant foods are plucked from branches. Pairs and family groups often forage close together. Pileated woodpeckers sometimes visit feeders.

Breeding

Pileated woodpeckers mate for life, and pairs jointly defend their territory year-round by drumming, calling and chasing intruders. When one member of a pair dies, the survivor remains in the territory, waiting for an unmated "floater" to join it. Nest cavities are excavated in large deciduous or coniferous trees, either live or dead. Pairs nest in a new cavity each year. Clutch size ranges from one to six, most commonly four. Nest-cavity entrance holes are about 4.5 inches (11.5 cm) high by 3.5 inches (9 cm) wide.

Migration

Pileated woodpeckers are generally nonmigratory. However, individuals that breed near the northern limits of the species' range may winter farther south, and those that breed in mountainous areas may move to lower elevations.

Conservation

Members of various native tribes traditionally killed pileated woodpeckers to use their body parts for ceremonial, medicinal and other purposes. European settlers and those who followed often shot these slow-flying, easily targeted birds for sport, and sometimes for food, until the early 1900s. Once the species was legally protected from hunting, populations increased significantly. Local declines have occurred where intensive forestry has eliminated suitable cavity trees and foraging trees and logs.

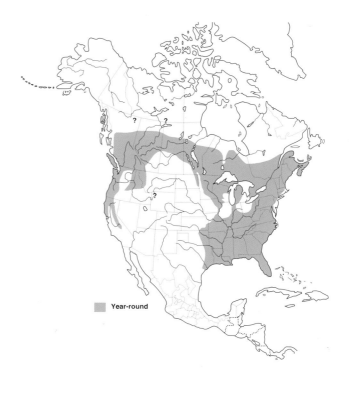

Year-round

IMPERIAL WOODPECKER
Campephilus imperialis (believed extinct)

The appropriately named imperial woodpecker was an aristocratic-looking bird and the largest member of the Picidae family. Once common in the mountains of western Mexico, it is now believed to be extinct. The last scientifically accepted record of an imperial woodpecker dates back to 1956. Since then there have been eight unsubstantiated reports of sightings from two remote areas. The last one was from an isolated part of Durango state, where a bird thought to be an imperial woodpecker was spotted in a wilderness canyon in 1996.

Researchers mounted an 11-month expedition to this region in 2001 and found some signs of imperial woodpecker activity, but no living proof of the species' continued existence. In 2003 a 16-day search that targeted the canyon area also came up empty-handed. The size of these distinctive woodpeckers and the almost complete elimination of suitable habitat within their historic range makes it doubtful that any survivors have been overlooked.

The imperial woodpecker's home was the high-elevation pine/oak forests of the Sierra Madre Occidental, the rugged mountain range that runs along Mexico's western flank from Jalisco to the U.S. border and continues a short distance north into Arizona. Because of the unique topography and climate of these mountains they feature some of the richest biodiversity in North America, with many types of flora and fauna that are found nowhere else. There are 23 different pine species and approximately 200 oak species in the Sierra Madre Occidental's pine/oak forests, which occur between about 4,900 and 10,800 feet (1,500 and 3,300 m) above sea level. Besides the imperial woodpecker, birds that are endemic to these forests include the tufted jay, eared quetzal, green-striped brush finch and thick-billed parrot. When the imperial woodpecker disappeared, the once-abundant thick-billed parrot lost a valuable source of nest holes, quite possibly contributing to the decline of these raucous green-and-red birds, which now number perhaps no more than 500 pairs.

Logging of the pine/oak forests began in the late 1800s with commercial timber harvesting operations and clearing of land for cultivation and cattle ranching. The large-diameter pine snags required by imperial woodpeckers for feeding and nesting were rapidly felled, and no second-growth trees were allowed to reach maturity to replace the lost ones. Eventually the impacts of mining, hydroelectric power generation and tourism development were added to the assault. By 2003 only about 2 percent of the original Sierra Madre Occidental pine/oak forest old growth remained – a mere 300,000 acres (121,400 ha) – not enough intact habitat to support a viable imperial woodpecker population. The point of no return was passed at some unremarked moment in the second half of the twentieth century.

Identification

This woodpecker, the largest in the world (length: 22 to 24 inches, or 56–61 cm), had an entirely black body, except for a narrow white line running down either side of the upper back like suspenders. A large area of white on the lower half of each wing contrasted with the black upper half. The ivory-white bill stood out against the black face. The male's large, tufted head crest was red behind and black along the front edge. The female's solid black crest was longer than the male's and curved strongly upward and forward.

Distribution

The imperial woodpecker's range extended through Mexico's western mountains from Chihuahua south to northern Jalisco and then west across to Michoacán.

Habitat

Imperial woodpeckers lived in old-growth pine/oak forests at elevations of about 5,900 to 9,800 feet (1,800 to 3,000 m). These forests featured large, widely spaced trees and a plentiful supply of snags.

Voice

The imperial woodpecker's call note apparently resembled that of the closely related ivory-billed woodpecker. It was described by pioneering ornithologist Edward William Nelson as consisting of "queer, nasal, penny-trumpet-like notes."

Drumming and Tapping

The only published scientific comment on the imperial woodpecker's drumming described it as loud and slow. This species probably drummed with the intermittent double raps (two beats in quick succession) that are characteristic of the genus *Campephilus*.

Feeding

Based on similarities between the foraging behavior of this species and the ivory-billed woodpecker's, the imperial woodpecker's primary prey are thought to have been beetle larvae, particularly the large larvae of long-horned beetles.

Breeding

Imperial woodpeckers maintained pair bonds year-round and were apparently monogamous and single-brooded. Clutch size ranged from one to four, but was usually two. Nest cavities were excavated in large dead pines and probably in suitably sized snags of other species.

Migration

Imperial woodpeckers were nonmigratory.

Conservation

This species is almost certainly extinct, largely because of habitat loss. Imperial woodpeckers were hunted for food, medicine and sport into the early 1900s, probably accelerating the decline of local populations.

IVORY-BILLED WOODPECKER
Campephilus principalis

By all accounts the ivory-billed woodpecker is a magnificent bird. John James Audubon wrote that ivory-billed woodpeckers invariably reminded him of the work of Flemish portrait painter Sir Anthony Van Dyck, who was renowned for conferring an air of elegance, dignity and refinement upon his sitters.

The chief cause of the species disappearance was loss of the vast old-growth forests on which it depended. What also stands out in the sad tale of its destruction is how much the killing of individual birds by or for acquisitive humans contributed to the eventual elimination of nearly all of them.

British artist-naturalist Mark Catesby, who undertook two scientific expeditions to the New World in the early 1700s, was the first person to publish an account of the far-reaching native trade in ivory-billed woodpecker body parts. Catesby wrote, "The bills of these Birds are much valued by the *Canada Indians*, who made Coronets of 'em for their Princes and great warriors, by fixing them round a Wreath, with their points outward. The Northern Indians having none of these Birds in their cold country, purchase them of the *Southern People* at the price of two, and sometimes three, Buck-skins a Bill."

Just over a century later Audubon reported that this form of adornment was still popular and had become more pervasive. "I have seen entire belts of Indian chiefs closely ornamented with the tufts and bills of this species," he wrote in *The Birds of North America*, "and have observed that a great value is frequently put upon them." He further described how the "rich scalp attached to the upper mandible forms an ornament for the war-dress of most of our Indians, or for the shot-pouch of our squatters and hunters, by all of whom the bird is shot merely for that purpose."

"Travellers of all nations are also fond of possessing the upper part of the head and the bill of the male," declared Audubon. Passengers on steamboats plying the Mississippi and other southern waterways to eagerly purchased these curios when the vessels stopped to refuel, paying 25 cents for two or three heads. By the early 1900s the bills alone sold for 5 dollars apiece in Florida to buyers who believed they were genuine ivory.

Ultimately the greatest profits in the ivory-billed woodpecker trade were made by those who provided specimens to museums, universities and private natural history collections during the Victorian era. The price rose as the supply dwindled. In 1884 a pair fetched 20 dollars. By 1905 each bird was worth 40 to 50 dollars. More than 400 individuals are known to have been killed by or for collectors, and the actual number probably exceeded 500. Most died between 1880 and 1910. Until the surprise reappearance of this species, fragile, faded skins and discolored bills were all that remained to substantiate reports of its uncommon beauty.

After the 1940s there were few sightings of ivory-billed woodpeckers, none of them confirmed by unambiguous photographic evidence. Although some people still held out hope for the species, many ornithologists believed it extinct. That changed when a report of a male seen in an area of bottomland swamp forest in eastern Arkansas in 2004 led to an intensive search that produced indisputable evidence—video footage that clearly showed the bird's distinctive plumage. This astounding discovery was kept secret until April 2005, while plans were put in place to protect as much habitat as possible. It remains to be seen how many living ivory-billed woodpeckers remain and whether the species will survive.

Identification

This very large woodpecker (length: 19–21 inches, or 48–53 cm) was named for its ivory-white bill, a feature shared with other members of the same genus. Its body and face are glossy blue-black, except for a white stripe running from below each eye down the sides of the neck to the sides of the back. The upper halves of the wings are black, contrasting with the white lower halves. Seen from below the extended wings show white along the leading edge, as well as a large expanse of white on the trailing edge. The male is distinguished by his large red head crest, the red extending back from just behind the eye. The female's crest is entirely black and slightly longer than the male's; it curls slightly upward.

Distribution

In the U.S., the ivory-billed woodpecker's range was mostly limited to the southernmost eastern states, from central Texas along the Gulf coast to Florida and north to southern North Carolina. It also extended north along the Mississippi and its tributaries to northeastern Texas, eastern Oklahoma, Arkansas and extreme southern Missouri, Illinois, Indiana and Ohio. A second subspecies of ivory-billed woodpecker, which was at one time considered a separate species, lived in Cuba.

Habitat

The ivory-billed woodpecker inhabited extensive tracts of continuous forest with large, probably widely spaced trees, including many snags. The last survivors were seen mostly in swamps and bottomlands, where human interference was least, but this species originally also inhabited upland areas. There is some evidence of nomadic movements in response to insect outbreaks, fire, flooding, hurricanes or other disturbances that killed large numbers of trees and produced a temporary abundance of beetle larvae. Where habitat quality was consistent, these woodpeckers were apparently sedentary.

Voice

The ivory-billed woodpecker's call note is a somewhat muted, nasal *kent*, similar to the sound made by blowing through the mouthpiece of a clarinet. It is given singly or in pairs, with a clear pause between repetitions. Quiet *pet* notes, uttered almost continuously throughout the day by family members foraging close together, were described as "social chatter" by Audubon. Other calls are poorly documented.

Drumming and Tapping

Drumming by ivory-billed woodpeckers is apparently in the form of a double rap: a loud first strike followed almost immediately by a second quieter, echo-like beat. One researcher heard a lone male give similar single raps.

Feeding

This species specializes in feeding on large beetle larvae taken from beneath the tight bark of recently dead trees. Some long-horned beetle larvae, which are probably the preferred prey, are 2 to 3 inches (5–8 cm) long and finger-thick. Ivory-billed woodpeckers use their powerful bills like chisels, angling them sideways under the bark. They strip sections of trunk bare, leaving marks described by one observer as resembling those "that a man might leave who knocked off the bark with a cross hatching motion with a heavy screwdriver." Less commonly they search for prey by splintering logs or excavating conical holes in snags. Nuts, berries and seeds are a seasonally important part of the diet.

Breeding

The scientific record suggests that ivory-billed woodpeckers were monogamous and that pairs produced one brood annually. Mates nearly always traveled together throughout the year. There are only about 35 scientifically useful nest records, from four states. Known cavity-tree species included bald cypress, pines, red maple, sugarberry and cabbage palmetto. Cavities were most often reported as being in snags or dead parts of live trees, but this kind of detail is missing from most of the reports. Clutch size ranged from one to six. Nest-cavity entrance holes were oval, measuring about 5 to 5.7 inches (12.7–14.5 cm) in height and 4 to 4.8 inches (10.2–12.2 cm) in width.

Migration

Ivory-billed woodpeckers are thought to have been nonmigratory.

Conservation

The most significant factor in this species' decline was habitat destruction and fragmentation, due mainly to 19th- and 20th-century logging. Killing for cultural uses, food, sport and scientific specimens undoubtedly hastened the demise of some local populations.

PALE-BILLED WOODPECKER

Campephilus guatemalensis

Members of the genus *Campephilus* are much larger than most other woodpeckers. The pale-billed woodpecker's two cousins – the imperial and the ivory-billed – are among the world's largest woodpeckers. Because of their size and the resulting strong gravitational forces acting on them as they climb and forage on trees, this group of birds has evolved some unique adaptations of their lower limbs.

Unlike other woodpeckers, the pale-billed and its *Campephilus* relatives have four long toes on each foot, with the fourth toe being the longest. Relative to body size these woodpeckers have the longest fourth toes of all the picids. When other woodpeckers climb or cling to a tree, they point their second and third toes upward so that these toes (along with their tail) overcome the downward pull of gravity. The fourth toe on each foot points out to the side and grips the tree like a pincer, resisting the outward component of the gravitational force. The heavy *Campephilus* woodpeckers need all four toes directed more or less upward to work with the tail in counteracting the downward force of gravity. With this arrangement the tarsus or lower leg comes in close contact with the tree, instead of being held away from it. A special callus-like "heel" pad on the upper end of the tarsus protects against abrasion when the leg presses against the rough bark.

Besides positioning their toes differently than other woodpeckers, *Campephilus* woodpeckers also adopt a distinctive stance when clinging to a tree trunk, extending their legs away from the center of the body as if hugging the tree. This posture helps resist gravity and stabilizes the bird as it delivers forceful blows with its bill.

To get at the beetle larvae that are their main prey, pale-billed woodpeckers excavate deep into decaying wood. If the tree is covered with bark, this is first stripped away. Bark removal typically starts with several horizontal strikes of the bill, leaving characteristic chisel-like marks on the wood. The bill is then used as a lever to pry the bark away from the trunk or branch, and the loosened bark is flicked aside. As they chop into the trunk, large woodchips and splinters are grasped in the bill and tossed to the ground.

Foraging pale-billed woodpeckers generally prefer to work between the middle and highest levels of trees, but will move lower when working on trees along forest edges, in clearings or in young stands.

Identification

This species, named for its whitish bill, is the largest surviving woodpecker in Mexico (length: 14–15 inches, or 35–38 cm). The neck and back are black, except for a white stripe running down each side of the neck and joining partway down the back to form a white V. The wings and tail are entirely black, as is the breast, with the rest of the underparts being whitish with black barring. Both sexes have a prominent bushy crest. The male's head is entirely red. The female's head is largely red, but distinguished by her black throat, forehead and forecrown.

Distribution

This species' range follows Mexico's Pacific slope south from southern Sonora and Atlantic slope south from southern Tamaulipas, converging where Mexico narrows, then re-separating and continuing south to western Panama.

Habitat

In Mexico pale-billed woodpeckers reside along both the Atlantic and Pacific slopes from sea level

to 6,600 feet (2,000 m). They occupy a wide range of humid to dry forest habitats, including pine/oak woodlands in the northern part of their range and rainforest, tall second-growth forest, plantations and mangrove habitats elsewhere. They often forage in relatively open areas, such as along forest edges, in gaps and in clearings with scattered trees.

Voice

Pale-billed woodpeckers are relatively quiet compared to many other woodpeckers. Their call note is a loud, nasal kint. Their loud, stuttering rattle, variously represented as *ka ka ka ka ka kay, nyuk, nyuk* or *kuh, kuh, kuh-uh-uh*, is probably used for long-distance communication. Intimate calls exchanged between mates in close quarters include moaning sounds and a repeated low *keeu* note.

Drumming and Tapping

The most common form of drumming by pale-billed woodpeckers is a loud double rap. The strikes are made in very quick succession, the first one harder than the second, which has a more vibratory quality. Double raps are produced at a rate of one or two a minute. Louder drumming with up to seven rapid single beats is infrequently heard.

During nest excavation pale-billed woodpeckers tap rapidly at the rim of the entrance hole or from within the cavity before exchanging places with their mates.

Feeding

Insects, mainly in their larval form, dominate the diet. Important prey species include long-horned beetles, other wood-boring beetles and ants. Pale-billed woodpeckers forage mostly on trunks and large branches, stripping the bark from dead trees, excavating deeply and probing. They also eat fruits and berries, which they often pluck and eat while clinging to a slender branch.

Breeding

Pale-billed woodpeckers are apparently monogamous. They maintain pair bonds throughout the year and mated birds generally travel and forage together. The usual clutch size is two. Limited information about nest cavities indicates that they are mostly excavated in dead trees.

Migration

Pale-billed woodpeckers do not migrate, but possibly make some seasonal local movements.

Conservation

Although generally common throughout its range and adaptable to some human alteration of its habitats, this species is rarely found in extensively deforested areas. Population trends are unknown.

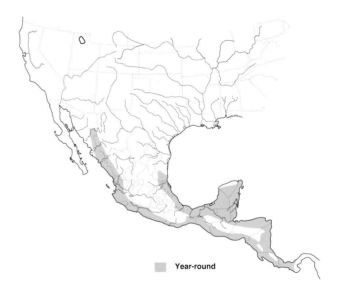

■ Year-round

Glossary

anisodactyl – describes the positioning of a bird's toes in which the first toe points backward and the other three toes are directed forward.

anting – a behavior exhibited by some woodpeckers and other birds in which the bird repeatedly picks up ants with its bill, inserts them among its feathers with a stroking or jabbing motion, then discarding it (active anting), or lies on the ground and allows ants to crawl through its plumage before picking them out (passive anting).

barbs – small rods or filaments that lie parallel to each other and extend outward from a feather shaft, forming the vanes of the feather.

barbules – tiny parallel filaments on either side of each barb on a feather. The barbules on adjacent barbs interlock to provide structural integrity for the feather vane.

brood – all of the young hatched from one clutch.

brood patch – an area on the belly of a bird that becomes temporarily featherless shortly before the incubation period begins. The skin in the area of the patch also becomes soft and engorged with blood vessels to assist in heat transfer to the eggs and, later, to the nestlings. Sometimes referred to as an incubation patch.

brooding – the warming of nestlings by an adult who covers them with its body.

cambium – the single layer of cells between the bark and the woody part of a tree.

cloaca – the common cavity into which a bird's intestinal, urinary and genital tracts open to the posterior; it is used for excretion of wastes, egg laying and copulation.

clutch – the full set of eggs laid by one female (or all of the co-breeding females in an acorn woodpecker group) during one nesting session.

columella – a rod-like bone in the middle ear that connects the eardrum to the inner ear and transmits sound vibrations.

displacement behavior – an irrelevant or out-of-context activity performed by a bird when it is unable to respond directly and appropriately to a source of stress or uncertainty.

extirpation – the elimination of a species from one part of its range; extinction at the local or regional level.

ectropodactyl – describes the positioning of the toes on the feet of most woodpecker species. The second and third toes face forward and the first toe faces backward. Depending on the bird's activity, the fourth toe may point backward or may be rotated to the side; some species have the ability to rotate the fourth toe to a forward-pointing position.

foraging – searching for and collecting food.

genus (*plural* **genera**) – a taxonomic category consisting of a group of closely related species. The genus is indicated in the first part of an organism's scientific name.

gleaning – foraging by picking food items from a surface.

hallux – the first toe, which is roughly equivalent to the human big toe.

hybridize – to cross-breed with a different species.

incubation patch – see *brood patch*.

malar stripe – a mustache-like marking that extends from the base of the bill down toward the throat on either side of a bird's face.

mandible – one half, either the upper or the lower, of a bird's beak. A mandible consists of a hard, thick sheath of modified skin cells molded around a bony core, which is part of the skull.

melanin – a naturally occurring pigment found in feathers, fur, hair or skin. Melanins produce black, dull yellow, red or brown colors.

montane – associated with mountainous regions.

nape – the back of the neck.

passerine – a bird belonging to the order Passeriformes, an immense group of approximately 70 families often referred to as perching birds. Woodpeckers belong to the order Piciformes.

phloem – the layer of tree tissue lying just inside the bark that transports sugars and other synthesized foods from the leaves to the stem and roots.

polyandry – a mating strategy in which one female breeds with two or more males in the same time period.

polygynandry – a rare mating strategy in which several females and several males form a breeding group. The females lay their eggs in a single nest and all the members of the group help incubate the eggs and care for the young.

polygyny – a mating strategy in which one male breeds with two or more females in the same time period.

population irruption – a substantial, rapid and temporary increase in population size or density in response to an episodic environmental change favorable to that species.

preening – a body-maintenance activity in which the bird uses its bill to remove dirt and parasites from its skin and feathers, straighten feather barbs and dis-tribute the oily secretions produced by the uropygial gland through its plumage.

primaries – the flight feathers on the outermost portion of the wing.

pygostyle – a plowshare-shaped bone formed by fusion of the last six vertebrae of a bird's spinal column. It provides the attachment point for the tail feathers and the muscles that move them.

rachis – the part of a feather shaft that lies between the two webs of the vane.

retrices – the flight feathers of the tail.

riparian habitat – distinctive habitat adjacent to a stream, river, lake or wetland. Elevated moisture levels typically make riparian areas lusher and often more treed than neighboring habitat farther from the water.

rufous – reddish.

savanna – open grassland with scattered trees.

snag – a standing dead tree.

tarsus – the lower leg of a bird; the segment to which the toes are attached.

understory – vegetation growing below the main tree canopy in a forest or woodland; includes young trees, shrubs, herbaceous plants and grasses.

uropygial gland – a gland located on the rump just above the base of the tail feathers; sometimes referred to as the preen gland or oil gland because it produces oils used for preening.

xylem – the main strengthening and water-conducting tissue in the trunk, branches, leaves and roots of a tree.

zygodactyl – describes the positioning of a bird's toes in which the second and third toes face forward and the first and fourth toes face backward.

Bibliography

Books

Audubon, J.J. *The Birds of America*. Vol. 4. 1840–44. Reprint, New York: Dover, 1967.

Bent, A.C. *Life Histories of North American Woodpeckers*. Bulletin 174. Washington, DC: U.S. National Museum, 1939.

Conner, R.C., D.C. Rudolph and J.R. Walters. *The Red-cockaded Woodpecker: Surviving in a Fire-maintained Ecosystem*. Austin: University of Texas Press, 2001.

del Hoyo, J., A. Elliott and J. Sargatal, eds. *Handbook of the Birds of the World*. Vol. 7, *Jacamars to Woodpeckers*. Barcelona: Lynx Edicions, BirdLife International, 2002.

Dickson, J.G., R.N. Connor, R.R. Fleet, J.A. Jackson and J.C. Kroll.. *The Role of Insectivorous Birds in Forest Ecosystems*. New York: Academic Press, 1979.

Ehrlich, P.R., D.S. Dobkin and D. Wheye. *The Birder's Handbook*. New York: Simon and Schuster, 1988.

Howell, S.N.G., and S. Webb. *A Guide to the Birds of Mexico and Northern Central America*. Oxford: Oxford University Press, 1995.

Kilham, L. *Life History Studies of Woodpeckers of Eastern North America*. Cambridge, MA: Nuttall Ornithological Club, Harvard University, 1983.

Lawrence, L. de K. *Mar: A Glimpse into the Natural Life of a Bird*. Toronto: Clarke, Irwin, 1976.

Ritchison, G. *Downy Woodpecker*. Mechanicsburg, PA: Stackpole Books, 1999.

Short, L.L. *Woodpeckers of the World*. Greenville, DE: Delaware Museum of Natural History, 1982.

Stokes, D., and L. Stokes. *The Complete Birdhouse Book*. Boston: Little, Brown, 1990.

Welty, J.C. *The Life of Birds*. Philadelphia: Saunders College Publishing, 1979.

Winkler, H., D.A. Christie and D. Nurney. *Woodpeckers: An Identification Guide to the Woodpeckers of the World*. Boston: Houghton Mifflin, 1995.

Other Publications

Poole, A., and F. Gill, eds. *The Birds of North America*. Philadelphia: Academy of Natural Sciences, and Washington, DC: American Ornithologists' Union. The 21 woodpecker accounts in *The Birds of North America* series were an invaluable source of information for this book. This series is a work in progress; the accounts are published separately, with new species added each year. More than 700 species accounts have been published to date. Each account summarizes the current scientific knowledge about every aspect of the species' biology and includes an extensive bibliography. *The Birds of North America* can be found in most major North American university libraries. Individual species accounts may be purchased from the American Ornithologists' Union's official distributor, Buteo Books (www.buteobooks.com).

Many of the following publications are available online.

Volumes 1–102 (1899–2000) of the *Condor* are available at http://elibrary.unm.edu/Condor/ Volumes 1–111 (1889–1999) of the *Wilson Bulletin* are available at http://library.unm.edu/wilson/

Aubry, K.B., and C.M. Raley. "Selection of Nest and Roost Trees by Pileated Woodpeckers in Coastal Forests of Washington." *Journal of Wildlife Management* 66 (2002): 392–406.

Austin, G.T., and E.L. Smith. "Winter Foraging Ecology of Mixed Insectivorous Bird Flocks in Oak Woodland in Southern Arizona." *Condor* 74 (1972): 17–24.

Bailey, A.M. "Ivory-billed Woodpecker's Beak in an Indian Grave in Colorado." *Condor* 41 (1939): 164.

Baptista, L.F. "A Revision of the Mexican *Piculus* (Picidae) Complex." *Wilson Bulletin* 90 (1978): 159–334.

Bednarz, J.C., D. Ripper and P.M. Radley. "Emerging Concepts and Research Directions in the Study of Cavity-nesting Birds: Keystone Ecological Processes." *Condor* 106 (2004): 1–4.

Bock, W.J., and W.D. Miller. "The Scansorial Foot of Woodpeckers with Comments on the Evolution of Perching and Climbing Feet in Birds." *Amer. Mus. Novitates* 1931 (1959).

Bonar, R.L. "Pileated Woodpecker Habitat Ecology in the Alberta Foothills." PhD diss. University of Alberta, 2001. http://www.fmf.ca/ PW/PW_report1.pdf

Burt, W.H. "Adaptive Modifications in the Woodpeckers." *University of California Publications in Zoology* 32 (1930): 455–524.

Dodenhoff, D.J., R.D. Stark and E.V. Johnson. "Do Woodpecker Drums Encode Information for Species

Recognition?" *Condor* 103 (2001): 143–50.

Duncan, Mrs. Sanford. "Flicker Captured by a Bullsnake." *Migrant* 3 (1932): 9.

du Plessis, M.A., W.W. Weathers and W.D. Koenig. "Energetic Benefits of Communal Roosting by Acorn Woodpeckers During the Nonbreeding Season." *Condor* 96 (1994): 631–37.

Eberhardt, L.S. "A Test of an Environmental Advertisement Hypothesis for the Function of Drumming in Yellow-bellied Sapsuckers." *Condor* 99 (1997): 798–803.

Ehrlich, P.R., and G.C. Daily. "Red-naped Sapsuckers Feeding at Willows: Possible Keystone Herbivores." *American Birds* 42 (1988): 357–65.

Farris, K.L., M.J. Huss and S. Zack. "The Role of Foraging Woodpeckers in the Decomposition of Ponderosa Pine Snags." *Condor* 106 (2004): 50–59.

Fayt, P., M.M. Machmer and C. Steeger. "Regulation of Spruce Bark Beetles by Woodpeckers: A Literature Review." *Forest Ecology and Management* (2004).

Gilman, M.F. "Woodpeckers of the Arizona Lowlands." *Condor* 17 (1915): 151–63.

Graber, R.R. "The Lineated Woodpecker." *Wilson Bulletin* 66 (1954): 5.

Husak, M.S. "Breeding Season Displays of the Golden-fronted Woodpecker." *Southwestern Naturalist* 41 (1996): 441–42.

——. "Observations of Survival by a Golden-fronted Woodpecker with an Injured Tongue." *Bulletin of the Texas Ornithological Society* 32 (1999): 42–44.

Husak, M.S., and T.C. Maxwell. "A Review of 20th Century Range Expansion and Population Trends of the Golden-fronted Woodpecker (*Melanerpes aurifrons*): Historical and Ecological Perspectives." *Texas Journal of Science* 52 (2000): 275–84.

Imbeau, L., and A. Desrochers. "Foraging Ecology and Use of Drumming Trees by Three-toed Woodpeckers." *Journal of Wildlife Management* 66 (2002): 222–31.

Ingold, D.J. "Influence of Nest-site Competition Between European Starlings and Woodpeckers." *Wilson Bulletin* 106 (1994): 227–41.

——. "The Influence of Starlings on Flicker Reproduction When Both Naturally Excavated Cavities and Artificial Nest Boxes Are Available." *Wilson Bulletin* 110 (1998): 218–25.

Inouye, R.S., N.J. Huntly and D.W. Inouye. "Non-random Orientation of Gila Woodpecker Nest Entrances in Saguaro Cacti." *Condor* 83 (1981): 88–89.

Jackson, J.A. "A Comparison of Some Aspects of the Breeding Ecology of Red-headed and Red-bellied Woodpeckers in Kansas." *Condor* 78 (1976): 67–76.

——. "How to Determine the Status of a Woodpecker Nest." *Living Bird* 15 (1976): 205–21.

Jackson, J.A., and E.E. Hoover. "A Potentially Harmful Effect of Suet on Woodpeckers." *Bird-banding* 46 (1975): 131–34.

Jackson, J.A., and B.J.S. Jackson. "Ecological Relationships Between Fungi and Woodpecker Cavity Sites." *Condor* 106 (2004): 37–49.

Jones, Z.F., and C.E. Bock. "Relationships Between Mexican Jays (*Aphelocoma ultramarina*) and Northern Flickers (*Colaptes auratus*) in Arizona Oak Savanna." *Auk* 120 (2003): 429–32.

Kerpez, T.A., and N.S. Smith. "Competition Between European Starlings and Native Woodpeckers for Nest Cavities in Saguaros." *Auk* 107 (1990): 367–75.

——. "Nest-site Selection and Nest-cavity Characteristics of Gila Woodpeckers and Northern Flickers." *Condor* 92 (1990): 193–98.

Kilham, L., and P. O'Brien. "Early Breeding Behavior of Lineated Woodpeckers." *Condor* 81 (1979): 299–303.

Kirby, V.C. "An Adaptive Modification in the Ribs of Woodpeckers and Piculets (Picidae)." *Auk* 97 (1980): 521–32.

Koenig, W.D. "European Starlings and Their Effect on Native Cavity-nesting Birds." *Conservation Biology* 17 (2003): 1134–40

——. "Geographical Ecology of Clutch Size Variation in North American Woodpeckers." *Condor* 88 (1986): 499–504.

Koenig, W.D., and R.L. Mumme. "The Great Egg-demolition Derby." *Natural History* 106 (1997): 32–37.

Laudenslayer, W.F., Jr., P.J. Shea, B.E. Valentine, C.P. Weatherspoon and T.E. Lisle, technical coordinators. *Proceedings of the Symposium on the Ecology and Management of Dead Wood in Western Forests.*

USDA Forest Service General Technical Report PSW-GTR-181. 2002. http://www.fs.fed.us/psw/publications/documents/gtr-181/.

Ligon, J.D. "The Role of Phylogenetic History in the Evolution of Contemporary Avian Mating and Parental Care Systems." *Current Ornithology* 10 (1993): 1–46.

Marsh, R.E. "Woodpeckers." In *Prevention and Control of Wildlife Damage.* Cooperative Extension Division, University of Nebraska, and USDA Animal and

Plant Health Inspection Service, Animal Damage Control. 1994. http://wildlifedamage.unl.edu/handbook/handbook/allPDF/bir_e139.pdf

Martin, K., K.E.H. Aitken and K.L. Wiebe. "Nest Sites and Nest Webs for Cavity-nesting Communities in Interior British Columbia, Canada: Nest Characteristics and Niche Partitioning." *Condor* 106 (2004): 5–19.

Martin, T.E., and P. Li. "Life History Traits of Open- vs. Cavity-nesting Birds." *Ecology* 73 (1992): 579–92.

Martindale, S., and D. Lamm. "Sexual Dimorphism and Parental Role Switching in Gila Woodpeckers." *Wilson Bulletin* 96 (1984): 116–21.

May, P.R.A., P. Newman, J.M. Fuster and A. Hirschman. "Woodpeckers and Head Injury." *Lancet* 1 (1976): 454–55.

McAuliffe, J.R., and P. Hendricks. "Determinants of the Vertical Distributions of Woodpecker Nest Cavities in the Sahuaro Cactus." *Condor* 90 (1988): 791–801.

Miller, A.H., and C.E. Bock. "Natural History of the Nuttall Woodpecker at the Hastings Reservation." *Condor* 74 (1972): 284–94.

Miller, R.S., and R.W. Nero. "Hummingbird–Sapsucker Associations in Northern Climates." *Canadian Journal of Zoology* 61 (1983): 1540–46.

Norberg, R.Å. "Why Foraging Birds in Trees Should Climb and Hop Upwards Rather Than Downwards." *Ibis* 123 (1981): 282–88.

Peterson, A.T., and A.G. Navarro-Sigüenza. "Western Mexico: A Significant Centre of Avian Endemism and Challenge for Conservation Action." *Cotinga* 14 (2000): 42–46.

Potter, E.F. "Anting in Wild Birds, Its Frequency and Probable Purpose." *Auk* 87 (1970): 692–713.

Repasky, R.R., R.J. Blue and P.D. Doerr. "Laying Red-cockaded Woodpeckers Cache Bone Fragments." *Condor* 93 (1991): 458–61.

Reynolds, P.S., and S.L. Lima. "Direct Use of Wings by Foraging Woodpeckers." *Wilson Bulletin* 106 (1994): 408–11.

Richardson, F. "Adaptive Modifications for Tree-trunk Foraging in Birds." *University of California Publications in Zoology* 46 (1942): 317–68.

Rumsey, R.L. "Woodpecker Nest Failures in Creosoted Utility Poles." *Auk* 87 (1970): 367–69.

Saab, V.A., and K.T. Vierling. "Reproductive Success of Lewis's Woodpecker in Burned Pine and Cottonwood Riparian Forests." *Condor* 103 (2001): 491–501.

Servín, J., S. Lyndaker Lindsey and B.A. Loiselle. "Pileated Woodpecker Scavenges on a Carcass in Missouri." *Wilson Bulletin* 113 (2001): 249–50.

Setterington, M.A., I.D. Thompson and W.A. Montevecchi. "Woodpecker Abundance and Habitat Use in Mature Balsam Fir Forests in Newfoundland." *Journal of Wildlife Management* 64 (2000): 335–45.

Sherman, Althea R. "At the Sign of the Northern Flicker." *Wilson Bulletin* 22 (1910): 135–71.

Short, L.L. "Burdens of the Picid Hole-excavating Habit." *Wilson Bulletin* 91 (1979): 16–28.

Skutch, A.F. Life *Histories of Central American Birds.* Vol. 3, *Pacific Coast Avifauna.* No. 35. Cooper Ornithological Society, 1969.

Smith, A.P. "Destruction of Imperial Woodpeckers." *Condor* 10 (1908): 91.

Spring, L.W. "Climbing and Pecking Adaptations in Some North American Woodpeckers." *Condor* 67 (1965): 457–88.

Stanback, M.T. "Getting Stuck: A Cost of Communal Cavity Roosting." *Wilson Bulletin* 110 (1998): 421–23.

Stark, R.D., D.J. Dodenhoff and E.V. Johnson. "A Quantitative Analysis of Woodpecker Drumming." *Condor* 100 (2001): 350–56.

Sutherland, G.D., C.L. Gass, P.A. Thompson and K.P. Lertzman. "Feeding Territoriality in Migrant Rufous Hummingbirds: Defense of Yellow-bellied Sapsucker (*Sphyrapicus varius*) Feeding Sites." *Canadian Journal of Zoology* 60 (1982): 2046–50.

Test, F.H. "Relation of Wing and Tail Color of the Woodpeckers *Colaptes auratus* and *C. cafer* to Their Food." *Condor* 71 (1969): 206–11.

Tobalske, B.W. "Scaling of Muscle Composition, Wing Morphology, and Intermittent Flight Behavior in Woodpeckers." *Auk* 113 (1996): 151–77.

U.S. Fish and Wildlife Service. *Recovery Plan for the Red-cockaded Woodpecker* (Picoides borealis). 2nd rev. Atlanta, GA: U.S. Fish and Wildlife Service, 2003.

Unitt, P. *San Diego County Bird Atlas.* San Diego, CA: San Diego Natural History Museum, 2004.

Weibe, K.L "First Reported Case of Classical Polyandry in a North American Woodpecker, the Northern Flicker." *Wilson Bulletin* 114 (2002): 401–3.

———. "Microclimate of Tree Cavity Nests: Is It Important for Reproductive Success in Northern Flickers?" *Auk* 118 (2001): 412–21.

Yom-Tov, Y., and A. Ar. "Incubation and Fledging Durations of Woodpeckers." *Condor* 95 (1993): 282–87.

Index

flying, 45
hitching, 31
nesting behavior, 50
physical characteristics, 24, 28–29
vocalization, 38, 40
pale-headed woodpecker, 138
parrots, 19, 214
passerine (perching) birds, 27
Peterson, A. Townsend, 206
Picidae. *See* woodpeckers
Picinae (true woodpeckers), 11–15
Picoides species (pied woodpeckers), 12, 137
aerial displays, 44–45
vocalization, 38, 39, 40
piculets (Picumninae), 11, 27, 33
Piculus species, 14, 85, 137, 206
Picus, 115
pied woodpeckers. *See Picoides* species
pileated woodpecker *(Dryocopus pileatus),* 14, **211–13**
diet, 85, 88, 112
drumming, 34, 35, 37
as excavator, 19–20, 103–4, 108
feeding behavior, 98, 124–25, 131
habitat, 46, 124–25
humans and, 116
mating behavior, 65, 76
nesting behavior, 74, 75, 103, 128
nestlings, 57, 58, 61–62, 63
observing, 135
and other woodpeckers, 128
physical characteristics, 15, 25, 117
roosting behavior, 79–80, 82, 83, 106–7
tapping, 37
vocalization, 39–40, 41
pines
as breeding sites, 126, 128
as food source, 86, 124, 162
pine siskin, 107
plumage. *See also* feathers
colors and patterns, 12–15, 133–34, 199–201
incubation (brood) patches, 51
polyandry, multiple-nest, 66
polygynandry, opportunistic, 67–68
polygyny, multiple-nest, 65
polytypic species, 203
Pomo people, 116
ponderosa pine, 74, 113, 124, 126, 162
predators, 70, 111–13
avoiding, 80, 109
birds as, 77, 78, 101, 111
cohabitation with, 106
feeding flocks and, 109, 110–11

forest fires and, 126
woodpeckers as, 87–88, 111–13
preening, 98–99
probing, 22, 25, 91–92
purple martin, 129
pygostyle, 26, 60

Ramphastidae (toucans), 17
red-bellied woodpecker *(Melanerpes carolinus),* 12, 77, **177–79**
breeding behavior, 63
diet, 112
drumming, 34
feeding behavior, 91–92, 96, 98, 108
humans and, 116, 131
mating behavior, 76, 77
nest cavities, 71, 104
nesting behavior, 34, 59, 60, 132
nestlings, 57, 58, 62
and other birds, 105, 108–9
and other woodpeckers, 107, 108, 171
physical characteristics, 117
plumage care, 99
tapping, 36, 37
territorial behavior, 46, 77–78
vocalization, 38, 40
red-breasted sapsucker *(Sphyrapicus ruber),* 12, **183–85**
breeding behavior, 68
hummingbirds and, 107
mating behavior, 75
and other sapsuckers, 195
physical characteristics, 12, 14
tapping, 37
visual displays, 43
vocalization, 40, 41
red-cockaded woodpecker *(Picoides borealis),* 12, **159–61**
breeding behavior, 63, 66–67
diet, 85, 88–89, 112
drumming, 34, 37
as endangered species, 127–28, 161
as excavator, 102, 104
feeding behavior, 91, 98, 124
and forest fires, 126
nest cavities, 72–73, 104, 133
nesting behavior, 51, 57, 66–67
nestlings, 56, 177
physical characteristics, 42, 117
sunbathing, 99
vocalization, 38, 41–42
red-headed woodpecker *(Melanerpes erythrocephalus),* 12, **180–82**
breeding behavior, 63
diet, 86, 89
European starlings and, 105

as excavator, 69
feeding behavior, 91, 92, 93, 94, 96–97
fledglings, 63
humans and, 119, 131, 132
mating behavior, 76, 77
nesting behavior, 50, 51, 70, 71, 104, 132
physical characteristics, 12, 99
tapping, 36
vocalization, 38, 41
red-naped sapsucker *(Sphyrapicus nuchalis),* 12, **187–89**
mating behavior, 75
nest cavities, 69–70
and other birds, 107, 110–11
and other sapsuckers, 183, 192, 195
tapping, 37
visual displays, 42–43
vocalization, 40, 41
red-shafted flicker, 198, 199, 201
regurgitation feeding, 57–58
Repasky, Richard R., 88
resin wells, 159
retrices, 25–26
reverse mounting, 77
Rocky Mountain grasshopper, 180
roosting, 79–83, 120. *See also* nest cavities
sites for, 81–83, 106–7
Rudolph, D. Craig, 128

saguaro cactus, 196–97
as food, 57
habitat, 128–29, 130–31
as nesting site, 71, 72, 103
saliva, 25
sallying. *See* hawking
salvage logging, 123, 126–27
sap wells, 63, 86–87, 107–8, 187, 193
sexual activity. *See* courtship; mating
sexual badges, 12–15, 42–43
sexual dimorphism, 169
Short, Lester L., 57
Sierra Madre Occidental, 35, 214
sink habitats, 125
Skutch, Alexander F., 208
sleep. *See* roosting
Smith, Austin Paul, 118
snags, 70, 123–24, 131
snakes, 70, 77, 78, 101, 159
Sonoran Desert, 128–29, 170, 196, 198
South America, 9, 14, 15
sparrows, 107
Sphyrapicus species (sapsuckers), 12–14, 137, 183, 187
diet, 86

Acknowledgements

Numerous biologists encouraged and assisted me in writing this book by sending me copies of their publications, directing me to additional sources of information and answering my questions; any errors in explaining or interpreting their work are my own. For their contributions I thank Suzanne Beauchesne, Rick Bonar (with whom I also spent an interesting day in the Foothills Model Forest in Alberta learning about his pileated woodpecker research), Richard Conner, John Cooper, Ralph Costa, Laurie Eberhardt, Philippe Fayt, Ted Fleming, Carol Hartwig, Michael Husak, Jeffrey Joy, Walter Koenig, Kenneth Parker, Michael Setterington, Jo Smith, Chris Steeger, Philip Unitt, Karen Weibe and Kathi Zimmerman. Thanks also to Karen Martin of the Nature Society in Griggsville, Illinois.

The highlight of my research was visiting a couple of red-cockaded woodpecker populations, a trip made possible by the gracious cooperation of five individuals. In Georgia, Craig Hedman and Jeremy Poirier welcomed me to Bainbridge and to International Paper's Southlands Experiment Forest where, with the assistance of Mark Register, they gave me a memorable intro-duction to these endangered birds. Frances James and Eric Walters of Florida State University toured me around their study sites in the Apalachicola National Forest near Tallahassee and shared their considerable knowledge about this species and longleaf pine forest ecosystems.

Eric deserves special thanks for being unfailingly helpful and supportive throughout this endeavor and replying promptly and comprehensively to all of my many e-mails. I am additionally grateful to him for his unpaid work as the moderator of CAVNET, a listserv for those with an interest in cavity-nesting birds, which allowed me to extend my inquiries much farther than would have been otherwise possible.

Literary agent Carolyn Swayze gave this book early momentum by connecting me with the right publisher and editor Charis Cotter carried it through its formative stages with her much appreciated enthusiasm, clarity and patience.

On the home front it is my good fortune to have the loving support and culinary talents of Mark Zuehlke, who invariably responds to my deadline panics with the welcome words "I'll cook."

Photo Credits

front cover:	Robert McCaw
back cover:	Maslowski Photo/Photo Researchers, Inc.
p. 1	Tom Vezo/Minden Pictures
p. 2-3	Gary W. Carter/CORBIS/MAGMA
p. 4 (left)	Tom & Pat Leeson/Photo Researchers, Inc.
p. 4 (right)	Tim Zurowski/CORBIS/MAGMA
p. 5 (left)	Terry Whittaker; Frank Lane Picture Agency/CORBIS/MAGMA
p. 5 (right)	Phyllis Greenberg/Maxximages.com
p. 8	John Cancalosi/DRK PHOTO
p. 10	Robert McCaw
p. 13	Tim Zurowski/CORBIS/MAGMA
p. 16	Anthony Mercieca/Maxximages.com
p. 18	Daybreak Imagery/Maxximages.com
p. 21	Michael Ederegger/DRK PHOTO
p. 23	Joe McDonald/CORBIS/MAGMA
p. 31	Tim Thompson/CORBIS/MAGMA
p. 32	Robert McCaw
p. 39	W. Perry Conway/CORBIS/MAGMA
p. 43	Gordon & Cathy Illg/Maxximages.com
p. 45	Tom Vezo/Minden Pictures
p. 47	Klaus Nigge/Foto Natura/Minden Pictures
p. 48	Donald Jones/ DRK PHOTO
p. 52	McDonald Wildlife Photography/Maxximages.com
p. 54	Dwight R. Kuhn/DRK PHOTO
p. 59	Fred Unverhau/Maxximages.com
p. 61	Anthony Mercieca/ Photo Researchers, Inc.
p. 64	Robert McCaw
p. 69	John Gerlach/Maxximages.com
p. 72	Anthony Mercieca/Photo Researchers, Inc.
p. 76	Marie Read/Maxximages.com
p. 80	Jack Wilburn/Maxximages.com
p. 81	Raymond Gehman/CORBIS/MAGMA
p. 84	Erwin & Peggy Bauer/Maxximages.com
p. 87	David Welling/Maxximages.com
p. 90	Robert McCaw
p. 92	Mickey Gibson/Maxximages.com
p. 95	Robert McCaw
p. 98	David Welling/Maxximages.com
p. 100	Matthias Breiter
p. 102	Sumio Harada/Minden Pictures
p. 110	Adam Jones/Photo Researchers, Inc.
p. 113	Esther Kiviat/Maxximages.com
p. 114	David Hosking /CORBIS/MAGMA
p. 118	Richard R. Hansen/Photo Researchers, Inc.
p. 123	Tom & Pat Leeson/Photo Researchers, Inc.
p. 130	James Robinson/ Maxximages.com
p. 134	Robert McCaw
p. 139	Steve Kaufman/CORBIS/MAGMA
p. 142	Gerald C. Kelley/Photo Researchers, Inc.
p. 145	S. C. Fried/Photo Researchers, Inc.
p. 148	Tom Edwards/Maxximages.com
p. 151	Robert McCaw
p. 154	Anthony Mercieca/Photo Researchers, Inc.
p. 156	Richard R. Hansen/Photo Researchers, Inc.
p. 160	Stephen G. Maka/DRK PHOTO
p. 163	Tim Zurowski/CORBIS/MAGMA
p. 166	Joe McDonald/DRK PHOTO
p. 169	Paul & Joyce Berquist/Maxximages.com
p. 172	David Welling/Maxximages.com
p. 175	Alan G. Nelson/Maxximages.com
p. 178	Maslowski Photo/Photo Researchers, Inc.
p. 181	Maslowski Photo/ Photo Researchers, Inc.
p. 184	Richard R. Hansen/ Photo Researchers, Inc.
p. 186	Robert McCaw
p. 188	Harry Engels/Photo Researchers, Inc.
p. 191	Maslowski Photo/ Photo Researchers, Inc.
p. 194	Marie Read/Maxximages.com
p. 197	Alan G. Nelson/Maxximages.com
p. 200	Wayne Lankinen/DRK PHOTO
p. 204	John Dunning/Photo Researchers, Inc.
p. 209	Norbert Wu/Minden Pictures
p. 212	David Macias/Photo Researchers, Inc.
p. 215	BirdLife International
p. 217	Robert Havell © Academy of Natural Sciences of Philadelphia/CORBIS/MAGMA
p. 220	A. M. Sada/VIREO